THE
COMPLETE LETTERS
OF
Lady Mary Wortley Montagu

VOLUME III

1752–1762

Mary, Countess of Bute
From a painting by Sir Joshua Reynolds, 1779

THE
COMPLETE LETTERS
OF
Lady Mary
Wortley Montagu

EDITED BY
ROBERT HALSBAND

VOLUME III

1752–1762

OXFORD
AT THE CLARENDON PRESS
1967

Oxford University Press, Ely House, London W. 1

GLASGOW NEW YORK TORONTO MELBOURNE WELLINGTON
CAPE TOWN SALISBURY IBADAN NAIROBI LUSAKA ADDIS ABABA
BOMBAY CALCUTTA MADRAS KARACHI LAHORE DACCA
KUALA LUMPUR HONG KONG TOKYO

PRINTED IN GREAT BRITAIN
AT THE UNIVERSITY PRESS, OXFORD
BY VIVIAN RIDLER
PRINTER TO THE UNIVERSITY

CONTENTS

LIST OF PLATES

INTRODUCTION TO VOLUME III

LETTERS 1752–1762

Tᴴɪs final volume contains the letters Lady Mary wrote during the last decade of her life. In 1752 she was still living in the Brescian village of Gottolengo, and paying long visits to Lovere, on Lago d'Iseo. Four years later, to disentangle her affairs from the mysterious Count Palazzi, she moved to Venice and Padua. She remained there until the death of her husband (in January 1761) made her resolve to return to England. A year later, after an expatriation of more than twenty-two years, she saw London again; but she survived her homecoming only six months, dying at the age of seventy-three.

During this decade she continued to correspond with her family. Although her letters to Wortley decreased in frequency and interest (their favourite topics being the weather and their health), those to Lady Bute sustained their range, variety, and fascination. New books sent from England still aroused her passionate, critical interest, particularly the novels of Richardson and Fielding and the writings of the egregious Lord Bolingbroke. She continued to offer counsel on the education of her granddaughters, and logically went on to discuss marriage and the status of women. In her rural retirement she also enjoyed the leisure to send long tales of local events; two that stand out are a comedy of cuckoldry[1] and a *Pamela*-like romance in real life.[2] After she left the provinces for the cosmopolitan city, the scope of her observations shifted; she now gossiped contentedly about English travellers passing through Venice, especially young men on the Grand Tour who might be suitable matches for her numerous granddaughters. But her

---

[1] Printed below, pp. 43–46.   [2] Below, pp. 70–75.

last years were agitated and embittered by her enmity towards John Murray, the British Resident, and by her distraught anxiety after her husband's death and by her son's machinations to upset his will.

In Venice she resumed her correspondence (in French) with two Italian friends. Her letters to Madame Chiara Michiel[1] are as gracious and affectionate as before. Those to Count Algarotti,[2] who had retired from Court life to live in his native country, are infused with witty *camaraderie*, instead of the hysterical passion of her initial infatuation for him.

When she was almost seventy years old she began a new friendship that stimulated her to a correspondence of remarkable vitality. Sir James Steuart, who had been attainted for Jacobite activity in 1745, lived on the Continent, occupying himself with scholarly pursuits. In 1757, when he visited Venice with his wife, he immediately won Lady Mary's ardent friendship, and retained it to the end of her life. Her letters to Sir James and his wife[3] are virtuoso in style, reminiscent of the intellectual enthusiasm and *esprit* of her Turkish Embassy Letters. Since the original manuscripts of these letters have apparently not survived, the present text is based on a transcript made by Lady Louisa Stuart for the 1837 edition of Lady Mary's letters and works. This has been collated with the privately printed edition of 1818, which had also been based on the original manuscripts (with some passages deleted).

Of the entirely new and previously unpublished letters in this volume (aside from those to Madame Michiel and to Algarotti), those from Lady Mary to James Stuart Mackenzie, Lord Bute's brother,[4] have recently been found among the Bute MSS. They not only express Lady Mary's affection for him, but also explain his involvement in her affairs when he served as British Ambassador to Turin. The strangest discovery of new letters, however, lies in a Commonplace Book of Lady Mary's, hitherto unrecorded, which was among the Wortley Manuscripts in 1925 when the late Lord Harrowby presented it to the University of

[1] Below, pp. 111 ff.   [3] Below, pp. 148 ff.
[2] Below, pp. 117 ff.   [4] Below, pp. 196 ff.

x

Sydney. A section of this Commonplace Book contains Lady Mary's summaries of letters she wrote from 1758 to 1761.[1] Although most of these refer to letters that still exist, twenty-one restore to her canon letters that have been lost, most of them to hitherto unknown correspondents. They vary in length and particularity, from one to Madame du Boccage that is provocatively terse ('War') to the long, elaborate ones of letters she sent to Wilhelmina Tichborne. Like all her known letters, these summaries—even as set down in a kind of shorthand—display her versatile intellect, imagination, and literary skill. Neither age nor exile could dim her brilliance.

PREVIOUS EDITIONS[2]

1803

The Works of the Right Honourable Lady Mary Wortley Montagu, Including Her Correspondence, Poems, and Essays . . . [ed. James Dallaway] . . . 1803.

1818

Original Letters from Lady Mary Wortley Montague, to Sir James and Lady Frances Steuart; also, Memoirs and Anecdotes of those Distinguished Persons. [ed. John Dunlop] Greenock: Printed by Robert Donaldson. 1818.

1837

The Letters and Works of Lady Mary Wortley Montagu. Edited by Her Great Grandson Lord Wharncliffe . . . 1837.

1861

The Letters and Works of Lady Mary Wortley Montagu. Edited by Her Great-Grandson Lord Wharncliffe. Third Edition, With Additions and Corrections. . . . By W. Moy Thomas. . . . MDCCCLXI.

1887

The Letters and Works [of 1861]. New Edition, Revised. (Bohn's Standard Library) 1887.

---

[1] See below, p. 156, n. 1.   [2] For detailed descriptions, see vol. 1, pp. xviii–xix.

MANUSCRIPT OWNERS

The following own letters, to or from Lady Mary, printed in the text of this volume: the Marquess of Bath (4), the Bodleian Library, Oxford (4), Mrs. R. G. Browne-Swinburne (1), the Marquess of Bute (25), the Earl of Harrowby (115), M. C. A. Lyell, Esq. (1), Lord Monson (1), Sir John Murray (2), the Duke of Newcastle (1), the Earl of Wharncliffe (27).

ACKNOWLEDGEMENTS

During the years I have worked on this edition I have incurred many more obligations than I can remember; and if the following list omits names of those who have helped me in one way or another, the fault lies with my imperfect memory (and files) and not with an ungrateful heart.

Owners of manuscripts and pictures I have used deserve first mention; they have without exception been extremely generous.

In addition I should like to thank the following: Rolando Anzilotti, Catherine Armet, John Barnard, E. S. de Beer, Theodore Besterman, Wallace Brockway, Paul Chamley, C. H. Clough, W. D. Coates, Mary Cosh, Duncan Eaves, Leon Edel, Roger Ellis, Claire-Éliane Engel, the Hon. David H. Erskine, John Fleming, Donald M. Frame, Lina Frizziero, Bernard Gagnebin, Peter Gay, Moses Hadas, Sherman Haight, John Harris, Evelyn B. Harrison, Joel Haynes, Olwen Hedley, John C. Hodges, Bernhard Knollenberg, George L. Lam, W. S. Lewis, John Lindon, Kenneth Lohf, R. Mackworth-Young, H. K. Miller, Jr., G. E. Mingay, E. L. C. Mullins, David Noakes, James M. Osborn, Dorothy Owen, Henry Pettit, David Piper, J. H. Plumb, Frederick A. Pottle, Kenneth Rose, A. L. Rowse, the Hon. Sir Steven Runciman, Viscount Sandon, H. C. Schulz, Miss A. Scott-Elliot, A. H. Scouten, Robert Shackleton, Mrs. John Shelley, Grant G. Simpson, Andrew S. Skinner, Warren H. Smith, Terence Spencer, Damie

Stillman, M. V. Stokes, H. A. Taylor, J. Trapp, Joan Varley, David M. Vieth, Frances Vivian, Jacques Voisine, Robert Warnock, Françoise Weil.

SHORT TITLES AND OTHER ABBREVIATIONS

All references to Lady Mary's published letters and works are cited by the dates of the editions (described on p. xi above).

The following standard biographical works and peerages have been used but will not be cited unless for a particular reason:

ENGLISH—G. E. Cokayne, *Complete Baronetage*, 1900–9; G. E. Cokayne, *The Complete Peerage*, ed. V. Gibbs *et al.*, 1910–59; Arthur Collins, *Peerage of England*, ed. Sir Egerton Brydges, 1812; *DNB*; *Scots Peerage*, ed. J. B. Paul, 1904–14; FRENCH—F.-A. A. de La Chenaye-Desbois, *Dictionnaire de la noblesse*, 3rd ed., 1863–76; J. C. F. Hoefer, *Nouvelle Biographie générale*, 1853–70; H. Jougla de Morenas, *Grand Armorial de France*, 1934–49; J. F. Michaud, *Biographie universelle ancienne et moderne*, [1870–3]; GERMAN—*Allgemeine Deutsche Biographie*, 1875–1912; C. von Wurzbach, *Biographisches Lexikon*, 1856–91; ITALIAN—G. B. Crollalanza, *Dizionario storico-blasonico*, 1886–90; P. Litta, *Famiglie celebri di Italia*, 1819–1902; V. Spreti, *Enciclopedia storico-nobiliare italiana*, 1928–35; ECCLESIASTICAL—C. Eubel, *Hierarchia Catholica*, 1901–58.

Standard encyclopaedias likewise have been used but will not generally be cited.

Add MS	Additional Manuscripts, British Museum.
BM	British Museum.
Bod.	Bodleian Library, Oxford.
Bute MS	Owned by the Marquess of Bute; at Mount Stuart, Isle of Bute.
CB MS	Commonplace Book (Manuscript), Fisher Library, University of Sydney.
Delany, *Corr.*	Mrs. Mary Delany, *Autobiography and Correspondence*, ed. Lady Llanover, 1861.
DNB	*Dictionary of National Biography.*
Eg MS	Egerton Manuscripts, British Museum.

H MS	Owned by the Harrowby Manuscripts Trust; at Sandon Hall, Stafford.
Halsband, *LM*	Robert Halsband, *The Life of Lady Mary Wortley Montagu*, 1956.
HMC	Historical Manuscripts Commission Reports.
D. B. Horn	D. B. Horn, *British Diplomatic Representatives 1689–1789*, 1932.
Isenburg	W. K. von Isenburg, *Stammtafeln zur Geschichte der europäischen Staaten*, revised ed., 1958–61.
LM	Lady Mary Wortley Montagu.
Monson MS	Owned by Lord Monson; at South Carlton, Lincoln.
MS	Manuscript *or* Manuscripts.
Murray MS	Owned by Sir John Murray, London.
OED	*Oxford English Dictionary*.
P.C.C.	Prerogative Court of Canterbury (wills), Somerset House.
PRO	Public Record Office, London.
Repertorium	F. Hausmann, *Repertorium der diplomatischen Vertreter aller Länder*, 1936–50.
SP	State Papers, Public Record Office.
W	Edward Wortley Montagu, senior.
W MS	Wortley Manuscripts (vols. i-viii: Harrowby MS, vols. 74–81).
Walpole, *Corr.*	Horace Walpole, *Correspondence*, ed. W. S. Lewis et al., 1937– .
Wh MS	Wharncliffe Muniments, owned by the Earl of Wharncliffe; on deposit in the Sheffield Central Library.

INDEX OF CORRESPONDENTS
AND LETTERS IN VOLUME III

[Symbols of first publication given in vol. i, p. xxiii]

---

¹ The next letter in chronological order, that of 22 June [1752], is printed in vol. ii, pp. 457–60.

[1] These four letters printed in HMC *Bath MSS*, ii, 1907, pp. 184–5.

To Wortley *29 Jan.* [*1752*][1]

Jan. 29. N.S.

I had the pleasure of receiving yours of Nov. 25 yester-day, and am very glad to find by it that you are arriv'd in London in good Health.[2] I heartily wish you the continuance of it. My Deafness lasted only a fortnight, thô it frighted me very much. I have had no return of it since.

Your advice to Mr. M. was certainly right, but I am not surpriz'd he did not follow it. I beleive there are few men in the World (I never knew any) capable [of] such a strength of Resolution as your selfe.

I have answer'd your Letter from Vienna, but as you do not mention having receiv'd mine, and perhaps it is lost, I shall add a word or two more concerning the use of Turkish Wheat. It is gennerally declaim'd against by all the Doctors, and some of them have wrote Treatises to show the ill Con-sequences of it, in which they say that since it has been sown (which is not above 100 years) it may be prov'd from the registers that the mortality is greater amongst the Country people than it was formerly. I beleive that may be true in regard to children, who are apt to eat greedily, it being very heavy of Digestion, but to those whose Stomachs can bear it and eat with moderation, I am perswaded it is a clean streng-thening Diet. I have made strict observations and enquirys on the Health and manner of Life of the Countrys in which I have resided, and have found little Difference in the length of Life. It is true, Gout, Stone and Small pox (so frequent with us) are little known here; in recompence, Pleurisys, Peripneumonys, and Fevers (especially malignant) are far more usual, and I am clearly of Opinion that if an exact

[1] Since 1746 LM had been living in the Venetian province of Brescia; she had a house in Gottolengo, about 18 miles south of the town of Brescia.

[2] W, LM's husband, had been on the Continent since the previous spring.

computation was made, as many dye in Brescia ⟨as⟩ in London in proportion to the different Numbers.

I have not heard from my Daughter of a long time. It may be occasion'd by the bad Weather. I hope both you and she are well. I have wrote to her many long Letters.

Text W MS ii. 225–6   *Address* To Edwd Wortley Esqr recommended to Samuel Child Esqr near Temple Bar London Angleterre [*in another hand*] Cavendish Square   *End. by W* [*Summary*] Ad 14 Apr. Recd 13 Mar.

To Lady Bute[1] [*16 Feb. 1752*]

Dear Child,

I receiv'd yesterday, Feb. 15 N.S., the case of Books you were so good to send to me. The entertainment they have allready given me has recompens'd me for the long time I expected them. I begun, by your direction, with Peregrine Pickle. I think Lady V[ane]'s memoirs contain more Truth and less malice than any I ever read in my Life.[2] When she speaks of her own being disinterested,[3] I am apt to beleive she really thinks her selfe so, as many highway men, after having no possibillity of retreiving the character of Honesty, please themselves with that of being Generous, because whatever they get on the road they allways spend at the next ale House, and are still as beggarly as ever. Her History, rightly consider'd, would be more instructive to young Women than any Sermon I know. They may see there what mortifications and variety of misery are the unavoidable consequences of Galant[r]ys. I think there is no rational Creature than [*sic*] would not prefer the life of the strictest Carmelite to the round of Hurry and misfortune she has gone through.

Her Style is clear and concise, with some strokes of Humour which appear to me so much above her I can't help being of opinion the whole has been modell'd by the

---

[1] LM's daughter.

[2] In *The Adventures of Peregrine Pickle*, published Feb. 1751, Smollett inserted (iii. 66–235) the 'Memoirs of

a Lady of Quality' by the notorious Lady Vane (see ii. 120).

[3] 'Interest and ambition have no share in my composition . . .' (iii. 225).

Author of the Book in which it is inserted, who is some subaltern admirer of hers.[1] I may judge wrong, she being no Acquaintance of mine, thô she has marry'd two of my relations.[2] Her first wedding was attended with Circumstances that made me think a visit not at all necessary, thô I disoblig'd Lady Susan by neglecting it;[3] and her second, which happen'd soon after, made her so near a Neighbour that I rather chose to stay the whole Summer in Town than partake of her Balls and partys of Pleasure, to which I did not think it proper to introduce you, and had no other way of avoiding it without incurring the censure of a most unnatural mother for denying you diversions that the péous Lady Ferrers permitted to her exemplary Daughters.[4] Mr. Sh[irley] has had uncommon Fortune in making the conquest of 2 such extrodinary Ladys,[5] equal in their heroic contempt of Shame, and eminent above their Sex, the one for Beauty, and the other Wealth, both which attract the persuit of all mankind, and have been thrown into his arms with the same unlimited Fondness. He appear'd to me gentile, well bred, well shap'd and sensible, but the charms of his Face and Eyes, which Lady V[ane] describes with so much warmth,[6] were, I confess, allwaies invisible to me, and the

[1] Although Lady Vane may have been acquainted with Smollett, it is uncertain which of them wrote the 'Memoirs'; the final version was almost certainly his (*Peregrine Pickle*, ed. J. L. Clifford, 1964, p. xxvi).

[2] She had m. (1733) Lord William Hamilton (d. 1734), 2nd son of 4th Duke of Hamilton; the 1st Duke had married a daughter of 1st Earl of Denbigh, ancestor of LM's mother. Lady Vane's second husband was William Vane (1714–89), 2nd Viscount, who on his mother's side was descended from the Hon. William Pierrepont.

[3] In her 'Memoirs', Lady Vane elopes with Lord William, and is visited the same day by his youngest sister. She was Lady Susan Hamilton (d. 1755), who m. (1736) Anthony Tracy Keck.

[4] Lady Ferrers, who lived in Twickenham, was widow of 1st Earl Ferrers—who had 17 children by his first wife,

10 by her, and about 30 by his mistresses. Two of her stepson's daughters were Methodists (see below, p. 223, n. 3).

[5] Sewallis Shirley, Lady Ferrers's son, became Lady Vane's lover soon after her second marriage in 1735; and in 1751 he married the widowed Lady Orford.

[6] As Mr. S—, he is 'absolutely master of those insinuating qualifications which few women of passion and sensibility can resist; and had a person every way adapted for profiting by these insidious talents. . . . He was tall and thin, which was perfectly agreeable to my taste, with large blue eloquent eyes, good teeth, and a long head turned to gallantry. . . . By these arts and advantages this consummate politician in love began by degrees to sap the foundations of my conjugal faith' ('Memoirs', p. 98). Walpole sarcastically calls him 'no great genius—but with all [Lady Orford's] affectation of parts', and

artificial part of his character very glareing, which I think her story shows in a strong light.

The next Book I laid my Hand on was the Parish Girl,[1] which interested me enough not to be able to quit it till it was read over, thô the author has fallen into the common mistake of Romance writers, intending a virtuous character and not knowing how to draw it, the first step of his Heroine (leaving her Patronesse's House) being alltogether absurd and ridiculous, justly entitleing her to all the misfortunes she met with.

Candles came, and my Eyes grown weary I took up the next Book meerly because I suppos'd from the Title it could not engage me long. It was Pompey the Little,[2] which has realy diverted me more than any of the others, and it was impossible to go to Bed till it was finish'd. It is a real and exact representation of Life as it is now acted in London, as it was in my time, and as it will be (I do not doubt) a Hundred years hence, with some little variation of Dress, and perhaps Government. I found there many of my Acquaintance. Lady T[ownshend] and Lady O[rford] are so well painted, I fancy'd I heard them talk, and have heard them say the very things there repeated.[3]

I also saw my selfe (as I now am) in the character of Mrs. Qualmsick. You will be surpriz'd at this, no English Woman being so free from Vapours, having never in my Life complain'd of low spirits or weak nerves, but our ressemblance is very strong in the fancy'd loss of Appetite, which I have been silly enough to be persuaded into by the Physician of this place.[4] He visits me frequently, as being one of the most

gives an example of his stupidity (*Corr.* xix. 309).

[1] *The History of Charlotte Summers, the Fortunate Parish Girl* (1749) was noticed in Feb. 1750 in the *Monthly Review*: 'All we shall say of this performance, is, that the author has kept his name unknown, which is an instance of his discretion. . . .' (ii. 352).

[2] *The History of Pompey the Little: or, The Life and Adventures of a Lap-Dog* (1751) by Francis Coventry. LM's copy remains in her library (Sotheby Catalogue, 1 Aug. 1928, p. 84).

[3] Lady Tempest has married a foolish man for his money and cuckolded him (or pretended to); she is 'the greatest Female Wit in *London*' (1751 ed., p. 45). Lady Sophister, full of affected wisdom, is divorced from her husband and has travelled abroad; she has read Hobbes, Malebranche, Shaftesbury, Wollaston, and especially Locke, and argues with her physicians 'at the Expence only of Christianity and the Gospel' (p. 66).

[4] 'Do you eat, Madam ?' Mrs. Qualmsick's physician asks her. 'Not at all, Sir, . . . not at all; I have neither

considerable men in the Parish, and is a grave, sober, thinking Great Fool, whose solemn appearance and deliberate way of delivering his sentiments gives them an Air of good Sense, thô they are often the most injudicious that ever were pronounc'd. By perpetual telling me I eat so little he is amaz'd I am able to subsist, he had brought me to be of his opinion, and I begun to be seriously uneasy at it.

This usefull Treatise has rouz'd me into a recollection of what I eat Yesterday, and doe almost every day the same. I wake generally about 7 and drink halfe a pint of warm asse's milk, after which I sleep two hours. As soon as I am risen, I constantly take 3 cups of milk coffee, and two hours after that a large cup of milk chocolate. Two hours more brings my Dinner, where I never fail swallowing a good Dish (I don't mean Plate) of gravy Soup with all the Bread, roots, etc. belonging to it. I then eat a Wing and the whole Body of a large fat capon, and a veal sweetbread, concluding with a Competent Quantity of custard and some roasted chestnuts. At 5 in the afternoon I take another Dose of Asse's milk, and for supper 12 chestnuts (which would weigh 24 of those in London), one new-laid Egg, and a handsome Poringer of white Bread and milk. With this Diet, notwithstanding the menaces of my wise Doctor, I am now convince'd I am in no danger of starving, and am oblig'd to little Pompey for this Discovery.

I open'd my Eyes this morning on Leonora,[1] from which I defy the greatest chymist in morals to extract any Instruction: the style most affectedly Florid and naturally insipid, with such a confus'd heap of admirable characters that never were, or can be, in Human Nature. I flung it aside after 50 pages[2] and laid hold of Mrs. Philips, where I expected to

Stomach, nor Appetite, nor Strength, nor any thing in the World; and I believe verily, I can't live a Week longer—I drank a little Chocolate yesterday Morning, Sir, and got down a little Bason of Broth at Noon, and eat a Pigeon for my Dinner, and made a shift to get down another little Bason of Broth at Night—but I can't eat at all, Sir; my Appetite fails me more and more every Day, and I live upon mere nothing' (p. 226).

[1] *Leonora: Or, Characters Drawn from Real Life. Containing A Great Variety of Incidents, Interspers'd with Reflections moral and entertaining*, 2 vols., 1745 (Andrew Block, *The English Novel 1740–1850*, 1961, p. 137).

[2] Yet in her copy of the second volume LM wrote: 'worse than 'tother' (Sotheby Catalogue, p. 91).

find at least probable, if not true, facts, and was not dis-
apointed.¹ There is a Great Similitude in the Genius and adventures (the one being productive of the other) between
Madam Con[stantia] and Lady Vane. The first mention'd has the Advantage in Birth and (if I am not mistaken)
in understanding. They have both had Scandalous law suits
with their Husbands² and are endow'd with the same
Intrepid Assurance. Con[stantia] seems to value her selfe also
on her Generosity, and has given the same proofes of it.
The Parallel might be drawn out to be as long as any of
Plutarch's, but I dare swear you are allready heartily weary
of my remarks and wish I had not read so much in so short
a Time, that you might not be trouble'd with my comments.
But you must suffer me to say something of the polite
Mr. S—te, whose name I should never have guess'd by
the rapturous Description his mistriss makes of his person,³
having allwaies look'd upon him as one of the most disagreable Fellows about Town, as odious in his outside as stupid
in his conversation, and I should as soon have expected to
hear of his Conquests at the Head of an Army as amongst
Women; yet he has been (it seems) the darling favourite of
the most experienc'd of the Sex, which ⟨shew⟩s me I am a
very bad Judge of Merit; b⟨ut⟩ I agree with Mrs. Ph[ilips]
that however profligate she may have been she is infinitely
his Superior in Virtue, and if her Penitence is as sincere as
she says,⁴ she may expect their Future Fate to be like that
of Dives and Lazarus.⁵

    This Letter is of a most immoderate length. I [hope] it
will find you at Cane Wood.⁶ Your Solitude there will

---

¹ *An Apology for the Conduct of Mrs.
T. C. Phillips* (1748-9). LM's comment
in vol. i: 'truly tho not finely wrote'
(Sotheby Catalogue, p. 93).

² Teresia Constantia Phillips (1709–
65) m. (1723) Henry Muilman, a Dutch
merchant; the next year he had the
marriage annulled.

³ Mrs. Phillips devotes a long section
(ed. 1750, ii. 94–191) to her five-year
liaison with Mr. P. S—te, son of a
Roman Catholic baronet; she describes
him as agreeable, with meaningful eyes

and artful tongue; graceful and delicately
clean; of dangerous address and robust,
lascivious constitution.

⁴ Mrs. Phillips is penitent throughout, referring to herself as a 'frail
Sinner' and warning her female readers
to profit by her sad experiences (ii.
148–9).

⁵ One in Heaven and one in Hell
(Luke xvi).

⁶ Kenwood House, Hampstead, occu-
pied by Lord Bute and his family since
1749.

permit you to peruse and even to forgive all the Impertinence of your most Affectionate Mother.

M. Wortley

My Blessing to our children and Complements to Lord Bute. I inclose a bill to pay the overplus due to you and serve for future little commissions.

Text W MS iii. 201–4   *Address* To the Rt Honble the Countess of Bute recommended to Samuel Child Esqr near Temple Bar London Angleterre [*in another hand*] Grosvenor Square [*sic*]

To Lady Bute *1 March* [*1752*]

March 1. N.S.

Dear Child,

I have now finish'd your Books, and I beleive you'l think I have made quick dispatch. To say truth, I have read night and Day. Mr. Loveill gave me some entertainment,[1] thô there is but one character in it that I can find out. I do not doubt Mr. Depy is design'd for Sir John Rawdon.[2] The adventure mention'd at Rome realy happen'd to him, with this addition, that after he was got quit of his Fear of being suspected in the Interest of the P[retender] he endeavor'd to manifest his Loyalty by railing at him in all Companys with all the warmth imaginable, on which his Companions perswaded him that his Death was absolutely determin'd by that Court, and he durst not stir out for sometime for Fear of being assasinated, nor eat for Fear of being poison'd. I saw him at Venice, where on hearing it said I had been at Constantinople, he ask'd Lord Mansel[3] by what accident I made that Journey. He answer'd, Mr. W[ortley] was Ambassador to the Port[e]. Sir John reply'd: To what Port? The Port of Leghorn? I could relate many speeches of his of equal Beauty, but

[1] *The Adventures of Mr. Loveill, Intersperse'd with many Real Amours of the Modern Polite World*, 1750 (Andrew Block, *The English Novel 1740–1850*, 1961, p. 3). James R. Foster (*History of the Pre-Romantic Novel in England*, 1949, p. 69) attributes it to Dr. John Hill (1716 ?–1775), as does the index to the *Monthly Review*.
[2] See ii. 457 (22 June [1752]).
[3] Mansell (see ii. 143) had befriended Rawdon in Venice.

I beleive you are allready tir'd of hearing of him as much as I was with the memoirs of Miss H[arriot] Steuart,[1] who, being intended for an Example of Wit and Virtue, is a Jilt and a Fool in every page; but while I was indolently peruseing the marvellous figures she exhibits, no more ressembling any thing in Human Nature than the wooden Cuts in the Seven Champions,[2] I was rouz'd into great surprize and Indignation by the monstrous abuse of one of the very, very few Women I have a real value for. I mean Lady B[ell] F[inch], who is not only clearly meant by the mention of her Library, she being the only Lady at Court that has one, but her very name at length, she being christen'd Cæcelia Isabella, thô she chuses to be call'd by the Latter. I allwaies thought her conduct in every light so irreproachable, I did not think she had an Enemy upon Earth.[3] I now see 'tis impossible to avoid them, especially in her Situation. It is one of the misfortunes of a suppos'd Court interest (perhaps you may know it by Experience), even the people you have oblig'd hate you if they do not think you have serv'd them to the utmost extent of a power that they fancy you are possess'd of, which it may be is only imaginary.

On the other Hand I forgive Jo. Thompson 2 volumes of Absurdities[4] for the sake of the Justice he has done the memory of the Duke of Montagu, who realy had (in my Opinion) one of the most humane dispositions that ever appear'd in the World.[5]

I was such an old Fool as to weep over Clarissa Harlowe[6]

[1] Charlotte Lennox, *The Life of Harriot Stuart* (1751).

[2] *Famous Historie of the Seaven Champions of Christendome*, a chivalric romance by Richard Johnson, first published in 1597.

[3] In 1747 Mrs. Lennox dedicated her first publication, a book of poems, to Lady Isabella Finch (d. 1771), da. of 7th Earl of Winchilsea, but apparently did not receive the patronage she expected (Miriam R. Small, *Charlotte Ramsay Lennox: An Eighteenth Century Lady of Letters*, 1935, pp. 4–5). Lady Isabella held a post at Court; and in the novel Mrs. Lennox, besides mentioning Lady Cecilia's library (i. 238),

castigates her for promising court-favours and failing to perform them (ii. 15).

[4] *The Life and Adventures of Joe Thompson* (1750) by Edward Kimber; it is treated in Philip B. Gove, *The Imaginary Voyage in Prose Fiction*, 1941, pp. 319–20. In vol. i of her copy LM wrote 'tolerable', and in vol. ii 'Intolerable' (Sotheby Catalogue, 1 Aug. 1928, p. 91).

[5] The 2nd Duke of Montagu (d. 1749) is eulogized as a 'godlike peer' and 'one of the greatest men that ever existed' (vol. ii, chap. xix).

[6] Samuel Richardson's *Clarissa* (1747–8). In the first volume of her

like any milk maid of sixteen over the Ballad of the Ladie's Fall.¹ To say truth, the first volume soften'd me by a near ressemblance of my Maiden Days, but on the whole 'tis most miserable stuff. Miss How, who is call'd a young Lady of sense and Honor, is not only extreme silly, but a more vicious character than Sally Martin, whose Crimes are owing at first to Seduction and afterwards to necessity,² while this virtuous Damsel, without any reason insults her mother at home and ridicules her abroad, abuses the man she marrys, and is impertinent and Impudent with great applause. Even that model of Perfection, Clarissa, is so faulty in her behaviour as to deserve little Compassion. Any Girl that runs away with a young Fellow without intending to marry him should be carry'd to Bridewell or Bedlam the next day. Yet the circumstances are so laid as to inspire tenderness, notwithstanding the low style and absurd incidents, and I look upon this and Pamela to be two Books that will do more general mischeif than the Works of Lord Rochester.³

There is something Humourous in R. Random that makes me beleive the Author is H[enry] Fielding.⁴ I am horridly afraid I guess too well the writer of those abominable insipidities of Cornelia, Leonora, and the Ladie's Drawing Room.⁵

I fancy you are now saying—'Tis a sad thing to grow old. What does my poor mama mean by troubling me with Criticisms on Books⁶ that no body but her selfe will ever read over?—You must alow something to my Solitude. I have a pleasure in writing to my dear child, and not many subjects to write upon. The adventures of people here would not at all amuse you, having no Acquaintance with the persons concern'd; and an account of my selfe would

copy LM wrote 'miserable stuff' (Sotheby Catalogue, p. 95).

¹ *A Lamentable Ballad of the Ladies Fall. . . .* , a broadside in black-letter [?1680].

² Sally Martin is a flirt who encourages Lovelace to seduce Clarissa.

³ John Wilmot (1647–80), 2nd Earl of Rochester, poet and libertine.

⁴ Other readers besides LM attributed to Fielding *The Adventures of Roderick Random* (1748), Smollett's first important

novel (Lewis M. Knapp, *Tobias Smollett*, 1949, p. 96).

⁵ *The History of Cornelia* (1750) was by Sarah Scott. For *Leonora*, see above, p. 5. *The Lady's Drawing Room* (1744): LM read the second edition (1748), on which she jotted 'very good' (Sotheby Catalogue, p. 90). LM's guess may have been Sarah Fielding.

⁶ For a discussion of LM's criticism, see essay by R. Halsband in *Philological Quarterly*, Jan. 1966.

hardly gain credit after having fairly own'd to you how deplorably I was misled in regard to my own Health, thô I have all my Life been on my Guard against the Information convey'd by the sense of Hearing; it being one of my earliest Observations, the universal Inclination of Humankind is to be led by the Ears, and I am sometimes apt to imagine that they are given to Men as they are to pitchers, purposely that they may be carry'd about by them. This consideration should abate my wonder to see (as I do here) the most astonishing Legends embrac'd as the most sacred Truths by those who have allwaies heard them asserted and never contradicted. They even place a Merit in complying with their Hearing in direct opposition to the evidence of all their other Senses.

I am very much pleas'd with the account you give me of your Father's Health. I hope your own and that of your Family is perfect. Give my Blessing to your little ones and my Compliments to Lord Bute, and think me ever Your most affectionate Mother,

M. Wortley.

Text W MS iii. 302–4   *Address* To The Rt Honble the Countess of Bute recommended to Samuel Child Esqr near Temple Bar London Angleterre

To Wortley *8 March* [*1752*]

March 8 N.S.

I receiv'd last night yours of Jan. 31 O.S., which has given me the greatest Anxiety. I cannot form to my selfe any Conjecture of the Adventure you mention. I have never heard from our Son since he was Secretary to the Embassy,[1] thô I wrote to him several times. I suppose he dropp'd his

---

[1] Edward Wortley Montagu, junior, had served at Aix-la-Chapelle in 1748 (see ii. 397, n. 2). His 'adventure' was the outcome of setting up as a gambler in Paris; in Nov. 1751 he was arrested for robbery and imprisoned for eleven days, but legally exonerated in Jan. 1752 (Jonathan Curling, *Edward Wortley Montagu*, 1954, pp. 131–41).

Correspondance with me from the time he thought it would be unnecessary. I was not surpriz'd at it, having never rely'd on his Proffessions. Mr. Anderson's[1] letter to me was only concerning Books which I desir'd him to purchase in Holland. Since I left Louvere in the beginning of November I have allways been in the Country, and seen no body that could menti⟨on⟩ to me any News from England. Indeed there is very little known here, since all public papers are forbidden excepting those printed in Italy.

I know not where to direct to my Son, nor in what manner to write on a Subject of which I am entirely ignorant, thô I should be very glad to do it as you think it proper, which no doubt you would not do if the affair had any thing Scandalous in it.

Text W MS ii. 229–30   *Address* To Edwd Wortley Esqr recommended to Sam. Child Esqr near Temple Bar London Angleterre *End. by W* [*Summary*] Ad 14 Apr. Recd 3 Apr.

To Lady Bute *16 March* [*1752*]

March 16. N.S.

Dear Child,

I receiv'd yours of Dec. 20th this morning, which gave me great Pleasure by the account of your good Health and that of your Father. I know nothing else could give me any at present, being sincerely afflicted for the Death of the Doge.[2] He is lamented here by all Ranks of people as their common Parent. He realy answer'd the Idea of Lord Bolingbroke's imaginary Patriot Prince,[3] and was the only Example I ever knew of having pass'd through the greatest employments and most important negotiations without ever making an Enemy. When I was at Venice[4] (which was some months before his Election) he was the leading voice in the

---

[1] See below, p. 16.
[2] Pietro Grimani (see ii. 152) died on 7 March 1752, aged 75 (Andrea da Mosto, *I Dogi di Venezia*, 1939, p. 298).

[3] *The Idea of a Patriot King* (1749), inspired by Frederick, Prince of Wales.
[4] From Sept. 1739 to Aug. 1740.

Senate, and possess'd of so strong a popularity as would
have been dangerous in the hands of a bad Man, yet he
had the art to silence Envy, and I never once heard an
Objection to his Character or even an Insinuation to his
disadvantage. I attribute this peculiar Happiness to be owing to the sincere Benevolence of his Heart, joyn'd with an
easy chearfullness of Temper, which made him agreable to
all companys, and a Blessing to all his Dependants. Authority
appear'd so aimable in him, no one wish'd it less except
himselfe, who would sometimes lament the weight of it as
robing him too much of the conversation of his Freinds, in
which he plac'd his cheife Delight, being so little Ambitious
that (to my certain knowledge) far from caballing to gain
that Elevation to which he was rais'd, he would have refus'd
it if he had not look'd upon the acceptation of it as a Duty
due to his Country.

This is only speaking of him in the public light. As to my
selfe, he allways profess'd (and gave me every demonstration
of) the most cordial Freindship.[1] Indeed I receiv'd every
good office from him I could have expected from a tender
Father or a kind Brother, and thô I have not seen him since
my last return to Italy, he never omitted an opertunity of
expressing the greatest regard for me, both in his discourse
to others, and upon all occasions where he thought he could
be usefull to me. I do not doubt I shall very sensibly miss the
Influence of his good Intentions.

You will think I dwell too long on this Melancholy
Subject. I will turn to one widely different in takeing
notice of the Dress of you London Ladies, who I find take
up the Italian Fashion of going in your Hair. It is here only
the custom of the Peasants and the unmarry'd Women of
Quality, excepting in the Heat of ⟨summer⟩ when any Cap
would be almost insupportable. ⟨I⟩ have often smile'd to
my selfe in viewing ⟨our⟩ assemblys (which they call conversations) at Louvere, the Gentlemen being all in light
nightcaps, nightgowns (under which I am inform'd they
wear no Breeches) and slippers, and the Ladys in their

---

[1] The British envoy in Venice wrote:
'His Serenity seemed to have retained
a partiality for the English Nation from
the time of His Embassy in the Reign
of Queen Anne' (Sir James Gray to
Holdernesse, 8 March 1752, SP 99/65).

stays, and smock sleeves ty'd with Ribands, and a single lutestring petticoat. There is not a Hat or a Hoop to be seen. It is true this dress is call'd Vestimenta di confidenza, and they do not appear in it in Town but in their own chambers, and that only during the Summer Months. My paper admonishes me to conclude, by assuring you that I am ever your most affectionate mother.

M. Wortley

My Complements to Lord Bute and blessing to my Grand children. You will send me Lord Orrery and Lord Bolingbroke's Books.[1]

Text W MS iii. 90–91   *Address* To The Rt Honble the Countess of Bute recommended to Samuel Child Esqr near Temple Bar London Angleterre [*in another hand*] Grosvenor Street

To Lady Bute *22 June* [*1752*]

[*This letter is printed in vol. ii, pp. 457–60*]

To Lady Bute *22 July* [*1752*]

July 22 N.S.

When I wrote to you last (my dear Child) I told you I had a great Cold, which ended in a very bad Fever, which continu'd a Fortnight without Intermission, and you may imagine has brought me very low. I have not yet left my chamber. My first care is to thank you for yours of May 8th.

I have not yet lost all my Interest in this Country by the Death of the Doge, having another very considerable Freind, thô I cannot expect to keep him long (he being near fourscore). I mean the Cardinal Querini, who is Archbishop of this Diocese,[2] and consequently of great Power, there being not one family high or low in this Province that has not some Eclesiastic in it, and therefore all of them have some dependance on him. He is of one of the

---

[1] See below, pp. 56, 59, 61-65.
[2] Angelo Maria Querini (1680–

1755), Bishop of Brescia and Cardinal (1727), Librarian of the Vatican (1730).

first Familys of Venice, vastly rich of himselfe, and has many
great Ben[e]fices beside his ArchBishoprick, but these
advantages are little in his Eyes in comparison of being the
first Author (as he fancys) at this day in Christendom; and
indeed if the merit of Books consisted in Bulk and Number
he might very justly claim that character.[1] I beleive he has
publish'd yearly several volumes for above fifty years, beside corresponding with all the Litterati of Europe, and
amongst these several of the Senior Fellows at Oxford, and
some members of the Royal Society that neither you nor
I ever heard of, whom he is persuaded are the most eminent
Men in England.[2] He is at present imploy'd in writeing his
own Life, of which he has already printed the first Tome,
and if he goes on in the same Style it will be a most volumnious performance.[3] He begins from the moment of his
Birth, and tells us that in that day he made such extraodinary faces, the Midwife, chambermaids, and Nurses all
agreed that there was born a shining light in church and State.

You'l think me very merry with the failings of my
Freind. I confess I ought to forgive a vanity to which I am
oblig'd for many good offices, since I do not doubt it is
owing to that, that he proffesses himselfe so highly attach'd
to my service, having an opinion that my suffrage is of
great weight in the Learned World, and that I shall not fail
to spread his Fame at least all over Great Brittain. He sent
me a present last week of a very uncommon kind, even his
own Picture, extreamly well done, but so flattering it is a
young old man, with a most pompous Inscription under it.
I suppose he intended it for the Ornament of my Library,
not knowing it is only a closet. However, these Distinctions
he shews me gives me a figure in this Town, where every

[1] The list of works written or edited
by him adds up to eighty (Alfred
Baudrillart, *De Cardinalis Quirini vita
et operibus*, 1889, pp. v–x).

[2] During his travels (1710–14)
Querini had visited England; he met
and later corresponded with Gilbert
and Thomas Burnet, theologians, Richard Bentley and John Hudson, classical
scholars, and Isaac Newton (Baudrillart,
p. 54). Charles de Brosses, who met him

in 1740, thought him 'pieux et savant,
mais d'une science lourde' (*Lettres
familières sur l'Italie*, ed. Y. Bezard,
1931, ii. 491).

[3] In 1749 he had published two
volumes, followed in 1750 by a one-
volume appendix—which carried the
story of his life up to 1740; and in 1754
he published commentaries in a folio
volume (Baudrillart, Nos. 58, 59, 73).

body has something to hope from him, and it was certainly in a view to that, they would have complemented me with a Statue, for I would not have you mistake so far as to imagine there is any set of people more gratefull or generous than another. Mankind is every where the same: like Cherries or Apples, they may differ in size, shape, or colour, from different soils, climates, or culture,[1] but are still essentially the same species; and the little black wood cherry is not nearer akin to the Dukes[2] that are serv'd at Great Tables, than the wild, naked Negro to the fine Figures adorn'd with Coronets and Ribands. This observation might be carry'd yet farther; all Animals are stimulated by the same passions, and act very near alike, as far as we are capable of observing them.

The conclusion of your Letter has touch'd me very much. I simpathize with you (my dear Child) in all the concern you express for your Family. You may remember I represented it to you before you was marry'd, but that is one of the sentiments it is impossible to comprehend till it is felt. A Mother only knows a Mother's fondness. Indeed, the pain so over balances the pleasure, that I beleive if it could be throughly understood, there would be no Mothers at all. However, take care that your Anxiety for the Future does not take from you the comforts you may enjoy in the present Hour. It is all that is properly ours, and yet such is the weakness of Humanity, we commonly lose what is, either by regretting the past, or disturbing our minds with Fear of what may be. You have many Blessings: a Husband you love and who behaves well to you, agreable hopefull children, a Handsome convenient House with pleasant Gardens, in a good Air and fine situation,[3] which I place amongst the most solid Satisfactions of Life. The truest Wisdom is that which diminishes to us what is displeasing, and turns our Thoughts to the advantages we possess.

I can assure you I give no precepts I do not daily practise. How often do I fancy to my selfe the pleasure I should take in seeing you in the midst of your little people! And how severe do I then think my destiny, that denys me that

---

[1] A variant of this idea in LM's Commonplace Book: 'as many diff[eren]t species of men, as of Birds'   (MS, f. 6).
[2] A kind of cherry.
[3] Kenwood House in Hampstead.

Happiness! I endeavor to comfort my selfe by refflecting that we should certainly have perpetual disputes (if not Quarrels) concerning the management of them. The affection of a Grand Mother has generally a tincture of Doatage. You would say I spoilt them, and perhaps not be much in the wrong. Speaking of them calls to my remembrance the Token I have so long promis'd my God daughter.[1] I am realy asham'd of it. I would have sent it by Mr. Anderson if he had been going immediately to London, but as he pro-pos'd a long Tour I durst not press it upon him.[2] It is not easie to find any one who will take the charge of a Jewel for a long Journey. It may be the value of it in Money, to chuse something for her selfe, would be as acceptable. If so, I will send you a Note upon Child. Ceremony should be banish'd between us. I beg you would speak freely upon that and all other occasions to your most affectionate Mother,

M. ⟨Wo⟩rtley.

Text W MS iii. 104–7   *Address* To The Rt Honble the Countess of Bute [recommended to S. Child Esqr near Temple Bar *struck out*] London [Angleterre *struck out*] [*in another hand*] Grosvenor Street

To Lady Bute [*Sept. 1752*]

It is very true (my Dear Child) we cannot now maintain a Family with the product of a Flock, thô I do not doubt the present sheep afford as much wool and milk as any of their Ancestors, and 'tis certain our natural wants are not more numerous than formerly; but the World is past its infancy, and will no longer be contented with spoon meat. ⟨Ti⟩me has added great Improvements, but those very improvements have introduce'd a train of artificial necessities. A Collective Body of men make a gradual progress in understanding, like

---

[1] Lady Bute's eldest daughter.
[2] John Anderson, a travelling tutor (formerly to LM's son), had visited her at Brescia in 1750 (see ii. 462) and re-turned to London in Feb. 1751.

that of a single Individual. When I refflect on the vast encrease of usefull as well as speculative knowledge the last three hundred years has produc'd, and that the peasants of this Age have more conveniencies than the first Emperors of Rome had any Notion of, I imagine we are now arriv'd at that period which answers to 15. I cannot think we are older when I recollect the many palpable Follys which are still (almost) universally persisted in. I place that of War amongst the most glareing, being full as senseless as the boxing of School Boys, and whenever we come to Man's estate (perhaps a thousand years hence) I do not doubt it will appear as ridiculous as the pranks of unlucky Lads. Several discoverys will then be made, and several Truths made clear, of which we have now ⟨no⟩ more Idea than the Ancients had of the Circulation of the Blood, or the optics of Sir I[saac] Newton.

You will beleive me in a very dull Humour when I fill my Letter with such Whims, and indeed so I am. I have just receiv'd the news of Sir J[ames] Gray's departure, and am exceedingly vex'd I did not know of his design'd Journey.[1] I suppose he would have carry'd my token, and now I utterly despair of an Opertunity of sending it, and therefore enclose a Note on Child for the value of it.

When you see Lady Rich pray do not fail to present my thanks and compliments.[2] I desire the same to every body that thinks it worth while to enquire after me. You mention a Collonel Rich as her Son; I thought he had been kill'd in Scotland.[3] You see my entire Ignorance of all English affairs, and consequently whatever you tell me of my acquaintance has the merit of Novelty to me, who correspond with nobody but your selfe and Lady Oxford, whose Retirement and ill Health does not permit her to send me much news.

I expect a Letter of thanks from my G[od] Daughter; I wrote to my G[rand] Mother[4] long before her Age. I desire you would not see it, being willing to judge of her Genius. I know I shall read it with some Partialty, which I

---

1 Gray, British Resident in Venice, departed on final leave soon after 20 Aug. 1752 (D. B. Horn, p. 85).
2 Lady Rich was an old friend (see i. 269).
3 Col. Robert Rich (1714–85) was

so seriously wounded in the battle of Culloden that his death was reported in the *Gentleman's Mag.* of May 1746 (p. 328).
4 The Dowager Lady Denbigh (see below, p. 27) was her step-grandmother.

cannot avoid to all that is yours, as I am your most affectionate Mother,

M. Wortley M.

My compliments to Lord Bute.

Text W MS iii. 148–9   *Address* To The Rt Honble the Countess of Bute recommended to Sam: Child Esqr near Temple Bar London Angleterre [*in another hand*] Grosevenors Street   *Postmark* oc ⟨3⟩

To Lady Bute *1 Oct.* [*1752*]

Oct. 1. N.S.[1]

I have wrote 5 Letters to my dear Child, of which you have not acknowledg'd the receit. I fear some if not all of them have miscarry'd, which may be attributed to Sir J[ames] Gray's leaving Venice. You must now direct (alas!) recommandée a Mons. Smith, consul de S[a] M[ajesté] B[ritannique].[2] The first of those Letters I mention spoke of Lord K.; the 2nd had a story of L. O.; the 3rd answer'd yours relateing to Miss Gunnings;[3] the 4th gave an account of our Cardinal;[4] and the last enclos'd a note upon Child.[5]

You need not excuse to me taking notice of your Carpet. I think you have great reason to value your selfe on the performance, but will have better luck than I have had if you can persuade any body else to do so. I could never get people to beleive that I set a stitch, when I work'd six hours in a day.

You will confess my Employments much more triffling than yours when I own to you (between you and I) that my cheife Amusement is writeing the History of my own Time. It has been my Fortune to have a more exact knowledge

---

[1] In Sept. 1752 England adopted the Gregorian calendar, in use on the Continent (except Russia), yet LM still writes N.S. occasionally.

[2] Gray was not replaced as Resident until 1754, by John Murray (D. B. Horn, p. 85). Joseph Smith had been Consul since 1744.

[3] In June 1751 all London talked of Maria and Elizabeth Gunning, Irish girls of no fortune and of such astonishing beauty that they were followed by crowds (Walpole, *Corr.* xx. 260). In Feb. 1752 Elizabeth (1733–90) m. 6th Duke of Hamilton; and in March, Maria (1732–60) m. 6th Earl of Coventry.

[4] On 22 July [1752].

[5] In her previous letter. The first three letters evidently were not received.

both of the Persons and Facts that have made the greatest figure in England in this Age than is common, and I take pleasure in putting together what I know, with an Impartialty that is altogether unusual. Distance of Time and place has totally blotted from my Mind all Traces either of Resentment or prejudice, and I speak with the same Indifference of the Court of G[reat] B[ritain] as I should do of that of Augustus Cæsar. I hope you have not so ill opinion of me to think I am turning Author in my old age. I can assure you I regularly burn every Quire as soon as it is finish'd, and mean nothing more than to divert my solitary hours.[1] I know Mankind too well to think they are capable of receiving Truth, much less of applauding it. Or were it otherwise, Applause to me is as insignificant as Garlands on the Dead. ⟨I⟩ have no concern beyond my own Family. ⟨But⟩ your Father's silence gives me great pain; I have not heard from him since last April. Let me know the reason of it, and write as often as you can to your most affectionate Mother,

M. Wortley M.

My Complements to Lord Bute and blessing to all yours.

Text W MS iii. 70–71   *Address* To The Rt Honble the Countess of Bute recommended to S. Child Esqr near Temple Bar London Angleterre   *Postmark* NO 14

To Wortley [*3 Dec. 1752*]

Yours of Aug't 24 did not come to my Hands till this morning, Dec. 3rd. It reliev'd me from a great deal of pain occasion'd by your Silence. I am glad you are in a place I have heard often celebrated for one of the prettiest in England.[2]

The last Summer has been as remarkable for Rain here as with you. It is now so rigid a Frost I am afraid we shall have

---

[1] Two fragments of historical memoirs, perhaps these, survived: a very brief one on the death of Queen Anne (1861, i. 122), and an account of the Court of George I in 1714 (W MS vii. 188–95; 1861, i. 123–34).

[2] Probably Newbold Verdon, Leics., which W had inherited in 1749.

as hard a Winter as the first I pass'd in Italy. It is so disagreeable both to my Inclination and Constitution that I am often tempted to remove to a warmer Situation. It is a long and expensive Journey, which deters me from undertaking it.

I hope your Health continues good, since you say nothing to the Contrary. I write long letters to my Daughter, and would do the same to you if it was as easy to me to write this large Hand as the small running one I am us'd to.

Text W MS ii. 231–2   *Address* To Edwd Wortley Esqr recommended to Samuel Child Esqr[1] near Temple Bar London Angleterre [*in another hand*] Cavendish Square   *Postmark* ⟨?⟩   *End. by W* [*Summary*] Recd 18 July 1753. Ad 1 Sept.

To Lady Bute 28 *Jan.* [*1753*]

Jan. 28 N.S.

Dear Child,

You have given me a great deal of Satisfaction by your account of your eldest Daughter. I am particularly pleas'd to hear she is a good Arithmetician; it is the best proofe of understanding. The knowledge of Numbers is one of the cheif distinctions between us and Brutes. If there is any thing in Blood, you may reasonably expect your children should be endow'd with an uncommon Share of good Sense. Mr. Wortley's Family and mine have both produce'd some of [the] greatest Men that have been born in England. I mean Admiral Sandwich, and my Great Grandfather who was distinguish'd by the name of Wise William.[2] I have heard Lord Bute's father[3] mention'd as an extroadinary Genius (thô he had not many oppertunitys of shewing it), and his uncle the present Duke of Argyle has one of the best Heads I ever knew.[4]

[1] LM did not know that he had died on 14 Oct. 1752 (*Gentleman's Mag.*, p. 478).

[2] Edward Montagu (1625-72), 1st Earl of Sandwich, was W's grandfather;

the Hon. William Pierrepont (1608–78), prominent politician.

[3] James Stuart (1690–1723), 2nd Earl.

[4] For Archibald Campbell, 3rd Duke of Argyll, see ii. 90.

I will therefore speak to you as supposing Lady Mary not only capable but desirous of Learning. In that case, by all means let her be indulg'd in it. You will tell me, I did not make it a part of your Education. Your prospect was very different from hers, as you had no deffect either in mind or person to hinder, and much in your circumstances to attract, the highest offers. It seem'd your business to learn how to live in the World, as it is hers to know how to be easy out of it. It is the common Error of Builders and Parents to follow some Plan they think beautifull (and perhaps is so) without considering that nothing is beautifull that is misplac'd. Hence we see so many Edifices raise'd that the raisers can never inhabit, being too large for their Fortunes. Vistos are laid open over barren heaths, and apartments contriv'd for a coolness very agreable in Italy but killing in the North of Brittain. Thus every Woman endeavors to breed her Daughter a fine Lady, qualifying her for a station in which she will never appear, and at the same time incapacitateing her for that retirement to which she is destin'd. Learning (if she has a real taste for it) will not only make her contented but happy in it. No Entertainment is so cheap as reading, nor any pleasure so lasting. She will not want new Fashions nor regret the loss of expensive Diversions or variety of company if she can be amus'd with an Author in her closet. To render this amusement extensive, she should be permitted to learn the Languages. I have heard it lamented that Boys lose so many years in meer learning of Words. This is no Objection to a Girl, whose time is not so precious. She cannot advance her selfe in any proffession, and has therefore more hours to spare; and as you say her memory is good, she will be very agreably employ'd this way.

There are two cautions to be given on this subject: first, not to think her selfe Learned when she can read Latin or even Greek. Languages are more properly to be calld Vehicles of Learning than Learning it selfe, as may be observ'd in many Schoolmasters, who thô perhaps critics in Grammar are the most ignorant fellows upon Earth. True knowledge consists in knowing things, not words. I would wish her no farther a Linguist than to enable her to read Books in their originals, that are often corrupted and allwaies injur'd by Translations. Two hours application every morning will bring this about much sooner than you can imagine, and she will have leisure enough beside to run over the English poetry, which is a more important part of a Woman's Education than it is generally suppos'd. Many a young Damsel has been ruin'd by a fine copy of Verses, which she would have laugh'd at if she had known it had been stoln from Mr. Waller. I remember when I was a Girl I sav'd one of my Companions from Destruction, who communicated to me an epistle she was quite charm'd with. As she had a natural good taste, she observ'd the Lines were not so smooth as Prior's or Pope's,[1] but had more thought and spirit than any of theirs. She was wonderfully delighted with such a demonstration of her Lover's sense and passion, and not a little pleas'd with her own charms, that had force enough to inspire such elegancies. In the midst of this Triumph, I shew'd her they were taken from Randolph's Poems,[2] and the unfortunate Transcriber was dismiss'd with the scorn he deserv'd. To say Truth, the poor Plagiary was very unlucky to fall into my Hands; that Author, being no longer in Fashion, would have escap'd any one of less universal reading than my selfe. You should encourrage your Daughter to talk over with you what she reads, and as you are very capable of distinguishing, take care she does not mistake pert Folly for Wit and humour, or Rhyme for Poetry, which are the common Errors of young People, and have a train of ill Consequences.

The second caution to be given her (and which is most absolutely necessary) is to conceal whatever Learning she attains, with as much solicitude as she would hide crookedness or lameness. The parade of it can only serve to draw on her the envy, and consequently the most inveterate Hatred, of all he and she Fools, which will certainly be at least three parts in four of all her Acquaintance. The use of knowledge in our Sex (beside the amusement of Solitude) is to moderate the passions and learn to be contented with a small expence, which are the certain effects of a studious Life and, it may

---

[1] Before Aug. 1712, when LM was married, Pope had published only the *Pastorals*, the *Essay on Criticism*, and the first version of *The Rape of the Lock*.

[2] Thomas Randolph (1605–35), *Poems* (1638).

be, preferable even to that Fame which Men have engross'd
to themselves and will not suffer us to share. You will tell me
I have not observ'd this rule my selfe, but you are mistaken;
it is only inevitable Accident that has given me any Reputation that way. I have allwaies carefully avoided it, and ever
thought it a misfortune.

The explanation of this paragraph would occasion a
long digression, which I will not trouble you with, it being
my present design only to say what I think usefull for the
Instruction of my Grand daughter, which I have much at
Heart. If she has the same inclination (I should say passion)
for Learning that I was born with, History, Geography,
and Philosophy will furnish her with materials to pass away
chearfully a longer Life than is allotted to mortals. I beleive
there are few heads capable of makeing Sir I[saac] Newton's
calculations, but the result of them is not difficult to be understood by a moderate capacity. Do not fear this should make
her affect the character of Lady ——, or Lady ——, or
Mrs. ——. Those Women are ridiculous, not because they
have Learning but because they have it not. One thinks
herselfe a compleat Historian after reading Eachard's
Roman History,[1] another a profound Philosopher having
got by heart some of Pope's uninteligible essays, and a third
an able Divine on the Strength of Whitfield's Sermons.[2]
Thus you hear them screaming Politics and Controversie.
It is a saying of Thucidides, Ignorance is bold, and knowledge reserv'd.[3] Indeed it is impossible to be far advance'd
in it without being more humble'd by a conviction of Human
ignorance than elated by Learning.

At the same time I recommend Books, I neither exclude
Work nor drawing. I think it as scandalous for a Woman not
to know how to use a needle, as for a Man not to know how
to use a sword. I was once extream fond of my pencil, and it
was a great mortification to me when my Father turn'd off
my Master, having made a considerable progress for the
short time I learnt. My over eagerness in the persuit of it had

[1] Lawrence Echard (1670?–1730), *The Roman History* (1695–8).

[2] George Whitefield (1714–70), famous Methodist preacher, published many sermons.

[3] 'Boldness means ignorance and reflection brings hesitation' (*Pelopon-nesian War*, II. xl. 3; transl. Loeb Library).

brought a weakness on my Eyes that made it necessary to leave it off, and all the advantage I got was the Improvement of my Hand. I see by hers that practise will make her a ready writer. She may attain it by serving you for a Secretary when your Health or affairs make it troublesome to you to write your selfe, and custom will make it an agreable Amusement to her. She cannot have too many for that station of Life which will probably be her Fate. The ultimate end of your Education was to make you a good Wife (and I have the comfort to hear that you are one); hers ought to be, to make her Happy in a Virgin state. I will not say it is happier, but it is undoubtedly safer than any Marriage. In a Lottery where there is (at the lowest computation) ten thousand blanks to a prize, it is the most prudent choice not to venture.

I have allwaies been so thoroughly persuaded of this Truth that notwithstanding the flattering views I had for you, (as I never intended you a sacrifice to my Vanity) I thought I ow'd you the Justice to lay before you all the hazards attending Matrimony. You may recollect I did so in the strongest manner. Perhaps you may have more success in the instructing your Daughter. She has so much company at home she will not need seeking it abroad, and will more readily take the notions you think fit to give her. As you were alone in my Family, it would have been thought a great Cruelty to suffer you no Companions of your own Age, especially having so many near Relations, and I do not wonder their Opinions influence'd yours. I was not sorry to see you not determin'd on a single Life, knowing it was not your Father's Intention, and contented my selfe with endeavoring to make your Home so easy that you might not be in hast to leave it.

I am afraid you will think this a very long and insignificant Letter. I hope the kindness of the Design will excuse it, being willing to give you every proofe in my power that I am your most affectionate Mother,

M. Wortley.

Text W MS iii. 78–81

To Lady Bute 6 *March* [*1753*]

March 6.

I cannot help writeing a sort of Apology for my last letter, foreseeing that you will think it wrong, or at least Lord Bute will be extremely shock'd at the proposal of a learned Education for Daughters, which the generality of Men beleive as great a prophanation as the Clergy would do if the Laity should presume to exercise the functions of the priesthood. I desire you would take notice I would not have Learning enjoin'd them as a Task, but permitted as a pleasure if their Genius leads them naturally to it. I look upon my Grand daughters as a sort of Lay Nuns. Destiny may have laid up other things for them, but they have no reason to expect to pass their time otherwise than their Aunts do at present,[1] and I know by Experience it is in the power of Study not only to make solitude tolerable but agreable. I have now liv'd almost seven years in a stricter Retirement than yours in the Isle of Bute,[2] and can assure you I have never had halfe an hour heavy on my Hands for want of something to do.

Whoever will cultivate their own mind will find full employment. Every virtue does not only require great care in the planting, but as much daily solicitude in cherishing as exotic fruits and flowers; the Vices and passions (which I am afraid are the natural product of the soil) demand perpetual weeding. Add to this the search after knowledge (every branch of which is entertaining), and the longest Life is too short for the persuit of it, which, thô in some regards confin'd to very strait limits, leaves still a vast variety of Amusements to those capable of tasting them, which is utterly impossible for those that are blinded by prejudices, which are the certain effect of an ignorant Education. My own was one of the worst in the World, being exactly the same as Clarissa Harlow's, her pious Mrs. Norton so perfectly ressembling my Governess (who had been Nurse to my Mother) I could

---

[1] Lord Bute's four sisters, all married, apparently lived in the country.

[2] Because of their small means, the Butes lived in the Isle of Bute for ten years after their marriage in 1736.

almost fancy the Author was acquainted with her.[1] She
took so much pains from my Infancy to fill my Head with
superstitious Tales and false notions, it was none of her
Fault I am not at this day afraid of Witches and Hobgoblins,
or turn'd Methodist.[2]

Allmost all Girls are bred after this manner. I beleive you
are the only Woman (perhaps I might say person) that
never was either frighted or cheated into any thing by your
parents. I can truly afirm I never deceiv'd any body in my
Life excepting (which I confess has often happen'd un-
designedly) by speaking plainly. As Earl Stanhope us'd to
say (during his ministry), he allwaies impos'd on the
Foreign Ministers by telling them the naked Truth, which
as they thought impossible to come from the mouth of a
statesman,[3] they never fail'd to write informations to their
respective Courts directly contrary to the assurances he
gave them, most people confounding the Ideas of Sense and
Cunning, thô there are realy no two things in Nature more
opposite. It is in part from this false reasoning, the unjust
custom prevails of debarring our Sex from the advantages
of Learning, the Men fancying the improvement of our
understandings would only furnish us with more art to
deceive them, which is directly contrary to the Truth. Fools
are allwaies enterprizing, not seeing the Difficulties of
Deceit or the ill Consequences of Detection. I could give
many examples of Ladies whose ill conduct has been very
notorious, which has been owing to that ignorance which
has expos'd them to Idleness, which is justly call'd the
Mother of mischeif.

There is nothing so like the Education of a Woman of
Quality as that of a Prince. They are taught to dance and
the exterior part of what is call'd good breeding, which if they
attain they are extroadinary Creatures in their kind, and
have all the accomplishments requir'd by their Directors.

[1] LM had criticized Richardson's
Clarissa the previous year (see above,
pp. 8–9).
[2] Mrs. Norton, in the novel, is more
pious than superstitious.
[3] James Stanhope (1673–1721), 1st
Earl, was Secretary of State 1714–21;

he was noted for his frank and open
manner (Basil Williams, *Stanhope*, 1932,
p. 168). In her Commonplace Book
LM put this idea in the form of a
maxim: 'Telling Truth deceives every
body when in the M[outh] of a Woman
or a Statesman' (MS, f. 7).

The same characters are form'd by the same Lessons, which inclines me to think (if I dare say it) that Nature has not plac'd us in an inferior Rank to Men, no more than the Females of other Animals, where we see no distinction of capacity,[1] thô I am persuaded if there was a Common-wealth of rational Horses (as Doctor Swift has suppos'd) it would be an establish'd maxim amongst them that a mare could not be taught to pace. I could add a great deal on this subject, but I am not now endeavoring to remove the prejudices of Mankind. My only Design is to point out to my Grand Daughters the method of being contented with that retreat to which probably their circumstances will oblige them, and which is perhaps preferable to all the show of public Life. It has allwaies been my Inclination. Lady Stafford[2] (who knew me better than any body else in the world, both from her own just discernment, and my Heart being ever as open to her as my selfe) us'd to tell me my true vocation was a monastery,[3] and I now find by experience more sincere pleasures with my Books and Garden than all the Flutter of a Court could give me.

If you follow my advice in relation to Lady Mary, my correspondance may be of use to her, and I shall very willingly give her those instructions that may be necessary in the persuit of her Studies. Before her age I was in the most regular commerce with my Grand mother, thô the difference of our time of Life was much greater, she being past 45 when she marry'd my Grand Father. She dy'd at 96, retaining to the last the vivacity and clearness of her understanding, which was very uncommon.[4] You cannot remember her, being then in your Nurse's Arms. I conclude with repeating to you, I only recommend, but am far from commanding, which I think I have no right to do. I tell you my sentiments because you desir'd to know them, and hope you will receive them with some partiality as coming from your most affectionate Mother,   M. Wortley.

[1] 'If Women are far inferior to Men, Nature has been more cruel to mankind than to any other species' (CB MS, f. 5).

[2] LM's intimate friend (see ii. 45), dead since 1739.

[3] For LM's advocacy of Protestant nunneries, see below, p. 97.

[4] Mary Carey (d. 1719), da. of 2nd Earl of Monmouth, was the second wife of LM's maternal grandfather, William Feilding (1640–85), 3rd Earl of Denbigh.

I have ask'd you over and over if you have receiv'd my
Letter to My Sister Mar.[1]

Text W MS iii. 86–89   *Address* To The Rt Honble the Countess of
Bute recommended to Samuel Child Esqr near Temple Bar London
Angleterre *Postmark* AP 17

To Wortley *22 March* [*1753*]

I have had no Letter from you in several months thô I
have wrote often, which silence gave me great concern for
your Health. My Daughter tells me (by one I receiv'd this
morning) that you are perfectly well, which I am very glad
to hear. I hope you will not disturb your selfe for the Follys
of a Person you mention.[2] The only way to avoid disapointment is never to Indulge any Hope on his Account. I am
convince'd his Conduct will ever be the same, and have
allways been of that Opinion. There is no Dependance on
any Intelligence on that subject. I know G[ibson][3] thinks it
a pious Fraud to deceive you on that occasion, and I am
afraid another (who engag'd for his good Behaviour) had
worse views, of which I have given you many hints not
proper to explain by the post. I shall speak no more on this
disagreable Topic.

I pray God preserve you.

March 22 N.S.

Text W MS ii. 237–8   *Address* To Edwd Wortley Esqr recommended to the care of Samuel Child Esqr near Temple Bar London Angleterre [*in another hand*] Cavendish Square *Postmark* AP 17 *End. by*
W [*Summary*] Ad 28 May Recd 19 Apr.

---

[1] Lady Mar, in the care of her
daughter, lived at Ampthill, Beds.,
where the Duke of Bedford—whose
wife was her niece—lent them a house
(Walpole, *Corr.* xx. 281; Duchess of
Bedford to Lady Mar, n.d., Mar and
Kellie MS).

[2] In Aug. 1752 their son returned to
England after his adventures in France
(Jonathan Curling, *Edward Wortley
Montagu*, 1954, p. 143). As an M.P. he
was protected from his creditors.

[3] John Gibson was W's agent in
dealing with his son.

To Lady Bute 2 *April* [*1753*]

Ap. 2. N.S.
My Dear Child,
I am very glad to hear of your Health and recovery, being allwaies uneasy till your danger is over. I wish you Joy of your young Son,¹ and that you may have comfort in your numerous Family.

I am not surpriz'd to hear the Duke of Kingston remains unmarry'd.² He is (I fear) surrounded with people whose Interest it is he should continu so.³ I desire to know the name of his present Inclination. By the manner you speak of it, I suppose there is no occasion of the nicety of avoiding her name.⁴

I am sorry the P[rince] has an Episcopal Education.⁵ He cannot have a worse both for himselfe and the nation. Thô the Court of England is no more personally to me than the Court of Pekin, yet I cannot help some concern for my native Country; nor can I see any good purpose from Church precepts except they design him to take orders. I confess if I was King of G[reat] B[ritain] I would certainly be also ArchBishop of Canterbury, but I beleive that is a refinement of Politics that will never enter into the headsofour Managers, thô there is no other way of having supreme power in church and State. I could say a great deal in favor of this Idea, but

---

¹ Charles (d. 1801), born 12 Jan. 1753.

² The 2nd Duke, LM's nephew, had discarded his French mistress, Madame de La Touche (see ii. 459, n. 2), and pensioned her off in a country village with £800 per annum. She was persuaded by emissaries from her husband to leave England, and in 1753 she settled in Brussels, where she died in 1765 aged 52 (Gustave Desnoiresterres, *Épicuriens et lettrés, XVIIᵉ et XVIIIᵉ siècles*, 1879, pp. 415–16).

³ The Duke's sister Lady Frances Meadows and her family lived with him; and her second son was his eventual heir (Delany, *Corr.* iv. 574).

⁴ The Duke's 'Inclination' was the notorious Elizabeth Chudleigh (1720–88). While Maid of Honour to the Princess of Wales, she secretly married (in 1744) Augustus John Hervey, second son of Lord Hervey, but they had been estranged since at least 1747. In 1769 she bigamously married the Duke.

⁵ In Jan. 1753 the Bishop of Peterborough had been appointed Preceptor to George, Prince of Wales, in place of the Bishop of Norwich, who had resigned in protest against alleged Jacobite influence on the Prince (George Bubb Dodington, *Political Journal*, ed. J. Carswell and L. A. Dralle, 1965, pp. 190–3).

as neither you nor I will ever be consulted on the Subject, I will not trouble you with my Speculative notions.

I am very much pleas'd to hear of your Father's good Health. That every Blessing may attend you is the earnest and sincere wish of (Dear child) your most affectionate Mother,

M. Wortley.

My complements to Lord Bute and blessing to all yours.

Text W MS iii. 45–46   *Address* To The Rt Honble the Countess of Bute recommended to Samuel Child Esqr near Temple Bar London Angleterre   *Postmark* MA 1

To Lady Oxford[1] 1 *June* [1753]

June 1. N.S.

Dearest Madam,

I receiv'd your Ladyship's obliging Letter of Ap. 14th this morning. It brought me the most sensible Joy I am capable of receiving, delivering me from the long uneasiness I have suffer'd in my fear of your Health. I find the post has been very unjust to me, or perhaps my own Servants; being 25 mile from any post Town, I beleive they sometimes save themselves the Trouble of going when I send them, and throw away my Letters, by which they also put the franking in their pockets.

Be assur'd, Dearest Madam, I should think my selfe the most worthless of Human Creatures, could I ever be wanting in the testimonys of my inviolable attachment and sincere Gratitude for your generous unmerited Freindship. Our Correspondance is the comfort of my Life. I am yours by every Tye that can bind a reasonable mind; I beg you would never think it possible for me to be guilty of a neglect in regard to your Ladyship. If it was in my power I would never be from Welbeck,[2] and should think my whole Life

[1] Widow of the 2nd Earl, and a correspondent of LM's (see ii. 310).   [2] Lady Oxford's seat in the Dukeries, Notts.

happily employ'd could I in any degree contribute to the
ease of yours. These are Castles I must not indulge, least I
murmur too much against that Destiny which confines me
at so great a distance from that only Freind in whom I
never saw any thing but what was worthy the highest
esteem, and who never gave me the least reason of complaint.
Depend upon it, Dearest Madam, it is impossible for any
one to have a juster sense of your value, or to be fonder of
giving every proofe of it, than your Ladiship's entirely
devoted and Faithfull Obedient Servant,

M. W. Montagu.

Text Portland MS (Longleat) ii. 327–8   *Address* To The Rt
Honble the Lady Henrietta Countess of Oxford in Dover Street near
St James's London Angleterre   *End. by Lady Oxford* R: Welbeck
Thursday July 19th 1753 Numbr (2)

To Lady Bute *3 June* [*1753*]

June 3. N.S.

My Dear Child,

You see I was not mistaken in supposing[1] we should
have disputes concerning your Daughters if we were together, since we can differ even at this distance. The sort of
Learning that I recommended is not so expensive, either
of Time or Money, as danceing, and in my opinion likely
to be of much more use to Lady M[ary], if her memory and
apprehension are what you represented them to me. However, every one has a right to educate their children after
their own way, and I shall speak no more on that subject.

I was so much pleas'd with the character you gave her
that had there been any possibillity of her undertaking so
long a Journey, I should certainly have ask'd for her, and
I think out of such a number you might have spar'd her.
I own my affection prevail'd over my Judgment in this
thought, since nothing can be more imprudent than undertaking the management of another's child. I verily beleive
that had I carry'd six daughters out of England with me, I

---

[1] On 22 July 1752 (above, p. 16).

could have dispos'd of them all advantageously. The Winter I pass'd at Rome there was an unusual concourse of English, many of them with great Estates, and their own masters. As they had no admittance to the Roman Ladies, nor understood the Language, they had no way of passing their Evenings but in my Apartment, where I had allwaies a full drawing room.[1] Their Governors encourrag'd their assiduities as much as they could, finding I gave them Lessons of Oeconomy and good conduct, and my Authority was so great it was a common Threat amongst them—I'll tell Lady M[ary] what you say.—I was judge of all their disputes, and my Decisions allwaies submitted to. While I staid there was neither gameing, drinking, quarrelling, or keeping. The Abbé Grant (a very honest, good natur'd North Briton, who has resided several years at Rome)[2] was so much amaz'd at this uncommon regularity, he would have made me beleive I was bound in conscience to pass my Life there for the good of my Countrymen. I can assure you my Vanity was not at all rais'd by this Influence over them, knowing very well that had Lady Charlotte de Roussi[3] been in my place, it would have been the same thing. There is that general Emulation in Mankind, I am fully persuaded if a dozen young Fellows bred a Bear amongst them and saw no other Creature, they would every day fall out for the Bear's favors, and be extreamly flatter'd by any mark of Distinction shewn by that ugly Animal.

Since my last return to Italy (which is now near 7 years) I have liv'd in a solitude not unlike that of Robinson Crusoe. Excepting my short trips to Louvere, my whole time is spent in my Closet and Garden, without regretting any Conversation but that of my own Family. The study of

[1] Corroborated by Lord Elcho, in Rome 1741 (Paul Chamley, *Documents relatifs à Sir James Steuart*, 1965, p. 98); see also ii. 228.

[2] Abbé Peter Grant (1708–84) represented the Scottish Mission in Rome for forty-six years (John Fleming, *Robert Adam and His Circle*, 1962, p. 349). He was 'all things to all men, a Jacobite to Jacobites, a Georgite to Georgites, and an agreeable companion to every one'

(Evan Charteris, *A Short Account of the Affairs of Scotland by David Lord Elcho*, 1907, p. 29).

[3] Charlotte de Roucy (1653–1743), a French Protestant refugee. Lord Hervey wrote that she was a miserable, boring drudge, who 'subsisted upon the scanty charity of the English Court' (*Memoirs of George II*, ed. R. Sedgwick, 1931, i. 252–3).

Simples is a new Amusement to me. I have no Correspondance with any body at London but your selfe and your
Father (whom I have not heard from of a long time). I am
much mortify'd that the post (or perhaps my own Servants)
take so little care of my Letters. By your account there are
at least 4 of mine lost, and some of yours. I have only receiv'd a few lines from you since you lay in, till this morning.
I have often ask'd you if you have had the Letter I enclos'd
for my Sister Mar. I have wrote to Lord Bute and to my
G[od] Daughter, of which you take no notice, which makes
me fear they have miscarry'd. My best wishes attend you
and yours, being with great Truth your most affectionate
Mother,

M. Wortley.

Text W MS iii. 94–95

To Wortley 22 *July* [*1753*]

July 22. N.S.

I receiv'd yesterday yours of May 28th, which gave me
great pleasure on many accounts, but cheiffly as I look upon
it as a proofe of your good Health, of which I heartily wish
the continuance.

I could send you in return Stories of the Courts round me
that would perhaps amuse you, but I dare not venture on
any thing of that kind for reasons I need not mention, and
have no other subject to write on but my insignificant selfe,
my frequent Indispositions confineing me almost wholly to
this Village. Indeed every body has been confine'd this
Summer. The great Snows that fell in the Winter, being
melted by excessive Rains in the Spring, have occasion'd
such general Inundations as have not been known of many
years. The Bridges have been broken down in most
places, a great number of cattle and many Houses with their
Inhabitants destroy'd; the roads are yet scarce practicable,
and several rivers not yet retir'd. This misfortune has been
in some measure repair'd to the Country people by an

extrodinary fertility. Their Harvest has been so abundant, the rich Farmers complain of it; and the appearance of the Vintage is so great, excellent Wine is now to be sold for halfe a crown (English) a Barrel, and finds no buyers. I am assur'd a great deal will be litteraly thrown away to empty the Vessels; and the silk worms have succeeded so well they have enrich'd all that have bred them. If I could establish a Correspondance with some English Merchant that would take the silk at a fix'd price at Venice, it would be very advantageous to me, but I know not to whom to address my selfe about it. I beleive I could buy a hundred Weight of silk in this Town for 15s. per pound (their pound is only 12 ounces), but the hazard of the sea is what I am not willing to venture on.

I have taken the Liberty of writeing in my usual running Hand. It is very uneasy to me to write larger, and I flatter my selfe from your Letter that you have no longer any complaint of your Eyes. I should take great pleasure in writeing to you if I thought I could give you any in reading.

Text W MS ii. 233–4   *Address* To Edwd Wortley Esqr recommended to Sam: Child Esqr near Temple Bar London Angleterre *Postmark* SE 8   *End. by W* [*Summary*] Recd in London 8 Sept.

To Lady Oxford *23 July* [*1753*]

July 23. N.S.

Dearest Madam,

Thô I wrote to your Ladiship not long since, to which I have yet had no Answer, I do not fear being thought impertinent by troubling you with a second. I am so fully persuaded of your partial Friendship to me, I beleive my imagin'd silence gave you some pain, and am resolv'd never to leave you in any doubt of the tender and inviolable Attachment I have for you. If one assurance of it amongst many reaches you, I am paid for my writeing, and my time can never be so well spent as in endeavouring to give you proofes of it. My daughter never told me of your Ladiship's kind enquiry; it would have sav'd me much concern, but she has so much employment both at home and abroad I do not wonder at her forgettfullness.

My constant Praiers are for your Health, which is certainly precious to all that know you, but I may venture to say, to none more than to your Ladiship's most faithfully affectionate Humble Servant,

M. W. Montagu.

Text Portland MS (Longleat) ii. 329–30   *Address* To The Rt Honble the Lady Henrietta Countess of Oxford in Dover Street near St James's London Angleterre   *Postmark* SE 8   *End. by Lady Oxford* R: Welbeck Monday Septr 10th 1753 Numbr (3)

To Lady Bute *23 July* [*1753*]

July 23. N.S.

My Dear Child,

I have just receiv'd two Letters from you (thô the dates are a month distant). The Death of Lady Carolina naturally raises the mortifying refflection on how slender a thread hangs all worldly prosperity![1] I cannot say I am otherwise much touch'd at it. It is true she was my sister, as it were, and in some sense, but her behaviour to me never gave me any Love, nor her general conduct any esteem. I own I cannot forgive her dishonnouring her Family by her mean marriage. It may be you will call this an old fashion'd way of thinking. The confounding of all Ranks and making a Jest of order has long been growing in England, and I perceive, by the Books you sent me, has made a very considerable progress. The Heros and Heroines of the age are Coblers and Kitchin Wenches. Perhaps you will say I should not take my Ideas of the manners of the times from such triffling Authors, but it is more truly to be found amongst them than from any Historian. As they write meerly to get money, they allwaies fall into the notions that are most acceptable to the present Taste. It has long been the endeavor of our

[1] Lady Caroline Brand, LM's half-sister (see ii. 431–2), died on 9 June 1753.

English Writers to represent people of Quality as the vilest and silliest part of the Nation. Being (gennerally) very low born themselves. I am not surpriz'd at their propagateing this Doctrine, but I am much mistaken if this Levelling Principle does not one day or other break out in fatal consequences to the public, as it has allready done in many private Families.

You will think I am influenc'd by living under an Aristocratic Government, where Distinction of Rank is carry'd to a very great height; But I can assure you my Opinion is founded on Refflection and Experience, and I wish to God I had allwaies thought in the same manner. Thô I had ever the utmost contempt for misalliances, yet the silly prejudices of my Education had taught me to beleive I was to treat no body as an Inferior, and that poverty was a degree of Merit. This imaginary Humility has made me admit many Familiar Acquaintance of which I have heartily repented every one; and the greatest examples I have known of Honor and Integrity has been amongst those of the highest Birth and Fortunes. There are many reasons why it should be so, which I will not trouble you with. If my Letter was to be publish'd, I know I should be rail'd at for pride, and call'd an Enemy of the poor, but I take a pleasure in telling you my real thoughts. I would willingly establish the most intimate Freindship between us, and I am sure no proofe of it shall ever be wanting on my Side.

I am sorry for the untimely death of poor Lord Cornbury. He had certainly a very good Heart; I have often thought it great pity it was not under the Direction of a better Head.[1] I had lost his favor sometime before I left England, on a pleasant account. He comes to me one morning with a Hat full of paper, which he desir'd me to peruse and tell him my sincere opinion. I tremble'd at the proposition, foreseeing the inevitable Consequence of this confidence. However, I was not so barbarous to tell him that his verses were extreme stupid (as, God knows, they were) and that he was no more inspir'd with the Spirit of Poetry than that of Prophecy.

[1] Henry Hyde (1710–26 April 1753), styled Viscount Cornbury, heir to 4th Earl of Clarendon. In Mrs. Delany's opinion: 'Of all the young men of quality with whom I have been acquain- ted he was the prime' (*Corr.* iii. 226–7). Walpole calls him 'amiable and dis- interested' (*A Catalogue of the Royal and Noble Authors of England*, in *Works*, 1798, i. 454).

I contented my selfe with representing to him (in the mildest terms) that it was not the busyness of a Man of Quality to turn Author, and that he should confine himselfe to the Applause of his Freinds and by no means venture on the press. He seem'd to take this advice with good Humour, promis'd to follow it, and we parted without any dispute; but alas, he could not help showing his performance to better judges, who with their usual Candor and good Nature earnestly exhorted him to oblige the World with this instructive piece, which was soon after publish'd and had the Success I expected from it; and Pope persuaded him (poor Soul!) that my declaiming against it occasion'd the ill reception it met with,[1] thô this is the first time I ever mention'd it in my Life, and I d⟨id⟩ not so much as guess the reason I heard of him no more, till a few days before I left London. I accidentally said to one of his Acquaintance his visits to me were at an end, I knew not why; and I was let into this weighty Secret. My Journey prevented all explanation between us, and perhaps I should not have thought it worth any if I had staid.

I am not surpriz'd he has left nothing to the D[uchess] of Q[ueensberry], knowing he had no value for her, thô I never heard him name her,[2] but he was of that Species of Mankind who without designing it discover all they think to any Observer that converses with them. His Desire of fixing his name to a certain Quantity of Wall is one Instance (amongst thousands) of the Passion Men have for perpetuateing their Memory.[3] This Weakness (I call every Sentiment so, that cannot be defended by Reason) is so universal it may be look'd on as Instinct; and as no Instinct is implanted but to some purpose, I could almost incline to an Opinion which was profess'd by several of the Fathers, and adopted by some of the best French Divines, that the Punishment of the next Life consists not only in the continuance but the redoubling our Attachment for this, in a more intense manner than we can now have any notion of. These Refflections

[1] When in 1735 Pope received Cornbury's commendatory verses on his *Essay on Man* he thought them 'fine', and printed them, along with other tributes, in the 1739 edition of his works (*Corr.*, ed. G. Sherburn, 1956, iii. 502).
[2] She was his sister (see ii. 48, n. 1).
[3] He is buried in Westminster Abbey.

would carry me very far. For your comfort my paper is at an end, and I have scarce room to tell you a Truth which admits of no Doubt, that I am your most affectionate Mother,

M. Wortley.

My complements to Lord Bute, and blessing to my Grand children. I have wrote to Lady Mary. Have you receiv'd that address'd ⟨to⟩ my Sister Mar?

Text W MS iii. 100–3   *Address* To The Rt Honble the Countess of Bute recommended to Sam: Child Esqr near Temple Bar London Angleterre   *Postmark* SE 8

To Lady Bute *10 Oct.* [*1753*]

This Letter will be very dull or very peevish (perhaps both). I am at present much out of Humour, being on the Edge of a Quarrel with my Freind and Patron the C[ardinal].[1] He is realy a good natur'd and Generous Man, and spends his vast revenue in (what he thinks) the service of his Country. Beside contributing largely to the building a new Cathedral, which (when finish'd) will stand in the first Rank of fine churches (where he has already the comfort of seeing his own Busto finely done both within and without), he has founded a magnificent College for one hundred Scholars, which I don't doubt he will endow very nobly, and greatly enlarg'd and embellish'd his Episcopall Palace. He has joyn'd to it a public Library, which when I saw it was a very Beautifull room. It is now finish'd and furnish'd, and open twice in a week with proper attendance.

Yesterday here arriv'd one of his cheif chaplains, with a long complement which concluded with desiring I would send him my Works. Having dedicated one of his cases to English Books, he intended my Labours should appear in the most conspicuous place. I was struck dumb for some time with this astonishing request. When I recover'd my vexatious surprize (foreseeing the Consequence) I made answer, I was highly sensible of the Honor design'd me, but upon

---

[1] Querini (see above, p. 13).

my word I had never printed a single line in my Life. I was answer'd in a cold tone, his Em[inence] could send for them to England but they would be a long time coming and with some hazard, and that he had flatter'd him selfe I would not refuse him such a favor, and I need not be asham'd of seeing my Name in a collection where he admitted none but the most Eminent Authors. It was to no purpose to endeavor to convince him. He would not stay dinner, thô earnestly invited, and went away with the air of one that thought he had reason to be offended. I know his Master will have the same Sentiments, and I shall pass in his opinion for a monster of Ingratitude, while 'tis the blackest of vices in my Opinion, and of which I am utterly incapable. I realy could cry for vexation.

Sure no body ever had such various provocations to print as my selfe. I have seen things I have wrote so mangle'd and falsify'd I have scarce known them. I have seen Poems I never read publish'd with my Name at length,[1] and others that were truly and singly wrote by me, printed under the names of others. I have made my selfe easy under all these mortifications by the refflection I did not deserve them, having never aim'd at the Vanity of popular Applause; but I own my Philosophy is not proof against losing a Freind, and, it may be, making an Enemy of one to whom I am oblig'd.

I confess I have often been complemented (since I have been in Italy) on the Books I have given the Public. I us'd at first to deny it with some Warmth, but finding I persuaded no body, I have of late contented my selfe with laughing when ever I heard it mention'd, knowing the character of a learned Woman is far from being ridiculous in this Country, the greatest Familys being proud of having produce'd female Writers, and a Milanese Lady being now proffessor of Mathematics in the University of Bologna, invited thither by a most obliging Letter wrote by the present Pope, who desir'd her to accept of the Chair not as a recompense for her merit, but to do Honor to a Town which is under his protection.[2]

[1] One instance is the attribution to her of Judith (Cowper) Madan's 'Progress of Poetry', translated into French by the Abbé Antoine Yart in *L'Idée de la poësie angloise*, 1753, ii. 98–122.

[2] Maria Gaetana Agnesi (1718–99),

To say Truth, there is no part of the World where our Sex is treated with so much contempt as in England. I do not complain of men for haveing engross'd the Government. In excluding us from all degrees of power, they preserve us from many Fatigues, many Dangers, and perhaps many Crimes. The small proportion of Authority that has fallen to my share (only over a few children and Servants) has all-waies been a Burden and never a pleasure, and I beleive every one finds it so who acts from a Maxim (I think an indispensible Duty) that whoever is under my power is under my protection. Those who find a joy in inflicting hardships and seeing objects of misery may have other sensations, but I have allwaies thought corrections (even when necessary) as painfull to the giver as to the Sufferer, and am therefore very well satisfy'd with the state of Subjection we are plac'd in.

But I think it the highest Injustice to be debarr'd the Entertainment of my Closet, and that the same Studies which raise the character of a Man should hurt that of a Woman. We are educated in the grossest ignorance, and no art omitted to stiffle our natural reason; if some few get above their Nurses' instructions, our knowledge must rest conceal'd and be as useless to the World as Gold in the Mine. I am now speaking according to our English notions, which may wear out (some ages hence) along with others equally absurd. It appears to me the strongest proofe of a clear understanding in Longinus (in every light acknowledg'd one of the greatest Men amongst the Ancients) when I find him so far superior to vulgar Prejudices as to chuse his two Examples of fine Writeing from a Jew (at that time the most despis'd people upon Earth) and a Woman.[1] Our modern Wits would be so far from quoteing, they would scarce own they had read the Works of such contemptible Creatures, thô perhaps they would condescend to steal from them at the same time they declar'd they were below their notice.

This subject is apt to run away with me; I will trou⟨ble⟩ you with no more of it. My Complements to Lord Bute and

who published *Instituzioni analitiche* in 1748, was invited to the university post by Benedict XIV in 1750.

[1] Longinus, in *On the Sublime*, mentions Moses and Sappho as writers of the sublime (chaps. ix, x).

blessing to all yours, which are truly dear to your most affectionate Mother,

M. Wortley.

Oct. 10. N.S.

Text W MS iii. 72–75   *Address* To The Rt Honble the Countess of Bute recommended to S. Child Esqr near Temple Bar London Angleterre   *Postmark* NO 8

To Wortley *10 Oct.* [*1753*]

I think I now know why our Correspondance is so miserably interupted and so many of my Letters lost to and from England, but I am no happier in the Discovery than a Man that has found out his Complaints proceed from a Stone in the Kidneys. I know the cause but am entirely ignorant of the remedy, and must suffer my uneasyness with what patience I can.

An old Priest made me a visit as I was folding my last Pacquet to my Daughter. Observing it to be large, he told me I had done a great deal of Business that morning. I made answer, I had done no business at all; I had only wrote to my Daughter on Family affairs or such triffles as make up Women's Conversation. He said gravely, people like your Excellenza do not use to write long letters upon Triffles. I assur'd him that if he understood English I would let him read my Letter. He reply'd (with a mysterious smile), if I did understand English I should not understand what you have written, except you would give me the Key, which I durst not presume to ask. What Key? (said I staring) there is not one Cypher beside the Date. He answer'd, Cyphers were only us'd by Novices in Politics, and it was very easy to write intelligibly under feign'd names of persons and places to a correspondant in such a manner as should be almost impossible to be understood by any body else.

Thus I suppose my innocent Epistles are severely sc[r]utiniz'd, and when I talk of my Grand children they are fancy'd to represent all the potentates of Europe. This is very provoking. I confess there are good reasons for extrodinary Caution at this juncture, but 'tis very hard I cannot pass for being as insignificant as I realy am.

The House at Acton was certainly left to Lady Carolina;[1] and whatever Lady Anne left, so little (when divided it [*sic*] 5 parts) it is not worth enquiring for, especially after so long silence.[2]

I heartily congratulate you ⟨on the⟩ recovery of your sight. It is a Blessing I prefer to Life, and will seek for Glasses whenever I am in a place where they are sold.

Oct. 10. N.S.

Text W MS ii. 235–6 *Address* To Edwd Wortley Esqr recommended to Sam: Child Esqr near Temple Bar London Angleterre *Postmark* NO 8 *End. by W* [*Summary*] Recd in London 10 Nov.

To Lady Bute [*30 Nov. (?)1753*]

My dear Child,

I receiv'd your agreable Letter of Sept. 24 yesterday, Nov. 29, and am very glad our Daughter (for I think she belongs to us both) turns out so much to your satisfaction; may she ever do so. I hope she has by this time receiv'd my Token. I am afraid I have lost some of your Letters. In last April you wrote me word the Box directed to me was to set out in a Week's time. Since that I have had no news of it, and apprehend very much that the Bill which I suppose you sent me has miscarry'd. If so, I am in danger of loseing the Cargo.

You please me extremely in saying my Letters are of any Entertainment to you. I would contribute to your Happiness in every shape I can, but in my solitude there are so few

[1] By his will, LM's father (1st Duke of Kingston) left this house to his Duchess (d. 1728), and then to his direct descendants as she should designate (P.C.C. Romney, f. 90).

[2] Lady Anne Pierrepont, LM's other half-sister, had died intestate; letters of administration were granted to Lady Caroline (P.C.C. Acts of Administration, Middlesex, Aug. 1739).

subjects present themselves, it is not easy to find one that would amuse you, thô as I beleive you have some leisure hours at Canewood, when any thing new is welcome, I will venture to tell you a small History in which I had some share. I have allready inform'd you of the Divisions and subdivisions of Estates in this Country, by which you will imagine there is a numerous Gentry of great names and little fortunes. Six of those familys inhabit this Town. You may fancy this forms a sort of Society, but far from it, as there is not one of them that does not think (for some reason or other) they are far superior to all the rest. There is such a settle'd aversion amongst them, they avoid one another with the utmost care, and hardly ever meet except by chance at the Castle (as they call my House)[1], where their regard for me obliges them to behave civilly, but it is with an affected coldness that is downright disagreable, and hinders me from seeing any of them often.

I was quietly reading in my closet, when I was interrupted by the chambermaid of the Signora Laura Bono, who flung her selfe at my Feet, and in an agony of sobs and tears begg'd me for the Love of the Holy Madona to hasten to her master's House, where the two Brothers would certainly murder one another if my presence did not stop their Fury. I was very much surpriz'd, having allwaies heard them spoke of as a pattern of Fraternal union. However, I made all possible speed thither, without staying for hoods or attendance. I was soon there (the House touching my Garden Wall) and was directed to the Bed chamber by the noise of Oaths and Execrations, but on opening the door was astonish'd to a degree you may better guess than I describe, by seeing the Signora Laura prostrate on the Ground, melting in Tears, and her Husband standing with a drawn stilletto in his Hand, swearing she should never see to morrow's Sun. I was soon let into the Secret.

The Good Man, having business of Consequence at Brescia, went thither early in the morning, but as he expected his cheif Tenant to pay his rent that day, he left orders with his Wife that if the Farmer (who liv'd 2 mile off) came him selfe or sent any of his Sons, she should take care

---

[1] Her house in Gottolengo stood on the site of a castle (see ii. 425).

to make him very welcome. She obey'd him with great punctuality. The money coming in the hand of a Handsome Lad of eighteen, she did not only admit him to her own Table and produce the best Wine in the cellar, but resolv'd to give him chere entiere. While she was exercising this generous Hospitality, the Husband met mid way the Gentleman he intended to visit, who was posting to another side of the Country. They agreed on another apointment, and he return'd to his own House, where, giving his Horse to be led round to the stable by the Servant that accompany'd him, he open'd his door with the pass-par-tout key, and proceeded to his chamber without meeting any body, where he found his beloved Spouse asleep on the bed with her Galant. The opening of [the] door wak'd them. The young Fellow immediately leap'd out of the Window, which look'd into the Garden and was open (it being summer), and escap'd over the Fields, leaving his Breeches on a chair by the Bed side, a very striking circumstance. In short, the Case was such I do not think the Queen of Fairies her selfe could have found an excuse, thô Chaucer tells us she has made a solemn promise to leave none of her Sex unfurnish'd with one, to all eternity.[1] As to the poor Criminal, she had nothing to say for her selfe but what I dare swear you will hear from your youngest daughter if ever you catch her stealing of sweetmeats: Pray, pray, she would do so no more, and indeed it was the first time.

This last article found no credit with me. I can not be persuaded that any Woman who had liv'd virtuous till forty (for such was her age) could suddenly be endow'd with such consummate Impudence to solicite a youth at first sight, there being no probabillity, his age and station consider'd, that he would have made any attempt of that kind. I must confess I was wicked enough to think the unblemish'd reputation she had hitherto maintain'd, and did not fail to put us in mind of, was owing to a series of such Frolicks; and to say truth, they are the only Amours that can reasonably hope to remain undiscover'd. Ladies that can resolve to make Love thus ex tempore may pass unobserv'd, especially if

[1] In the Merchant's Tale of the *Canterbury Tales.* Among the books sent to LM in 1739 was 'Chaucer's Works' (Wh MS 135).

they can content themselves with Low Life, where fear may oblige their Favourites to Secrecy. There wants only a very Lewd Constitution, a very bad Heart, and a moderate understanding, to make this conduct easy, and I do not doubt it has been practis'd by many prudes beside her I am now speaking of.

You may be sure I did not communicate these refflections. The first word I spoke was to desire Signor Carlo to sheath his ponjard, not being pleas'd with its glittering. He did so very readily, begging my pardon for not have[ing] done it on my first appearance, saying he did not know what he did; and indeed he had the Countenance and Gesture of a Man distracted. I did not endeavor a defence that seem'd to me impossible, but represented to him as well as I could the Crime of a Murder which, if he could justify before Men, was still a crying Sin before God, the disgrace he would bring on himselfe and posterity, and irreparable injury he would do his eldest Daughter (a pretty Girl of 15, that I knew he was extreme fond of). I added that if he thought it proper to part from his Lady he might easily find a pretext for it some months hence, and that it was as much his Interest as hers to conceal this affair from the knowledge of the World. I could not presently make him taste these reasons, and was forc'd to stay there near 5 hours (almost from 5 to ten at night) before I durst leave them together, which I would not do till he had sworn in the most serious manner he would make no future attempt on her Life. I was content with his Oath, knowing him to be very devout, and found I was not mistaken.

How the matter was made up between them afterwards I know not, but 'tis now two year since it happen'd, and all appearances remaining as if it had never been. The secret is in very few hands; his Brother, being at that time at Brescia, I beleive knows nothing of it to this day. The chambermaid and my selfe have preserv'd the strictest silence; and the Lady retains the satisfaction of insulting all her acquaintance on the foundation of a spotless Character that only She can boast in the Parish, where she is most heartily hated, from these airs of impertinent virtue, and another very essential reason, being the best dress'd Woman amongst them, thô one of the plainest in her figure.

The discretion of the Chambermaid in fetching me, which possibly sav'd her mistresse's Life, and her taciturnity since, I fancy appears very remarkable to you, and is what would certainly never happen in England. The first part of her behaviour deserves great praise, coming of her own accord, and inventing so decent an excuse for her admittance; but her silence may be attributed to her knowing very well that any Servant that presumes to talk of his Master will most certainly be incapable of talking at all in a short time, their Lives being entirely in the power of their Superiors. I do not mean by Law but by Custom, which has full as much force. If one of them was kill'd, it would either never be enquir'd into at all or very slightly pass'd over; yet it seldom happens, and I know no instance of it, which I think is owing to the great Submission of Domestics, who are sensible of their Dependance, and the national temper not being hasty and never enflam'd by Wine, Drunkeness being a vice abandonn'd to the Vulgar and spoke of with greater detestation than Murder, which is mention'd with as little concern as a Drinking bout in England, and is almost as frequent. It was extream shocking to me at my first coming, and still gives me a sort of Horror, thô Custom has in some degree familiariz'd it to my Imagination. Robbery ⟨w⟩ould be persu'd with great Vivacity and punish'd with the utmost rigour, therefore is ⟨ve⟩ry rare, thô stealing is in daily practise; but ⟨as a⟩ll the peasants are suffer'd the use of Fire Arms, the slightest provocation is su⟨ffic⟩ient to shoot, and they see one of their own Species lye dead before them with as little remorse as a Hare or a Partridge, and when Revenge spurs them on, with much more pleasure. A disertation on this subject would engage me in a discourse not proper for the post.

My Compliments to Lord Bute. His kindness to you ought to obtain the Freindship of all that love you. My Blessing to your little ones. Think of me as ever your most affectionate Mother,

M. Wortley.

Have you receiv'd my Letter to my Sister Mar?

Text W MS iii. 35–40   *Address* To The Rt Honble the Countess of

Bute recommended to the Care of Samuel Child Esqr near Temple Bar London Angleterre

To Lady Bute *1 March* [*1754*]

I pity Lady M[ary] Cooke extreamly. You will be surpriz'd at this Sentiment when she is the present Envy of her Sex, in the possession of Youth, Health, Wealth, Wit, Beauty and Liberty.[1] All these seeming Advantages will prove snares to her. She appears to me walking blindfold upon Stilts, amidst precipices. She is at a dangerous time of Life, when the passions are in full vigour, and we are apt to flatter our selves the understanding arriv'd at Maturity. People are never so near playing the Fool as when they think themselves wise. They lay aside that distrust which is the surest Guard against Indiscretion, and venture on many steps they would have tremble'd at, at fiveteen, and like children are never so much expos'd to falling as when they first leave off leading-strings. I think nothing but a miracle or the support of a Guardian Angel can protect her. It is true (except I am much mistaken) Nature has furnish'd her with one very good defence. I took particular notice of her, both from my own likeing her, and her uncommon obliging behaviour to me. She was then of an age not capable of much disguise, and I thought she had a great Turn to Oeconomy. It is an admirable shield against the most fatal weaknesses. Those who have the good fortune to be born with that Inclination seldom ruin themselves, and are early aware of the Designs laid against them. Yet with all that precaution she will have so many plots contriv'd for her Destruction, she will find it very difficult to escape, and if she is a second time unhappily engag'd it will make her much more miserable than the first, as all misfortunes brought on by our own Imprudence are the most wounding to a sensible Heart. The most certain security would be that diffidence

[1] The unhappy marriage of Lady Mary Campbell to Edward, Viscount Coke (see ii. 385), was terminated by his death on 31 Aug. 1753. As she grew older she became increasingly eccentric.

which naturally arises from an impartial selfe-examination. But this is the hardest of all Tasks, requiring great Refflection, long Retirement, and is strongly repugnant to our own Vanity, which very unwillingly reveals even to our selves our common Frailty, thô it is every way a usefull study. Mr. Locke (who has made a more exact disection of the Human mind than any Man before him) declares he gain'd all his knowledge from the consideration of himselfe.[1] It is indeed necessary to judge of others.

You condemn Lord Cornbury without knowing what he could say in his Justification. I am persuaded he thought he perform'd an Act of rigid Justice in excluding the D[uchess] of Q[ueensberry] from an Inheritance to which she had no Natural, thô a Legal, right, especially having had a large portion from her real Father.[2] I have heard him talk on that subject (without naming names) and call it a robbery within the Law. He carry'd that notion to a great height. I agreed with him that a Woman that produc'd a false child into a Family incurr'd the highest Guilt (being irreparable), but I could not be of his Opinion that it was the Duty of the child in such a case to renounce the Fortune the Law entitle'd it to. You see he has acted by a Maxim he imagin'd Just, Lady Essex being inside and out ressembling Lord Clarendon; and whoever remembers Lord Carleton's Eyes must confess they now shine in the Dutchesse's Face.[3] I am not brib'd by Lord Cornbury's behaviour to me to find excuses for him, but I have allwaies endeavor'd to look on the conduct of my Acquaintance without any regard to their way of acting towards me. I can say (with Truth) I have strictly adhere'd to this principle whenever I have been injur'd, but I own (to my shame be it spoken) the Love of

---

[1] In his *Essay Concerning Human Understanding*; for example: 'It is the contemplation of our own abstract ideas that alone is able to afford us general knowledge' (ed. A. C. Fraser, 1894, ii. 266).

[2] Cornbury (see above, p. 36) and the Duchess of Queensberry had the same mother, the Countess of Clarendon; but the Duchess was fathered by Lord Carleton (see ii. 48, n. 1).

[3] Jane (d. 1724), da. of Henry Hyde (1672–1753), 4th Earl of Clarendon, m. (1718) 3rd Earl of Essex. She was called by Thomas Hearne a 'most celebrated Beauty' (*Remarks and Collections*, 1885–1921, vi. 256). LM implies that she, unlike the Duchess, was Clarendon's real as well as legal daughter; and this is borne out by Cornbury's leaving the bulk of his estate to *her* surviving daughter, Lady Chalrotte Villiers.

Flattery has sometimes prevail'd on me (under the Mask of Gratitude) to think better of people than they deserv'd when they have proffess'd more value for me than I was conscious of meriting.—I slide, insensibly, into talking of my selfe, thô I allwaies resolve against it. I will re⟨leiv⟩e you from so dull a subject by concluding my Letter, with my Compliments to Lord Bute, my Blessing to my Grand children, and the assurance of my being ever your most affectionate Mother.

M. Wortley

March 1.

    I have receiv'd a Letter from Lady Mary and will answer it the next post.

Text W MS iii. 129–30   *Address* To The Rt Honble the Countess of Bute recommended to Sam: Child Esqr near Temple Bar London Angleterre   *Postmark* AP 3

To Lady Oxford *1 March* [*1754*]

Dearest Madam,

    I owe your Ladiship many thanks for the Honor of your obliging Letter of Sept'r 22. I have waited long for it, being come to my Hands but Yesterday, but I receiv'd so much pleasure from the account of your Health and Happiness that it has paid me the pain of expectation. You cannot have more prosperity than you deserve, yet it must be confess'd an unusual Blessing to see two Generations answer the Wishes of a Parent. I am much oblig'd to the Duke and Dutchess of Portland[1] for remembering me; their just behaviour to you gives me the highest Esteem for them. No Mother can have a better right to a return of Filial affection than your selfe; But this World is so often unjust it is no common Merit when people perform their duty. I should be greatly defective in mine if I could be ungratefull to so many proofes of Friendship as I have receiv'd from your

---

[1] Lady Oxford's son-in-law and daughter.

Ladiship's goodness, or omit any occasion of professing my selfe (Dearest Madam) your most faithfully devoted Obedient Servant,

M. Wortley Montagu.

March 1.

Text Portland MS (Longleat) ii. 331   *Address* To The Rt Honble the Lady Henrietta Countess of Oxford in Dover street near St James's London Angleterre   *Postmark* AP 3   *End. by Lady Oxford* R: Cav: Lodge Saturday April 6th 1754 Numbr (1)

To Lady Bute 28 April 1754

April 28. 1754

My Dear Child,

I am quite sick with vexation at the Interuptions of our Correspondance. I have sent you six Letters since the Date of the last that you say you have receiv'd, and 3 enclos'd address'd to my Sister, none of which are arriv'd. I have had but 2 from you (including this of March 25) since October. You have had no loss farther than in the testimonies of my real affection. My long storys of what passes here can be little entertainment to you, but every thing from England is interesting to me, who live the Life (as I have already told you) of Robinson Crusoe. His Goats and kids were as much companions as any of the people I see here. My Time is wholly dedicated to the care of a decaying Body, and endeavoring (as the old Song says) to grow wiser and better as my Strength wears away. I have wrote two long Letters to your Father to which I have had no Answer, therefore suppose they have miscarry'd. I know not how to remedy this misfortune, and cannot help feeling it very sensibly.

I imagine the Duke of Newcastle will soon have the Treasurer's Staff; the Title of first Commissioner is not equal to his Importance. You do not tell me how Mr. Pelham has dispos'd his affairs.[1] You should be particular in your

[1] Henry Pelham, First Commissioner of the Treasury, died on 6 March 1754, and was succeeded in his office by his brother, Thomas (1693–1768), Duke of Newcastle, Secretary of State. There had not been a Lord Treasurer since 1714.

Relations; I am as ignorant of every thing that passes at London as if I inhabited the Desarts of Africa. I am not surpriz'd at Mr. Spencer's Choice. I guess some accident has occasion'd a familiar acquaintance with the Girl, and that is sufficient to make a Conquest of a Boy of his Age,[1] while perhaps the Dutchess of Marlbrô's prudence kept him at an awfull Distance from her fair Daughter.[2] I have never seen him since he could speak plain, but I thought there was something in his Countenance too much ressembling his Cousin Lord Weymouth.[3]

The Boxes you have been so kind to send me have been sometime safely arriv'd at Venice, but are not yet come to my Hands, greatly to my affliction. I wish you would send the other, or the season will be too far advanc'd. I am very glad of Lord Mountstuart's[4] recovery, and pity very much the pain you have suffer'd during his Danger. It would be terrible to lose so agreable a child. I dare not advise you to moderate your tenderness, finding ⟨it⟩ impossible to overcome my own, notwithstanding my ⟨m⟩elancholy experience.

This Letter is so incomparably Dull, I cannot res⟨olve⟩ to own it by setting my Name to it.

My Complements to Lord Bute. God Bless you and yours.

Text W MS iii. 115–16   *Address* To The Rt Honble the Countess of Bute recommended to Sam: Child Esqr near Temple Bar London Angleterre *Postmark* MA 25

[1] John Spencer (1734–83), later 1st Earl, m. (20 Dec. 1755) Margaret Georgiana Poyntz (1737–1814). Mrs. Delany's opinion was kinder: 'he has not been won by any arts on her side, but attached by the strong bent of his inclination. . . . She was born a gentlewoman, greatly allied by her mother's side, well educated, a most sensible, generous, delicate mind, and I think a very agreeable person; he has rank and an immense fortune, and I hope good qualities—I have never heard of any bad ones' (*Corr.* iii. 340).

[2] The Duchess was Elizabeth (d. 1761), da. of 2nd Baron Trevor, who m. (1732) Charles Spencer (uncle of John above), later 3rd Duke of Marlborough. They had two daughters: Lady Diana (1734–1808) and Lady Elizabeth (1737–1831).

[3] Thomas Thynne (1734–96), 3rd Viscount Weymouth; he and John Spencer were first cousins. This paragraph has been omitted by previous editors.

[4] Courtesy title of Bute's eldest son, John Stuart (1744–1814), who succeeded as 4th Earl, later 1st Marquess of Bute.

To Lady Bute *23 June* [*1754*]

Louvere, June 23. N.S.

Soon after I wrote my last letter to my Dear child, I was seiz'd with so violent a Fever, accompany'd with so many bad Symptoms, my Life was despair'd of by the Physician of Gottolengo, and I prepar'd my selfe for Death with as much resignation as that Circumstance admits. Some of my Neighbours (without my knowledge) sent express for the Doctor of this Place[1] (whom I have mention'd to you formerly as having uncommon secrets). I was surpriz'd to see him at my Bed side. He declar'd me in great Danger, but did not doubt my recovery if I was wholly under his care, and his first prescription was transporting me hither. The other Physician asserted positively I should die on the road. It has allways been my opinion that it is a matter of the utmost Indifference where we expire, and I consented to be remov'd. My Bed was plac'd on a Brancard, my servants follow'd in chaises, and in this equipage I set out. I bore the first Day's Journey of 15 mile without any visible Alteration. The Doctor said as I was not worse I was certainly better, and the next day proceeded 20 mile to Iseo, which is at the Head of this Lake. I lay each night at Noblemen's Houses which were empty. My Cook, with my Physician, allwaies preceded two or 3 hours, and I found my chamber and all necessaries ready prepared with the exactest attention. I was put into a Bark in my Litter bed, and in 3 hours arriv'd here. My Spirits were not at all wasted (I think rather rais'd) by the Fatigue of my Journey.

I drank the Water next morning, and with a few doses of my Physician's prescription, in three days found my selfe in perfect Health, which appear'd almost a Miracle to all that saw me. You may imagine I am willing to submit to the orders of one that I must acknowledge the Instrument of saving my Life, thô they are not entirely conformable to my Will and pleasure. He has sentence'd me to a long continuance here, which (he says) is absolutely necessary for the

[1] Dr. Baglioni (see ii. 436, n. 1).

confirmation of my Health, and would persuade me that my illness has been wholly owing to my omission of drinking the Waters these two years past. I dare not contradict him, and must own he deserves (from the various surprizing Cures I have seen) the name given him in this Country, of the Miraculous Man.

Both his Character and practice are so singular I cannot forbear giving you some account of them. He will not permit his patients to have either Surgeon or Apothecary. He performs all the operations of the first with great dexterity, and whatever compounds he gives, he makes in his own House. Those are very few, the juice of Herbs and these Waters being commonly his sole prescriptions. He has very little learning, and professes drawing all his knowledge from experience, which he possesses perhaps in a greater degree than any other Mortal, being the 7th Doctor of his Family in a direct line. His Fore Fathers have all of them left Journals and registers solely for the use of their Posterity, none of them having publish'd any thing, and he has recourse to these manuscripts on every difficult case, the veracity of which (at least) is unquestionable. His vivacity is prodigious, and he is indefatigable in his Industry, but what most distinguis[h]es him is a disinterestness I never saw in any other. He is as regular in his attendance on the poorest peasant, from whom he never can receive one farthing, as on the richest of the Nobility, and when ever he is wanted will climb 3 or 4 mile in the mountains, in the hottest Sun or heaviest rain, where a Horse cannot go, to arrive at a Cottage where, if their condition requires it, he does not only give them advice and med'cines Gratis, but Bread, Wine, and whatever is needfull. There never passes a Week without one or more of these expeditions. His last visit is generally to me. I often see him as dirty and tir'd as a foot post, having eat nothing all day but a roll or two that he carrys in his pocket, yet blest with such a perpetual flow of Spirits, he is allwaies Gay to a degree above chearfullness. There is a peculiarity in this character that I hope will incline you to forgive my drawing it.

I have allready describ'd to you this extrodinary Spot of earth, which is almost unknown to the rest of the World, and indeed does not seem to be destin'd by Nature to be inhabited by Human Creatures, and I beleive would never have been so without the cruel Civil War between the Guelphs and Gibillines. Before that time here was only the Huts of a few Fisher men, who came at certain Seasons on account of the fine Fish with which this Lake abounds, particularly Trouts as large and red as Salmon. The Lake it selfe is different from any other I ever saw or read of, being the colour of the sea, rather deeper ting'd with Green, which convinces me that the surrounding Mountains are full of Minerals, and it may be, rich in Mines yet undiscover'd, as well as Quarries of Marble, from whence the churches and Houses are ornamented and even the streets pav'd, which if polish'd and laid with art would look like the finest mosaic work, being a variety of Beautifull Colours. I ought to retract the Honorable Title of Street, none of them being broader than an Alley, and impassible for any wheel carriage except a Wheelbarrow.

This Town (which is the largest of 25 that are built on the Banks of the Lake) is near 2 mile long, in the Figure of a semi circle. If it was a regular range of Building it would appear magnificent, but being founded accidentally by those who sought a refuge from the violencies of those bloody Times, it is a mixture of Shops and Palaces, Gardens and Houses, which ascend a mile high, in a confusion which is not disagreable. After this salutary water was found and the purity of the Air experienc'd, many people of Quality chose it for their Summer residence, and embellish'd it with several fine edifices. It was populous and flourishing till that fatal plague which overran all Europe. In the year 1626 it made a terrible ravage in this Place.[1] The poor were almost destroy'd, and the rich deserted it. Since that time it has never recover'd its former Splendour; few of the Nobillity return'd.

It is now only frequented during the Water-drinking season, several of the ancient Palaces degraded into Lodging Houses, and others stand empty in a ruinous Condition. One of these I have bought. I see you lift up your Eyes in wonder at my Indiscretion. I beg you to hear my reasons before you

---

[1] LM may refer to a devastating plague in Brescia in 1629–30 (*Le Cronache bresciane inedite dei secoli XV–XIX*, ed. P. Guerrini, 1922–, iv. 355, 423 ff.).

condemn me. In my infirm state of Health the unavoidable noise of a public Lodging is very disagreable, and here is no private one. Secondly and cheiffly, the whole purchase is but one hundred pound, with a very pretty Garden in Terrases down to the Water, and a Court behind the House. It is founded on a rock, and the Walls so thick they will probably remain as long as the Earth.

It is true the Apartments are in most tatter'd circumstances, without doors or Windows. The Beauty of the great salon gain'd my affection. It is 42 foot in length by 25, proportionably high, opening into a Balconey of the same length, with marble Ballustres. The ceiling and Flooring are in good repair, but I have been forc'd to the expence of covering the Wall with new Stucco, and the Carpenter is at this minute taking measure of the Windows in order to make frames for sashes. The great stairs are in such a declineing way, it would be a very hazardous exploit to mount them. I never intend to attempt it. The State bed chamber shall also remain for the sole use of the spiders that have taken possession of it, along with the Grand Cabinet and some other pieces of magnificence quite useless to me, and which would cost a great deal to make habitable. I have fitted up 6 rooms, with Lodgings for 5 servants, which are all I ever will have in this place; and I am persuaded that I could make a profit if I would part with my purchase, having been very much befreinded in the sale, which was by Auction, the owner having dy'd without Children, and I beleive he had never seen this Mansion in his Life, it having stood empty from the Death of his Grand Father. The Governor bid for me, and no body would bid against him; thus I am become a Citizen of Louvere, to the great Joy of the Inhabitants, not (as they would pretend) from their respect for my person, but I perceive they fancy I shall attract all the travelling English; and to say Truth the Singularity of the Place is well worth their Curiosity, but as I have no correspondants I may be bury'd here 50 years and nobody know any thing of the matter.

I receiv'd the Books you were so kind to send me, 3 days ago, but not the china, which I would not venture amongst the precipices that lead hither. I have only had time to read

Lord Orrery's Work,[1] which has extremely entertain'd and
not at all surpriz'd me, having the Honor of being acquainted
with him, and know him for one of those Danglers after Wit
who (like those after Beauty) spend their time in humbly
admiring, and are happy in being permitted to attend, thô
they are laugh'd at, and only encourrag'd to gratify the insa-
tiate Vanity of those proffess'd Wits and Beauties who aim at
being publickly distinguish'd in those characters. D[ean]
S[wift] (by his Lordship's own account) was so intoxicated
with the Love of Flattery, he sought it amongst the lowest
of people and the silliest of Women,[2] and was never so
well pleas'd with any Companions as those that worship'd
him while he insulted them. It is a wonderfull condescention
in a Man of Quality to offer his Incense in such a croud,[3]
and think it an Honor to share a Freindship with Sheridan[4]
etc., especially being himselfe endow'd with such universal
merit as he displays in these Letters, where he shews that he
is a Poet, a Patriot, a Philosopher, a Physician,[5] a Critic,
a compleat Scholar, and most excellent Moralist, shineing in
private Life as a submissive Son, a tender Father, and zealous
Freind. His only Error has been that love of learned ease,
which he has indulg'd in a Solitude which has prevented the
World from being blest with such a General, Minister, or
Admiral, being equal to any of these employments if he
would have turn'd his Talents to the use of the Public.
Heaven be prais'd, he has now drawn his Pen in its service,
and given an Example to Mankind that the most villainous
Actions, nay, the coarsest nonsense, are only small Blemishes
in a great Genius.

I happen to think quite contrary. (Weak Woman as I am!)
I have allwaies avoided the Conversation of those who
endeavour to raise an opinion of their understanding by

---

[1] In 1751 John Boyle (1707–62), 5th
Earl of Orrery, published his *Remarks
on the Life and Writings of Swift*.

[2] In her Commonplace Book LM
wrote 'Dr. S[wift] in the midst of his
Women, like a master E[unuch] in a
seraglio' (MS, f. 6). Orrery writes of
Swift's 'constant seraglio of very virtuous women' (3rd ed., 1752, p. 83).

[3] 'His friendship was an honour to

me', writes Orrery of Swift. '. . . He
was open to adulation, and could not,
or would not distinguish between low
flattery, and just applause' (p. 3).

[4] Thomas Sheridan, D.D. (1687–
1738), schoolmaster. Orrery discusses
his friendship with Swift (pp. 53–55).

[5] Orrery discusses lunacy at great
length (pp. 171–9).

ridiculeing what both Law and Decency obliges them to revere, but whenever I have met with any of those bright Spirits who would be smart on sacred Subjects, I have ever cut short their discourse by asking them if they had any Lights and Revelations by which they would propose new articles of Faith? No body can deny but Religion is a comfort to the distress'd, a Cordial to the Sick, and sometimes a restraint on the wicked; therefore whoever would argue or laugh it out of the World without giving some equivalent for it ought to be treated as a common Enemy. But when this Language[1] comes from a churchman who enjoys large benefices and Dignitys from that very church he openly despises, it is an Object of Horror for which I want a Name, and can only be excus'd by Madness, which I think the Dean was allwaies strongly touch'd with. His character seems to me a Parallel with that of Caligula, and had he had the same power, would have made the same use of it. That Emperor erected a Temple to himselfe, where he was his own High Priest, preferr'd his Horse to the highest Honors in the state, proffess'd Enmity to [the] Human Race, and at last lost his Life by a nasty Jest on one of his Inferiors,[2] which I dare swear Swift would have made in his place.

There can be no worse picture made of the Doctor's morals than he has given us himselfe in the Letters printed by Pope.[3] We see him Vain, triffling, ungratefull to the memory of his Patron the Earl of Oxford,[4] making a servile Court where he had any interested views, and meanly abusive when they were disapointed, and as he says (in his own Phrase) flying in the Face of Mankind in company with his adorer Pope.[5] It is pleasant to consider that had it not been for the good nature of these very mortals they contemn, these two superior Beings were entitle'd by their Birth and hereditary Fortune to be only a couple of Link Boys. I am of Opinion their Freindship would have continu'd thô they had remain'd

[1] In *A Tale of a Tub* (1705).

[2] The chief assassin of Caligula was one of his guards, whom he had provoked with accusations of voluptuousness and effeminacy (Suetonius, *Lives*).

[3] In 1737.

[4] Robert Harley (1661-1724), 1st Earl.

[5] The phrase 'Fly in its [the world's] face' is actually used in a letter from Pope and Bolingbroke to Swift in the collection published by Pope (*Corr.*, ed. G. Sherburn, 1956, ii. 349). A similar sentiment does occur in a letter from Swift to Pope (ibid. ii. 342).

in the same Kingdom.[1] It had a very strong Foundation: the Love of Flattery on one side and the Love of Money on the other.

Pope courted with the utmost assiduity all the old men from whom he could hope a Legacy: the Duke of Buckingham, Lord Peterborrough, Sir G[odfrey] Kneller, Lord Bolingbroke, Mr. Wycherly, Mr. Congreve, Lord Harcourt[2] etc., and I do not doubt projected to sweep the Dean's whole inheritance if he could have persuaded him to throw up his Deanery and come die in his House; and his general preaching against money was meant to induce people to throw it away that he might pick it up. There cannot be a stronger proofe of his being capable of any Action for the sake of Gain than publishing his Literary Correspondance, which lays open such a mixture of Dullness and iniquity that one would imagine it visible even to his most passionate admirers,[3] if Lord O[rrery] did not show that smooth lines have as much influence over some people as the Authority of the Church in these Countrys, where it can not only veil but sanctifye any absurdity or Villainy whatever.

It is remarkable that his Lordship's Family have been smatterers in Wit and Learning for 3 Generations. His [Great] G[rand] Father[4] has left monuments of his good taste in several Rhimeing Tragedys and the romance of Parthenissa. His Father begun the World by giving his name to a treatise wrote by Atterbury and his club, which gain'd him great Reputation,[5] but (like Sir Martin Marall,

---

[1] Orrery conjectures that the friendship between Pope and Swift remained constant not only because they pursued different roads in poetry but because they lived in different kingdoms (*Remarks*, pp. 147, 149–50).

[2] John Sheffield (1648–1721), 1st Duke of Buckingham; Peterborough (1658–1735); Kneller (1646–1723); Bolingbroke (1678–1751); Wycherley (1640 ?–1716); Congreve (1670–1729); Simon Harcourt (1661–1727), 1st Viscount. All these were friends of Pope's, but apparently his only 'legacy' from any of them was Peterborough's deathbed gift of a watch presented to him by the King of Sicily (*Corr.* iii. 509).

[3] LM had expressed her indignation, when the letters were published, with a short prose piece entitled 'A Letter to A.P. in answer to the preface of His Letters' (W MS v. 8; printed in George Paston [E. M. Symonds], *Lady Mary Wortley Montagu and Her Times*, 1907, pp. 351–2), but it apparently remained unpublished.

[4] Roger Boyle (1621–79), 1st Earl of Orrery, statesman and soldier as well as dramatist—for whom see Kathleen M. Lynch, *Roger Boyle, First Earl of Orrery* (1965).

[5] Charles (1674–1731), 4th Earl, was involved in the controversy with Dr. Bentley over the epistles of Phalaris; and

who would fumble with his Lute when the music was over)[1]
he publish'd soon after a sad Comedy of his own, and what
was worse, a dismal Tragedy he had found amongst the
first Earl of Orrery's papers.[2] People could easier forgive
his being partial to his own silly Works (as a common Frailty)
than the want of Judgment in produceing a piece that dis-
honor'd his [Grand] Father's memory. Thus fell into dust
a Fame that had made a Blaze by borrow'd Fire. To do
justice to the present Lord, I do not doubt this fine performance is all his own, and is a public benefit if every Reader
has been as well diverted with it as my selfe. I verily beleive
it has contributed to the establishment of my Health.

I have wrote two long letters to your Father to which I
have had no Answer. I hope he is well. The prosperity of
you and yours is the warmest wish of (my Dear child) your
most affectionate Mother.

M. Wortley

This Letter is of a horrible Length. I dare not read it over.
I should have told you (to justifye my Folly as far as I can)
here is no ground rent to be paid, Taxes for church and
poor, or any Imposition whatever on Houses.

I desire in your next parcel you would send me Lady
Frail, the Adventures of G. Edwards,[3] and the Life of Lord
Stair,[4] which I suppose very superficial and partly fictitious,
but as he was my Acquaintance I have some Curiosity to see
how he is represented.

Text W MS iii. 63–67   *Address* To The Rt Honble the Countess of
Bute recommended to Sam: Child Esqr near Temple Bar London
Angleterre *Postmark* SE ⟨12⟩

---

assisted by Francis Atterbury (1662–
1732), later Bishop of Rochester, and by
George Smalridge, he published *Dr.
Bentley's Dissertations . . . Examined*
(1698).

[1] In Dryden's comedy Sir Martin
pretends to serenade a lady; and his
servant, who supplies the real music,
signals that the song is over, but 'Sir
Martin continues fumbling' (*Sir Martin
Mar-All*, 1668, Act v).

[2] The 4th Earl wrote a comedy, *As
You Find It* (1703), and produced
Altemira (1702) by his grandfather the
1st Earl.

[3] *The Adventures of Lady Frail* (1751)
and *The Adventures of Mr. George
Edwards, A Creole* (1751), both by
Dr. John Hill.

[4] *The Life of John, Earl of Stair* by
Andrew Henderson, published in 1748,
a year after Stair's death.

To Lady Oxford *10 July* [*1754*]

Louvere, July 10 N.S.

Dearest Madam,

I should have sooner return'd my thanks for your Lady-ship's obliging Letter if I had not been so ill I was unable to do any thing. I am now at this Place by the doctor's orders, and the Waters and Air have so far recover'd my Health, I have reason to hope the perfect reestablishment of it. I am much in pain about yours; I wish your Ladyship here on many Accounts, but realy cheiffly to be some time under the care of this Physician. I have seen so many wonderfull cures by his skill (beside my own) I should expect he might be usefull to you, and cannot help desiring you would send your Case.

I know not how to mend the direction I gave your Ladi-ship, thô I am sensible there is a great difference between the Care of Sir J. Gray and him I am now forc'd to employ.[1] Sir James is long since return'd to England, to my great Sorrow; thô I never saw him, he was in the civilest manner attentive to every thing that concern'd me. I rejoice in the Prosperity of your Ladiship's family; what ever contributes to your Happiness is dear to me. My Daughter tells me Lady Pomfret is a Widow, but not in what circumstances,[2] and that the Duke of K[ingston] is again engag'd in a persuit that cannot do him much Honor.[3]

I beleive I lose the sight of many disagreeable things by my Retirement, but I want your Conversation, which will ever be sensibly regretted by (Dearest Madam) your Ladyship's most Faithfull and Devoted Servant,

M. W. Montagu.

Text Portland MS (Longleat) ii. 333–4   *Address* To The Rt Honble the Lady Henrietta Countess of Oxford in Dover Street near St James's London Angleterre   *Postmark* AV ⟨?⟩   *End. by Lady Oxford* R: Cav: Lodge Thursday Aug 22 1754 (2)

[1] Consul Smith.

[2] After Pomfret's death in July 1753, Walpole told Mann of the widow's circumstances: 'The Countess has two thousand a year rent charge for jointure, five hundred as lady of the Bedchamber to the late Queen, and £14,000 in money, in her own power, just recovered by a lawsuit—what a fund for follies!' (*Corr.* xx. 389–90).

[3] Probably his pursuit of Elizabeth Chudleigh (see above, p. 29, n. 4).

To Lady Bute *20 July* [*1754*]

July 20. N.S.

My Dear Child,

I have now read over the Books you were so good to send, and intend to say something of them all, thô some are not worth speaking of. I shall begin, in respect to his Dignity, with Lord B[olingbroke][1], who is a glareing proofe how far Vanity can blind a Man, and how easy it is to varnish over to one's selfe the most Criminal Conduct. He declares he allwaies lov'd his Country, thô he confesses he endeavor'd to betray her to Popery and Slavery, and lov'd his Freinds, thô he abandonn'd them in Distress with all the blackest Circumstances of Treachery.

His account of the Peace of Utrecht[2] is (almost) equally unfair or Partial. I shall alow that perhaps the views of the Whigs at that time were too vast, and the nation, dazled by Military Glory, had hopes too sanguine, but sure the same terms that the French consented to at the Treaty of Gertruydenberg might have been obtain'd;[3] or, if the displaceing of the Duke of Marlbrô rais'd the spirits of our Enemies to a degree of refusing what they had before offer'd, how can he excuse the guilt of removing him from the Head of a victorious Army, and exposing us to submit to any Articles of Peace, being unable to continue the War? I agree with him that the Idea of conquering France is a wild extravagant Notion,[4] and would (if possible) be impolitic, but she might have been reduce'd to such a state as would have render'd her incapable of being terrible to her neighbours for some ages. Nor should we have been oblig'd (as we have done

---

[1] In answer to LM's request on 16 March 1752, Lady Bute had sent Bolingbroke's *Letters on the Study and Use of History* (1752), which also contained two other letters and 'Reflections upon Exile'.

[2] In Letter VIII (*Works*, 1809, iv. 118).

[3] In 1710 the Whigs began negotia-

tions at Gertruydenburg to end the War of the Spanish Succession, but failed because of their excessive demands. In 1713 the Tories put through the Treaty of Utrecht, which the Whigs considered a betrayal of British interests.

[4] Bolingbroke refers to 'chimerical projects about changing her government' (iv. 121).

almost ever since) to bribe the French ministers to let us live in Quiet.

So much for his political reasonings, which I confess are deliver'd in a florid easy style, but I cannot be of Lord Orrery's Opinion that he is one of the best English Writers.[1] Well turn'd periods or smooth lines are not the perfection either of Prose or verse; they may serve to adorn, but can never stand in the Place of good Sense. Copiousness of words, however rang'd, is allwaies false Eloquence, thô it will ever impose on some sort of understandings. How many readers and admirers has Madame de Sevigny, who only gives us, in a lively manner and fashionable Phrases, mean sentiments, vulgar Prejudices, and endless repetitions![2] Sometimes the tittle tattle of a fine Lady, sometimes that of an old Nurse, allwaies tittle tattle; yet so well gilt over by airy expressions and a Flowing Style, she will allwaies please the same people to whom Lord Bolingbroke will shine as a first rate Author. She is so far to be excus'd as her Letters were not intended for the Press, while he labours to display to posterity all the Wit and Learning he is Master of, and sometimes spoils a good Argument by a profusion of Words, running out into several pages a thought that might have been more clearly express'd in a few lines, and what is worse, often falls into contradictions and repetitions, which are almost unavoidable to all Voluminous Writers, and can only be forgiven those Retailers whose necessity compels them to Diurnal scribbling, who load their meaning with Epithets and run into Digressions because (in the Jockey Phrase) it rids ground; that is, covers a certain Quantity of Paper to answer the Demand of the Day.

A great part of Lord B[olingbroke]'s Letters are design'd to shew his Reading, which indeed appears to have been very extensive, but I cannot perceive that such a minute account of it can be of any use to the Pupil he pretends to instruct;[3] nor can I help thinking he is far below either Tillotson[4] or Addison even in style, thô the latter was

---

[1] Along with Addison and Swift (*Remarks on the Life and Writings of Swift*, 1751; 3rd ed., 1752, p. 153).

[2] For LM's opinion in 1726, see ii. 66. Orrery praised the French-woman in his book (p. 166).

[3] The *Letters on the Study and Use of History* were addressed to Lord Cornbury.

[4] John Tillotson (1630–94), theo-

sometimes more diffuse than his Judgment approv'd, to furnish out the length of a daily Spectator.[1] I own I have small regard for Lord B[olingbroke] as an Author, and the highest contempt for him as a Man. He came into the World greatly Favor'd both by Nature and Fortune, blest with a noble Birth, Heir to a large estate, endow'd with a strong Constitution, and (as I have heard) a Beautifull Figure, high Spirits, a good memory and a lively apprehension, which was cultivated by a learned Education. All these glorious advantages being left to the Direction of a Judgment stiffle'd by unbounded Vanity, he dishonour'd his Birth, lost his estate, ruin'd his Reputation and destroy'd his Health by a wild persuit of Eminence, even in Vice and Triffles.[2]

I am far from making misfortune a matter of reproach. I know there are accidental occurrences not to be foreseen or avoided by Human prudence, by which a character may be injur'd, Wealth disipated, or a constitution impair'd; but I think I may reasonably dispise the understanding of one who conducts himselfe in such a manner as naturally produces such lamentable Consequences, and continus in the same destructive paths to the end of a long Life, ostentatiously boasting of Morals and Philosophy in print, and with equal ostentation bragging of the scenes of low debauchery in public conversation, tho deplorably weak both in Mind and Body, and his Virtue and his Vigour in a state of non-Existence. His confedracy with Swift and Pope puts me in mind of that of Bessus and his sword men (in the King and No King), who endeavor to support themselves by giving certificates of each other's merit.[3] Pope has triumphantly declar'd that

logian and writer. LM read and 'liked' his sermons (Lady Oxford to LM, 17 Aug. 1745, Harley MS in BM).

[1] In his *Remarks* Orrery calls Swift and Addison 'more diffusive writers' than Tillotson (p. 40).

[2] In a long poem, probably written *c*. 1738, LM attacked Bolingbroke for his vices, particularly his political treason ('An Epistle from Pope to Lord Bolingbroke', 1861, ii. 474–6).

In 1757, Mme du Boccage, a literary lady, called on LM in Venice and re-

ported that she owned portraits of men she admired, including the Pope. Mme du Boccage continues: 'J'y vis aussi celui de Mylord Bolinbrook fort connu d'elle ainsi que ses ouvrages qui lui paroissent d'un penseur érudit, mais prolixe' (*Lettres sur l'Angleterre . . . et l'Italie* in *Recueil des œuvres*, 1762, iii. 178).

[3] The braggart Bessus in Beaumont and Fletcher's *A King and No King*, 1619, Act IV, Scene ii.

they may do and say whatever silly things they please, they will still be the greatest Geniuses Nature ever exhibited. I am delighted with the comparison given of their Benevolence, which is indeed most aptly figur'd by a circle in the Water, which widens till it comes to nothing it [*sic*] all.

But I am provok'd at Lord B[olingbroke]'s misrepresentation of my Favorite Atticus,[1] who seems to have been the only Roman that from good sense had a true Notion of the Times in which he liv'd, in which the Republic was inevitably perishing, and the two factions who pretended to support it equally endeavoring to gratify their Ambition in its ruin. A wise Man in that case would certainly declare for neither, and try to save himselfe and Family from the general wreck, which could not be done but by a superiority of understanding acknowledg'd on both sides. I see no Glory in loseing Life or Fortune by being the Dupe of either, and very much aplaud that conduct which could preserve a universal Esteem amidst the Fury of opposite Parties. We are oblig'd to act vigorously where action can do any good, but in a storm when it is impossible to work with success, the best hands and ablest Pilots may laudably gain the Shore if they can. Atticus could be a Freind to Men without engaging in their passions, disapprove their Maxims without awaking their Resentment, and be satisfy'd with his own Virtue without seeking popular Fame. He had the reward of his Wisdom in his Tranquillity, and will ever stand amongst the few examples of true Philosophy either ancient or modern.

You must forgive this tedious Dissertation. I hope you read in the same Spirit I write, and take as proofes of affection what ever is sent you by your truly tender Mother.

M. Wortley

I must add a few words on the Essay on Exile, which I read with attention (as a subject that touch'd me). I found the most Abject Dejection under a pretended Fortitude. That the Author felt it, can be no doubt to one that knows

---

[1] 'Atticus, whose great talents were usury and trimming, who placed his principle merit in being rich, and who would have been noted with infamy at Athens, for keeping well with all sides, and venturing on none. . . .' ('Reflections upon Exile', 1752, in *Works*, 1809, i. 153.)

(as I do) the mean submissions and solemn promises he made to obtain a return, flattering himselfe (I suppose) he need ⟨on⟩ly appear, to be at the Head of the administration,[1] a⟨s a⟩n Ensign of sixteen fancies he is in a fair way to be a ⟨general⟩ on the first sight of his commission.

    You will think I have been too long on the Chara⟨cter of⟩ Atticus. I own I took pleasure in explaining it. ⟨?⟩ Pope thought himselfe covertly very severe on M⟨r. Addison⟩ by giving him that name, and I feel indignation ⟨when⟩ he is abus'd, both from his own merit, and ha⟨ving been⟩ your Father's Freind. Besides that, it is naturally sh⟨ocking to see⟩ an⟨y one⟩ lampoon'd after his Death by the same m⟨an who⟩ had ⟨paid⟩ him the most servile court while he ⟨lived, and was⟩[2] highly oblig'd by him.[3]

Text W MS iii. 131–3   *Address* To The Rt Honble the Countess of Bute recommended to Samuel Child Esqr near Temple Bar London Angleterre

To Lady Bute *23 July* [*1754*]

                              July 23, Louvere

My Dear Child,

    I have promis'd you some remarks on all the Books I have receive'd. I beleive you would easily forgive my not keeping my word; however, I shall go on. The Rambler is certainly a strong misnommer. He allwaies plods in the beaten road of his Predecessors, following the Spectator (with the same pace a Pack horse would do a Hunter) in the style that is proper to lengthen a paper. These writers may perhaps be of Service to the Public (which is saying a great deal in their

---

[1] On his return in 1725, Bolingbroke was still barred from holding office.

[2] MS torn; text restored from 1861, ii. 259.

[3] Although LM had told Spence that Pope wrote his satiric portrait of Addison (as Atticus) during his lifetime (*Anecdotes*, ed. J. M. Osborn, 1966, § LM 4), she was apparently ignorant of the fact that Pope had sent Addison a draft of the lines in 1716. They were anonymously printed in a newspaper in 1722, three years after Addison's death, and were ultimately used by Pope in his *Epistle to Dr. Arbuthnot*, 1735 (George Sherburn, *Early Career of Pope*, 1934, pp. 145–8; Pope, *Minor Poems*, ed. N. Ault and J. Butt, 1954, p. 144).

Favor). There are numbers of both Sexes who never read
any thing but such productions, and cannot spare time from
doing nothing to go through a sixpenny Pamphlet. Such
gentle Readers may be improv'd by a moral hint which,
thô repeated over and over from Generation to Generation,
they never heard in their Lives. I should be glad to know the
name of this Laborious Author.[1]

H. Fielding has given a true picture of himselfe and his
first Wife[2] in the Characters of Mr. and Mrs. Booth (some
Complement to his own figure excepted) and I am persuaded
several of the Incidents he mentions are real matters of Fact.[3]
I wonder he does not perceive Tom Jones and Mr. Booth
are Sorry Scoundrels. All these sort of Books have the same
fault, which I cannot easily pardon, being very mischeivous.[4]
They place a merit in extravagant Passions, and encourrage
young people to hope for impossible events to draw them
out of the misery they chuse to plunge themselves into,
expecting legacys from unknown Relations, and generous
Benefactors to distress'd Virtue, as much out of Nature as
Fairy Treasures. Fielding has realy a fund of true Humour,
and was to be pity'd at his first entrance into the World,
having no choice (as he said himselfe) but to be a Hackney
Writer or a Hackney Coachman. His Genius deserv'd a
better Fate, but I cannot help blaming that continu'd
Indiscretion (to give it the softest name) that has run through
his Life, and I am afraid still remains. I guess'd R. Random
to be his, thô without his Name. I cannot think Fadom
wrote by the same hand; it is every way so much below it.[5]
Sally [Fielding] has mended her style in her last Volume

---

[1] In 1752 Johnson's *Rambler*
(1750–2) was collected in six volumes
duodecimo (W. P. Courteney and
D. N. Smith, *Bibliography of Samuel
Johnson*, 1915; repr. 1925, p. 33); this
was probably the edition sent by Lady
Bute. Johnson's authorship was generally known in London.

[2] Charlotte Cradock (d. 1744) m.
(1734) Henry Fielding.

[3] In *Amelia*, published Dec. 1751.
Since LM was Fielding's cousin, her
remark is valuable; it is discussed in
Wilbur L. Cross, *History of Henry

Fielding, 1918, ii. 328–35, and F. Homes
Dudden, *Henry Fielding, His Life,
Works, and Times*, 1952, ii. 855–9. On
her copy of vol. i of the book LM
wrote: 'inferior to himselfe, superior to
most others' (Sotheby Catalogue, 1 Aug.
1928, p. 86).

[4] On her copy of *Tom Jones* LM gave
a different opinion: '*Ne plus ultra*' (Lady
Louisa Stuart, 1861, i. 107).

[5] *Roderick Random* (1748) and *Ferdinand Count Fathom* (1753) were both by
Tobias Smollett.

of D[avid] Simple, which conveys a usefull moral (tho' she does not seem to have intended it); I mean, shews the ill consequences of not providing against Casual losses, which happen to almost every body. Mrs. Orgueil's character is well drawn, and is frequently to be met with.[1] The Art of Tormenting, the Female Quixote, and Sir C. Goodville are all sale work.[2] I suppose they proceed from her pen, and heartily pity her, constrain'd by her Circumstances to seek her bread by a method I do not doubt she despises. Tell me who is that accomplish'd Countess she celebrates.[3] I left no such person in London; nor can I imagine who is meant by the English Sapho mention'd in Betsy Thoughtless,[4] whose adventures, and those of Jenny Jessamy,[5] gave me some amusement. I was better entertain'd by the Valet, who very fairly represents how you are bought and sold by your Servants.[6] I am now so accustom'd to another manner of treatment, it would be difficult for me to suffer them. His adventures have the uncommon Merit of ending in a surprizing manner.

The General Want of Invention which reigns amongst our Writers inclines me to think it is not the natural Growth of our Island, which has not Sun enough to warm the Imagination; the Press is loaded by the servile Flock of Imitators. (Lord B[olingbroke] would have quoted Horace[7] in this place.) Since I was born, no original has appear'd excepting

[1] By 1750 LM had read Sarah Fielding's earlier works (ii. 470). In the third ('last') volume of *The Adventures of David Simple* (1753) Mrs. Orgueil is a villainous, cruel, and hypocritical character. The novel ends tragically as David and his family suffer a series of misfortunes. On her copy of this volume LM wrote 'Natural' (Sotheby Catalogue, p. 86).

[2] *An Essay on the Art of Ingeniously Tormenting* (1753) by Jane Collier; *The Female Quixote; or, The Adventures of Arabella* (1752) by Charlotte Lennox; *Memoirs of Sir Charles Goodville and His Family* (1753). All three had been praised in the *Monthly Review* (viii. 274–81, vi. 249–62, viii. 187–9).

[3] 'The celebrated Countess of——...

who among her own sex had no superior in wit, elegance and ease, was inferior to very few of the other in sense, learning and judgment' (*The Female Quixote*, book viii, chap. v).

[4] *The History of Miss Betsy Thoughtless* (1751) by Eliza Haywood; LM's copy survives (Sotheby Catalogue, p. 88). A couplet by the unidentifiable 'English Sappho' is quoted in the novel (4th ed., 1768, iii. 76).

[5] *The History of Jemmy and Jenny Jessamy* (1753), also by Haywood.

[6] *The Adventures of a Valet. Written by Himself* (1752) was favourably noticed in the *Monthly Review* (vi. 110–23).

[7] 'O imitatores, servum pecus . . .' (*Epistles* I. xix. 19).

Congreve, and Fielding, who would I beleive have approach'd nearer to his excellencies if not forc'd by necessity
to publish without correction, and throw many productions
into the World he would have thrown into the Fire if meat
could have been got without money, or money without
Scribbling. The Greatest Virtue, Justice, and the most
distinguishing prerogative of Mankind, writeing, when duly
executed do Honor to Human nature, but when degenerated
into Trades are the most contemptible ways of getting Bread.
I am sorry not to see any more of P[eregrine] Pickle's per-
formances; I wish you would tell me his name.[1]

I can't forbear saying something in relation to my Grand
Daughters, who are very near my Heart. If any of them are
fond of reading, I would not advise you to hinder them
(cheiffly because it is impossible) seeing Poetry, Plays or
Romances; but accustom them to talk over what they read,
and point to them, as you are very capable of doing, the
Absurdity often conceal'd under fine expressions, whe⟨re⟩
the Sound is apt to engage the Admiration of young People.
I was so much charm'd at fourteen with the Dialogue of
Henry and Emma,[2] I can say it by heart to this Day, without
refflecting on the monstrous folly of the story in plain prose,
where a young Heiress to a fond Father is represented falling
in love with a Fellow she had only seen as a Huntsman,
a Faulkner [Falconer], and a Beggar, and who confesses,
without any circumstances of excuse, that he is oblig'd to
run his country, having newly committed a Murder. She
ought reasonably to have suppos'd him (at best) a Highway
man, yet the Virtuous Virgin resolves to run away with him
to live amongst the Banditti, and wait upon his Trollop if
she had no other Way of enjoying his Company. This senseless Tale is, however, so well varnish'd with melody of
Words and pomp of Sentiments, I am convince'd it has
hurt more Girls than ever were injur'd by the lewdest Poems
extant.

I fear this Counsel has been repeated to you before, but
I have lost so many Letters design'd for you, I know not

---

[1] Smollett (see above, p. 2).
[2] Matthew Prior's 'Henry and Emma',
1709 (*Literary Works*, ed. H. B. Wright
and M. K. Spears, 1959, pp. 278-300,
909-10). For LM's early quotations
from it see i. 120, 121, 177, 178.

which you have receiv'd. If you would have me avoid this fault, you must take notice of those that arrive, which you very seldom do.

My dear child, God bless you and yours. I am ever your most affectionate Mother,

M. Wortley.

Text W MS iii. 117–18   *Address* To The Rt Honble the Countess of Bute recommended to Samuel Child Esqr near Temple Bar London Angleterre

To Wortley *23 July* [*1754*]

It is long since I have wrote two letters to you without receiving any Answer. I am afraid that some Indisposition in your Eyes occasions your silence, my Daughter telling me you are in good Health. I have sent her my opinion of Lord Bolingbroke and Lord Orrery's performances.¹ You may perhaps have some curiosity to read it, having once before desir'd to know my thoughts on a like subject.²

I have had a very bad Fever, but am now recover'd by this Air and drinking the Waters, which the Doctor orders me to continue a month longer.

I have heard a story of your Freind Lord R[avensworth]³ which I am ⟨sorry⟩ for, beleiving it a Mortific⟨ation⟩ to him. If the same case ⟨had⟩ happen'd in this Country, the Lawyer would not have liv'd 24 hours after.⁴

I could write many customs here that would (perhaps) amuse you, but I dare venture nothing of that kind by the Post. The certainty of Letters being open'd puts a great restraint on my pen.

¹ In her letters of 20 July and 23 June [1754] respectively.

² In 1749 she had sent W a critique on Bolingbroke's *Letters, on the Spirit of Patriotism*, but it was lost (see ii. 448).

³ Henry Liddell, 1st Baron (see ii. 91, n. 2).

⁴ In Jan. 1753, on information of a lawyer, Edward Fawcett (d. 1768), Ravensworth had accused several prominent men of Jacobitism; but the accusations were rejected in Feb. by the Cabinet Council and the lawyer was discredited (*Letters from George III to Lord Bute 1756–1766*, ed. R. Sedgwick, 1939, pp. xxxi–xxxvii).

I hope you are well and heartily wish you to continue so many Years.

July 23. N.S.

Text W MS ii. 239–40 *Address* To Edwd Wortley Esqr recommended to S. Child Esqr near Temple Bar London Angleterre *End.* by *W* [*Summary*] Arrived in London 16 Sept. Ad at Newc[astle] 6 Oct.

To Lady Bute *8 Dec.* [*1754*]

Louvere, Dec. 8. N.S.

My dear Child,

This Town is at present in a General Stare, to use their own expression, Sotto Sopra,[1] and not only this Town but the Capital Bergamo, the whole province, the neighbouring Brescian, and perhaps all the Venetian Dominion, occasion'd by an Adventure exactly ressembling and, I beleive, copy'd from Pamela. I know not under what constellation that Foolish stuff was wrote, but it has been translated into more Languages than any modern performance I ever heard of.[2] No proofe of its Influence was ever stronger than this present story, which in Richardson's hands would serve very well to furnish out 7 or 8 Volumes. I shall make it as short as I can.

Here is a Gentleman's Family [Ardenghi] consisting of an old Batchelor and his Sister, who have fortune enough to live with great elegance, thô without any Magnificence, possess'd of the Esteem of all their Acquaintance, he being distinguish'd by his Probity, and she by her virtue. They are not only suffer'd but sought by all the best Company, and indeed are the most conversable reasonable people in the place. She is an excellent Huswife, and particularly remarkable for keeping her pretty House as neat as any in Holland. She appears no longer in public, being past 50, and passes

---

[1] Topsy-turvy.
[2] Since its publication in 1740, *Pamela* had been translated into Dutch, German, and Danish as well as French and Italian.

her time cheiffly at Home with her Work, receiving few visitants.

This Signora Diana, about ten years since, saw at a Monastery a Girl of 8 years old who came thither to beg Alms for her Mother. Her Beauty, thô cover'd with Rags, was very observable, and gave great compassion to the Charitable Lady, who thought it meritorious to rescue such a modest sweetness as appear'd in her Face from the ruine to which her wretched circumstances expos'd her. She ask'd her some Questions, to which she answer'd with a natural Civility that seem'd surprizing, and finding the head of her Family (her Brother) to be a Cobler who could hardly live by that trade, and her Mother too old to work for her maintenance, she bid the child follow her Home, and sending for her Parent, propos'd to her to breed the little Octavia for her servant. This was joyfully accepted, the old Woman dismiss'd with a piece of money, and the Girl remain'd with the Signora Diana, who bought her decent cloaths, and took pleasure in teaching her whatever she was capable of learning. She learn'd to read, write, and cast accompts, with uncommon Facility, and had such a Genius for Work that she excell'd her mistriss in Embrodiery, point, and every operation of the needle. She grew perfectly skill'd in Confectionary, had a good insight into Cookery, and was a great proficient in Distillery. To these accomplishments, she was so handy, well Bred, humble and modest, that not only her master and mistrisse but every body that frequented the House took notice of her.

She liv'd thus near 9 years, never going out but to church. However, Beauty is as difficult to conceal as Light; hers begun to make a great noise. Signora Diana told me she observ'd an unusual concourse of pedling Women that came on pretext to sell pen'norths of Lace, china etc., and several young Gentlemen, very well powder'd, that were perpetually walking before her door and looking up at the Windows. These prognostics alarm'd her prudence, and she listen'd very willingly to some honourable proposals that were made by many honest thriving Trademen. She communicated them to Octavia, and told her that thô she was sorry to lose so good a Servant, yet she thought it right to advise her to choose a Husband. The Girl answer'd modestly, that it was her Duty to obey all her commands, but she found no Inclination to marriage, and if she would permit her to live single she should think it a greater obligation than any other she could bestow. Signora Diana was too Conscientious to force her into a state from which she could not free her, and left her to her own Disposal.

However, they parted soon after. Whither (as the neighbours say) Signor Aurelio Ardinghi, her Brother, look'd with too much attention on the young Woman, or that she her selfe (as Diana says) desir'd to seek a place of more profit, she remov'd to Bergamo, where she soon found preferment, being strongly recommended by the Ardinghi Family. She was advanc'd to be first waiting Woman to an Old Countess, who was so well pleas'd with her service, she desir'd on her Death Bed Count Jeronimo Sosi,[1] her Son, to be kind to her. He found no repugnance to this Act of Obedience, having distinguish'd the beautifull Octavia from his first sight of her, and during the six months that she had serv'd in the House had try'd every Art of a fine Gentleman accustom'd to Victorys of that sort, to vanquish the virtue of this fair virgin. He has a handsome Figure and has had an Education uncommon in this Country, having made the Tour of Europe and brought from Paris all the improvements that are to be pick'd up there, being celebrated for his Grace in Dancing and skill in Fencing and rideing, by which he is a favourite amongst the Ladies and respected by the Men. Thus Qualify'd for Conquest, you may judge of his surprize at the firm yet modest resistance of this Country Girl, who was neither to be mov'd by address, nor gain'd by Liberality, nor on any Terms would be prevail'd on to stay as his Housekeeper after the Death of his Mother.

She took that post in the House of an old Judge, where she continu'd to be solicited by the Emissaries of the Count's passion, and found a new Persecutor in her Master, who, after 3 months endeavor to corrupt her, offer'd her marriage. She chose to return to her former Obscurity, and escap'd from his persuit without asking any wages, and privately return'd to the Signora Diana. She threw her selfe

[1] The family Sozzi of Bergamo.

at her Feet, and kissing her hands begg'd her with Tears to conceal her at least some time, if she would not accept of her service. She protested she had never been happy since she left it.

While she was making these submissions, Signor Aurelio enter'd. She intreated his intercession on her knees, who was easily persuaded to consent she should stay with them, thô his sister blam'd her highly for her precipitate Flight, having no reason from the Age and Character of her Master to fear any violence, and wonder'd at her declining the Honor he offer'd her. Octavia confess'd that perhaps she had been too rash in her proceedings, but said that he seem'd to resent her refusal in such a manner as frighted her, she hop'd that after a few days search he would think no more of her, and that she scrupul'd entering into the Holy Bands of Matrimony where her Heart did not sincerely accompany all the words of the Ceremony. Signora Diana had nothing to say in Contradiction to this pious Sentiment, and her Brother applauded the Honesty which could not be perverted by any Interest whatever. She remain'd conceal'd in their House, where she help'd in the Kitchin, clean'd the rooms, and redouble'd her usual Diligence and officiousness. Her old Master came to Louvere on pretence of adjusting a law suit 3 days after, and made private enquiry after her, but hearing from her mother and Brother (who knew nothing of her being here) that they had never heard of her, he concluded she had taken another Route, and return'd to Bergamo; and she continu'd in this Retirement near a fortnight.

Last Sunday, as soon as the day was clos'd, arriv'd at Signor Aurelio's door a Handsome Equipage in a large Bark attended by 4 well arm'd servants on Horseback. An old Priest stepp'd out of it, and desiring to speak with Signora Diana, inform'd her he came from the Count Jeronimo Sosi to demand Octavia, that the Count waited for her at a Village 4 mile from hence, where he intended to marry her, and had sent him, who was engag'd to perform that Divine Rite, that Signora Diana might resign her to his Care without any Difficulty. The Young Damsel was call'd for, who intreated she might be permitted the company of another Priest with whom she was acquainted. This was readily granted, and she sent for a young Man that visits me very often, being remarkable for his Sobriety and learning. Mean while a valet de chambre presented her with a Box in which was a compleat gentile undress for a Lady. Her lac'd Linnen and fine Nightgown were soon put on, and away they march'd, leaving the Family in a Surprize not to be describ'd.

Signor Aurelio came to drink coffee with me next morning. His first words were, he had brought me the History of Pamela. I said, laughing, I had been tir'd with it long since. He explain'd himselfe by relating this story, mix'd with great Resentment for Octavia's Conduct. Count Jeronimo's Father had been his ancient Freind and Patron, and this escape from his House (he said) would lay him under a Suspicion of having abetted the young Man's Folly, and perhaps expose him to the anger of all his Relations for contriving an Action he would rather have dy'd than suffer'd if he had known how to prevent it. I easily beleiv'd him, there appearing a latent Jealousy under his affliction, that shew'd me he envy'd the Bridegroom's Happiness at the same time he condemn'd his Extravagance.

Yesterday noon, being Saturday, Don Joseph return'd (who has got the name of Parson Williams[1] by this Expedition). He relates that when the Bark which carry'd the Coach and train arriv'd, they found the Amorous Count waiting his Bride on the Bank of the Lake. He would have proceeded immediately to the Church, but she utterly refus'd it till they had each of them been at Confession, after which the happy Knot was ty'd by the Parish Preist. They continu'd their Journey and came to their Palace at Bergamo in a Few Hours, where every thing was prepar'd for their Reception. They receiv'd the Communion next morning, and the Count declares that the Lovely Octavia has brought him an inestimable Portion, since he owes to her the Salvation of his Soul. He has renounce'd Play, at which he had lost a great deal of Time and money. She has already retrench'd several superfluous Servants and put his Family into an exact method of Oeconomy, preserving all the Splendor necessary to his

[1] In *Pamela* the parson tries to help the heroine escape from her would-be seducer; he ultimately officiates at their marriage.

Rank. He has sent a Letter in his own Hand to her mother, inviteing her to reside with them, and subscribing himselfe her Dutyfull Son; but the Countess has sent another privately by Don Joseph, in which she advises the old Woman to stay at Louvere, promising to take care she shall want nothing, accompany'd with a Token of 20 sequins, which is at least 19 more than ever she saw in her Life. I forgot to tell you that from Octavia's first serving the old Lady, there came frequent charitys in her name to her poor Parent, which no body was surpriz'd at, the Lady being celebrated for Pious Works, and Octavia known to be a great Favourite with her. It is now discover'd that they were all sent by the Generous Lover, who has presented Don Joseph very handsomly, but he has brought neither Letter nor message to the House of Ardinghi, which affords much Speculation.

I am afraid you are heartily tir'd with this tedious Tale. I will not lengthen it with Refflections; I fancy yours will be [the] same with mine. All these adventures proceed from Artifice on one side and weakness on the other. An Honest, open, tender mind is betraid to Ruin by the charms that make the Fortune of a designing Head, which when join'd with a Beautifull Face can never fail of advancement, except barr'd by a Wise Mother who locks up her Daughters from view till no body cares to look on 'em. My poor Freind the D[uche]ss of Bolton was educated in Solitude, with some choice Books, by a Saint-like Governess. Cramm'd with virtue and good Qualitys, she thought it impossible not to find Gratitude, thô she fail'd to give Passion, and upon this plan threw away her Estate, was despis'd by her Husband, and laugh'd at by the Public.[1] Polly, bred in an Alehouse and produce'd on the stage, has obtain'd Wealth and Title and found the way to be esteem'd.[2] So usefull is early Experience; without it halfe of Life is disipated in correcting the Errors that we have been taught to receive as indisputable Truths.

[1] Anne, Duchess of Bolton (c. 1689–1751), wife of the 3rd Duke, had been very unhappily married (see i. 233, n. 2 and 237, n. 1).

[2] Lavinia Fenton (1708–60), famous as the original Polly Peachum of *The* *Beggar's Opera* in 1728, by which time the Duke of Bolton had taken her into keeping. He married her a month after his first wife's death. (He himself died on 26 Aug. 1754.) Both as mistress and wife her conduct was notably discreet.

Make my Complements to Lord Bute. I am out of Humour with Lady Mary for neglecting to answer my Letters. However, she shares my Blessing with her Brothers and Sisters. I have a little Ring for Lady Jane,¹ but God knows when I shall have an oppertunity to send it. I am ever Your truly affectionate mother.

M. Wortley

It is a long time since I have heard from your Father, thô I have wrote several times.

Text W MS iii. 56–60 *Address* To The Rt Honble the Countess of Bute recommended to Sam: Child Esqr near Temple Bar London Angleterre

To Wortley *19 Dec.* [*1754*]

Louvere, Dec. 19. N.S.

I receiv'd yours of Oct. 6 yesterday, which gave me great pleasure. I am flatter'd by finding that our Sentiments are the same in regard to Lord Bolingbroke's writeings, as you will see more clearly if you ever have the long Letter I have wrote to you on that subject. I beleive he never read Horace or any other Author with a design of instructing himselfe, thinking he was born to give precepts and not to follow them. At least, if he was not mad enough to have this opinion, he endeavor'd to impose it on the rest of the World. All his works (being well consider'd) are little more than a Panegyric on his own universal Genius, many of his pretensions as preposterously inconsistent as if Sir Isaac Newton had aim'd at being a Critic in Fashions, and wrote for the Information of Tailors and Mantuamakers. I am of your opinion that he has never look'd into halfe the authors he quotes, and am much mistaken if he is not oblig'd to Mr. Bayle for the Generality of his Criticisms, for which reason he affects to despise him, that he may steal from him with less suspicion.² A diffusive style (thô often admir'd as Florid

¹ Like her eldest sister, she was a god-daughter of LM.

² Pierre Bayle (1647–1706), philosopher, famous for his *Dictionnaire*

by all halfe witted Readers) is commonly obscure and allwaies triffling. Horace has told us that where words abound,
sense is thinnly spread, as Trees over-charg'd with leaves
bear little Fruit.[1]

You do not mention Lord O[rrer]y, or perhaps would not
throw away Time in perusing that extraodinary Work
address'd to a Son[2] who he educates with an Intention he
should be a first Minister, and promises to pray to God for
him if ever he plays the Knave in that Station.[3] I perceive
that he has already been honnor'd with five Editions. I wish
that Encourragement may prevail with him to give the World
more Memoirs. I am resolv'd to read them all, thô they should
multiply to as many Tomes as Erasmus.

Here are no news papers to be had but those printed under
this Government; consequently I never learn the Births or
Deaths of private persons. I was ignorant of that of my poor
Freind the D[uchess] of Bolton, when my Daughter's last
letter told me the Death of the Duke and the Jointure he has
left his second Dutchess.[4]

I am very glad your Health is so good. May that and every
other Blessing be ever yours.

Text W MS ii. 241-2   *Address* To Edwd Wortley Esqr recommended to Sam: Child Esqr near Temple Bar London Angleterre
Postmark IA 16   *End. by W* [*Summary*] Recd 17 Jan. Ad 6 May

---

historique et critique (1697); Bolingbroke
criticizes him in the fourth of his *Letters
on the Study and Use of History.*
  1 LM is apparently thinking of Pope's
Essay on Criticism:
  Words are like *Leaves;* and where they
      most abound,
  Much *Fruit* of *Sense* beneath is rarely
      found
                         (lines 309-10).

  2 Orrery's *Remarks on Swift* (see
above, p. 56) is a series of letters to his
2nd son, Hamilton Boyle (1730–64),
then an undergraduate at Christ Church,
Oxford. He succeeded his father as
6th Earl.
  3 *Remarks,* 3rd ed., 1752, pp. 210–12.
  4 The Duke bequeathed all his real
and personal estate to her, and appointed
her sole executrix.

To Lady Bute *1 Jan. 1755*

Jan. 1. 1755. N.S.

My dear Child,

I wish you many new years, accompany'd with every Blessing that can render them agreable, and that it was in my power to send you a better new year's gift than a dull Letter. You must however accept it as well meant thô ill perform'd. I am glad you have found a House to please you.[1] I know nothing of that part of the Town you mention. I beleive London would appear to me as strange as any place I have pass'd in my Travells, and the streets as much alter'd as the Inhabitants.

I did not know Lady H. Wentworth was marry'd, thô you speak of her children;[2] you see my total Ignorance. It would be amusing to me to hear various things that are as indifferent to you as an old Almanack.

I am sorry my Freind Smallet [*sic*] loses his time in Translations. He has certainly a Talent for Invention, thô I think it flags a little in his last work.[3] Don Quixote is a difficult undertaking.[4] I shall never desire to read any attempt to new dress him; thô I am a meer pidler in the Spanish Language, I had rather take pains to understand him in the Original than sleep over a stupid Translation.[5]

I thank you for your Partiality in my Favor. It is not my Interest to rectifye mistakes that are so obliging to me. To say truth, I think my selfe an uncommon kind of Creature, being an old Woman without superstition, peevishness or

---

[1] Bute had moved to South Audley Street [No. 75], Mayfair.

[2] Lady Henrietta Wentworth (d. 1786), da. of 1st Earl of Strafford, m. (1743) Henry Vernon (1718–65). They had, in all, three sons and five daughters (J. Venn, *Alumni Cantab. to 1751*, iv. 299; Burke, *Landed Gentry*, 1852–3, ii. 1478).

[3] The previous year LM had read Smollett's *Ferdinand Count Fathom* without knowing its authorship (see above, p. 66). In calling him her friend, she refers only to her fondness for his

writing; they had never met.

[4] Smollett's translation had been announced in newspapers as early as Nov. 1748; it was published in Feb. 1755 (Lewis M. Knapp, *Tobias Smollett*, 1949, pp. 44, 165). Whether he translated it himself or plagiarized from Charles Jervas's version (1742) is disputed (C. R. Linsalata, *Smollett's Hoax: Don Quixote in English*, 1956).

[5] Among LM's books in 1739 was a copy of *Don Quixote* (Wh MS 135). Her general opinion was: 'Translations [are like] Scowr'd Silks' (CB MS, f. 7).

censoriousness. I am so far from thinking my Youth was past in an age of more virtue and sense than the present, I am of opinion the World improves every day. I confess I remember to have dress'd for St. James' chappel with the same thoughts your Daughters will have at the Opera, but am not of the Rambler's mind that the Church is the proper place to make Love in;[1] and the peepers behind a Fan, who divided their glances between their Lovers and their Praier book, were not at all modester than those that now laugh aloud in public Walks.—I tattle on, and forget you're in Town and consequently I ought to shorten my Letters, knowing very well that the same Letter that would be read thrice over in the Country will be cramm'd into the pocket before 'tis halfe gone through when people are in a Hurry to go to the Court or Play House.

My Compliments to Lord Bute and blessing to you and yours, to whom I am ever a most affectionate Mother.

M. Wortley

Text W MS iii. 125–6   *Address* To The Rt Honble the Countess of Bute recommended to Sam: Child Esqr near Temple Bar London Angleterre   *Postmark* IA 14

To Lady Bute *23 Jan.* [*1755*]

Louvere, Jan. 23. N.S.

I am very sorry for your past Indisposition and, to say truth, not heartily glad of your present Condition; but I neither do nor will admit of your excuses for your silence. I have already told you some ten or twelve times over that you should make your eldest Daughter your secretary; it would be an ease to your selfe and highly improving to her in every regard. You may, if you please, at once oblige your Mother and instruct your Daughter by only talking halfe an hour over your tea in a morning.

The D[uches]s of Queensbury's misfortune would move

1 *Rambler* No. 97 (19 Feb. 1751), contributed to Johnson's periodical by Samuel Richardson.

Compassion in the hardest Heart, yet all circumstances cooly consider'd I think the Young Lady deserves most to be pity'd, being left in the terrible situation of a young (and I suppose) rich widowhood,[1] which is (as I have allready said of Lady M. Cook)[2] walking blindfold upon stilts amidst precipices, thô perhaps as little sensible of her Danger as a child of a Quarter old would be in the paws of a Monkey leaping on the Tiles of a House.[3]

I beleive (like all others of your age) you have long been convince'd there is no real Happiness to be found or expected in this World. You have seen a Court near enough to know neither riches nor power can secure it, and all Human endeavors after Felicity are as childish as running after Sparrows to lay salt on their Tails; but I ought to give you another Information, which can only be learn'd by Experience: that Liberty is an Idea equally chimerical, and has no real existence in this Life. I can truly assure you I have never been so little mistrisse of my own Time and Actions as since I have liv'd alone. Mankind is plac'd in a state of Dependency, not only on one another (which all are in some degree); but so many inevitable accidents thwart our Designs and limit our best laid projects, the poor efforts of our utmost prudence and political schemes appear (I fancy) in the eyes of some superior Beings like the pecking of a young Linnet to break a Wire Cage, or the climbing of a Squirrel in a Hoop. The Moral needs no explanation. Let us sing as chearfully as we can in our impenetrable Confinement and crack our Nuts with pleasure from the little Store that is allow'd us.

My old Freind the Cardinal is dead of an apoplectic Fit, which I am sorry for, notwithstanding the disgust that happen'd between us on the ridiculous Account of which I gave you the History a year ago.[4] His memory will probably last as long as this province, having embellish'd it with so

---

[1] Elizabeth Hope (1736–56), da. of 2nd Earl of Hopetoun, m. (24 July 1754) Henry Douglas (1722–19 Oct. 1754), styled Earl of Drumlanrig, son and heir of 3rd Duke of Queensberry. The young man accidentally shot himself three months after his marriage (Delany, *Corr.* iii. 292, 296–7).

[2] Lady Mary Coke (see above, p. 47).

[3] LM may have borrowed the image of the monkey from *Gulliver's Travels*, part II, chap. v.

[4] Cardinal Querini (see above, pp. 13, 38–39) died on 6 Jan. 1755.

PLATE 2

*Letter of Lady Mary Wortley Montagu to Mary, Countess of
Bute, 23 Jan. [1755]*
Wortley MSS iii. 127

many noble Structures, particularly a public Library well furnish'd and richly adorn'd, and a college built for ⟨100⟩ scholars, with salarys for Masters, and plentifully endow'd many charitable Foundations; and so large a part of the new Cathedral (which will be one of the finest Churches in Lombardy) has been built at his Expence, he may be almost call'd the Founder of it. He has left a considerable Annuity to continue it, and deserves an eminent Place amongst the few Prelates that have devoted what they receiv'd f⟨rom⟩ the church to the use of the public, which is not here (as in some countrys) so ungratefull to overlook Benefits. Many statues have been erected and medals cast to his Honor, one of which has the figures of Piety, Learning, and Munificence on the reverse in the attitude of the three Graces. His Funeral has been celebrated by the City with all the Splendor it was capable of bestowing, and waited on by all the Ranks of the Inhabitants.

You told me some months since that a box was made up for me. I have never had the bill of lading, and know not whither you have receiv'd the little bill of Exchange sent by your most affectionate Mother,

M. Wortley.

Text W MS iii. 127–8   *Address* To The Rt Honble the Countess of Bute recommended to Sam: Child Esqr near Temple Bar London Angleterre [*in another hand*] Audley Street

To Lady Bute *15 April* [*1755*]

April 15. N.S.

My dear Child,

I receiv'd yours of Feb. 10th with great Pleasure as it brought me the news of your Health and that of your Family, thô mix'd with some mortification to find that some of yours have been lost, and several of mine. I never had that in which you mention'd the Death of Lord Gower, and should be glad to hear in what state he has left his Affairs. I do not doubt as Madam had the carving of the whole she has taken care to reserve some good Bits for her selfe.[1]

I cannot guess who you mean by Lord Montfort, there being no such Title when I left England,[2] nor any Lord Hertford (who I hear is nam'd Ambassador to France).[3] These are all new people to me. I wish you would give me some Information concerning them. None can be so agreeable as the continuation of your Father's Health. You see in him the good Effect of a strict Abstinence and regular Exercise. I am much pleas'd (but not at all surpriz'd) at his kindness to you. I know him to be more capable of a Generous action than any Man I ever knew. I am afraid my last long Letter to him has miscarry'd, and perhaps he thinks me very negligent or very stupid in delaying to answer that which he sent me. You may assure him no part of the merit of it was lost upon me. I took all possible care my thanks for it should be safely deliver'd into the post master's own hand. I suspect my cautions have been all in vain, and also that you have not had mine in which was enclos'd a small bill on Mr. Child. I have never heard one word of the Books that you told me were pack'd up last June.

These things are very provoking. Fretting mends nothing; I will continue to write on, thô the uncertainty of your receiving my Letters is a strong Abatement of my pleasure in writeing, and will be of heavy Consequence to my Style. I feel at this minute the spirit of Dullness chill my Heart, and I am ready to break out into Alacks and allass's, with many murmurs against my cruel Destiny that will not even permit this distant Conversation between us, without such allaying Circumstances. However, I beg you not to be

[1] John Gower, 1st Earl, whose first wife had been LM's sister Evelyn, died on 25 Dec. 1754. His third wife was Mary Tufton (1701–85), da. of 6th Earl of Thanet and widow of the Earl of Harold. By his will Gower left his estate to his children, and £1,000 p.a. clear of taxes and deductions to his widow 'in lieu of such Dower and thirds as she might claim out of my Estate at Common Law' (P.C.C. Paul, f. 44).

[2] Henry Bromley (1705–1 Jan. 1755),

cr. (1741) Baron Montfort, died a suicide.

[3] Francis Seymour Conway (1718–94), cr. (1750) Earl of Hertford, named ambassador by Feb. 1755 in place of Lord Albemarle, who had died in Paris on 22 Dec. 1754; but he did not go (Walpole, *Letters*, ed. Mrs. P. Toynbee, 1903, iii. 286). Diplomatic relations between England and France were interrupted from July 1755 until 1763 because of the Seven Years War (D. B. Horn, pp. 20–22).

discourrag'd. I am persuaded from the goodness of your
Heart that you are willing to give me Happiness, and I can
have none here so great as a Letter from you. You can never
want subjects, and I can assure you that your eldest Daughter
cannot be more delighted with a Birthday suit, or your
youngest with a paper of sugar plumbs, than I am at the
sight of your Hand.

You seem very anxious on the account of your children's
Education. I have said all I have to say on that Head, and am
still of the same Opinion, that Learning is necessary to the
Happiness of Women, and ignorance the common foundation of their Errors, both in Morals and Conduct. I was
well acquainted with a Lady (the D[uchess] of M[anchester])
who I am persuaded ow'd all her misfortunes to the Want
of Instruction in her youth.[1] You know another who, if she
had had her natural good understanding cultivated by
Letters, would never have mistaken Johnny Gay for a Wit,[2]
and much less have printed that he took the Liberty of calling
her his Laura——.[3]

I am pleasingly intterupted by the welcome Information
from Lord Bute that you are safely deliver'd of a Son.[4]
I am never in pain for any of that Sex. If they have any Merit
there are so many roads for them to meet good Fortune, they
can no way fail of it but by not deserving it. We have but
one of establishing Ours, and that surrounded with precipices, and perhaps, after all, better miss'd than found. I have
allready told you I look on my Grand Daughters as Lay
Nuns. Lady Mary might avoid that Destiny if Religion was
not a Bar to her being dispos'd of in this Country. You will
laugh to hear it, but it is realy true; I had propos'd to me a
young man of Quality, with a good Estate. His Parents are

[1] The Duchess's 'misfortunes' were
her engagement to Lord Scarborough,
which ended with his suicide, and her
second marriage, in 1746, to Edward
Hussey (see ii. 178, 371).

[2] LM wrote in her Commonplace
Book: 'Gay a good compiler thô a mean
poet' (MS, f. 11).

[3] LM refers to the intimate friendship
between Gay and the Duchess of Queensberry, for whom he wrote 'To a Lady

on her Passion for Old China', a play-
fully romantic poem (Gay, *Poetical
Works*, ed. G. C. Faber, 1926, pp. 179–
80). Published anonymously, it was
advertised in 1725 as being by Gay
(H. Williams in *Review of English
Studies*, vii, 1931, pp. 79–80); and it was
presumably issued with the Duchess's
permission.

[4] William Stuart (12 March 1755–
1822), later Primate of Ireland.

both dead. She would find a fine Palace, and neither want
Jewells nor Equipage, and her name (with a present from me)
be thought sufficient Fortune.

I shall write to Lord Bute this post. My Blessing to you
and yours are sincerely sent from your most affectionate
Mother,

M. Wortley.

Text W MS iii. 47–48   *Address* To The Rt Honble The Countess
of Bute recommended to Sam: Child Esqr near Temple Bar London
Angleterre

To Lady Bute *24 July* [*1755*]

July 24.

It is allwaies a great pleasure to me (my Dear Child) to
hear of your Health and that of your Family. This year has
been fatal to the Litteratti of Italy. The Marquis Maffei[1]
soon follow'd Cardinal Quirini. He was in England when you
was marry'd; perhaps you may remember his coming to see
your father's Greek Inscription.[2] He was then an old Man,
and consequently now a great age, but preserv'd his memory
and senses in their first vigour.

After having made the Tour of Europe in the search of
Antiquitys he fix'd his Residence in his native Town of
Verona, where he erected himselfe a little Empire from the
general esteem, and a Conversation (so they call an Assembly)
which he establish'd in his Palace, which is one of the largest
in that place and so luckily situated that it is between the
Theatre and the ancient Amphitheatre. He made Piazzas
leading to each of them, fill'd with shops where was sold
Coffee, The, Chocolate, all sort of cool and sweet meats,
and in the midst a court well kept and sanded for the use of

[1] Francesco Scipione Maffei (1675–
11 Feb. 1755), savant and writer.
[2] From May to Aug. 1736 Maffei
visited England, where he was elected to
the Royal Society and to the Society of
Antiquaries (Antonio Spagnolo, 'Scipione Maffei e il suo viaggio all'estero
(1732–1736)', *Atti e memorie dell'*
accademia d'agricoltura scienze lettere
arti e commercio di Verona, serie IV,
vol. iii, 1902–3, pp. 335–8). For W's
Greek inscription, see i. 417–18.

those young Gentlemen who would exercise their manag'd
Horses or shew their mistrisses their skill in riding. His
Gallery was open every evening at 5 o' clock, where he had
a fine collection of Antiquitys and 2 large Cabinets of
medals, intaglios and Camæos rang'd in exact order. His
Library join'd to it, and on the other side a suitte of 5 rooms,
the first of which was destin'd to Dancing, the second to
Cards (but all games of Hazard excluded), and the others
(where he himselfe presided in an easy chair) sacred to Conversation, which allways turn'd upon some point of Learning,
either Historical or Poetical, Controversie and Politics being
utterly prohibited. He generally propos'd the subject and
took great Delight in Instructing the young people, who
were oblig'd to seek the medal or explain the Inscription
that illustrated any Fact they discourse'd of.

  Those who chose the diversion of the public Walks or
Theatre went thither, but never fail'd returning to give an
account of the Drama, which produce'd a critical Dissertation on that subject, the Marquis having given shining
proofes of his skill in that art, his Tragedy of Merope (which
is much injur'd by Voltaire's Translation) being esteem'd
a master piece, and his Comedy of the Ceremonies[1] being so
just a ridicule of those Formal Fopperys it has gone a great
way in helping to banish them out of Italy. The Walkers contributed to the entertainment by an account of some herb or
Flower, which led the way to a Botanical conversation, or
if they were such inaccurate observers as to have nothing of
that kind to offer, they repeated some pastoral Description.
One day in the week was set apart for Music, vocal and
instrumental, but no mercenarys admitted to the consort.[2]

  Thus at very little expence (his fortune not permitting a
large one) he had the happiness of giving his Countrimen a
Tast of Polite Pleasure and shewing the youth how to pass
their Time agreably without Debauchery; and (if I durst say

[1] *Merope* (1713) and *Le Cerimonie*
(1728). Voltaire's *Mérope*, an adaption of
Maffei's, was produced in 1743.
[2] In 1731 Joseph Spence had observed
Maffei's benign activities: 'he has just
built a very pretty opera-house, with
rooms for dancing, conversation, and

concerts, all contrived and carried on
by him, and at his expense' (*Anecdotes*,
ed. S. W. Singer, 1820, p. xx). About ten
years later Charles de Brosses also described Maffei's establishment (*Lettres
familières sur l'Italie*, ed. Y. Bezard,
1931, i. 140–1).

it) in so doing has been a greater benefactor to his Country than the Cardinal with all his Magnificent Foundations and volumnious writeings to support superstition and create Disputes on things (for the most part) in their own Nature Indifferent.

The Veronese Nobillity, having no road open to advancement, are not tormented with Ambition or its child, Faction; and haveing learn'd to make the best of the Health and Fortune allotted them, terminate all their views in Elegant Pleasure. They say, God has reserv'd Glory to himselfe and permitted Pleasure to the persuit of Man. In the Autumn (which is here the pleasantest season of the year) a Band of about Thirty join their hunting Equipages, and carrying with them a Portable Theatre and a set of music, make a progress in the neighbouring Provinces, where they hunt every morning, perform an Opera every Sunday and other plays the rest of the Week, to the Entertainment of all the Neighbourhood. I have had many honourable invitations from my old Freind Maffei to make one of this Society; some accident or other has allwaies prevented me. You, that are accustom'd to hear of deep Political Schemes and wise Harrangues, will dispise perhaps this triffling Life. I look upon them in another Light, as a Sect of rational Philosophers:

> Who sing and dance and laugh away their Time,
> Fresh as their Groves, and happy as their clime.[1]

My paper is out.

Text W MS iii. 119–20   *Address* To The Rt Honble The Countess of Bute recommended to Sam: Child Esqr near Temple Bar London Angleterre *Postmark* AV 27

To Lady Bute *22 Sept.* [*1755*]

Sept. 22, Louvere

My Dear Child,

I receiv'd 2 days ago the Box of Books you were so kind to send, but I can scarce say whither my pleasure or

---

[1] LM repeats this verse from an Embassy Letter (i. 422).

disapointment was greatest. I was much pleas'd to see before me a fund of amusement, but heartily vex'd to find your Letter consisting only of 3 lines and a halfe. Why will you not employ Lady Mary as Secretary if it is troublesome to you [to] write? I have told you over and over, you may at the same time oblige your mother and improve your Daughter, both which I should think very agreable to your selfe. You can never want something to say. The Historys of your Nursery, if you had no other subject to write on, would be very acceptable to me. I am such a stranger to every thing in England, I should be glad to hear more particulars relating to the Familys I am acquainted with: if Miss Liddal marrys the Lord Euston I knew, or his Nephew who has succeeded him;[1] if Lord Berkeley has left children;[2] and several triffles of that sort, that would be a satisfaction to my Curiosity.

I am sorry for H[enry] Fielding's Death,[3] not only as I shall read no more of his writeings, but I beleive he lost more than others, as no Man enjoy'd life more than he did, thô few had less reason to do so, the highest of his preferment being raking in the lowest sinks of vice and misery.[4] I should think it a nobler and less nauseous employment to be one of the staff officers that conduct the Nocturnal Weddings. His happy Constitution (even when he had, with great pains, halfe demolish'd it) made him forget every thing when he was before a venison Pasty or over a Flask of champaign, and I am perswaded he has known more happy moments than any Prince upon Earth. His natural Spirits gave him Rapture with his Cookmaid,[5] and chearfullness when he was Fluxing in a Garret. There was a great similitude between his character and that of Sir Richard Steele. He had the

---

[1] The Lord Euston known to LM (see ii. 343, n. 1) had died in 1747. He was succeeded as heir to the Duke of Grafton by his nephew Augustus Henry Fitzroy (1735–1811), later 3rd Duke, who m. (29 Jan. 1756) Anne Liddell (1738–1804), da. of 1st Baron Ravensworth. After their marriage was dissolved (in 1769) she married the Earl of Upper Ossory.

[2] Augustus Berkeley (1716–19 Jan. 1755), 4th Earl, left four children, born between 1745 and 1753.

[3] On 8 Oct. 1754 in Portugal, where he had gone for the restoration of his health.

[4] As a Justice of the Peace, Fielding was chosen (in 1749) Chairman of the Quarter-Sessions of the Peace for Westminster.

[5] As his second wife Fielding m. (1747) Mary Daniel (1721–1802), who —according to LM's granddaughter— was his first wife's maid, and devoted to him and his children (Lady Louisa Stuart, 1861, i. 106).

advantage both in Learning and, in my Opinion, Genius. They both agreed in wanting money in spite of all their Freinds, and would have wanted it if their Hereditary Lands had been as extensive as their Imagination, yet each of them so form'd for Happiness, it is pity they were not Immortal.

I have read the Cry,[1] and if I would write in the Style to be admir'd by good Lord Orrery, I would tell you the Cry made me ready to cry, and the Art of Tormenting tormented me very much. I take them to be Sally Fielding's, and also the Female Quixote. The Plan of that is pretty, but ill executed.[2] On the contrary, the Fable of the Cry is the most absurd I ever saw, but the Sentiments generally just, and I think (if well dress'd) would make a better body of Ethics than Bolingbroke's. Her inventing new words that are neither more harmonious or significant than those allready in use is intolerable.[3] The most edifying part of the Journey to Lisbon is the history of the Kitten.[4] I was the more touch'd by it, having a few days before found one in deplorable Circumstances in a neighbouring Vineyard. I did not only releive her present wants with some excellent milk, but had her put into a clean Basket and brought to my own House, where she has liv'd ever since very comfortably.

I desire to have Fielding's posthumous works with his Memoirs of Jonathan Wild and Journey to the Next World, also the Memoirs of Verocand a Man of Pleasure,[5] and those of a Young Lady.[6] You will call all this Trash, Trumpery etc. I can assure you I was more entertain'd by G. Edwards

---

[1] Subtitled *A New Dramatic Fable* (1754), it was a collaboration by Sarah Fielding and Jane Collier. On her copy of vol. i LM wrote: 'Thorday [Thoroly ?] trite and insignificant' (Sotheby Catalogue, 1 Aug. 1928, p. 86).

[2] LM had mentioned these two latter books on 23 July [1754]. On her copy of *The Female Quixote* she wrote: 'pretty plan, ill executed' (Sotheby Catalogue, p. 94).

[3] Portia, the heroine, proposes introducing three new words into the language: *turba* (angry passions), and *dextra* and *sinistra* (rightness and wrongness of mind) (vol. i, scene xi; vol. ii, scene i).

[4] In Fielding's *Journal of a Voyage to Lisbon*, published Feb. 1755, a kitten falls into the sea, and is rescued and revived; but some time later she is found suffocated under a feather bed (*Works*, ed. L. Stephen, 1882, vii. 51–52, 103).

[5] *Memoirs of a Man of Pleasure; or the Adventures of Versorand*, translated from the French [of H.-F. de La Solle] (1751). On her copy LM wrote the word 'Parisian' (Sotheby Catalogue, p. 90).

[6] Probably *The Memoirs of a Young Lady of Quality, A Platonist* (1756), which LM again asked for (on 3 April [1757]) and received.

than H. St. John, of whom you have sent me duplicates.[1]
I see new story Books with the same pleasure your eldest
Daughter does a new dress, or your youngest a new Baby.
I thank God I can find play things for my Age. I am not of
Cowley's mind that this World is

a Dull ill acted Comedy,[2]

nor of Mrs. Philips's that it is

a too well acted Tragedy.[3]

I look upon it as a very pretty Farce for those that can see it
in that Light. I confess a severe Critic that would examine
by ancient Rules might find many deffects, but tis ridiculous
to judge seriously of a puppet show. Those that can laugh
and be diverted with absurditys are the wisest Spectators,
be it of writeings, actions, or people.

The Stage Coach has some Grotesque Figures that
amuse.[4] I place it in the rank of Charlotte Summers,[5] and
perhaps it is by the same Author. I am pleas'd with Sir
Herald for recording a generous action of the Duke of
Montagu (which I know to be true, with some variation of
Circumstances).[6] You should have given me a key to the
Invisible Spy, particularly to the Catalogue of Books in it;
I know not whether the Conjugal Happiness of the D[uke]
of B. is intended as a Compliment or an Irony.[7]

This Letter is as Long and as Dull as any of Richardson's.
I am asham'd of it, notwithstanding my Maternal Privelege
of being tiresome.

[1] *George Edwards, A Creole*, which
LM had requested on 23 June [1754];
and Bolingbroke's books (see above,
pp. 61–65).
[2] From *The Mistress*, 1668 (*Poems*, ed.
A. R. Waller, 1905, p. 87). The phrase
is quoted in *The Invisible Spy* (book I,
chap. iv), mentioned in this same letter.
[3] From 'A Resvery' by Katherine
Philips (1631–64) (*Poems*, 1669, p. 86).
[4] *The Stage-Coach: containing the
character of Mr. Manly and the History
of his Fellow-Travellers* (1753). LM's
brief comment: 'very well' (Sotheby
Catalogue, p. 96). The author was Miss
Smythies (*Times Lit. Supp.*, 26 Sept.
1935, p. 596).

[5] See above, p. 4 and n. 1.
[6] In *The History of Sir Harry Herald
and Sir Edward Haunch* (1754), a
gentleman identified as the D— of
M–nt–g–u gives money and an army
commission to a poor, worthy man (ed.
1755, pp. 164 ff.).
[7] In Eliza Haywood's *The Invisible
Spy by Exploralibus* (1755), book VI,
chap. iv, a list of forty-two titles is
found in Hyde Park; for example,
No. 30: 'The Beauties of Domestick
Life, illustrated with Examples. A
Pastoral Eclogue. By the D— of B—.
Neatly bound.' On her copy of the
book LM wrote: 'displeasing' (Sotheby
Catalogue, p. 88).

I return many thanks to Lord Bute for the china, which I am sure I shall be very fond of, thô I have not yet seen it. I send you a third bill of exchange, supposing the 2nd, sent last June, has not reach'd you. In the next Box put up the History of London,[1] and also 3 of Pinchbec's[2] watches, [with] shagrine cases and enamell'd Dial plates. When I left England they were 5 guineas each; I do not now know the price. Whatever it is, pray take it of Mr. Samuel Child.[3] You may imagine they are for presents; one for my Doctor, who is exactly Parson Adams in another proffession,[4] and the other for 2 Priests to whom I have some obligations.

This Richardson is a strange Fellow. I heartily despise him and eagerly read him, nay, sob over his works in a most scandalous manner. The 2 first Tomes of Clarissa touch'd me as being very ressembling to my Maiden Days.[5] I find in the pictures of Sir Thomas Grandison and his Lady what I have heard of my Mother and seen of my Father.[6]

This Letter is grown (I know not how) into an immeasurable Length. I answer it to my Conscience as a just Judgment on you for the shortness of yours. Remember my unalterable Maxim, where we love we have allways something to say. Consequently my pen never tires[7] when expressing to you the thoughts of your most affectionate Mother,

M. Wortley.

My Complements to Lord Bute and blessing to all your dear young ones, even the last commer.

Text W MS iii. 134–6

[1] Probably *The History of an Old Lady and Her Family*, noticed in the *Monthly Review* of May 1754: 'The old lady here intended, is the city of London. Her family are the aldermen, &c. . . .' It was evidently a satire on the recent elections.

[2] Edward and Christopher Pinchbeck were well-known clock-makers.

[3] Although this member of the banking firm had died in 1752, LM continued to address many of her letters through him until 1756.

[4] Dr. Baglioni and the admirable parson of Fielding's *Joseph Andrews* (1742).

[5] LM had already expressed her opinion of *Clarissa* in 1752 (see above, pp. 8–9).

[6] In an autobiographical fragment, written before her marriage, LM sketches both her pleasure-loving father and her 'noble Mother' (Halsband, *LM*, p. 2). In Richardson's last novel, *Sir Charles Grandison* (1753), the hero's parents are described in vol. ii, letters 6 and 7 (ed. 1931). In her own copy (3rd ed., 1754) LM wrote: 'mean Sentiments meanly express'd' (Sotheby Catalogue, p. 95).

[7] 'Hard mouth'd Pen, hard to rein' (CB MS, f. 9).

To Lady Bute *20 Oct.* [*1755*]

October 20 N.S.

Dear Child,

I have now read over Richardson;[1] he sinks horribly in his third Volume. (He does so in his story of Clarissa). When he talks of Italy, it is plain he is no better acquainted with it than he is with the Kingdom of Mancomugi.[2] He might have made his Sir Charles's amour with Clementina begin in a Convent, where the Pensioners sometimes take great Libertys, but that such familiarity should be permitted in her Father's House is as repugnant to Custom as it would be in London for a young Lady of Quality to dance on the Ropes at Bartholomew Fair. Neither does his Hero behave to her in a manner suitable to his nice Notions. It was impossible a discerning Man should not see her passion early enough to check it if he had realy design'd it. His conduct puts me in mind of some Ladys I have known who could never find out a Man to be in love with them (let him do or say what he would) till he made a direct attempt, and then they were so surpriz'd, I warrant you! Nor do I approve Sir Charles's offer'd compromise (as he calls it).[3] There must be a great Indifference as to Religion on both sides to make so strict a union as marriage tolerable between people of such distant persuasions. He seems to think Women have no Souls by agreeing so easily that his Daughters should be educated in Bigotry and Idolatry.

You will perhaps think this last a hard Word, yet it is not difficult to prove that either the Papists are guilty of Idolatry, or the Pagans never were so. You may see in Lucian (in his vindication of his Images) that they did not take their Statues to be real Gods, but only the representations of them.[4] The same Doctrine may be found in Plutarch, and it is all the modern Priests have to say in excuse for their Worshiping Wood and Stone, thô they cannot deny, at the same time, that the Vulgar are apt to confound that Distinction.

[1] *Sir Charles Grandison.*
[2] Possibly from Manco, crowned emperor of the Incas in 1534.
[3] In planning to marry the Roman Catholic Clementina, he agrees that he educate the sons and she the daughters.
[4] 'Of Sacrifice' (*Works*, transl. H. W. and F. G. Fowler, 1905, i. 188).

I allways (if possible) avoid controversal disputes. Whenever I cannot do it, they are very short. I ask my adversary if he beleive the Scripture. When that is answer'd affirmatively, their church may be prov'd by a child of ten year old contradictory to it in their most important points.[1] My second Question is, if they think St. Peter and St. Paul knew the True Christian Religion. The Constant reply is, O Yes! Then, say I, Purgatory, Transubstantiation, invocation of Saints, adoration of the Virgin, Reliques (of which they might have had a cart Load), and observation of Lent is no part of it since they neither taught nor practice'd any of these things. Vows of Cœlibacy are not more contrary to Nature than to the positive precept of St. Paul. He mentions a very common Case in which people are oblig'd by Conscience to marry.[2] No mortal can promise that case shall never be theirs, which depends on the Disposition of the Body as much as a Fever, and 'tis as reasonable to engage never to feel the one as the other. He tells us the marks of the Holy Spirit are Charity, Humility, Truth and long Suffering. Can any thing be more uncharitable than damning eternally so many millions for not beleiving what they never heard? or prouder than calling their Head a Vice-God? Pious Frauds are avowedly permitted, and persecution applauded. These maxims cannot be dictated by the Spirit of peace which is so warmly preach'd in the Gospel.

The Creeds of the Apostles and Council of Nice [Nicaea] do not speak of the Mass or real presence as Articles of beleife, and Athanasius asserts whosoever beleives according to them shall be sav'd. Jesus Christ in answer to the Lawyer bids him Love God above all things and his Neighbour as himselfe, as all that is necessary to Salvation.[3] When He describes the last Judgment, he does not examine what Sect or what Church Men were of, but how far they had been beneficent to Mankind.[4] Faith cannot determine reward or Punishment, being involuntary and only the Consequence of

---

[1] This idea, as noted in her Commonplace Book: 'if the S[cripture] is true the R.C. Religion is false because contrary; if the S[cripture] is false the R.C. Religion is false because founded on it' (MS, f. 6).

[2] 'But if they cannot contain, let them marry: for it is better to marry than to burn' (1 Cor. vii. 9).

[3] Matt. xxii. 35–40.

[4] Matt. xxv. 31–46.

Conviction. We do not beleive what we please, but what appears to us with the Face of Truth.

As I do not mistake Exclamation, invective, or Ridicule for Argument, I never recrimminate on the Lives of their Popes and Cardinals when they urge the Character of Henry the 8th. I only answer, good Actions are often done by ill Men through interested Motives, and tis the common Method of Providence to bring good out of Evil. History both Sacred and profane furnishes many Examples of it. When they tell me I have forsook the Worship of my Ancestors, I say I have had more Ancestors Heathen than Christian, and my Faith is certainly ancienter than theirs, since I have added nothing to the Practice of the Primitive proffessors of Christianity.

As to the Prosperity or extent of the Dominion of their Church, which Cardinal Bellarmin[1] counts amongst the proofes of its Orthodoxy, the Mahometans, who have larger Empires and have made a quicker progress, have a better plea for the visible protection of Heaven. If the Fopperies of their Religion were only Fopperies, they ought to be comply'd with wherever it is establish'd, like any ridiculous Dress in Fashion; but I think them Impietys. Their Devotions are a Scandal to Humanity from their Nonsense, the mercenary Deceits and barbarous Tyranny of their Ecclesiastics inconsistent with Moral Honesty. If they object the diversity of our Sects as a mark of Reprobation, I desire them to consider that Objection has equal Force against Christianity in General. When they thunder with the Names of Fathers and Councils, they are surpriz'd to find me as well (often better) acquainted with them than themselves. I shew them the variety of their Doctrines, their virulent contests, and various Factions instead of that union they boast of.

I have never been attack'd a second Time in any of the Towns where I have resided, and perhaps shall never be so again after my last Battle, which was with an Old Priest, a learned Man, particularly esteem'd as a Mathematician, and who has a Head and Heart as warm as poor Whiston's.[2] When I first came hither he visited me every day, and talk'd

---

[1] Roberto Francesco Bellarmine (1542–1621), influential controversialist.

[2] William Whiston, energetic churchman and writer (see i. 317).

of me every where with such violent praise that had we been young People, God knows what would have been said. I have allways the advantage of being quite calm on a subject which they cannot talk of without Heat. He desir'd I would put on paper what I had said. I immediately wrote one side of a sheet, leaving the other for his Answer. He carry'd it with him, promising to bring it the next Day, since which time I have never seen it, thô I have often demanded it, being asham'd of my defective Italian. I fancy he sent it to his Freind the Arch Bishop of Milan.[1] I have given over asking for it, as a desperate Debt. He still visits me, but seldom and in a cold sort of a way.[2]

When I have found Disputants I less respected I have sometimes taken pleasure in raising their Hopes by my Concessions. They are charm'd when I agree with them in the number of the Sacraments, but are horridly disapointed when I explain my selfe by saying the Word Sacrament is not to be found either in Old or New Testament, and one must be very ignorant not to know it is taken from the listing Oath of the Roman Soldiers, and means nothing more than a solemn, irrevocable Engagement. Parents vow in Infant Baptism to educate their children in the Christian Religion, which they take upon themselves by Confirmation; the Lord's Supper is frequently renewing the same Oath; Ordination and Matrimony are solemn vows of a different kind; Confession includes a vow of revealing all we know and reforming what is amiss; Extream Unction, the last vow, that we have liv'd in the Faith we were Baptis'd. In this sense they are all sacraments. As to the Mysteries preach'd since, they were all invented long after, and some of them repugnant to, the primitive Institution.

This Digression has carry'd me far from my Criticism; you will laugh at my making any on a Work below Examination. It may of be [*sic*] use to my Grandaughters. I am perswaded it is a favorite Author in all the Nurserys in England, and has done much harm in the Boarding Schools, therefore ought to have his Absurditys detected. You will think me

---

[1] Giuseppe Pozzobonelli (1696–1784), Archbishop since 1743.
[2] LM's Commonplace Book: 'an Ecclesiastic b[oun]d to defend his C[hur]ch as a Chambermaid her Lady's Complexion' (MS, f. 7).

angry with him for repeating a saying of mine, accompany'd with a description of my person which ressembles me as much as one of the Giants in Guild Hall,[1] and plainly shews he never saw me in his Life.[2] Indeed, I think after being so many years dead and bury'd, I might be suffer'd to enjoy the right of the Departed and rest in peace. I cannot guess how I can possibly have incurr'd his Indignation except he takes for Truth the Literary Correspondance between me and the Marquis Argens,[3] whom I never saw, and who with many high Complements has attributed to me Sentiments that never came into my Head, and amongst them a criticism on Pamela, who is, however, more favorably treated than she deserves. The Book of Letters I mention never came to my Hands till sometime after it was printed, accidentally at Tholouse.[4] I have need of all my Philosophy on these occasions, thô they happen so often I ought to be accustom'd to them. When I print, I submit to be answer'd and criticis'd, but as I never did, 'tis hard to be abus'd for other people's Follys. A light thing said in Gay Company should not be call'd upon for a serious Defence, especially when it injures no body.

It is certain there are as many marriages as ever. Richardson is so eager for the multiplication of them, I suppose he is some parish Curate, whose cheife profit depends on Weddings and christenings. He is not a Man Midwife, for he would be better skill'd in Physic than to think Fits and Madness

---

[1] Gog and Magog, grotesque giants with enormous heads.

[2] In letter 10 of *Grandison*, Harriet Byron describes Miss Barnevelt: 'a Lady of masculine features, and whose mind belied not those features; for she has the character of being loud, bold, free, even fierce when oppos'd; and affects at all times such airs of contempt of her own Sex, that one almost wonders at her condescending to wear petticoats. . . . One reason indeed, she everywhere gives, for being satisfied with being a woman; which is, *that she cannot be married to a* WOMAN.' This last remark paraphrases one in LM's letter to Mrs. Calthorpe in 1723 (ii. 33), and

in her Commonplace Book (MS, f. 3).

[3] Jean-Baptiste de Boyer (1703–71), marquis d'Argens, prolific novelist and journalist (Newell R. Bush, *The Marquis d'Argens and His Philosophical Correspondence*, 1953).

[4] The book LM refers to cannot be definitely identified. It would have been published before 1746, when she visited Toulouse. Possibly she means the *Lettres amusantes et critiques* (1743) by François de La Chesnaye-Desbois and issued anonymously. 'Myledy W', to whom the letters are addressed, regards *Pamela* more favourably than LM does in her letters but less so than Richardson presumably would have liked.

any Ornament to the Characters of his Heroines, thô his Sir Charles had no thoughts of marrying Clementina till she had lost her Wits, and the Divine Clarissa never acted prudently till she was in the same Condition, and then very wisely desir'd to be carry'd to Bedlam, which is realy all that is to be done in that Case. Madness is as much a corporal Distemper as the Gout or Asthma, never occasion'd by affliction, or to be cur'd by the Enjoyment of their extravagant wishes. Passion may indeed bring on a Fit, but the Disease is lodg'd in the Blood, and it is not more ridiculous to attempt to releive the Gout by an embrodier'd Slipper than to restore Reason by the Gratification of wild Desires.

Richardson is as ignorant in Morality as he is in Anatomy, when he declares abusing an obliging Husband or an Indulgent Parent to be an innocent Recreation. His Anna How[e] and Charlotte Grandison are recommended as Patterns of charming Pleasantry, and applauded by his saint-like Dames, who mistake pert Folly for Wit and humour, and Impudence and ill nature for Spirit and Fire.[1] Charlotte behaves like a humoursome child, and should have been us'd like one, and have had her Coats flung over her Head and her Bum well whipp'd in the presence of her Freindly Confidante Harriet. Lord Halifax very justly tells his Daughter that a Husband's Kindness is to be kindly receiv'd by a Wife even when he is drunk, and thô it is wrapp'd up in never so much impertinence.[2] Charlotte acts with an Ingratitude that I think too black for Human Nature, with such coarse Jokes and low expressions as are only to be heard amongst the Lowest Class of People. Women of that Rank often plead a right to beat their Husbands when they don't cuckold them, and I beleive this Author was never admitted into higher Company, and should confine his Pen to the Amours of Housemaids and the conversation at the Steward's Table, where I imagine he has sometimes intruded, thô oftner in the Servants' Hall;[3] yet if the Title Page be not a puff, this Work has pass'd 3 Editions.

[1] Anna Howe is Clarissa's confidante, and Charlotte Grandison is Harriet Byron's.
[2] 'The Lady's New-Year's-Gift: Or, Advice to a Daughter', *Miscellanies* (1700) by George Saville (1633–95), 1st Marquess of Halifax. His daughter Elizabeth (d. 1708) m. (1692) Philip Stanhope, later 3rd Earl of Chesterfield.
[3] Portrayal of upper-class life in the

I do not forgive him his disrespect of old china,[1] which is below no body's tast since it has been the Duke of Argyle's, whose understanding has never been doubted either by his Freinds or Enemys. Richardson never had (probably) money enough to purchase any, or even a Ticket for a Masquerade, which gives him such an aversion to them, thô his intended Satyr against them is very absurd on the account of his Harriet, since she might have been carry'd off in the same manner if she had been going from supper with her Grandmama.[2] Her whole behaviour, which he designs to be examplary, is equally blamable and ridiculous. She follows the Maxim of Clarissa, of declaring all she thinks to all the people she sees, without refflecting that in this Mortal state of Imperfection Fig leaves are as necessary for our Minds as our Bodies, and tis as indecent to shew all we think as all we have.

He has no Idea of the manners of high Life. His old Lord M. talks in the style of a Country Justice,[3] and his virtuous young Ladies romp like the Wenches round a May pole. Such Libertys as pass between Mr. Lovelace and his cousins are not to be excus'd by the Relation. I should have been much astonish'd if Lord Denbeigh should have offer'd to kiss me, and I dare swear Lord Trentham never attempted such an Impertinence to you.[4]

With all my Contempt, I will take notice of one good thing, I mean his project of an English Monastery. It was a favorite Scheme of mine when I was fifteen, and had I then been mistriss of an Independant fortune, would certainly have executed it and elected my selfe Lady Abbess.[5]

novels of the 1750's was generally un-realistic (R. B. Pierce in *Philological Quarterly*, xliv, 1965, p. 86).

[1] It is Charlotte Grandison (and not Richardson) who shows disrespect for old china (vol. iv, letter 10).

[2] Early in *Grandison* Harriet is abducted while returning in a sedan chair from a masquerade; this form of entertainment is then condemned.

[3] Lord M., in *Clarissa*, continually speaks in proverbs.

[4] Denbigh, the 5th Earl, was LM's first cousin; Trentham, now 2nd Earl Gower, was Lady Bute's.

[5] Sir Charles Grandison advocates Protestant nunneries 'in which single women of small or no fortunes might live with all manner of freedom, under such regulations as it would be a dis-grace for a modest or good woman not to comply with, were she absolutely on her own hands; and to be allowed to quit it whenever they pleased' (vol. iii, letter 32). LM's feminist friend Mary Astell had promoted a similar project (Florence M. Smith, *Mary Astell*, 1916, pp. 21–22); and so had Bishop Burnet (*History of His Own Time*, 1724–34, ii. 653).

There would you and your 10 children have been lost for ever. Yet such was the disposition of my early youth; so much was I unlike those Girls that declare if they had been born of the male kind they should have been great Rakes, which is owning they have strong Inclinations to Wh—ing and drinking, and want only Oppertunity and impunity to exert them vigorously.

This tedious miscellany of a Letter is promis'd to be deliver'd into your own hand, nay farther, that I shall have an Account how you look, how you're dress'd, and in what manner your room is furnish'd. Nothing relating to you is trivial to me, and if the performance answers the engagement it will be a vast pleasure to your most affectionate Mother.

M. Wortley

Text W MS iii. 154–9   *Address* To The Rt Honble the Countess of Bute in South Audley Street near Hide Park London

To Lady Bute *2 Nov.* [*1755*]

Nov. 2.

My Dear Child,

I am allwaies pleas'd when I hear you have been with the D[uke] and D[uches]s of Portland, being persuaded they are both worthy and sincere Freinds of yours. I had wrote so many Letters to dear Lady Oxford without receiving any Answer, I was in great pain on her account. I will write again, thô I lose so much of my writeing I am afraid it will only be more time and paper thrown away.

I pity poor Lady Dalkeith, who (perhaps) thinks her selfe at present an Object of envy. She will be soon undeceiv'd. No rich Widow can marry on prudential motives, and where Passion is only on one side every marriage must be miserable. If she thought justly, she would know no Man ever was in Love with a Woman of 40, since the Deluge. A Boy may be so, but that blaze of straw only lasts till he is old enough to distinguish between Youth and Age, which generally happens about 17; till that time, the whole Sex

appears angelic to a warm Constitution. But as that is not
Mr. Townshend's case, all she can hope is a cold complaisance
founded on Gratitude, which is the most uncertain of all
Foundations for a lasting union.¹ I know not how it is, whither
obligers are apt to exact too large returns, or whither human
Pride naturally hates to remember obligations, but I have
seldom seen Freindships continue long where there has
been great Benefits conferr'd, and I should think it the
severest suffering to know I was a burden on the good
nature of a man I lov'd, even if I met a mind so generous
to dissemble a disgust which he could not help feeling. Lady
Dalkeith had fond Parents² and (as I have heard) an obliging Husband. Her sorrowfull hours are now coming on.
They will be new to her, and tis a cruel addition to refflect
(as she must do) that they have been her own purchasing.
I wish my favorite Lady Mary [Coke]³ may make use of her
bitter experience to escape the snares laid for her. They are
so various and so numerous, if she can avoid them I shall
think she has some supernatural assistance, and her Force
more wonderfull than any of Don Quixot's Heros, thô they
vanquish'd whole armys by the strength of a single lance.

I have sent Lady J[ane] Stuart a little Ring. If it comes
safe, I will find something for Lady Anne. I expect a Letter
of thanks. I think I have ill luck if none of my many Grandaughters have a turn for writeing. She that has will be
distinguish'd by me.

I have sent you 3 bills of exchange. It does not appear
you have receiv'd one. What method to take I cannot imagine. I must depend on my new Freind who is a merchant
of the Valteline.⁴ If the War breaks out,⁵ Difficulties will

¹ Caroline Campbell (1717–94), da.
of 2nd Duke of Argyll, m. (1742)
Francis Scott (1721–50), Earl of
Dalkeith. She remarried (18 Sept. 1755)
Charles Townshend (1725–67), prominent in Parliament and son of the witty
and gallant Lady Townshend. Although
Walpole told one friend that Lady Dalkeith was marrying prudently because
her husband's family were 'the best sort
of people in the world' (*Corr.* ix. 171),
to another friend he said that Town-

shend's 'parts and presumption are prodigious. He wanted nothing but inde-
pendence to let him loose . . .' (*Letters*,
ed. Mrs. P. Toynbee, 1903, iii. 321).
² For the Duke and Duchess of
Argyll, see ii. 312, 430.
³ Lady Dalkeith's sister.
⁴ Valtellina, a district near Milan.
The merchant was Pitrovani (see
below, p. 109 and n. 1).
² The Seven Years War broke out
the next year.

encrease, thô our Correspondance can hardly be more
interupted than it is allready. I must endure it, as set down
by Destiny in the long list of Mortifications allotted to, Dear
child, your most affectionate Mother,

M. Wortley.

My compliments to Lord Bute and blessing to all yours.

Text W MS iii. 54–55   *Address* To The Rt Honble the Countess of
Bute in South Audley Street near Hide Park London Angleterre
Postmark PENY POST PAYD PTV

To Lady Bute *22 March* [*1756*]

March 22nd

I have receiv'd but this morning the first Box of china
Lord Bute has been so obliging to send me. I am quite
charm'd with it, but wish you had sent in it the Note of the
contents. It has been so long deposited that it is not impossible some dimunition may have happen'd. Every thing
that comes from England is precious to me, to the very Hay
that is employ'd in Packing. I should be glad to know any
thing that could be an agreable return from hence. There
are many things I could send, but they are either Counter-
band, or the Custom would cost more than they are worth.
I look out for a Picture; the few that are in this part of Italy
are those that remain in Familys where they are entail'd, and
I might as well pretend to send you a Palace.

I am extreamly pleas'd with the account you give of your
Father's Health. I have wrote to desire his consent in the
disposal of poor Lady Oxford's Legacy.[1] I do not doubt
obtaining it. It has been both my Interest and my Duty to
study his character, and I can say with Truth I never knew
any Man so capable of a Generous Action.

A late Adventure here makes a great Noise, from the

---

[1] Lady Oxford died on 9 Dec. 1755.
In her will (dated 9 June 1754), which
was not proved until 11 Aug. 1756,
she left LM £200 (P.C.C. Glazier,
f. 228).

Rank of the People concern'd—the Marchioness Lyscinnia Bentivoglio, who was Heiress of one branch of the Martinenghi, and brought 40 thousand gold Sequins to her Husband,[1] and the expectation of her Father's estate, £3,000 per Annum, the most magnificent Palace at Brescia (finer than any in London), another in the country, and many other advantages of Woods, Plate, Jewells etc. The Cardinal Bentivoglio, his uncle,[2] thought he could not chuse better, thô his Nephew might certainly have chose amongst all the Italian Ladies, being descended from the Sovereigns of Bologna, actually a Grandee of Spain, a Noble Venetian, and in possession of £25 thousand st[erling] per Annum, with immense Wealth in Palaces, Furniture, and absolute Dominion in some of his Lands. The Girl was pretty, and the match made with the Satisfaction of both Familys; but she brought with her such a Diabolical temper and such Luciferan Pride than [*sic*] neither Husband, Relations or Servants had ever a moment's Peace with her.

After about 8 years Warfare, she elop'd one fair Morning and took Refuge in Venice, leaving her 2 Daughters,[3] the eldest scarce 6 years old, to the Care of the exasperated marquis. Her Father was so angry at her extravagant conduct he would not for some time receive her into his House, but after some months and much solicitation, Parental Fondness prevail'd, and she remain'd with him ever since, notwithstanding all the Efforts of her Husband, who try'd kindness, submission, and threats, to no purpose. The Cardinal came twice to Brescia, her own Father join'd his intreaties, nay, his Holiness wrote a Letter with his own Hand and made use of the Church Authority, but he found it harder to reduce one Woman than ten Heretics. She was inflexible, and liv'd ten years in this State of Reprobation. Her Father dy'd last Winter and left her his whole Estate for her Life, and afterwards to her children. Her eldest was now marriagable, and dispos'd of to the Nephew of Cardinal Valentino Gonzagua, first minister at Rome.[4] She would neither

---

[1] Marchese Guido Bentivoglio (1705–59) m. Licinia, da. of Pietro Martinengo.

[2] Cornelio (1668–1732), Cardinal since 1719.

[3] The younger was Matilde, who m. (1759) Marcantonio Erizzo; the elder, Beatrice.

[4] Beatrice Bentivoglio m. marchese Carlo Valenti of Mantua. For the Cardinal, see ii. 227

appear at the Wedding, nor take the least notice of a Dutifull
Letter sent by the Bride. The old Cardinal (who was pas-
sionately fond of his illustrious Name) was so much touch'd
with the apparent Extinction of it, that it was thought to
have hasten'd his Death.

She continu'd in the Enjoyment of her ill humour, living
in great Splendor, thô almost Solitary, having by some
Impertinence or other disgusted all her Acquaintance, till
about a month ago, when her Woman brought her a bason
of Broth, which she usually drank in her Bed. She took a few
spoonfulls of it and then cry'd out it was so bad it was
impossible to Endure it. Her chamber maids were so us'd
to hear her Exclamations, they had not the worse opinion of
it, and eat it up very comfortably. They were both seiz'd
with the same Pangs and dy'd the next Day. She sent for
Physicians, who judg'd her poison'd, but as she had taken a
small Quantity, by the Help of Antidotes she recover'd, yet
is still in a languishing Condition. Her cook was examin'd
and rack'd, allways protesting entire Innocence, and swearing he had made the Soupe in the same Manner he was
accustom'd.

You may imagine the noise of this affair. She loudly
accus'd her Husband, it being the Interest of no other
person to wish her out of the World. He resides at Ferrara
(about which the greatest part of his Lands lie) and was
soon inform'd of this Accident. He sent Doctors to her,
whom she would not see, sent vast Alms to all the Convents
to pray for her Health, and order'd a number of Masses to be
said in every church of Brescia and Ferrara. He sent Letters
to the Senate at Venice and publish'd manifestos in all the
Capital Citys, in which he professes his affection to her and
abhorrence of any attempt against her, and has a cloud of
Wittnesses that he never gave her the least reason of complaint, and even since her leaving him has allways spoke of
her with kindness and courted her Return. He is said to be
remarkably sweet temper'd, and has the best character of
any Man of Quality in this Country.

If the Death of her Women did not seem to confirm it,
her Accusation would gain Credit with nobody. She is certainly very sincere in it her selfe, being so persuaded he has

resolv'd her Death that she dare not take the air, apprehending to be assasinated, and has imprison'd her selfe in her chamber, where she will neither eat nor drink any thing that she does not see tasted by all her Servants. The Physicians now say that perhaps the Poison might fall into the Broth accidentally. I confess I do not perceive the possibillity of it. As to the Cook suffering the Rack, that is a meer jest where people have money enough to bribe the Executioner. I decide nothing; but such is the present Destiny of a Lady who would have been one of Richardson's Heroines, having never been suspected of the least Galantry, hateing and being hated universally, of a most noble Spirit, it being proverbial,—as Proud as the Marchioness Lyscinnia.[1]

I am afraid I have tir'd you with my long story. I thought it singular enough to amuse you. I beleive your censure will be different from that of the Ladies here, who all range themselves in the party of the Marquis Guido. They say he is a handsome Man, little past forty, and would easily find a second Wife, notwithstanding the suspicion rais'd on this occasion. Many customs and some Laws are as extraordinary here as the situation of the Capital.[2]

I would write to Lord Bute to thank him if I did not think it would be giving him trouble. I have not less Gratitude; I desire you would assure him of it, and that I am to you both your most affectionate Mother,

M. Wortley.

My Blessing to your Little ones.

[*Postscripts*] Let me know if you have receiv'd the fifty pound bill. Since I wrote this, I have heard of a picture, which if I can get shall be sent to Lord Bute.

Text W MS iii. 139–41   *Address* To The Rt Honble the Countess of Bute in South Audley Street near Hide Park London Angleterre

---

[1] She must have died soon after, for her husband at his death in 1759 was married to Elena, da. of Michele Grimani, by whom he had a son and two daughters (Litta *sub* Bentivoglio).

[2] 'Several Customs in V[enice] as singular as the situation of their Capital' (CB MS, f. 5).

To Lady Bute *1 April* [*1756*]

April 1.

My Dear Child,

I have this minute receiv'd yours of Feb. 1. I had one before (which I have answer'd) in which you mention some changes amongst your ministerial subalterns. I see theMotions of the Puppets but not the Master that directs them, nor can guess at him. By the help of some miserable news papers, with my own refflections, I can form such a dimm Telescope as serves Astronomers to survey the moon. I can discern spots and inequalitys, but your Beauties (if you have any) are invisible to me, your Provinces of Politics, Galantry, and litterature all terra Incognita.

The merchant who undertook to deliver my ring to Lady Jane assures me it is deliver'd, thô I have no advice of it either from her or you.

Here are two new Fortunes, far superior to Miss Crawleys.[1] They are become so by an Accident which would be very extraordinary at London. Their Father was a Greek, and had been several years cheife Farmer of the Customs at Venice. About ten days ago, a Creditor who had a demand of 500 Crowns was very importunate with him. He answer'd he was not satisfy'd it was due to him, and would examine his accounts. After much pressing without being able to obtain any other reply, the Fellow drew his Stiletto, and in one stroke stabb'd him to the Heart. The noise of his Fall brought in his Servants. The resolute Assassin drew a pistol from his pocket and shot himselfe throû the Head. The Merchant has left no Will and is said to have been worth 4 millions of Sequins, all which will be divided between 2 Daughters. If it be only halfe as much, they are (I beleive) the greatest Heiresses in Europe; it is certain he has dy'd immensly rich. The eldest Lady is but 18, and both of them reported to be very Beautifull. I hear they declare

---

[1] Elizabeth (1728–81), da. of John Crowley, Alderman of London, m. (28 June 1756) 2nd Earl of Ashburnham; her fortune was £200,000. Her sister Theodosia (c. 1725–65), called by Walpole 'the fat rich Crawley', m. (1762) Charles Boone (*Corr.* x. 32 and n. 6).

they will chuse Husbands of their own Country and Religion, and refuse any other proposals. If they keep their Resolution I shall admire them much. Since they are destin'd to be a prey, 'tis a sort of Patriotism to enrich their own Country with their Spoils.

You put me out of patience when you complain you want Subjects to entertain me. You need not go out of your own Walls for that purpose. You have within them ten strangers to me, whose characters interest me extreamly. I should be glad to know something of them inside and out. What proportion of Wit and Beauty has heaven allotted them? I shall be sorry if all the Talents have fallen into the male part of your Family.

Do not forget, amongst the Books, Fielding's Posthumous Works, his Journey to the Next World, and J[onathan] Wild's Memoirs; also those of a Young Lady, and the History of London. I have said this already,[1] but am afraid my Letter is lost, amongst many others.

I congratulate Mrs. Dunch[2] on her good Fortune. She ⟨is a p⟩roofe of the force of Industry. Without any other Qualification, she has brought more projects to bear than any body I ever knew, many which I am sure I should have fail'd in. Tell me if her pension is continu'd, which was one of her views when I left England.[3]

This [is] a strange miscellaneous Letter. Consider my Age, and forgive the weaknesses of your most affectionate Mother.

M. Wortley

Compliments to Lord Bute and Blessings to the rest of your dear ones.

Text W MS iii. 269–70   *Address* To The Rt Honble the Countess of Bute in South Audley Street near Hide Park London Angleterre

[1] On 22 Sept. [1755].
[2] Elizabeth Dunch (see ii. 128).
[3] Perhaps her pension after the death

(in 1719) of her husband, who had been Comptroller of the Royal Household under George I.

To Lady Bute *19 May* [*1756*]

May 19.

My Dear Child,

I am sorry to begin this Letter with a sort of Complaint, thô I am persuaded Mr. Prescot[1] is more to blame than you. However, I am realy concern'd that he imagines he has reason to be offended. I never saw him, but I know those sort of people are apt to be very punctilious, and he is so much displeas'd (as he says) at the reception you gave him, he desires to decline the Correspondance, which I hop'd would have been more safe and expeditious than any other I have hitherto hit upon. I wish you would enquire whither the D[uke] and D[uches]s of Portland have receiv'd my Letters, which I sent at the same time with yours, but have had no return.

I congratulate my Grand Daughters on being born in an age so much enlighten'd. Sentiments are certainly extream silly, and only qualify young People to be the Bubbles of all their acquaintance. I do not doubt the frequency of assemblies has introduce'd a more enlarg'd way of thinking. It is a kind of public Education, which I have allways thought as necessary for Girls as Boys. A Woman marry'd at five and twenty from under the Eye of a strict Parent is commonly as ignorant as she was at five, and no more capable of avoiding the snares or struggling with the Difficulties she will infaillibly meet with in the commerce of the World. The knowledge of mankind (the most usefull of all knowledge) can only be acquir'd by conversing with them. Books are so far from giving that Instruction, they fill the Head with a set of wrong Notions, from whence spring the Tribes of Clarissas, Harriots etc. Yet such was the method of Education when I was in England, which I had it not in my power to correct. The young will allways adopt the opinions of their Companions rather than the advice of their Mothers.

---

[1] George Prescot (*c.* 1711–90), merchant in the Italian trade, and later banker and M.P. (History of Parlia- ment, *House of Commons 1754–1790*, ed. L. Namier and J. Brooke, 1964, iii. 324–5).

There is no thing talk'd of here but Earthquakes,[1] the greatest part of which I beleive wholly imaginary, but the panic is so spread that if a Rat runs over the ceiling it is suppos'd a shock, and here is daily processions, pilgrimages etc. to deprecate divine Vengeance. I am tempted to laugh, but restrain'd by prudential considerations.

Here is a second Bill for £50 on Child. I have already told you, 15 is to pay for the Watches, 30 to buy a Watch as my token to Lady Anne, and the odd five to pay for such Books as you may occasionally send.[2]

I am very well pleas'd with Lady Jane's Letter, and wish it was longer.

My Complements and thanks to Lord Bute. I am afraid his picture will be long in coming if I can get it at all.

Text W MS iii. 267–8

To Lady Bute *30 May* [*1756*]

May 30

My dear Child,

I sent you a long Letter very lately and enclos'd one to Lady Jane, and also a 2nd bill for [£]50, which I hope you have receiv'd. Thô I fear I cannot prevail on Mr. Prescot to take care of my Letters, if he should do it I beg you would be very obliging to him. Remember Civillity costs nothing, and buys every thing. Your Daughters should engrave that maxim in their Hearts.

I am sorry Sir William Louther dy'd unmarry'd. He ought to have left some of his Breed, which are almost extinct. He dy'd unluckily for his acquaintance, thô I think fortunately for himselfe, being yet ignorant of the ingratitude and vileness of Mankind. He knew not what it was to lament misplac'd obligations, and thought himselfe blest in many

[1] On 1 Nov. of the previous year Lisbon had been destroyed by earthquake.

[2] Here the bill has been cut out of the letter.

Freinds whom a short time would have shewn to be worthless, mercenary, designing Scoundrels.[1] The most tender disposition grows callous by miserable Experience. I look upon it as the reason why so many old people leave immense wealth in a Lump to Heirs they neither love nor esteem, and others, like Lord Sundon, leave it at random to they know not who. He was not a Covetous Man, but had seen so little merit and was so well acquainted with the vices of Mankind, I beleive he thought there was none amongst [them] deserv'd any particular Distinction.[2]

I have pass'd a long Life, and may say with Truth, have endeavor'd to purchase Freinds. Accident has put it in my power to confer great Benefits, yet I never met with any return, nor indeed any true Affection but from dear Lady Oxford, who ow'd me nothing. Did not these considerations restrain natural Generosity, I am of opinion we should see many Sir William Louthers. Neither is it saying much in favor of the Human Heart: it is certain the highest Gratification of Vanity is found in Bestowing; but when we plainly foresee being expos'd by it to Insults, nay, perhaps abuses, which are often Liberally dispers'd by those who wish to hide they are oblig'd, we abandonn the pleasure rather than suffer the Consequence. The first shocks receiv'd from this conduct of protesting Freinds are felt very severely. I now expect them, and they affect me with no more surprize than Rain after Sunshine. The little good I do is scatter'd with a spareing Hand, against my Inclination, but I now know the necessity of managing Hopes, as the only links that bind attachment or even secure us from Injuries. Was it possible for me to elevate any body from the station in which they are born, I now would not do it. Perhaps it is a Rebellion against that Providence that has plac'd them, and all we ought to do is to endeavor to make them easy in the Rank assign'd them.

I hope you will not forget to send me the bill of Ladeing,

---

[1] Sir William Lowther (1727–15 April 1756) left thirteen legacies of £5,000 each to friends (Walpole, *Corr.* ix. 184 and n. 6). His cousin and heir, Sir James (who inherited £2,000,000 from him), m. (1761) LM's granddaughter Mary; he was later created Earl of Lonsdale.

[2] William Clayton (1671–1752), 1st Baron Sundon, died intestate (P.C.C. Bettesworth, f. 141). According to Egmont, he was 'esteemed covetous' (HMC *Diary of First Earl of Egmont*, 1920–3, iii. 220).

without which I may chance to lose the Box, which is very precious to (my Dear child) Your most affectionate Mother, M. Wortley.

My Complements to Lord Bute and Blessing to all yours.

Text W MS iii. 142–3   *Address* To The Rt Honble The Countess of Bute in South Audley Street near Hide Park London Angleterre

To Lady Bute [*22 Aug. 1756*]

My Dear Child,
I receiv'd with great pleasure yours of June 29th yesterday, August 21. You are too gratefull for Triffles, but you are no Woman of Business; when you send me a Box you should at the same time send me a bill of ladeing, and take care it is noted in the Captain's Book. I had some difficulty in obtaining the last, and am afraid I shall never get this at all, at least as I collect from your Letter that you have sent it to Mr. Prescot without having any receit from him. It is impossible to be too cautious in dealings with Mankind, especialy with Merchants, who are often suppos'd rich, and break the next day. I know nothing of him. His Correspondant here[1] I met accidentally at the Waters of Louvere. As I then complain'd to every body I saw of the Interuption of our Correspondance, he heard of my distress, and assur'd me that He knew how to remedy it, and that he would take care any Letter or whatever else I was pleas'd to send should be safely deliver'd to your own Hand. I snatch'd at this Oportunity and sent that Bauble of a ring to Lady Jane as an essay to venture something of higher value to your selfe.

About the Time that I receiv'd your notice of its arrival, I heard from the Duke of Portland the Death of my dear Freind Lady Oxford, and the kind remembrance she had bequeath'd me. I wrote immediately a Letter to him and another to the Dutchess, in which I told them I intended to employ it in the purchase of a Ring inscrib'd with both our

[1] Pitrovani (named later in this letter). In her 'Italian Memoir' LM confirms her account of dealing with him, and mentions the significant fact that he had been recommended to her by Palazzi (Wh MS 510, ff. 24–25).

names, and after I had worn it my short remainder of Life, I desir'd her Grace would accept it in memory of us both.[1] To neither of these Letters I have had any Answer. Soon after, Signor Pitrovani wrote to me to say he heard I had a Legacy to receive in England, and as he was oblig'd to pay a sumn of money and should lose by the Exchange, he hop'd in consideration of his care and faithfull delivery of the Ring I would favor him with a Bill on the Person who was to pay it. I made answer I would not draw a Negotiable Note on the Duke of Portland as on a common Banker, but on his pressing me, I wrote a respectfull Demand payable to the Bearer, since which time I have no notice of its being paid. As I do not doubt but it was, I hope the Duke has had the precaution of takeing the receit, and will let me know the name of the Merchant to whom he paid it.

I have already told you I ask'd your father's permission to dispose of the money in the manner I have mention'd. I did not doubt readily obtaining it, but have never heard either from him or you on this subject. I am determin'd to go to Venice my selfe to try to settle our commerce in a better manner. I am actually on the road, and this is wrote from an Inn in Mantua,[2] the 22nd of August, by (Dear child) your most affectionate mother,

M. Wortley.

My Complements to Lord Bute. Both his and your conduct is so obliging to me, whatever I can do shall be wholly for you and yours. I have a necklace for you which you need not be asham'd to wear.

Text W MS iii. 249–50   *Address* To The Rt Honble the Countess of Bute recommended to Sam: Child Esqr near Temple Bar London Angleterre [*in another hand*] North Audley Street   *Postmark* 20 SE

[1] See LM's will (p. 294 below).

[2] In her 'Italian Memoir' LM relates that in the late spring of 1756 she prepared to go to Venice, but when Count Palazzi constantly interfered with her plans she realized that she was his prisoner. In August, after further adventures (that read like the libretto of an *opéra bouffe*), she finally succeeded in leaving for Mantua, accompanied by the Count and his brother. The Count followed her to Padua, where she took a house, and then to Venice (ff. 26–36; summarized in Halsband, *LM*, pp. 257–60). She arrived in Venice on 8 Sept. (John Murray to Henry Fox, 10 Sept. 1756, SP 99/66). Later she brought suit against Palazzi to recover what she had paid for a house in the province of Mantua (William Graeme to Lord Bute, 8 Sept. 1758, Bute MS).

To Mme Chiara Michiel[1] [*Sept. 1756*]

Ma chere et tres aimable Madame,
   Je ne sçaurois exprimer a quel point je suis mortifiée d'estre a Venise sans avoir l'honneur de vous voir; je vous jure que c'étoit le bût principal de mon voiage. Je me desespererois si je ne me flattai que le temps, qui racomode tant des choses, ajustera encore ce desagreable suspension.[2] En tout cas, nous nous reverrons a Padoûe. J'ÿ ritorne incessement; j'aurois par tout le mesme Coeur, zelé pour vous et remplie d'une tendresse respectueuse pour elle qui fait la gloire de (ma tres chere et tres aimable Madame) vostre tres obligée et obeissante Servante,

                                 M. W. Montagu.

Text Bute MS

To Mme Chiara Michiel *4 Nov. 1756*

Tres chere et aimable Madame,
   J'ai reçeu avec un plaisir inexprimable l'aimable Lettre dont vous m'avez honorée. Je suis enchantée que vous avez faites l'honneur a ma Langue de vous donner la peine de l'aprendre. Vous ettes douée d'une facilité merveilleuse a sçavoir tout ce vous voudra. Je me flatte que nous avons quelques Livres digne de vous amuser, et peutestre ma petite Biblioteque vous pouriez estre de quelque usage. J'en serois bien glorieuse.

1 A Venetian lady, LM's friend since 1739 (see ii. 170). This is the first extant letter to her since 31 Dec. 1746. The letters to Mme Michiel are translated in Appendix I below.

2 The explanation is to be found in a dispatch dated 1 Oct. 1756 from John Murray, British Resident, to Holdernesse, Secretary of State: 'The Imperial Ambassador Count Rosenbergh has been guilty of an Indiscretion that has fallen heavily upon me. He was so unguarded some time past to converse in publick with an old noble Venetian Lady, Madam Michieli, for which she was banished into the Country for some Weeks, but since recalled and confined in her own House for some Months—and I hear she is just now allowed to receive Visitors. This has thrown the Women into such a Pannick that they dare not look at the same Side of the Canal where the Ministers pass' (Eg MS 3464, f. 274).

Je cours a Venise vous embrasser puis qu'il est permis. Aussi tost que je serois arrivée, je'n manquerai pas de vous rendre mes devoirs, et toute occasion vous me trouver⟨ez⟩, avec un attachment éternel, Madame, vostre tres humble et Obeissante Servante,

M. W. Montagu.

Nov. 4. 1756, Padoua

Je n'ai pas écrite en Anglois; je suis bien aise, en cas qu'on ouvre ma Lettre, qu'on voit l'innocence de nostre Commerce. Si on sçavoit a quel point je hai et meprise la Politique on ne m'en soupçonnera jamais.

Text Bute MS   *Address* A Sua Excellenza La Signora Signora Chiara Michielli Bragadina a Venezia

To Mme Chiara Michiel *18 Nov.* [*1756*]

Ma tres chere et aimable Amie,

Je ne sçaurois exprimer a quel point je suis mortifiée d'avoir été obligée de quitter Venise sans vous dire Adieu. Je suis persuadée que vous rendez Justice a mon Cœur, qui est toute a vous, mais j'ai mon Guignon comme vous avez le vostre. Je me flatte pourtant que bon temps viendra. Je n'aspire qu'a passer ma vie aupres de vous, en vous donnant des preuves que je suis avec la plus parfait attachment, ma chere Madame, vostre tres humble et tres obeisante Servante,

M. W. Montagu.

Padoua, Nov. 18.

Text Bute MS   *End. by Mme Michiel* risposto.

To Lady Bute *23 Nov.* [*1756*]

My Dear Child,

I heartily wish you joy of your present situation. Lord Bute has attain'd it by a very uncommon road; I mean an acknowledg'd Honor and Probity.[1] I have but one short Instruction (pardon that word) to give on his account, that he will never forget the real interest of Prince and People cannot be divided, and are almost as closely united as that of Soul and Body. I could preach long on this subject, but I ought to consider your time is now fully taken up, and you can have no leisure for reading my tedious Letters. I shall henceforward relinquish the motherly Prerogative I have hitherto indulg'd of tireing your patience with long Discourses.

I went to Venice a few Days ago, and in the House of General Graham (whose obliging Freindship I shall ever gratefully own)[2] I saw Mr. Cunningham[3] and his Lady. They appeard to me to have great Merit and Politeness. They offer'd in a very Freindly manner to carry my Present to you, but designing to proceed on their Journey in these perillous Times, I thought it better to delay it. I hope to send it early in the Spring by the Hand of Lord Archer's Son,[4] who is now at Rome. It is possible a Peace may be treating by that Time.[5] God Bless you and yours, which is the Constant Praier of (Dear child) your most affectionate Mother.

M. Wortley

Padoua, Nov. 23.

I have wrote you several Letters since my arrival here,

---

[1] Through his friendship with the Dowager Princess, Bute had won the affection and loyalty of the young Prince of Wales, who insisted—against the King's wishes—that he be appointed Groom of the Stole. In Sept. the King agreed (*Letters from George III to Lord Bute 1756–1766*, ed. R. Sedgwick, 1939, p. 2, n. 3).

[2] William Graeme (d. 1767), a Scotsman who after military service for Holland had risen to be Commander-in-Chief of the Venetian forces (Louisa G. Græme, *Or and Sable: A Book of the Græmes and Grahams*, 1903, p. 428). LM had met him that spring in Brescia when at her daughter's request he visited her to find out why her letters were not reaching England ('Italian

Memoir', Wh MS 510, f. 25). Boswell, who stayed at his house in 1765, found him 'a very sensible polite man' (*Grand Tour: Italy, Corsica and France*, ed. F. Brady and F. A. Pottle, 1955, pp. 103–4).

[3] See below, p. 116.

[4] Andrew Archer (1736–78), only son of Thomas (1695–1768), 1st Baron.

[5] In Oct. 1756 William Pitt was asked by Newcastle to join his ministry; and LM evidently thought that a peace treaty with France would result. But Pitt, who was appointed Secretary of State on 15 Nov. (and received the seals on 4 Dec.), continued the war (Basil Williams, *The Whig Supremacy 1714–1760*, 2nd ed., 1962, pp. 354–5; 472).

which I hope you have receiv'd, thô you do not mention them.

My complements to Lord Bute.

Text W MS iii. 209–10   *Address* To The Rt Honble The Countess of Bute

To Wortley *8 Dec.* [*1756*]

Padoua, Dec. 8.

I wrote to you when I first came here, which is near 3 months ago. I have never receiv'd any Answer, which I fear is occasion'd by the weakness of your Eyes which you complain'd of in your last letter. I will not therefore trouble you with a long one. I have sent many to our Daughter, which I suppose she communicates to you.

I have taken here a pretty convenient House at a reasonable Rate. Venice is too expensive, and this Air esteem'd the best in Italy. I have reason to think well of it, having my Health better than it has been of a long time.

I send this to Mr. Murray, the English Resident,[1] and desire you would recommend your next to him.

Text W MS ii. 243   *End. by W* [*Summary*] Ad 4 Jan. 1757. Recd 28 Dec.

To Mme Chiara Michiel [*23 Dec. 1756*]

J'ai reçeu ce matin, Dec. 23, deux cheres Lettres de mon Aimable Amie, dont l'une est datée du 26 du dernier mois, et l'autre du 13 de celui ci. J'enrage contre la negligence de la poste, et crains d'avoir beaucoup soufferte en vostre

[1] John Murray (*c.* 1715–75), Resident in Venice 1754–66 (*Miscellanea Genealogica et Heraldica*, 2nd series, 1886, i. 347; D. B. Horn, p. 85). By May 1757 he had become LM's *bête noire*.

Opinion. Vous avez eue raison de m'accuser d'ingratitude ou d'insensiblety, quand j'étois toute occupée de vous, demandant des vos nouvelles a tous ceux que je voyois, et toute triste de vostre silence, dont je ne pouvois deviner la cause — mais je m'oublie de vous écrire en françois, quand vous ettes aussi capable d'ecrire en anglois que moi.

I am charm'd with your English; I cannot naturally account for the perfection you have attain'd, and begin to have Faith in the Fairy Tales, and fancy you have met with some Genius, who has endow'd you with the gift of Tongues. You have all the Qualitys that are necessary to attract the Care of those benevolent Spirits; but do not suffer your commerce with those superior beings to make you forget a little bit of Earth, which miserable as it is, is wholly attach'd to you, call'd amongst Mortals your faithfull Servant,

M. W. M.

Text Bute MS   *Address* A S. E. La Signora Signora Chiara Michielli Bragadini a Venise

To Lady Bute *28 Dec.* [*1756*]

Padoua, Dec. 28.

My Dear Child,

I receiv'd yours of Nov. 29th with great Pleasure; some days before, I had the box of Books, and am highly delighted with the Snuff Box. That manufacture is at present as much in Fashion at Venice as at London. In General, all the Shops are full of English Merchandize, and they boast every thing coming from London, in the same Style they us'd to do from Paris.

I was show'd, of their own Invention, a set of Furniture in a taste entirely New. It consists of 8 large Arm'd Chairs, the same Number of Sconces, a Table and prodigious Looking Glass, all of Glass. It is impossible to imagine their Beauty. They deserve being plac'd in a Prince's Dressing room or Grand Cabinet. The Price demanded is

£400. They would be a very proper Decoration for the Apartment of a Prince so young and beautifull as ours.

The Present Ministry[1] promises better Counsels than have been follow'd in my Time. I am extreamly glad to hear the Continuation of your Father's Health, and that you follow his advice. I am realy persuaded (without any Dash of Partiality) no man understands the Interest of England better or has it more at Heart. I am oblig'd to him for what ever he does for you. I will not indulge my selfe in troubling you with long letters or Commissions when you are charg'd with so much business at home and abroad. I shall only repeat the Turkish Maxim which I think includes all that is necessary in a Court Life: Carress the favorites, avoid the Unfortunate, and trust no body. You may think the second Rule ill natur'd. Melancholy experience has convince'd me of the ill Consequence of mistaking Distress for Merit. There is no mistake more productive of evil. I could add many arguments to enforce this Truth, but will not tire your Patience.

I am exceedingly oblig'd to General Graham for his Civillitys. He tells me he has wrote to you the account of poor Mr. Cunningham's sad story.[2] I wish it do not come too late. The news paper says the mean Capitulator is rewarded.[3] I fear the Generous Defender will be neglected.[4]

I intend to correspond with Lady Jane. I confess I was much pleas'd with her little Letter, and supposing Lady Mary is commence'd fine Lady, she may have no leisure to ⟨read⟩ or Answer an old Grandmother's Letters. ⟨I⟩ presume

---

[1] Formed by Pitt after Newcastle's resignation.

[2] Major William Cunningham (d. 1759) had been engineer at Minorca; at Nice on his way home with his wife and children he heard that the French were about to attack his former garrison on the island. After buying supplies with his own money he reached Fort Mahon just before the siege. In the attack (27 June 1756) he was wounded; and the garrison, not receiving help from the fleet under Admiral Byng, surrendered (Brian Tunstall, *Admiral Byng and the Loss of Minorca*, 1928,

pp. 99, 164). Cunningham had arrived on 17 Nov. in Venice, where Murray reported: 'He seems in a weak State of Health, and still fears a Mortification in his Arm' (to Henry Fox, 19 Nov. 1756, SP 99/66).

[3] William Blakeney (1672–1761) had gallantly defended Fort Mahon for seventy days before capitulating. On 27 Nov. he was made a Knight of the Bath, and three weeks later created Baron Blakeney.

[4] Cunningham was rewarded the same year with promotion to a lieutenant-colonelcy (Tunstall, p. 208).

Lady Jane is to play least in sig⟨ht⟩ till her sister is dispos'd of. If she loves writeing, it may be an Employment not disagreable to her selfe, and will be extreamly gratefull to me, who am ever (my Dear Child) your most affectionate Mother,

M. Wortley.

My Compliments to Lord Bute and blessing to all yours.

Text W MS iii. 146–7   *Address* To The Rt Honble The Countess of Bute recommended to Francis Child Esqr¹ near Temple Bar London Angleterre [*in another hand*] North Audley Street   *Postmark* IA 31

To Francesco Algarotti² *30 Dec. 1756*

I gratefully accept your obliging offer of your delightfull Mirabella,³ but am resolv'd to see it in full Beauty, which it cannot be without the Presence of the Master. I receiv'd your Iphigenia and immediately return'd my thanks for the Pleasure it gave me; the Essay on Painting never came to my Hands.⁴ I cannot refuse the General's⁵ solicitation, and shall pass (at least) some part of the Carnival at Venice. I propose to be the Lent in Padoua, or if you are there, at Mirabella.

You should advise your Roial Patron⁶ a mutare suoi Pazzie heroicé per la sapientia Rustica, ed lasciare gli Piaceri

¹ Banker (*c.* 1735–63).

² His early friendship with LM had ended in 1741 (see ii. 237). Since 1753, when he retired from Frederick the Great's Court on account of ill health, Algarotti had lived in Italy. Even before LM left Brescia, he had apparently written to her at Gottolengo, and an unnamed correspondent then told him that LM would have replied 'si l'on ne l'avait pas assure la que vous etiez morte d'un appoplexie peu de jours apres que vous l'aviez ecrit. Enfin elle vous fait les excuses et desire de vous conoitre elle sera a Venise en 10 ou 12 jours. Si vous voullez faire conoissence avec elle je vous prie d'avance de manger la soup avec Madame Zenobiro et Lady Mary'

(Padua, 30 Oct. [1756], Murray MS).

³ Algarotti's 'delightful villa', 10 miles outside Padua (Ida Treat, *Francesco Algarotti*, 1913, pp. 161, 195). He had moved to Bologna in June 1756, and remained there for the rest of his life except for short, infrequent visits elsewhere.

⁴ Algarotti's *Iphigénie en Aulide*, an opera libretto, was published in 1755 as part of his *Saggio sopra l'opera in musica* (*Saggi*, ed. G. da Pozzo, 1963, pp. 197–223, 550). His *Saggio sopra la pittura* was published in 1756 (ibid., pp. 53–144, 550).

⁵ William Graeme.

⁶ Frederick the Great, who had given him the title of Count (Dec. 1749).

Diaboliche dell' Destrutione, per godere di quelli di Paradiso nell gli diletti d'una Giardino ornato di tutti les gratie della mano della Natura. Alcinous in Homero mi para piu Heroe che Achilles; certo e piu amabile, comme la Benevolentia è piu degno che la Crudelta. Quel Example du vrai Heroism! Si on pouvoit voir un Conquerant qui n'a jamais receû d'échec mettre des bornes a ses Triomphes et se retirer comme Dioclesian, mille fois plus grand dans sa retraitte que dans son Elevation! Vous voyez que j'imite Homere, au moins par un endroit, en écrivant d'un style composé des Differens patois,¹ car au bout du Compte tous nos Langues modernes non sono altro che vernaculi della Romana antiqua.²

Padoua, Dec. 30. 1756

Text Murray MS

From Wortley [*4 Jan. 1757*]

[*Passage omitted*] I bundle up all your letters and keep a list of the dates of what I send you so that I cannot mistake as to either. I do not recollect that any letter sent me from a foreign country besides yours ever miscarried. As to those I send abroad, I always send two servants with them to the Post office, so that I do not trust to one servant's honesty; and the officer of the Post sees there is evidence of the delivery, so that his neglect or fraud may easily appear. This method is taken by all foreign ministers at all Courts.

I have now something to mention which I believe will be agreable to you. I mean some Particulars relating to my Lord Bute, which you have not learned from the Prints or from our minister at Venice. He stood higher in the late Prince of Wales's favour than any man. His attendance at Leicester House, where this young Prince has resided ever since his father's Death, continued without intermission till new officers were to be placed about him. It is said that another Person was

---

¹ As expressed by Alexander Pope in the preface to his translation of the *Iliad* (1715), Homer 'was not satisfy'd with his Language as he found it settled in any one Part of *Greece*, but search'd thro' its differing *Dialects* with this particular View, to beautify and perfect his Numbers' (*Prose Works*, ed. N. Ault, 1936, p. 234).

² LM's letters to Algarotti are translated in Appendix I below.

designed to be Groom of the Stole but that the Prince's earnest Request was complied with in my Lord's favour.[1] It is supposed that the Governors, Preceptors etc. that were before about him are now laid aside and that my Lord is his principal adviser.

It is not easy to express how well bred and reasonable the Prince always appears at his Publick Levee every Thursday and on all other occasions. The King of France and the Empress of Germany always shew themselves to great advantage, and this young Prince's behaviour is equal that of either of them. He is supposed to know the true State of this Country and to have the best inclinations to do all in his power to make it flourish.

These appearances do much honour to my Lord, and the Continuance of his favour is, I believe, wished by all that are unconnected with some of those who have been ministers of State.

Text W MS i. 139–40 (draft)   *End. by* W To L.M. 4 Jan. 1757

To Wortley 23 *Jan.* 1757

Padoua, Jan. 23. 1757.

Yours of the 4th instant came to me this morning, which is quicker than I have ever receiv'd any from England. It brought me the most sensible pleasure, both as a proofe of your Health and the account of Lord Bute's Prosperity; God continue those blessings to me. But you know Court Favor is no more to be depended on than fair weather at Sea. I intend to send my Daughter my Jewels as I see occasion offers.[2] You were so good to promise me at Avignon that she should have them after my Death.[3] I hope you will permit me to give them to her, now they may be, in some degree, necessary in her Court attendance.

I find this Air agree very well with me. I am as well as I can reasonably expect in my Time of Life, notwithstanding the present sharpness of the Weather. I write this post to my Daughter. I cannot help ⟨?⟩ her the Advantage I know it will

[1] As Groom of the Stole to the young Prince of Wales the King had proposed James, 2nd Earl Waldegrave (1715–63), who had been his Governor since 1752 (*Letters from George III to Lord Bute 1756–1766*, ed. R. Sedgwick, 1939, pp. 1–2).

[2] In Sept. 1758 she had still not sent them all (see below, p. 175).

[3] See ii. 361, 369.

be to her Lord to consult you in his conduct. It is possible there is no occasion for my advising what his own good Sense already dictates, but I think they cannot take amiss the Zeal I have to serve them.

Text W MS ii. 244–5   *Address* To Edwd Wortley Esqr [*struck out*] recommended to Fran: Child Esqr near Temple Bar London Angleterre [*in another hand*] at ⟨Bath⟩¹   *End. by W* L.M. 23 Jan. 1757 Recd in London 21 Feb.

To Francesco Algarotti [*Feb. 1757*]

Vous n'avez pas encore reçeu les injures que je vous a dit, et je reçoy de vous une Lettre capable de calmer toute ma colere. Me voici radoucie au point de me croire obligée de vous remercier des eaux precieux, qui viennent fort a propos, apres que j'ai passée la Nuit alla Regina d'Inghilterra.²

Vous voyez que je donne tête baissée dans tous les desordres du Carnival. J'avoüe que je ne suis plus en droit de me moquer des monarques qui dissipent leur tresors et diminuent leur sujets pour une fantome d'Ambition;³ moi, qui dissipe ma Santé et diminue le peu de jours qui me restent pour courir apres une fantome de plaisir que je cherche par le sang et la Destruction. Je puis dire pour m'excuser (vous savez qu'on croit toujours trouver quelque chose a dire en faveur de ses sottises) que Faisans et Perdrix sont couvez pour estre la proye des hommes, qu'ils sont fait pour nostre nouriture, qu'il est permis de leur mettre a toute sauce, et qu'on les retranchent un si petite espace du temps en leur ostant la vie qu'il ne vaut pas la peine d'ÿ penser. Un Heros pouroit

---

¹ W fell ill in Jan., and visited Bath and Tunbridge Wells to restore his health (W to LM, 15 Oct. 1757, W MS i. 141).

² An elegant hotel, near St. Mark's Square, patronized by the English (E. Zaniboni, *Alberghi italiani e viaggiatori stranieri*, 1921, p. 78). Goethe, who stayed there thirty years later, found it comfortable and convenient;

today it is called the Hotel Vittoria (*Italienische Reise*, ed. E. Trunz, 1951, pp. 64, 589).

³ LM probably refers to Frederick II, whom Algarotti continued to defend from afar. Having profited from the War of the Austrian Succession (1740–8), Frederick had invaded Saxony in 1756 to start what was to be the Seven Years War.

justifier sa conduitte, peut estre, avec plus de raison. Il dira
que le genre humain est né pour mourir, et quand ils peris-
sent par l'épee ou le feu ils échappent a des maladies mille
fois plus cruelles, a les quelles la Nature les ont destinez,
sans compter le plaisir qu'ils doivent trouver a mourir pour
la Gloire de leur Maitre, et qu'entre cent milles on trouvera
pas dix qui n'ont pas merité la corde par leur Crimes. Les
oisaux innocents sont creez pour joüir d'une vie douce et
paisible, sans vice ou Ambition. Ils bornent leur Desseins
a peupler les Bois de leur posterité, et c'est leur oster un vrai
bien de leur plonger dans le néant. Je suis frappée de cette
verité, et je regarde les Conquerants comme les vengeurs
des Bêtes qui sont sacrifiez si impitoyablement a nos caprices
et nostre Luxure. Est-il juste de regarder avec horreur un
champ de Battaile jonchez de corps morts, et avec joye un
Souper pour le quel on a fait un masacre de cents especes
differents?

Si j'etois d'humeur a écrire, je ferai un epistre au nom
de tous les animaux au plus grand Guerrier du Siecle, pour
l'encourager au Carnage de ces Tyrants, qui s'imaginent
estre privelegiez d'exerciser la cruauté le plus enorme.[1]

Vous m'avouerez que la debauche m'inspire des belles
moralitez. Si on voudroit faire les refflections apres la victoire
que je fais en sortant de Table, on conveindroit avec moi que
l'amitie seule peut faire le bonheur. Ferme en ce sentiment,
jugez de celle que je ressens pour vous.

Text Bod. MS Don. c. 56, ff. 48–49   *Address* A Monsieur Monsieur le Comte Algarotti a Bologna

To Francesco Algarotti *19 Feb. 1757*

Il faut avoüer (Monsieur) que vous sçavez vous venger
d'une maniere fine et vraiment apostoliques, en rendant des
bien faits pour des injures. Vous desarmez vos ennemis, et

[1] Although no such epistle by LM
is known, she wrote a prose fable in
French on the same theme (W MS vii.
308–9; printed in Halsband, 'Algarotti
as Apollo', *Friendship's Garland: Essays
Presented to Mario Praz*, 1966).

vous vous flattez (sans doute) d'attirer sur eux les feux du Ciel.

Je n'ai pas manquée de faire vos compliments au General.[1] Il vous embrasse de tout son Cœur, dit-il; mais (entre nous) je lui croi un peu piqué d'avoir assiegé une Place six mois, sans qu'il peut se vanter d'avoir fait grand progres, que vous avez emporté d'assaut en moins de quinze jours. Il faut pardonner des Froideurs qui viennent d'une cause si legitime. Il a beau donner des Fêtes, servir a l'opera, et qui pis est, perdre son Argent a Pharon. Si l'inclination ne trahit point, le chateau est invincible. Je me garde bien de lui annoncer cette triste nouvelle. La chasse est souvent agreable quoy qu'on ne prend rien.

J'aime beaucoup Madame de Barbarigo. Elle a une bonté de Cœur qui m'enchante. Si sa Cour estoit moins nombreuse elle seroit plus belle.[2] Elle me plaist beaucoup, mais je m'imagine qu'elle me plaira encore plus a Padoue. Je voudrois y retourner, mais je suis enchainée ici de milles façons. Nous nous reverrons. Que j'aurois des choses a vous dire!

Fev. 19. 1757.

Text Bod. MS Don. c. 56, ff. 39–40   *Address* A Monsieur Monsieur le Comte Algarotti Bologna

From Francesco Algarotti *3 March 1757*

A Milady Mans [*sic*] Wortley Mantaigu [*sic*] a Padova[3]

Bologna, 3 Marzo 1757

Da questa dotta Città in cui sono io trasmetto un breve saggio sopra gli Antichi e i Moderni[4] a voi, Milady, che dimorando in

[1] Graeme.

[2] Caterina Sagredo m. (1739) Gregorio Barbarigo (Archivio di Stato, Venice). She was a beauty and wit; the French Ambassador, François-Joachim de Bernis, who greatly admired her, considered that of all the Venetian ladies she had the most important friends

(*Mémoires et lettres*, ed. F. Masson, 1878, i. 184).

[3] This letter is translated on p. 301 below.

[4] Although none of his published essays bears such a title, Algarotti dealt with the topic in various works.

Padova vi avete fermate le Muse. Niuno potrebbe meglio decider
di voi la bella lite che pende tuttavia quali dei due abbiano il vanto
della dottrina e dell'ingegno. Mercè la molta vostra lettura, e i molti
viaggj da voi intrapresi sono da voi ragguagliati con la giusta bilancia
di un sapere libero da ogni prevenzione il valore di ciascun secolo,
e di ciascun paese: Di quanto hanno scritto di migliore gli Antichi
avete conservato nella mente; e di quanto scrivete voi, Milady,
fanno già tesoro i Moderni, e molto più il faranno coloro,
      Che questo tempo chiameranno antico.

Text Algarotti, *Opere*, 1764–5, vii. 319

To Francesco Algarotti *12 March* [*1757*]

Adieu la Philosophie; voici des beaux commencements
de Radottage. J'en ai fait mes preuves hier au soir a l'acade-
mie de M. Barberigo en presence de trois ou quatre cents
personnes. Il faut vous en faire l'histoire. Il y avoit une
Musique excellente. Vous ne sçavez pas, peutestre, que
j'aime la Musique jusqu'a la Haine. Je ne sçaurois l'écouter
impunement; je suis aussi sensible qu'Alexandre, et un
autre Timothée me feroit courir, le Flambeau a la main,
mettre le feu a la ville. Mais comme je n'ai pas gagnée
assez de Battailes pour faire respecter mes folies, je me
suis tenüe eloignée tant que j'ai pû de cette charmante
seductrice, et je me flattai qu'on ne savoit pas mon Foible.
Pauvre Sagesse humaine! c'est ton dernier effort: tu peut
cacher les passions, jamais tu parveindrai a les exterminer.
Cet Refflection sent furieusement le Marivaux.[1]
  —Reprenons mon Histoire. Je m'abandonai au Plaisir
d'écouter de sons enchanteur qui remuent l'ame, croiant la
mienne assez glacée par le temps pour y pouvoir resister
aux Sirenes mêmes. Mademoiselle de Barberigo[2] avec sa

[1] Pierre de Marivaux (1688–1763), dramatist and novelist, whose delicate analysis and affected style are termed *marivaudage*.

[2] Caterina, da. of Gregorio and Caterina Barbarigo, who m. (1765) Marino Zorzi (Archivio di Stato, Venice).

figure d'Ange joint sa voix aux Instruments, les Aplaudisements sont juste et generale; les yeux de Madame sa mere petillent de joie. Un certain Chevalier Sagromoso[1] (qui je hairai toute ma vie) me dit tout bas, par une maudite Politesse, qu'il avoit entendu chanter ma Fille a Londres. Mille images a la fois se presentent a mon esprit, l'Impression devint trop fort et, moi miserable, je fonds en larmes, et suis obligée de sortir pour ne pas troubler le concert par mes sanglots. Je retourne chez moi, outrée de m'avoir attirée le mepris public, a juste titre: une vieille tendre, quel Monstre!

J'en sens le ridicule en toute sa force. Deffendez moi, si vous pouvois, contre les plaisanteries qu'on ne manqueroit pas de faire. Je voudrois tenir encore un petit coin dans vostre estime. Si cela est impossible, songez au moins qu'il y est de vostre Interêt de me sauver des railleurs impitoyable. Mon Amitie perdroit tout son prix si je tombe en odeur de Sottise. Elle est toute a vous. Vous serez aussi imprudent en vous moquant de ma Foiblesse qu'un Peintre qui conviendroit de l'inutilité des Tableaux.

Venise, ce 12 de mars.

Text Bod. MS Don. c. 56, ff. 45–46   *Address* A Monsieur Monsieur le Comte Algarotti a Bologne

To Lady Bute *3 April* [*1757*]

My Dear Child,

Yours of Feb. 20th releiv'd me from a great deal of uneasyness that I had suffer'd a long time from your silence. Why will you not order one of your Daughters to write when you are unable to do it? But I have said so much on that subject, I will mention it no more. Many of my Letters to you remain unanswer'd, particularly that in which is enclos'd the Captain's note for the Box I have directed to Lady Augusta Stuart.[2]

---

[1] Michele Sagramoso (1720–91), Knight of Malta, had been in London 1749 or 1750, and was in Venice in 1757 as Ambassador from the Order of Malta (Claire-Éliane Engel, *L'Ordre de Malte* *en Méditerranée*, 1957, pp. 194–5).

[2] LM's granddaughter (1749–78). She m. (1773) Capt. Andrew Corbett of the Horse Guards.

Several English are expected here at the Ascention. I hope to find an opportunity of sending you the Necklace. I have been persuaded to take a little House here, as living in Lodgings is realy disagreable. However, I still retain my favorite Palace at Padoua, where I intend to reside the greatest part of the Year.[1] In the mean time I amuse my selfe with buying and placeing Furniture, in which I only consult neatness and Convenience, having long renounce'd (as it is fit I should) all things bordering on Magnificence. I confess I sometimes indulge my taste in Baubles, which is as excusable in our second childhood as our first.[2]

I am sorry the Dutchess of Portland has not receiv'd my thanks for her obliging Letter. I also desir'd to know the name of the merchant to whom the Duke consign'd the Legacy Left me by Lady Oxford, which I have not yet heard of. General Graham is gone into the Country for his Health. I hope [for] his return soon, but he is preparing for a Tour on the Frontiers of these Dominions.[3]

I see in the news papers the names of the following Books: Fortunate Mistriss, Accomplish'd Rake, Mrs. Charke's Memoirs, Modern Lovers, History of 2 Orphans, Memoirs of David Ranger, Miss ⟨Mos⟩tyn, Dick Hazard, History of a Lady Platonist, Sophia Shakespear, Jasper Banks, Frank Hammond, Sir Andrew Thompson, Van a Clergyman's Son, Cleanthes and Celemena.[4] I do not doubt

---

[1] On 18 April LM left Venice for Padua, accompanied by three servants and her secretary: 'S. E. Miledi Montagù Inglese, Giuseppe Frannzese suo Agente, Servo Battista Friberare e Maddalena Giulei sua serva e Dottor Moro da Bressa suo Segretario. Partiti disse il giorno sudetto alogiando in casa sudetta' (Busta 758, Forestieri, Inquisitori di Stato, Archivio di Stato, Venice).

[2] Gen. Graeme observed: 'She is as fond of bables [*sic*] as a child and is constantly buying some triffle of no price' (to Bute, 8 Sept. 1758, Bute MS).

[3] After his return in May 1758 Graeme wrote to Bute, 'I was near 14 [months] in making the tour of Istria, Dalmatia, Albany, and the Grecian

islands, by ordre of the Senat' (ibid.).

[4] *The Fortunate Beauty* (not *Mistress*), listed in the *London Mag.* for July 1757; *The Accomplished Rake* by Mary Davys, listed in the *Monthly Rev.* for Dec. 1755; *A Narrative of the Life of Mrs. Charlotte Charke, by Herself*, 1755; *The Modern Lovers; or, The Adventures of Cupid*, listed in the *Monthly Rev.* for Nov. 1756; *The History of Two Orphans* by William Toldervy, severely dealt with in the *Monthly Rev.* for Nov. 1756; *The Juvenile Adventures of David Ranger*, listed in the *London Mag.* for Oct. 1756; *Miss [?Mos]tyn*, apparently unrecorded; *The Adventures of Dick Hazard*, noticed contemptuously in the *Monthly Rev.* for Dec. 1754, and by LM as 'pert' (Sotheby Catalogue, 1 Aug. 1928, p. 82); *The*

at least the greatest part of these are Trash, Lumber etc.; however, they will serve to pass away the Idle time, if you will be so k⟨in⟩d to send them to your most affectionate Mother.

M. Wortley

My Complements to Lord Bute and hearty Blessing ⟨to⟩ all my Grand Children.

Venice, April 3.

Lord Roseberry is in this Town at present; no bad Figure, But ——. I am sorry for him. He is as Ridiculous as a Man that would carry Oysters to Colchester; he is at the expence of the Carriage and may find as good in every Corner.[1]

Text W MS iii. 164–5 *Address* To The Rt Honble the Countess of Bute recommended to Fran: Child Esqr near Temple Bar London Angleterre [*in another hand*] North Audley Street *Postmark* AP 26

To Lady Bute *30 May* [*1757*]

Venice, May 30

It is a Long time since I have heard from my Dear child, thô I have wrote several times, and indeed never fail to do it at least once in a fortnight, but I hear many pacquets have been lost, which may occasion this interuption of our

Memoirs of a Young Lady of Quality, A Platonist, noticed in the *Monthly Rev.* for Feb. 1757, and by LM as 'insufferable' (p. 92); *The History of Sophia Shakespear*, called 'beneath censure' in the *Monthly Rev.* for March 1753, and 'trash' by LM (p. 90); *The History of Jasper Banks*, noticed in the *Monthly Rev.* for June 1754, and by LM as 'Ribaldry' (p. 89); *The History and Adventures of Frank Hammond*, listed in the *Monthly Rev.* for May 1754; *The Fortunate Villager; or, Memoirs of Sir Andrew Thompson*, noticed in the *Monthly Rev.* for March 1757; *The Life* of Mr. *John Van, a Clergyman's Son* by George Smith Green, severely noticed in the *Monthly Rev.* for March 1757; *The History of Cleanthes, an Englishman of the Highest Quality, and Celemene, the Illustrious Amazonian Princess*, listed in the *London Mag.* for April and the *Monthly Rev.* for June 1757.

1 Neil Primrose (1729–1814), 3rd Earl of Rosebery; in Rome the year before, Robert Adam had met 'little Roseberry and his whore', who was shortly expected to 'bring furth' (John Fleming, *Robert Adam and His Circle*, 1962, p. 221).

Correspondance. I will not frighten my selfe by supposing that you or your Family are indispos'd.

I seize with great pleasure the oportunity of writeing by a sure hand. I send this by Mr. Anderson, who has also promis'd to deliver to you a Pearl Necklace consisting of 46 Pearls, and a pair of Earrings which are not altogether worthy to accompany it,[1] but if you do not like them present them to Lady Jane to make up for the small value of her Ring. It is some Months since I sent Lady Augusta a Plaything, which I intended to be follow'd by a Box of various others, if that came safe. I have hitherto had no account of it from you, nor no Answer to a Question I have desir'd you to ask more than once: what is the Name of the Merchant to whom the Duke of Portland consign'd the Legacy left me by dear Lady Oxford?

Here are a great Number of English Travellers, and 2 Ladies, one of them Mrs. Greville,[2] sister in law to your old Freind Mrs. Boughton.[3] Unavoidable visits, joyn'd with the occupation of fitting and furnishing, hardly leaves me any time to dispose on to my own Taste, which is (as it ought to be) more solitary than ever. I left my Hermitage that what Effects I have might not be disipated by servants, as they would have been, probably, if I had dy'd there. I begg'd of your Father (when I was at Avignon) that they might be yours, which he Generously promis'd me.

To say truth I am very uneasy, knowing no body here I can confide in, General Graham being gone for a long time, and the Brittish Minister here such a scandalous Fellow in every Sense of that word, he is not [to] be trusted to change a Sequin, despis'd by this Government for his smuggling, which was his original proffession, and always surrounded with Pimps and Brokers, who are his privy Councellors.[4]

---

[1] John Anderson, again on the Continent as a bear-leader, was with Andrew Archer, by whom LM had intended to send the jewels (see above, p. 113).

[2] Frances (d. 1789), da. of James Macartney, m. (1748) Fulke Greville; she was both a beauty and a poetess (Boswell, *Life of Johnson*, ed. G. B. Hill and L. F. Powell, 1934, iv. 535; Walpole, *Corr.* xi. 47, n. 41).

[3] Mary (d. 1786), da. of Algernon Greville, m. (1736) Shuckburgh Boughton (*c.* 1705–63) (Jos. Foster, *Alumni Oxon. 1715–1886*, i. 136; William Betham, *Baronetage*, 1801–5, i. 419–20).

[4] John Murray (see above, p. 114) had aroused LM's hatred, perhaps because they differed in regard to Pitt's coalition ministry. To Casanova this 'aimable épicurien' was a 'bel homme,

Sir John [*sic*] Gray was, as I am told, universally esteem'd, but alas, he is at Naples.[1] I wish the Maxims of Queen Elizabeth were reviv'd, who always chose for her Foreign Ministers Men whose Birth and Behavior would make the Nation respected, people being apt to look upon them as a Sample of their Country Men. If those now employ'd are ⟨so⟩, Lord have mercy upon us.—I have seen only Mr. Villette at Turin who knew how to support his character.[2] How much the Nation has suffer'd by false Intelligence, I beleive you are very sensible of, and how impossible it is to get Truth either from a Fool or a Knave.

Company forces me upon an Abrupt Conclusion. I am ever, my dear child, Your most affectionate Mother,

M. Wortley.

My Compliments to Lord Bute and Blessing to all yours.

Text W MS iii. 225–6   *Address* To The Rt Honble The Countess of Bute

To Lord Lincoln[3] *5 June 1757*

My Lord,

I ask pardon for troubling your Lordship with a Letter from an old Relation, who, probably, you have forgot that you have ever seen, but it is in favor of a Man I have long been acquainted with, and know to be that extraodinary Character, *truly an Honest Man*. He had the Honor of being distinguish'd by Mr. Pelham, whose memory I am sure you reverence.[4] Your Rank and merit will allwaies give you

---

plein d'esprit, savant, et prodigieusement amateur du beau sexe, de Baccus et de la bonne chère. . . . sautant d'une à l'autre il avait toujours les plus jolies filles de Venise' (*Histoire de ma vie*, ed. F. A. Brockhaus, 1960–2, iv. 136, 138).

   [1] Sir James Gray, who had left Venice in 1752, was appointed to Naples in 1753 (D. B. Horn, p. 76).

[2] Arthur Villettes (see ii. 149).

[3] Henry Fiennes-Clinton (1720–94), 9th Earl of Lincoln, later 2nd Duke of Newcastle. For his distant relationship to LM, whom he had seen in Rome and Genoa, see ii. 221.

[4] Since Lincoln had married his cousin Catherine in 1744, Henry Pelham (d. 1754) had been both his uncle and father-in-law.

power, and I am persuaded you will be ever glad to employ it in making the Happiness of those who deserve it. Mr. Anderson will never abuse any trust you please to charge him with, and it is as much for your service as his that he is recommended by, My Lord, Your Lordship's most obedient Humble Servant,

M. Wortley Montagu.

Venice, June 5. 1757

Text MS owned by the Duke of Newcastle; on deposit at the University of Nottingham *Address* To The Rt Honble the Earl of Lincoln

To Wortley 7 *June* [*1757*]

I have wrote very often both to you and my Daughter, but have heard from neither of a long time. I have, however, had the pleasure of knowing from a Letter of Mr. Gibson to Mr. Anderson that you enjoy good Health, which I heartily pray God to continue. Having this Opportunity of a private Conveyance I cannot forbear writeing, but will not trouble you with a tedious Letter.

I have taken the Liberty of sending by Mr. Anderson my Pearl Necklace and Earings to my Daughter, which I suppose you will permit.

I am at present very well, and think I have fewer Infirmities than most people of my Age. Here are 2 or 3 English Ladies, but their time of Life and mine are so different we do not meet often, they being generally engag'd in Diversions which I have neither Inclination nor Spirits to pertake.

Venice, June 7th

Text W MS ii. 246 *End. by W* Ad L.M. 7 June 1757 Brought by Mr. Anderson 14 Aug. [*Summary*]

To Lady Bute 7 *July* [*1757*]

Padoua, July 7.

My dear Child,

I receiv'd yours last night, which gave me a pleasure beyond what I am able to express (this is not according to the common Expression, but a simple Truth). I had not heard from you of some months, and was, in my Heart, very uneasy from the apprehension of some misfortune in your Family. Thô, as I allwaies endeavor to avoid the Anticipation of Evil, which is a Source of Pain and can never be productive of any Good, I stiffled my Fear as much as possible, yet it cost me many a Midnight Pang. You have been the Passion of my Life. You need thank me for nothing; I gratify my selfe whenever I can oblige you.

I have allready given into the hands of Mr. Anderson a long Letter for you, but it is now of so old a Date I accompany it with another. His Journey has been delaid by a very extraordinary Accident, which might have prov'd as Fatal as that of Lord Drumlanrig[1] or that (which I think worse) which happen'd to my Convert, Mr. Butler.[2] Fortunately it has only serv'd to set the Characters of both the Governor and Pupil in a more aimable Light.

Mr. Archer[3] was at Breakfast with six other English Gentlemen, and handling a Blunderbuss, which he did not know to be charg'd. It burst, and distributed amongst them six chain'd Bullets, beside the Splinters which flew about in the manner you may imagine. His own hand was considerably wounded, yet the first word he spoke (without any regard to his own smart and danger) was: I hope no body is hurt. No body was Hurt but himselfe, who has been ever since under Cure to preserve two of his Fingers, which were very much torn. He had also a small razure on his cheek, which is now quite heal'd.

The Paternal Care and tenderness Mr. Anderson has shewn on this occasion has recommended him to every body. I wanted nothing to raise that Esteem which is due to his

---

[1] Who shot himself by accident (see above, p. 80, n. 1).

[2] Not identified.

[3] Andrew Archer (see above, p. 113).

Sterling Honesty and good Heart, which I do not doubt you value as much as I do. If that Wretch Hickman had been ———. But this is a melancholy Thought, and as such ought to be suppress'd.[1] How Important is the charge of Youth! And how useless all the advantages of Nature and Fortune without a well turn'd Mind! I have lately heard of a very shineing instance of this Truth from two Gentlemen (very deserving ones they seem to be) who have had the Curiosity to travel into Moscovy, and now return to England with Mr. Archer.

I enquir'd after my old Acquaintance Sir Charles Williams, who I hear is much broken both in his spirits and Constitution.[2] How happy might that Man have been if there had been added to his natural and acquir'd Endowments a dash of Morality! If he had known how to distinguish between false and true Felicity, and instead of seeking to encrease an Estate already too large, and hunting after Pleasures that have made him rotten and ridiculous, he had bounded his desires of Wealth and follow'd the Dictates of his Conscience! His servile Ambition has gain'd him two yards of red Riband[3] and an exile into a miserable Country where there is no Society and so little Taste that I beleive he suffers under a Dearth of Flatterers.[4]

This is said for the use of your growing Sons, who I hope no Golden Temptations will induce to marry Women they cannot love, or comply with Measures they do not approve. All the Happiness this World can afford is more within reach than is generally suppos'd. Whoever seeks Pleasure will undoubtedly find Pain; whoever will persue ease will as certainly find Pleasures. The World's esteem is the highest

[1] Nathan (or Nathaniel) Hickman (d. 1746), F.R.S., had been tutor and physician to LM's nephew the 2nd Duke of Kingston. The learned Abbé Le Blanc and the naturalist Buffon considered him a cultivated and learned connoisseur (Hélène Monod-Cassidy, *Un Voyageur-Philosophe au XVIIIe siècle: l'abbé Jean-Bernard Le Blanc*, 1941, pp. 16, 41).

[2] Sir Charles Hanbury Williams (see ii. 394), Ambassador to Russia since 1755, had asked to be recalled in the spring of 1757, and left for England in Oct. Soon after his return in Feb. 1758, he became insane, and had to be confined (Lord Ilchester and Mrs. Langford Brooke, *Life of Sir Charles Hanbury-Williams*, 1928, pp. 406–23 *passim*; D. B. Horn, p. 115).

[3] In 1744 he had been named a Knight of the Bath.

[4] LM's opinion of Williams was so severe because she had sided with his estranged wife (Ilchester and Langford-Brooke, p. 437).

Gratification of Human Vanity, and that is more easily obtain'd in a moderate Fortune than an overgrown one, which is seldom possess'd, never gain'd, without Envy. I say Esteem, for as to Applause, it is a youthfull persuit, never to be forgiven after twenty, and naturally succeeds the childish desire of catching the setting Sun, which I can remember running very hard to do: a fine Thing truly if it could be caught, but experience soon shews it to be impossible.

A Wise and Honest Man lives to his own Heart, without that silly Splendor that makes him a prey to Knaves, and which commonly ends in his becoming one of the Fraternity. I am very glad to hear Lord Bute's decent Oeconomy sets him above any thing of that kind. I wish it may become National. A Collective Body of Men differs very little from a single Man; Frugality is the Foundation of Generosity. I have often been complimented on the English Heroism, who have thrown away so many Millions without any prospect of advantage to them selves, purely to succour a Distress'd Princess.[1] I never could hear these praises without some Impatience; they sounded to me like the Panegyrics made by the dependants on the Duke of N[ewcastle] and poor Lord Oxford,[2] Bubbled when they were commended, and laugh'd at when undone. Some late events will, I hope, open our Eyes. We shall see we are an Island, and endeavor to extend our Commerce rather than the Quixote Reputation of redressing wrongs and placeing Diadems on Heads that should be equally indifferent to us. When Time has ripen'd Mankind into common Sense, the Name of Conqueror will be an odious Title. I could easily prove that had the Spainyards establish'd a Trade with the Americans, they would have enrich'd their Country more than by the addition [of] 22 Kingdoms and all the Mines they now work; I don't say possess, since thô they are the proprietors, others enjoy the Profit.

My letter is too long; I beg your pardon for it. 'Tis seldom I have an opportunity of speaking to you, and I would have you know all the Thoughts of your most affectionate Mother.

M. Wortley M.

[1] Maria Theresa in the War of the Austrian Succession.   [2] 1st Earl.

I desire you would thank your Father for the Jewels; you know I have nothing of my own.[1]

Text W MS iii. 168–70   *Address* To The Rt Honble The Countess of Bute

To Lord Bute *24 Sept.* [*1757*]

I return your Lordship many thanks for your obliging notice of my daughter's Health and safety.[2] I wish you joy of the encrease of your Family, and am much flatter'd by the Esteem you express for me. I wish I was as well known to you as you are to me; thô I was only acquainted with you in your early Youth, your character then appear'd to me the same which is now universally allow'd you. It is the greatest Happiness of my Life to hear it is so, being, My Lord, with a tender esteem, sincerely and affectionately Your Lordship's Obedient Humble Servant,

M. W. Montagu.

Venice, Sept. 24

Text Bute MS   *Address* To The Rt Honble the Earl of Bute recommended to Francis Child Esqr near Temple Bar London Angleterre [*in another hand*] North Audley Str.   *Postmark* OC ⟨?⟩

To Lady Bute *30 Sept. 1757*

My Dear Child,
Lord Bute has been so obliging as to let me know your safe delivery and the Birth of another Daughter; may she be

---

[1] That is, no marriage jointure; and the £6,000 left to her by her father was entailed on Lady Bute.

[2] On 12 Aug. 1757 Lady Bute gave birth to her thirteenth and last child, christened Louisa (Bute MS). Lady Mary Coke stood proxy for LM as godmother (Coke, *Letters and Journals*, 1889–96, I. xiii, n. 1). Lady Louisa Stuart (d. 1851) was the only one of LM's grandchildren distinguished as a writer.

as meritorious in your Eyes as you are in mine. I can wish nothing better to you both, thô I have some reproaches to make you. Daughter, Daughter, don't call names. You are allwaies abusing my Pleasures, which is what no mortal will bear. Trash, Lumber, sad stuff, are the Titles you give to my favorite Amusements. If I call'd a white staff a stick of Wood, a Gold key gilded Brass, and the Ensigns of Illustrious Orders colour'd strings, this may be Philosophycally true, but would be very ill receiv'd. We have all our Playthings; happy are they that can be contented with those they can obtain. Those hours are spent in the wisest manner that can easiest shade the ills of Life, and are the least productive of ill Consequences. I think my time better employ'd in reading the Adventures of imaginary people, than the Dutchess of Marlbrô's, who pass'd the latter years of her Life in padling with her Will,[1] and contriving schemes of plagueing some and extracting Praise from others, to no purpose, eternally disapointed and eternally fretting.

The active scenes are over at my Age. I indulge, with all the art I can, my taste for reading. If I would confine it to valuable Books, they are allmost rare as valuable Men. I must be content with what I can find. As I approach a second childhood, I endeavor to enter into the Pleasures of it. Your youngest Son is, perhaps, at this very moment riding on a Poker with great Delight, not at all regretting that it is not a gold one, and much less wishing it an Arabian Horse, which he would not know how to manage; I am reading an Idle Tale, not expecting Wit or Truth in it, and am very glad it is not Metaphisics to puzzle my Judgment, or History to mislead my Opinion.[2] He fortifys his Health by Exercise, I calm my Cares by Oblivion. The methods may appear low to busy people, but if he improves his strength, and I forget my Infirmitys, we attain very desirable ends.[3]

---

[1] See ii. 347, n. 2.
[2] Similar sentiments in LM's Commonplace Book: 'Metaphysicians: Moles' and 'Scholiastic Works: spiders' webs' (MS, ff. 5, 6).
[3] When Mme du Boccage visited LM in Venice in May 1757, she observed many Latin authors in her library; but

LM said, '. . . le temps m'a appris que tous les systêmes métaphysiques, même les faits historiques donnés pour vérités, ne le sont gueres; ainsi je m'amuse des plus agréables mensonges, je ne lis plus que des romans' (*Lettres sur l'Angleterre . . . et l'Italie* in *Recueil des œuvres*, 1770, iii. 178).

I shall be much pleas'd if you would send your Letters in Mr. Pit's Pacquet.[1]

I have not heard from your Father of a long time. I hope he is well, because you do not mention him.

I am ever, dear child, your most affectionate Mother,

M. W. M.

My compliments to Lord Bute and blessing to all yours.

Sept. 30. 1757

Text W MS iii. 152–3   *Address* To The Rt Honble The Countess of Bute

To Lady Bute *8 Oct.* [*1757*]

I am sorry (my Dear child) you fatigue'd your selfe with writeing during your lying in. You need thank me for nothing. I have already told you (and tis litteraly true) that I please my selfe when ever it is in my power to do any thing obliging to you.

I explain'd my selfe ill, or you did not take the right sense of my Demand. I would know of Mr. Prescot the name of the Merchant to whom he consign'd Lady Oxford's Legacy.[2]

I have receiv'd both your bills of ladeing, and am in daily expectation of the ship, which is not yet arriv'd. I am very glad to hear of your Father's Health; mine is better than I ought to expect at my Time of Life. I beleive Mr. Anderson talks partialy of me, as to my looks; I know nothing of the Matter. It is eleven Year since I have seen my Figure in a Glass. The last Refflection I saw there was so disagreable, I resolv'd to spare my selfe such mortifications for the Future, and shall continue that resolution to my Live's end. To indulge all pleasing Amusements and avoid all Images that give Disgust is in my opinion the best method to attain of

[1] As Secretary of State for the Southern Department, William Pitt would be in correspondence with the Resident in Venice.

[2] To be paid by the Duke of Portland (see above, pp. 109-10).

confirm Health.—I ought to consider yours, and shorten my Letter, while you are in a Condition that makes reading uneasy to you.

God Bless you and yours, my Dear child; it is the most ardent Wish of Your affectionate Mother,

M. Wortley.

Oct. 8, Venice

Text W MS iii. 178–9   *Address* To The Rt Honble the Countess of Bute recommended to Francis Child Esqr near Temple Bar London Angleterre   *Postmark* NO 7

To Lady Bute [*9 Oct. 1757*]

My Dear Child,

I receiv'd yours of September 15 this morning, October 9th, and am exceeding Glad of the Health of you and your Family. I am fond of your little Louisa.¹ To say truth, I was afraid of a Bess, a Peg, or a Suky, which all give me the Ideas of washing Tubs and scowring of Kettles.

I am much oblig'd to Mr. Hamilton,² which is, according to the Academy of Complements, more his goodness than my Deserts. I saw him but twice and both times in mix'd Company; but am surpriz'd you have never mention'd Lord Roseberry, by whom I sent a pacquet to you, and took some pains to shew him Civillitys.³ He breakfasted with me at Padua. I gave him Bread and Butter of my own Manufacture, which is the admiration of all the English. He promis'd to give you full Information of my selfe and all my employments. He seem'd delighted with my House and Gardens, and perhaps has forgot he ever saw me or any thing that belong'd to me.

We have had many English here. Mr. Greville, his Lady and her suitte of adorers deserve Particular mention.⁴ He

¹ Her new god-daughter.
² Not identified. He was in a foreign military service.
³ See above, p. 126. He reached

London only on 2 Oct. (*Daily Advertiser*, 4 Oct. 1757).
⁴ Fulke Greville (*c.* 1717–*c.* 1806), M.P. 1747–54 (Gerrit P. Judd,

was so good to present me with his curious Book.[1] Since the
Days of the Honorable Mr. Ed[ward] Howard, nothing
has ever been publish'd like it.[2] I told him the Age wanted
an Earl of Dorset to celebrate it properly,[3] and he was so
well pleas'd with that speech that he visited me every day, to
the great Comfort of Madame, who was entertain'd mean
while with partys of pleasure of another kind. Thô I fear I
lost his esteem at last by refusing to correspond with him,
however, I qualify'd my Denial by complaining of my bad
Eyes not permitting me to multiply my Correspondants.

I could give you the characters of many other Travellers
if I thought it would be of any use to you. It is melancholy
to see the pains our Pious Minister[4] takes to debauch the
younger sort of them. But, as you say, all is melancholy
that relates to Great Brittain. I have a high value for Mr.
Pit's probity and understanding, without having the Honor
of being acquainted with him; I am persuaded he is able to
do whatever is within the bounds of possibility.[5] But there is
an Augæan stable to be clean'd and several other labours
that I doubt if Hercules himselfe would be equal to.

If the Duke of Kingston only intends to build a hunting
seat at Thorsby, I think it is most proper for the Situation,
which was certainly by Nature never design'd for a Palace.[6]
I hope he will not employ the same architect that built his
House in London. You see I am not entirely devested of
Family prejudices, thô I thank the Lord they are not lively

Members of Parliament 1734–1832,
1955, p. 213). He and his wife (see above,
p. 127) seemed 'very agreeable people'
to James Adam, who met them in
Naples in 1761 ('Journal of a Tour in
Italy', *Library of the Fine Arts*, ii, 1831,
p. 243).

[1] *Maxims, Characters, and Reflections,
critical, satyrical, and moral* (1756). To
Walpole, some of the maxims were
'pretty' but all the characters 'absurd'
(*Letters*, ed. Mrs. P. Toynbee, 1903,
iii. 414).

[2] Edward Howard (1624–c. 1700),
dramatist—called by the actor John
Lacy 'more a fool than a poet'.

[3] Charles Sackville (1638–1706), 6th

Earl of Dorset, ridiculed Howard in
two poems: "On his incomparable,
incomprehensible poem, called The
British Princess" and "On his Plays".

[4] John Murray.

[5] Describing Pitt's coalition cabinet,
LM wrote in her Commonplace Book:
'the present English Ministry: Arle-
quin's Coat' (MS, f. 6).

[6] Thoresby had been burnt down in
1745; and the Duke did not rebuild
until 1762—when he erected a house
costing £30,000 (John Harris, 'Thoresby House, Nottinghamshire', *Architec-
tural History*, iv, 1961, p. 17; G. E.
Mingay, *English Landed Society in the
Eighteenth Century*, 1963, p. 160).

enough to give me violent uneasiness. I cannot help wishing
well to my ever-dear Brother's children.[1] However, I have
the conscious satisfaction of knowing I have done my Duty
towards them, as far as my power extended; no body can
be serv'd against their Will. May all your Young Ones grow
up an Honor to you. I am told one Objection to Lord
Mount Stuart: that he is too handsome, which is a Fault
that will certainly mend every day. I should be glad to hear
your Daughters accus'd of the same Deffect.—My paper is
out; I have scarce room to assure my Dear child I am ever
your most Affectionate Mother.

M. Wortley

Text W MS iii. 123–4   *Address* To The Rt Honble the Countess of
Bute recommended to Francis Child Esqr near Temple Bar London
Angleterre   *Postmark* NO 7

To Wortley [*12 Nov. 1757*]

I receiv'd yours of Oct'r 15[2] yesterday, Nov. 11th. I was
quite frighted at the relation of your Indisposition, and am
very glad I did not know it till it was over. I hope you will
no more suffer the Physicians to try Experiments with so
good a Constitution as yours. I am persuaded Mineral
Waters, which are provided by Nature, are the best (perhaps the only real) remedies, particularly that of Tunbridge,
of which I have a great Opinion. I would not trouble you
with a long letter, which may be uneasy to you to read. My
most fervent wishes are for your Health and Happiness.
What ever I write to my Daughter is for you.

Text W MS ii. 247   *End. by* W L.M. 12 Nov. 1757. Recd 6 May
1758 [*Summary*] Ad 10 June 1758.

[1] William (1692–1713), Earl of Kingston, left a son who became 2nd Duke,
and a daughter, Lady Frances Pierrepont, who m. Philip Meadows.

[2] Sent from Wharncliffe Lodge
(W MS i. 141–2).

To Lady Bute [*12 Feb. 1758*]

My Dear Child,
I am realy very miserable from your Silence. Your last Letter is dated September 15;[1] it is now Feb. 12. I can alow a great deal to Avocations abroad and attention to your numerous Family at home, but why will you not order one of your Daughters to write? I have desir'd it over and over. I never pass a fortnight without writeing to you. I do not expect in your present Situation you should do the same, yet it is just to releive me from the concern I am in for your Health, and which indeed affects my own. I sent you a long Letter by a private Hand (Mr. Law),[2] who promis'd to deliver it to your selfe, and several since by the post, to which I have no return. I wish you would write to me with that openess of Heart I do to you. I have trusted this to a merchant of your Country.[3] He seems an honest, sensible Man. He has engag'd it should [be] safely convey'd. I beg you would answer ⟨?⟩ you value the repose of a most affectionate Mother,

M. Wortley.

My Complements to Lord Bute. I gave him thanks[4] for his obliging Letter the post after I receiv'd it.

Text W MS iii. 277–8 *Address* A Madame Madame la Comtesse de Bute recommandee a Monsieur Monsieur Child Banquier near Temple Bar London Angleterre

To Lady Bute *21 Feb.* [*1758*]

My Dear Child,
If halfe of the Letters I have sent to you have reach'd you, I beleive you think I have allwaies a pen in my Hand, but

---

[1] LM answered it on 9 Oct. 1757.
[2] Law was bear-leader to a Mr. Oliver (see below, p. 150).
[3] Scotland.
[4] On 24 Sept. [1757].

I am realy so uneasy by your long silence, I cannot forbear enquiring the reason of it by all the methods I can imagine. My time of Life is naturally inclin'd to Fear, and thô I resist (as well as I can) all the Infirmitys incident to Age, I feel but too sensibly the Impressions of Melancholy when I have any Doubt of your Welfare.

You fancy, perhaps, that the public papers give me Information enough, and that when I do not see in them any misfortune of Yours, I ought to conclude you have none. I can assure you I never see any excepting by Accident. Our Resident has not the good Breeding to send them to me, and after having ask'd for them once or twice, and being told they were engag'd, I am unwilling to demand a triffle at the expence of thanking a Man who does not desire to oblige me. Indeed, since the Ministry of Mr. Pit, he is so desirous to signalize his zeal for the contrary Faction, he is perpetually saying ridiculous things to manifest his attachment; and as he looks upon me (no body knows why) to be the Freind of a Man I never saw, he has not visited me once this Winter. The misfortune is not great.

I cannot help laughing at my being mistaken for a Politician. I have often been so, thô I ever thought Politics so far remov'd from my Sphere I cannot accuse my selfe of dabling in them even when I heard them talk'd over in all Companys. But as the old Song says,

> Thô through the wide World we should range,
> 'Tis in vain from our Fortune to Fly.

I forget my selfe and tattle on, without remembering you are too much imploy'd to throw away time on reading insignificant Letters. You should, however, forgive them in consideration of the real affection of your very loving Mother,

M. Wortley.

Venice, Feb. 21.

My Complements to Lord Bute and Blessing to all yours.

Text W MS iii. 180–1   *Address* To The Rt Honble The Countess of Bute

To Francesco Algarotti 5 *March* [*1758*]

Vous me flattez, Monsieur, mais vous sçavez assaisoner la flatterie de tant des Graces, il est impossible de ne pas s'ÿ plaire. Avouons la Dette: l'humanité est petrie de vanité. Nous sommes tous logez la, Saints, Heros, Philosophes. La chere Flatterie est nostre nouriture favorite. Il n'ÿ a qu'a sçavoir l'apprester pour la faire gouter. Vous possedez l'Art de l'habiler legerement, d'ÿ mettre un sel picquant; vous le rendez si tendre, si delicat, je l'avale avidement, et je ne veux pas m'apercevoir que ma pauvre Tête s'en trouve mal. Trop heureux ceux qui osent se flatter eux mêmes! J'ai vüe une piece de Voltaire ou il s'encense de la plus belle maniere. Avec quel Feu chante-il ses propres louanges! Voila, c'est que s'appelle un Panegyrique sincere! chose presq'unique.—Je me sens des tentations violents de l'imiter. L'imagination s'échauffe aisement quand on veut traiter de son propre merite, mais Helas! j'ai quelque lueur de sens commun, qui me represente impitoyablement telle que je suis. Tout ce j'ai puis dire avec verité, j'etois jeune sans coquetterie, affectation, ou étourderie; je suis vieille sans humeur, superst[it]ion, ou medisance. Voici bien des negatives, miserable resource pour mon Amour propre! Je tache de sauver ses droits en me persuadant que je suis moins sotte qu'une autre, en voiant mes sottises au moment même que je m'ÿ laisse entrainer.

Mars cinquieme, Venise
On dit que le Pape est mort;[1] comme Citoyenne du Monde j'en suis au desespoir.

Text Bod. MS Don. c. 56, ff. 42–43   *Address* A Monsieur Monsieur le Comte Algarotti a Bologna

---

[1] Benedict XIV, who had been seriously ill for several years, did not die until 3 May 1758. When visited by Mme du Boccage in 1757, LM remarked: 'malgré . . . mon opposition aux lois de Rome, admirez, regardez le portrait du Pape régnant au nombre des hommes choisis peints dans mon cabinet' (*Lettres sur l'Angleterre . . . et l'Italie* in *Recueil des œuvres*, 1762, iii. 178).

To Lady Bute *12 April 1758*

My Dear Child,

I receiv'd about a week ago yours dated November 20th. Those you mention sent before it never came to my Hands. I cannot guess why or how, but 'tis certain the greatest part of my Letters are lost, thô I should think it worth no body's while to stop them. The last news Paper inform'd me Lord Elgin is likely to be one of your Family, which I am very glad to hear. I have seen no young Man more proper to adorn a Court, having an agreable figure, with a large proportion of good Humour and good breeding.[1] I do not doubt you have had good Success in presenting our Daughter to the Princess. I can judge of your Anxiety by what I felt on the same Occasion. I had the pleasure to hear you universally commended, and beleive to this day you deserv'd it. I flatter my selfe I shall find an opportunity this Ascension to send you a pacquet. Hitherto I have had none since Mr. Anderson. I wish you could find some way of serving that honest Man, but I suppose I need not recommend it to you, whenever it is in your Power.

General Graham is expected every Day. I stay here on purpose to see him; otherwise I am, on many Accounts, better pleas'd at Padoua. Our great Minister, the Resident, affects to treat me as one in the Opposition. I am inclin'd to laugh rather than be displeas'd at his political Airs, yet as I am amongst strangers they are disagreable, and could I have foreseen them, would have settled in some other part of the World; but I have taken leases of my Houses, been at much pains and expence in furnishing them, and am no longer of an Age to make long Journeys.

I saw some months ago a Countriman of yours (Mr. Adams) who desires to be introduce'd to you.[2] He seem'd

---

[1] Charles Bruce (1732–71), 5th Earl of Elgin, was married in June 1759— but not to Lady Mary, LM's eldest granddaughter; or LM may refer to a rumoured Court post. In Rome two years before, Robert Adam had found Elgin entertaining and merry (John

Fleming, *Robert Adam and His Circle*, 1962, p. 226).

[2] Robert Adam (1728–92) had been in Venice in the summer of 1757. Through other friends he was introduced to Bute, apparently in May 1758, and to his disappointment and indigna-

to me, in one short visit, to be a Man of Genius, and I have heard his knowledge of Architecture much applauded. He is now in England.

My Dear Child, God Bless you and yours; it is the hearty and daily praier of your most affectionate Mother,

M. Wortley.

My complements to Lord Bute.

Venice, April 12. 1758

Text W MS iii. 205–6   *Address* To The Rt Honble The Countess of Bute recommended to Fran: Child Esqr near Temple Bar London Angleterre par Amsterdam   *Postmark* AP 29

To Wortley *17 April* [*1758*]

I very seldom trouble you with Letters, finding what I send by the post generally miscarry. I am not much surpriz'd at it at present. I perceive the Factions in England run so high the most innocent actions are suspected. If people knew my Heart, they would see such a total Indifference for every thing that does not personally regard You or my Daughter, I shall hardly have more when I am remov'd from the Face of the Earth.

I hear you have been at the Bath. I hope it has been beneficial for your Health; may it long continue.

Venice, April 17

Text W MS ii. 248   *End. by W* [*Summary*] Recd in London 6 June. Ad 10 June 1758

To Lady Bute [*3 May 1758*]

Dear Child,

I receiv'd yours of the 20th of Feb. yesterday, May the 2nd, so irregular is the post. I could forgive the delay, but I cannot pardon the loss of so many that have never arriv'd at all.

tion was very coldly received (Fleming, pp. 235, 254). Not until 1761 did Bute patronize him, with a commission to design a house in Berkeley Square.

Mr. Hamilton is not yet come, nor perhaps will not of some Months; I hear he is at Leghorn. General Graham has been dangerously ill, but I am told he is now on his return.[1] We have at present the most extravagant Weather [that] has been known of some years. It is as cold and Wet as an English November. Thursday next is the Ceremony of the Ascention. The shew will be entirely spoilt if the Rain continues, to the serious Affliction of the fine Ladies, who all make new cloaths on that Occasion. We have had lately two Magnificent Weddings. Lord Mandevile[2] had the pleasure of danceing at one of them. I appear'd at Neither, being formal Balls where no Masques were admitted, and all people set out in high Dress, which I have long renounce'd, as it is very fit I should, thô there were several Grandmothers there who exhibited their Jewells. In this Country no body grows old till they are bed rid.

I wish your Daughters to ressemble me in nothing but the Love of Reading, knowing by experience how far it is capable of softening the cruelest Accidents of Life. Even the happiest cannot be pass'd over without many uneasy hours, and there is no Remedy so easy as Books, which if they do not give chearfullness at least restore quiet to the most trouble'd Mind. Those that fly to Cards or Company for releife generally find they only exchange one misfortune for another.

You have so much business on your Hands I will not take you from more proper employment by a long Letter. I am (My dear child), with the warmest affection, ever your tender Mother,

                M. Wortley.

My Complements to Lord Bute and blessing to all yours.

Text W MS iii. 166–7   *Address* To the Rt Honble the Countess of

[1] In May, when Graeme returned from his fourteen months' tour of the Venetian territories, he 'prefferd a retreat to the country to dresse my raporte to the [Venetian] Senat of the Countrys I had been sent to visite, for all gos in writing betwixt us, and had I been bred to the pen in stead of the sword I should have been a much fitter General for this Republick' (to Bute, headed Valdagno, 30 Aug., and concluded Venice, 8 Sept. 1758, Bute MS).

[2] George Montagu (1737–88), Viscount Mandeville, son and heir of 3rd Duke of Manchester.

PLATE 3

Sir James and Lady Frances Steuart
From paintings by Meyer of Tübingen, [1761]

Bute recommended to Fran: Child Esq near Temple Bar London
Angleterre par Amsterdam *Postmark* MA 18

To Lady Bute [*13 May 1758*]

It was with great Pleasure I receiv'd my dear child's
Letter of April 15th this Day, May 13. Do not imagine I
have had hard thoughts of you when I lamented your
silence. I think I know your good Heart too well to suspect
you of any unkindness to me. In your Circumstances many
unavoidable accidents may hinder your writeing, but having
not heard from you of many Months, my Fears for your
Health made me very uneasy.

I am surpriz'd I am not oftener low spirited, considering
the vexations I am expos'd to by the Folly of Murray. I
suppose he attributes to me some of the marks of Contempt
he is treated with, without remembering that he was in no
higher Esteem before I came. I confess I have receiv'd great
Civillities from some Freinds that I made here so long ago
as the Year 40, but upon my Honor have never nam'd
his Name or heard him mention'd by any noble Venetian
whatever; nor have in any shape given him the least provocation to all the low malice he has shewn me, which I have
overlook'd as below my Notice, and would not trouble you
with any part of it at present if he had not invented a new
Persecution which may be productive of ill Consequences.

Here arriv'd a few days ago Sir James Stuart with his
Lady.[1] That name was sufficient to make me fly to wait on
her. I was charm'd to find a Man of uncommon Sense and
Learning, and a Lady that without Beauty is more Aimable
than the fairest of her Sex. I offer'd them all the little good

[1] Sir James Steuart (1713–80), who
took the name of Denham in 1773, m.
(1743) Lady Frances (1723–89), da. of
5th Earl of Wemyss. Sir James, a
lawyer, was implicated in the Jacobite
rebellion of 1745, and had since then
lived first in France and then Germany.
In the spring of 1758, on account of
his ill health, they left Tübingen, where
they had settled, and travelled through
the Tyrol to Venice (Andrew Kippis,
'Memoir of Sir James Steuart Denham',
Coltness Collections 1608–1840, ed. J.
Dennistoun, 1842, pp. 295–309 *passim*).

offices in my power, and invited them to Supper,[1] upon which our wise Minister has discover'd that I am in the Interest of Popery and Slavery.[2] As he has often said the same thing of Mr. P[itt], it would give me no Mortification if I did not apprehend that his fertile imagination may support this wise Idea by such circumstances as may influence those that do not know me. It is very remarkable that after having suffer'd all the rage of that Party at Avignon for my attachment to the present reigning Family, I should be accus'd here of favouring Rebellion, when I hop'd all our Odious Divisions were forgotten.

I return you many thanks, my dear child, for your kind Intention of sending me another set of Books. I am still in your debt 9*s.* and send you enclos'd a Note on Child to pay for whatever you buy; but no more duplicates—as well as I love Nonsense, I do not desire to have it twice over in the same Words—no Translations, no Periodical papers, thô I confess some of the World entertain'd me very much, particularly Lord Chesterfield, and Hory Walpole whom I knew at Florence, but whenever I met Dodsley I wish'd him out of the World with all my Heart.[3] The Title was a very lucky one, being as you see productive of Puns World without end, which is all the Species of Wit some people can either practice or understand.

I beg you would direct the next Box to me without passing through the Hands of Smith. He makes so much merit

---

[1] Lady Frances recollected LM's extraordinary 'humanity and benevolence.... This celebrated woman, being informed of their afflicted situation, flew to them with eagerness, and, quitting all other company, made it her sole business to administer to their consolation and entertainment. . . . Her temper was warm and keen, and, wherever she conceived an attachment, she carried it to the utmost height. . . . her friendship for them partook of all the ardour of her disposition. She even entirely changed her hours of living, that she might accommodate them to those which were suitable to Sir James's state of indisposition' (Kippis, 'Memoir', pp. 309-10).

[2] On 12 May, Murray reported: 'Sir James Stewart arrived here ten days ago with his Family from Suabia. He has taken pains to induce me to receive him, but I could by no means comply with it. I don't find that he has any other call into Italy but on account of his Health, and I am told he intends to take a House in the Venetian State' (to Pitt, SP 99/67).

[3] *The World* (1753–6) was extremely popular; collected editions were published in 1756 and 1757. Walpole and Chesterfield contributed to it; Robert Dodsley (1703–64), who published it, wrote only one paper (No. 32) and was mentioned in several others (Ralph Straus, *Robert Dodsley: Poet, Publisher & Playwright*, 1910, pp. 184–99).

of giving himselfe the trouble of asking for it that I am quite weary of him, beside that he imposes on me in every thing. He has lately marry'd Murray's Sister, a Beauteous Virgin of 40, who after having refus'd all the peers in England because the Nicety of her Conscience would not permit her to give her Hand when her Heart was untouch'd, she remain'd without a Husband till the charms of that fine Gentleman Mr. Smith, who is only 82, determin'd her to change her Condition.[1] In short, they are (as Lord Orrery says of Swift and Company) an illustrious Groupe,[2] but with that I have nothing to do. I should be sorry to ruin any body or offend a Man of such strict Honor as Lord Holderness, who like a great Politi[ci]an has provided for a worthless Relation without any Expence.[3] It has long been a Maxim not to consider if a Man is fit for a Place, but if the Place is fit for him, and we see the Fruit of these Machivilan [*sic*] proceedings. All I desire is that Mr. Pit would require of this noble Minister to behave civilly to me, the contrary conduct being very disagreable. I will talk farther on this Subject in another Letter if this arrives safely. Let me have an Answer as soon as possible, and think of me as Your most affectionate Mother,

M. Wortley.

[1] Joseph Smith (*c.* 1675–1770) had been consul since 1744. His first wife (d. 1756) was Catherine Tofts, the singer; his second was Elizabeth Murray (d. 1788). Their courtship was described by her brother, John Murray, on 1 Oct. 1756: 'The Old Consul Smith, who buried his Wife about 9 Months ago, has thrown himself at my Sister's Feet, but he has not yett been able to prevail upon her' (to Holderness, Eg MS 3464, f. 275). By the spring of 1757 they were married; Robert Adam found her 'facetious, frank and of a sweet turn of behaviour' (John Fleming, *Robert Adam and His Circle*, 1962, p. 236).

[2] 'As fine a groop of friends, as have appeared since the Augustan age' (*Remarks on the Life and Writings of Swift*, 3rd ed., 1752, p. 165).

[3] Holdernesse had been appointed Secretary of State in March, and Murray as Resident in Venice in July 1754 (D.B. Horn, p. 85). Murray m. (1748) Bridget (d. 1774), da. of Sir Ralph Milbanke and Elizabeth Darcy, and widow (since 1741) of Sir Butler Cavendish Wentworth. She was first cousin to Holdernesse, to whom Murray had expressed gratitude: 'As to my Family, we all enjoy perfect Health and good Spirits. My Lady Wentworth laughs and grows fatt, my Sister the same. . . . In short, my Lord, you have putt us into so good a Pasture that if we dont Change the Soil we shall all burst.' In 1760 he expressed it more concisely: '. . . I must always look upon your Lordship as the Fountain from whence all my good Fortune springs' (1 Oct. 1756, 12 Dec. 1760, Eg MS 3464, ff. 275, 285).

My Complements to Lord Bute and blessing to all yours, who are very near my Heart.

Text W MS iii. 307–8[1]

To Sir James and Lady Frances Steuart[2] [*May 1758*]

I am in great pain both for your health and situation, and wish you would permit me to be of any service to you. I know what it is to be without servants in a strange country, and how far people are imposed on that bear the name of English and heretics into the bargain; the folly of British boys and stupidity or knavery of governors have gained us the glorious title of Golden Asses all over Italy. I never was in the Padua Locanda, but except they are more virtuous than any I ever met with, you will be very ill served and very well robbed.

Here is a fellow recommended to me by Baron [Talman],[3] who says he will answer for his honesty and capacity: he can serve as cook, valet de chambre, purveyor and steward; he speaks no German, but is very willing to follow you and presumes he shall soon learn it. I think recommending servants almost as dangerous as making matches (which, I thank the Lord, I never engaged in). Nothing could oblige me to venture on it but your distress and the good opinion I have of the probity of Baron [Talman], who is a German man of quality I have known some time and am much obliged to. He has earnestly pressed me to make you this offer on hearing me lament the seduction of your woman.

This minute I am shown a letter of my Gastaldi (in French Concierge; I know no proper title for him in English). I can

---

[1] A copy exists, perhaps made by Lady Bute (W MS iii. 251).

[2] LM's letters to Sir James and Lady Frances were privately printed in 1818 (see above, pp. x, xi). When Lady Louisa Stuart helped prepare the 1837 edition of LM's letters, she borrowed the original manuscripts from Sir James's son, and transcribed them (Sir James Steuart the younger to [Lady Louisa

Stuart], 23 April 1827; Lady Louisa to Lord Wharncliffe, 11 Dec. 1836: Wh MS 439). Since the original letters have not been found, Lady Louisa's transcript has been used as copy text.

[3] Probably Freiherr Leopold von Talmann, who had been Imperial Ambassador to Turkey 1728–37 (*Repertorium*, ii. 87). Lady Louisa misread his name as Talmua; 1818 gives Talman.

assure you, Sir and Madam, his *stile grossier* gave me more pleasure than ever I received from the points of Voiture[1] or the puns of Swift or Pope, since my secretary[2] assured me that it contained an account of your well-being and having honoured my mansion with your presence; he brags of having done his duty in waiting on the two Milordi, and that you found the Palazzo very clean, and he hopes you took nothing ill, tho' you refused the Portantina.[3] In this manner were his Hieroglyphics explained to me, which I am forced and pleased to give faith to as I do to the translators of Hebrew, tho' I can make nothing of the figures myselfe. I have read over your book,[4] Sir James, and have a great deal to say about it tho' nothing to object, but must refer to another time, having literally six people in the room, according to their laudable custom talking all at once. I hardly know what I say, but I know what I think: that I will get to Padua as fast as I can to enjoy the best company I ever knew.

Text Wh MS 509 (transcript)[5] *End.* by *Lady Frances (transcript)* May 1758 from Venice to Padua (the 1st letter after parting with her ladyship and coming to Padua)

To Francesco Algarotti [*?May 1758*]

I receiv'd yours by General Graham with great Pleasure, but as I am destin'd never to taste Pleasure without a strong

---

[1] Vincent Voiture (1598-1648), letter-writer, famous for his preciosity.

[2] Dr. Julio Bartolomeo Moro or Mora had been LM's secretary since 1755. In her 'Italian Memoir', where she speaks of his 'carattere dolce e sincero', she credits him with having helped her to escape from Palazzi (Wh MS 510, f. 22); Gen. Graeme suspected he had done so in order to swindle her himself (to Bute, 8 Sept. 1758, Bute MS).

[3] A sedan chair.

[4] *Apologie du sentiment de monsieur le*

chevalier Newton sur l'ancienne chronologie des Grecs (1757).

[5] On her transcript Lady Louisa noted: 'The original spelling has been copied in all these letters—except in the termination *ed*, which Lady Mary always wrote thus *'d*—as refus'd, admir'd, serv'd. She spelt hon*o*r, fav*o*r, etc. in the modern way (disapproved by Dr. Johnson). It was a peculiarity of her own to say *fiveteen* for fifteen. Possibly she thought the number ought to be given at length, like *six*teen, *seven*teen, etc.' (Wh MS 509).

Dash of Mortification, I am very sorry to find my two Letters miscarry'd, and also the Copy of the Ode¹ you desir'd. Here is another, which I hope may reach you, notwithstanding the Mountains between us.² If we ever meet, the Memory of Lord Hervey shall be celebrated; his Gentle Shade will be pleas'd in Elysium with our Gratitude. I am insensible to every thing but the remembrance of those few Freinds that have been dear to me.

Text Murray MS *End. in margin by LM* Hymn to the Moon.³

To Lady Bute *29 May 1758*

May 29, Padoua

My Dear Child,

My last Letter was wrote in such a fright I do not remember one word I said, and presume you could make nothing out of it. I am now restor'd to my usual calmness of mind, and hope I was more afraid than Hurt, being assur'd (I think from good Hands) that my Civillity to a Distress'd Lady and Gentleman⁴ can no way be an Injury to you, or give any Suspicion of my being engag'd in an Interest that was allways foreign both to my Principles and Inclination. You mention the Letter you receiv'd from Mr. Law, but say nothing of his Pupil Mr. Oliver,⁵ who if his Estate be as large as I have been told, may be worthy the regard of my Grand Daughters, being a Generous, good natur'd Man, and willing to do right whenever he sees it. Mr. P[itt] is oblig'd to him, having had high words with Murray upon his Account. I did not charge him with my Letter, suspecting the carelessness incident to Youth, thô I no way mistrusted his Integrity. But as they propos'd staying

---

¹ Probably the 'Hymn to the Moon'.
² Bologna, where Algarotti lived at this time, is on the same side of the Apennines as Padua and Venice. He may, however, have been on a short visit to Pisa.

³ Algarotti printed this 'oda' as LM's, accompanied by a very flattering eulogy of her abilities (*Opere*, 1764–5, vii. 70–71; ode reprinted in LM, 1861, ii. 487).
⁴ Sir James and Lady Frances.
⁵ Not identified.

sometime in Germany, I did not send my token to you by either of them, expecting many English this Ascension; but by the Political contrivances of our great Minister I have seen few, and those in such a cool way that I did not think it proper to ask a favor. I mention'd it to Lord Mandevile and Collonel Otway who travells with him.[1] They promis'd to wait on me for it, but left the Town suddenly, on which I heard lamented the slavery the Young Nobillity were under to formal Governors, and easily guess'd the reasons for their Departure.

I am afraid you may think some imprudent behavior of mine has occasion'd all this ridiculous persecution. I can assure you I have allways treated him and his Family with the utmost Civillity, and am now retir'd to Padoua to avoid the comments that will certainly be made on his extraordinary Conduct towards me. I only desire privacy and Quiet, and am very well contented to be without Visits which oftener disturb than amuse me. My sole concern is the Design He has form'd of securing (as he calls it) my Effects immediately on my decease. If they ever fall into his Hands I am persuaded they will never arrive intire into yours, which is a very uneasy thought to, Dear child, your most affectionate Mother,

M. Wortley.

My Blessing to all yours and compliments to Lord Bute.

To Fran: Child and Comp.

Sir,

Pray pay to the Countess of Bute or order five pounds sterling and place it to the account of, Sir, Your Humble Servant,

M. Wortley.

Padoua, May 29. 1758

I fear I forgot this bill, which I intended to put in my last Letter; there can be no harm in a second.

---

[1] Francis Otway had begun his army career in 1718 as ensign, and retired in 1751 (Charles Dalton, *George the First's Army 1714–1727*, 1910–12, ii. 166). He was governor to Mandeville (see above, p. 144). On 30 May 1758 they were in Milan, a week later in Verona; on 31 Oct. they arrived in London (Otway's letters to the Duke of Manchester, Huntingdon Record Office, Box 49B, Bundle 7).

I never saw Mr. Ferguson[1] but twice, and know little of him, but as he was polite enough to ask my commands I recommended your Letter to his care.

Text W MS iii. 207–8   *Address* To The Rt Honble the Countess of Bute recommended to Fran: Child Esqr near Temple Bar London Angleterre par Amsterdam   *Postmark* IV 26

To Mme Chiara Michiel *13 June* [*1758*]

J'ai reçeû vos deux Lettres charmantes, il n'ẙ a qu'un moment; je m'empresse a vous remercier. Je suis, il y a longtemps, toute accoutumée a vos Bontez, sans qu'elles perdent rien de leur prix. Elles me parroissent toujours nouvelles et precieuses.

Vous sçavez que la maison d'Oldembourg est celle du Roi de Danmarc.[2] La Dame en question est sa parente, et souve-raine d'un petit état. Elle a prit fantaisie (il y a quelques années) d'epouser un frere Cadet du Duc de Portland.[3] Ma belle mere (qui estoit sa Sœur) m'en a parlée autrefois,[4] mais j'avoue franchement que j'ai oubliois tout ce qu'elle m'en a dit. Tout ce que je sçai, c'est une personne dont la figure et le discours vaut la peine d'etre depeint par Scuderi ou Calprenede.[5] Elle alloit porter des Lettres de l'Impera-trice a la Princesse de Modene,[6] et ensuitte chercher un Azile (disoit elle) en Suisse. Si elle n'en trouve point a son gre, elle veut retourner a Venise. Elle ajouta que toute l'Europe

[1] Not identified.

[2] Frederick V (1723–66), king since 1746.

[3] Charlotte Sophia, Countess von Aldenburg (1715–1800), m. (1733) William Bentinck (1704–74), son of 1st Earl of Portland and half-brother of Henry Bentinck (1682–1726), 1st Duke (Isenburg, iii. 8). Christian I, King of Denmark in 1448, had been Count von Oldenburg (ibid. ii. 72).

[4] LM's step-mother, the Duchess of Kingston (d. 1728), was William Bentinck's half-sister.

[5] Like Madeleine de Scudéry, Gau-thier de La Calprenède (1614–63) wrote long historical romances.

[6] Charlotte de Valois (1700–61), da. of Philip II d'Orléans, m. (1720) Francesco III (1698–1780), in 1737 Duke of Modena (Isenburg, ii. 125). After the Duchy was invaded in 1733 they separated, and she eventually moved to Paris, remaining there even after her husband's restoration in 1748 (Édouard Barthélemy, *Les Filles du Régent*, 1874, ii. 221, 226). The Empress was Maria Theresa.

estoit instruitte de ses Malheurs; je n'osois confesser mon Ignorance apres cette declaration.

Je suis tres touchée de la Maladie de la Procuratessa,[1] l'estimant infiniment pour son Merite, et sachant a quel point elle vous estes chere.

Profitez de la force de vostre Esprit (Ma belle Dame); soyez persuadée que le Ciel n'a jamais favorisée personne de tant des Graces dont vous estes ornée sans l'accompagner d'assez d'accidents facheuses pour exercer ces Talents superieurs.

Mlle Brown[2] ne s'attend pas a une visite; elle seroit honteuse de vous voir dans son petit Apartement, et se croirez trop heureuse d'estre admise chez vous. C'est une bonne personne; je suis seure que vous n'auroit jamais raison de vous repentir de l'avoir connue.

Voici des visites, qui m'oblige de vous dire precipitement que je suis toujours avec la plus forte estime et les plus tendres Sentiments (ma charmante Amie) toute a vous.

M. W. M.

Ce 13 de Juin, Padou

Text Bute MS   *Address* A S. E. La Signora Signora Chiara Michielli Bragadino   *End. by Mme Michiel* Risposto li 9 Lugo 1758

To Sir James and Lady Frances Steuart [*June 1758*]

Here is Predestination in abundance! I am not born to be happy. Perhaps nobody can be so without great allays; all philosophers, ancient and modern, agree in that sentiment. I cannot come to you for reasons I will whisper to Lady Fanny, and I dare not accept your company for fear of affecting Sir James's health, which is more precious to me than to any body, alwaies excepting sua amabilissima Consorte.

Text Wh MS 509 (transcript)   *End. by Lady Frances* from Venice or Padua when we were with her ladyship.

---

1 Mme Michiel's mother (see below, p. 286).
2 Probably Elizabeth Brown, to

whom LM paid £350 a year later (see below, p. 225).

To Lady Bute [*4 July 1758*]

My Dear Child,

I am extreamly delighted by your Letter of May 6th, which I receiv'd yesterday, July 3rd. Your pleasure in your Daughters' company is exactly what I have felt in yours, and recalls to me many tender Ideas—perhaps better forgot. You observe very justly my affection, which was confin'd to one, must be still more intense than yours, which is divided amongst so many. I cannot help being anxious for their future welfare, thô throughly convince'd of the folly of being so. Human prudence is so short sighted, it is common to see the wisest schemes disapointed, and things often take a more favorable Turn than there is any apparent reason to expect. My poor Sister Gower, I realy think, shorten'd her Life by fretting at the disagreable prospect of a numerous Family slenderly provided for, yet you see how well Fortune has dispos'd of them.[1] You may be as lucky as Lady Selina Bathurst.[2]

I wish Lady Mary's Destiny may lead her to a Young Gentleman I saw this Spring. He is Son to Judge Hervey, but takes the name of Desbouverie on inheriting a very large Estate from his Mother.[3] He will not charm at first sight, but I never saw a young Man of better understanding, with the strictest notions of Honor and Morality, and, in my opinion, a peculiar sweetness of temper.[4] Our Acquaintance was short, he being summon'd to England on the

---

[1] Of Lady Gower's five daughters still alive, Gertrude was wife of 4th Duke of Bedford, Mary of Sir Richard Wrottesly, Elizabeth of 3rd Earl Waldegrave, Evelyn of 1st Earl of Upper Ossory, and Frances of Lord John Sackville (their son became 3rd Duke of Dorset).

[2] Lady Selina Shirley (1701–77), da. of 1st Earl Ferrers, m. (after 1720) Peter Bathurst (1687–1748), brother of 1st Lord Bathurst, and bore him (besides five sons) ten daughters, of whom only one died unmarried (*Stemmata Shir-leiana*, 1841, p. 165).

[3] Christopher (d. 1786), B.A. 1755 (J. Venn, *Alumni Cantab. to 1751*, ii. 322), son of John Hervey (1696–1764), M.P. and a King's Justice in Wales. His mother was Anne (d. 1757), da. of Sir Christopher Des Bouverie (History of Parliament, *House of Commons 1754–1790*, ed. L. Namier and J. Brooke, 1964, ii. 619).

[4] Robert Adam thought him 'a very goodnatured sensible young fellow' (John Fleming, *Robert Adam and His Circle*, 1962, pp. 204, 359).

Death of his Younger Brother.[1] I am persuaded he will never marry for Money, nor even for Beauty. Your Daughter's character perfectly answers the Description of what he wish'd his Bride. Our conversation happen'd on the subject of Matrimony in his last visit, his mind being much perplex'd on that subject, supposing his Father (who is old and Infirm) had sent for him with some view of that sort.— You will laugh at the Castles I build in relation to my Grand children, and will scarce think it possible those I have never seen should so much employ my Thoughts. I can assure you that they are (next to your selfe) the Objects of my tenderest Concern, and it is not from custom but my Heart when I send them my Blessing and say that I am y⟨our⟩ most affectionate Mother.

M. Wortley

My complements to Lord Bute.

My Dear Child, I am glad you do not know (by dear bought Experience) the most despicable Enemy can do great Mischeife, and, alas, the most valuable Freind little good. Such is Humankind!

Text W MS iii. 121–2 *Address* To The Rt Honble the Countess of Bute recommended to Fran: Child Esqr near Temple Bar London Angleterre *Postmark* ⟨?⟩ 26

To Mme Chiara Michiel 5 *July* [1758]

Je craigne de vous importuner (Ma belle Dame) mais je ne sçaurois m'empecher de vous donner la Nouvelle que M. Mackensie va remplacer my Lord Bristol a Turin.[2]

[1] John Hervey, matric. 1756 (J. A. Venn, *Alumni Cantab. 1752 to 1900*, iii. 344).

[2] James Stuart Mackensie, Bute's brother, was very fondly regarded by Mme Michiel and LM, who had both met him in 1740 (see ii. 217). He had been an M.P. since 1742, and through his brother's influence was appointed

Envoy Extraordinary to Savoy and Sardinia, replacing George William Hervey, 2nd Earl of Bristol. On 7 June he was to kiss hands; and Walpole sent the news to Mann in Florence: 'He is very well-bred, and you will find him an agreeable neighbour enough' (D. B. Horn, p. 125; Walpole, *Corr.* xxi. 212 and n. 14).

Je me flatte que vous en serez aussi aise que moi. Il y a longtemps qu'il soupire pour un établissement en Italie. Je fabrique la dessus des Chateaux en Espagne charmant, dont je vous ferois la Confidence quand j'aurois l'honneur de vous voir. Conservez vostre Santé, mon Aimable Amie, et je serois trop heureuse, etant a vous de tout mon Cœur.

Padoue, ce 5 de Juillet

Text Bute MS

To Wortley [*July 1758*]

I am very glad to hear you have receiv'd so much Benefit from the Bath Waters, and hope you will continue the use of them. There are some here which I take to be of the same Nature. They are much esteem'd, but having no occasion I have never tasted them.

I suppos'd the Partys stronger than ever from the behavior of our Resident, who makes great Distinctions. To say truth I was in the wrong to draw any Consequences from his Actions.

We have had few English here this Ascention, which has prevented me from sending a Token that I had prepar'd for my Daughter. I heartily pray for her Health and that of her Family, and for yours in the first place, which is the cheife wish I have on Earth.

Text W MS ii. 251   *End. by W* Ad 7 Oct. L.M. No Date   Recd in London 21 Jul. 1758 [*Summary*]

To Lady Bute *14 July* [*1758*][1]

My Dear Child,

I hope this will find you in perfect Health. I had a Letter from your Father last post dated from Newbold,[2] which

[1] In her Commonplace Book, LM wrote summaries of fifty-four of her letters from 1758 to 1761; of these, twenty-one supply the place of letters no longer surviving. Here LM fre-

quently shortens words; they are expanded in this text. The present letter is summarized in CB MS, f. 15.

[2] Newbold Verdon, Leics., where W had a house.

tells me a very agreable piece of news, that the contests of Partys so violent formerly (to the utter destruction of peace, civillity and common sense) are so happily terminated that there is nothing of that sort mention'd in good Company. I think I ought to wish you and my Grand children joy on this general pacification when I remember all the vexation I have gone through from my Youth upwards on the account of those Divisions, which touch'd me no more than the disputes between the Followers of Mahomet and Ali,[1] being allways of Opinion that Politics and Controversie were as unbecoming to our Sex as the dress of a Prize Fighter, and I would as soon have mounted Fig's Theatre[2] as have stew'd all Night in the Gallery of a Committee, as some Ladies of bright parts have done.[3]

Notwithstanding this habitual (I beleive I might say natural) Indifference, here am I involv'd in adventures as surprizing as any related in Amadis de Gaul, or even by Mr. Glanville.[4] I can assure you I should not be more surpriz'd at seeing my selfe riding in the Air on a broom stick than in the Figure of a first rate Politician.[5] You will stare to hear that your nurse[6] keeps her corner (as Lord Bolingbroke says of Misse Oglethorp)[7] in this illustrious Conspiracy. I realy think the best head of the Junto is an English Washer woman who has made her fortune with all Partys by her Complaisance in changing her religion, which gives her the merit of a new convert; and her charitable Disposition of keeping a House of fair Reception for the English Captains,

---

[1] The question of Ali's right to succeed Mohammed divided the Moslem world into its two major sects.

[2] An amphitheatre in Marylebone built by James Figg, celebrated prize-fighter.

[3] In the House of Lords in 1739 (see ii. 135–7).

[4] *Amadis de Gaul*, a sixteenth-century chivalric romance; Joseph Glanvill (1636–80) was author of *Sadducismus Triumphatus: Or, A full and plain Evidence concerning Witches and Apparitions* (1681). Among the books sent abroad to LM in 1739 was 'Glanvil on Witches' (Wh MS 135), probably

the same copy (3rd ed., 1689) still in her library (Sotheby Catalogue, 1 Aug. 1928, p. 87).

[5] The occasion for these remarks is clear from LM's summary: 'Murray's impertinence'.

[6] For an explanation of this, see below, pp. 187–8.

[7] In *A Letter to Sir William Windham* (1753) Bolingbroke described the Pretender's court in Paris in 1715: 'No sex was excluded from this ministry. Fanny Oglethorpe [reputed mistress of the Pretender] . . . kept her corner in it . . .' (*Works*, 1809, i. 53–54).

Sailors etc. that are distress'd by long sea voiages (as Sir
Sam[p]son Legend remarks in Love for Love)[1] gains her
Freinds amongst all public spirited People. The Scenes are
so comic they deserve the Pen of a Richardson to do them
Justice.

I begin to be persuaded the surest way of preserving
Reputation and haveing powerfull Protectors is being openly
Lewd and Scandalous. I will not be so censorious to take
examples from my own Sex, but you see Dr. Swift, who set
at defiance all Decency, Truth, or Reason, had a croud of
Admirers, and at their Head the virtuous and Ingenious
Earl of Orrery, the polite and learned Mr. Greville,[2] with a
number of Ladies of fine Taste and unblemish'd Characters,
while the Bishop of Salisbury (Burnet I mean), the most
Indulgent Parent, the most Generous Churchman, and the
most Zealous Assertor of the rights and Liberties of his
Country, was all his Life defam'd and vilify'd,[3] and after his
Death most barbarously calumniated for having had the
courage to write a History without Flattery.[4] I knew him in
my very early Youth, and his condescention in directing a
Girl in her studies is an Obligation I can never forget.[5]

A propos of Obligations, I hope you remember yours to
Lady Knatchbull. Her only Son is here. His father has been
dead 9 years;[6] he gave me the first news of it (so little do I
know of what passes amongst my Acquaintance). I made
him the bad complement of receiving him with Tears in my
Eyes, and told him bluntly I was extream sorry for the loss
of so good a Freind, without refflecting that it was telling
him I was sorry he was in possession of his Estate. However,
he did not seem offended but rather pleas'd at the esteem I
express'd for his Parents. I endeavor'd to repair my Blunder
by all the Civillities in my power, and was very sincere in

1 In Congreve's *Love for Love* (1695), Act III, Scene ix.

2 Fulke Greville (see above, p. 136). In his book he calls Swift a genius and a 'man of fun' (*Maxims, Characters, and Reflections*, 1756, p. 157).

3 By the Tories, including Swift (mentioned by Orrery, *Remarks on Swift*, 3rd ed., 1752, p. 138).

4 Gilbert Burnet's *History of His Own Times*, published posthumously in 1723 and 1734.

5 See i. 43–46.

6 Sir Wyndham Knatchbull, later Knatchbull-Wyndham (d. 1749), m. (1730) Catharine Harris (d. 1741) of Salisbury. Their son, 6th Baronet, was Sir Wyndham Knatchbull-Wyndham (1737–63).

saying I wish'd him well for the sake of his dead and living Relations. He appears to me to be what the Duke of K[ingston] was at Thorsby, tho more happy in his Guardians and Governor.[1] The Gentleman who is with him is a Man of Sense, and I beleive has his Pupil's Interest realy at Heart,[2] but there is so much pains taken to make him despise Instruction, I fear he will not long resist the alurements of pleasures which his Constitution cannot support.[3]

Here is great Joy on the nomination of Mr. Mackensie for Turin, his Freinds hoping to see him on his Journey. My Token for you lies dormant and is likely to do so sometime. None of the English have visited me (excepting Sir W[yndham]) or in so cold a way that it would be highly improper to ask favors of them. He is going to Rome, and it may be I may be oblig'd to wait till he returns next Ascention before I have an Opportunity of conveying it. Such is the behaviour of my loving Countrimen! In recompence I meet with much Freindship amongst the noble Venetians, perhaps the more from being no favourite of a Man they dislike. It is the peculiar Glory of Mr. Mackensie that the whole Sardinian Court rejoyce in the Expectation of his Arival, notwithstanding they have been very well pleas'd with Lord Bristol. To say truth they are the only young Men I have seen abroad that have found the secret of introduceing themselves into the best Company. All the others, now living (however dignify'd and distinguish'd) by herding together, and throwing away their Money on worthless Objects, have only acquir'd the Glorious Title of Golden Asses; and since the Birth of the Italian Drama, Goldoni has adorn'd his scenes with gli Milordi Inglese,[4] in the same manner as Moliere represented his Parisian Marquises.

If your agreable Brother-in-law is still at London, I

---

[1] For Kingston's guardians, see ii. 62; for his governor, Hickman, see above, p. 131.

[2] Louis Devismes (1720–76), Knatchbull's tutor, had been appointed chaplain to Lavinia, Duchess of Bolton, in 1754 (Lambeth Palace Archives). From 1765 until his death he was in the diplomatic service.

[3] Murray assured the Secretary of State, who had sent a letter with Devismes and Knatchbull: 'I shall take a particular Pleasure in shewing them all the Civilities in my power' (to Pitt, 7 July 1758, SP 99/67).

[4] In *La Vedova scaltra* (1748) Goldoni depicts a rich Englishman. He reflected the general opinion in Venice of the English as wealthy spendthrifts (Charles Rabany, *Carlo Goldoni*, 1896, p. 196).

desire you would wish him Joy in my Name. If it be no
trouble to him, you may take that occasion of sending me
some Books, particularly 2 small volumes lately wrote by
Mr. Horace Walpole.[1]

My Dear Child, I ask your pardon for the Intolerable
Length of this triffling Letter. You know Age is tatling,
and something should be forgiven to the sincere Affection
with which I am ever Your most affectionate Mother,

M. Wortley M.

Padoua, July 14

Do not tell your Father these foolish squabbles; it is the
only thing I would keep from his knowledge. I am appre-
hensive he should imagine some misplac'd Railery or vivacity
of mine has drawn on me these ridiculous Persecutions.
'Tis realy incredible they should be carry'd to such a height
without the least provocation.

My best Complements to Lord Bute. I think my selfe
much oblig'd to him and shall not forget it. My Blessing to
all my Grand children. I would have sent my pacquet by
Mr. Hervey [Des Bouverie] if I could have foreseen that I
should not be visited by any other. I do not doubt Sir Wyndham Knatchbull would accept of the care of it, but he is
making the Tour to Rome and Naples and does not intend
for England till next Spring.

Text W MS iii. 171–3

To Mme Chiara Michiel [*c. 15 July 1758*]

Mia Carissima Amica,

J'ai reçeû avec grand plaisir vostre chere Lettre, quoique
melé avec beaucoup d'Amertume voiant l'état de vostre
Santé. Au nom de Dieu, ma belle, ayez soin de vous; c'est
un bien public qu'une vie aussi precieuse que la vostre. Je

---

[1] *A Catalogue of the Royal and Noble
Authors of England*, published April
1758. Walpole printed only 300 copies
of this private edition; the trade edition
came out in Dec. though dated 1759
(Allen Hazen, *Bibliography of Straw-
berry Hill Press*, 1942, pp. 34–36).

viendrois vous trouver sans la crainte de vous incommoder;
la même raison me force de finir, en vous asseurant d'une
tendresse eternelle.

M. W. M.

Text Bute MS   *End. by Mme Michiel* Risposto li 23 Lugo.

To Lady Bute *29 July* [*1758*]

My Dear Child,
   I am sure you laugh at my Philosophy. I own I dare make
no more pretences to it, after appearing so much heated on a
Subject that (I agree with you) ought to seem a Triffle, but the
Idea of injuring you or offending your Father by any part
of my Conduct is so sensible a Pain, it puts an end to all
the stoicism that Time and Refflection have furnish'd me
with. I will talk no more of things disagreable.
   I am glad to hear Lady Betty Mackensie is so aimable.[1]
I have din'd with her at the Duke of Argyle's and seen her
several times, but she was then of an Age when young
Ladies think silence becomeing in the presence of their
Parents. Lady Mary, hardly past her childhood, was more
free, and I confess was my favorite in the Family.[2]
   The rejoyceing[s] in this Town for the Election of the
Pope who was ArchBishop of this City[3] are not yet over, and
have been magnificent to the last degree. The illuminations,
Fire works, and Assemblys have been finer than any known
of many years. I have had no share in them, going to Bed at
the Hour they begun. It is remarkable the present Pope has
his mother yet living at Venice; his Father dy'd only last
Winter.[4] If he follows the steps of his Predecessor, he will

---

[1] James Stuart Mackenzie's wife (see ii. 429–30).

[2] One of the sisters was Lady Mary Coke. '. . . fear of their father kept them all in silence and decorum, Lady Mary excepted' (Lady Louisa Stuart, *Selections from Her Manuscripts*, ed. J. Home, 1899, p. 26).

[3] Cardinal Carlo Rezzonico (1693–1769), Bishop of Padua, elected 6 July 1758 as Clement XIII.

[4] His father was Giambattista Rezzonico; and his mother, Vittoria (Barbarigo), died on 28 July, the day before LM wrote her letter (Ludwig von Pastor, *The History of the Popes*, transl. E. F. Peeler, 1938–53, xxxvi. 157–8).

be a great Blessing to his Dominions. I could with pleasure to my selfe enlarge on the character of the deceas'd Prelate,[1] which was as extraordinary as that of the Czar Peter, being equally superior to the prejudices of Education, but you would think me brib'd by the Civilities I receiv'd from him. I had the Honor of a most obliging message by his particular Order the post before that which brought the news of his Death.

I am not surpriz'd you are not much delighted with Lady Irwin's conversation, yet on the whole I think her better than many other Women. I am persuaded there is no blackness in her Heart. Lord Carlisle was the most intimate Freind of my Father. They were near of the same Age, and if he had not been dedicated to Retirement, would have been one of the Duke of K[ingston]'s Guardians, and I firmly beleive would have acted in a different manner from those who were intrusted, being (with all his Failings) a Man of great Honor. I was early acquainted with his Daughters, and giving way to the vanity and false pretentions of Lady Irwin, allways liv'd well with her.[2] It was possible to laugh at her, but impossible to be angry with her. I never saw any Malice in her Composition. A Court Life may have alter'd her, But when I saw her last (a few weeks before I left London) she was ⟨the⟩ same as I knew her at Castle Howard. I tire you with these old Wives' Tales, and will put an end to my dull Epistle by the sincere assurance of my being ever Your most affectionate Mother,

M. Wortley.

My complements to Lord Bute and blessing to all yours.

Padoua, July 29

I wish you would mention the Dates of your Letters. I think I have receiv'd but one of 3 that you tell me you have wrote.

I hope Mr. Mackensie intends to pass by Venice.[3]

---

[1] Benedict XIV.

[2] The daughters of Charles Howard, 3rd Earl of Carlisle, were early friends of LM's (see i. 211, n. 2). Lady Anne, widow of Viscount Irwin and of Col. Douglas, had been Lady of the Bed-chamber to the Princess of Wales since 1736. She had been inordinately proud of her appointment (HMC *Carlisle MSS*, 1897, pp. 165–6).

[3] En route to his new post at Turin.

Text W MS iii. 176–7¹   *Address* To The Rt Honble the Countess
of Bute recommended to Fran: Child Esqr near Temple Bar London
Angleterre par Amsterdam   *Postmark* AV 17

To Lady Bute *10 Aug.* [*1758*]

Aug't 10, Padoua

My Dear Child,

I receiv'd yours by Mr. Hamilton with exceeding pleasure. It brought me all the news I desire to hear, your
Father's Health and your Prosperity being all the wishes
I have on Earth. I think few people have so much reason
to bless God as your selfe, happy in the Affection of the Man
you love, happy in seeing him high in the general Esteem,

Lov'd by the Good, by the Oppressor fear'd,

happy in a numerous beautifull posterity. Mr. Hamilton
gave me such an Account of them as made me shed Tears of
Joy, mix'd with Sorrow that I cannot pertake the blessing of
seeing them round you. He says Lady Anne is the Beauty
of the Family, thô they are all agreable. May they ever continue an Honor to you and a pleasure to all that see them.

There are preparations at Venice for a Regata. It can
hardly be perform'd till the middle of next month. I shall
remove thither to see it, thô I have already seen that which
was exhibited in Complement to the Prince of Saxony.²
It is by far the finest Sight in Europe (not excepting our
own Coronations). 'Tis hardly possible to give any notion
of it by Description.

The General has shewn me a Letter from Lord Bute very
obliging to me,³ and which gives a very good Impression
both of his Heart and understanding, from the honest
resolutions and just refflections that are in it.

---

¹ Summary in CB MS, f. 15.
² In 1740 (see ii. 190–2).
³ In his letter to Bute, 8 Sept. 1758,
Graeme wrote: 'I went up to Padua two

or three days after Col. Hamilton's
arival and showd your letter to Lady
Mary, knowing it would give her
pleasure, as it realy did' (Bute MS).

My Time here is entirely imploy'd in rideing, walking and reading. I see little Company, not being of a Humour to join in their Diversions. I feel greatly the loss of Sir James Stewart and Lady Fanny, whose Conversation was equally pleasing and instructive. I do not expect to have it ever replace'd; there are not many such Couples. One of my best Freinds at Venice I beleive your Father remembers. It is Signor Antonio Mocenigo,[1] Widower of that celebrated Beauty the Procuratessa Mocenigo.[2] He is 82, in perfect Health and Spirits, his Eloquence much admir'd in the Senate, where he has great weight. He still retains a degree of that Figure which once made him esteem'd one of the Handsomest Men in the Republic. I am particularly oblig'd to him and proud of being admitted into the number of 7 or 8 select Freinds, near his own age, who pass the Evenings with him.

God bless you (my Dear Child) and all yours. Pray make ⟨my co⟩mplements to Lord Bute and return him thanks for the kind manner in which he has mention'd me to ⟨the⟩ General. I am ever your most affectionate Mother,

M. W. Montagu.

Text W MS iii. 189–90   *Address* To The Rt Honble the Countess of Bute recommended to Fran: Child Esqr near Temple Bar London Angleterre par Amsterdam   *Postmark* AV 28

To Mme Chiara Michiel *11 Aug.* [*1758*]

Je ne sçaurois vous exprimer (ma Belle Dame) a quel point je suis touchée par la relation que vous me faittes de vos Souffrances, mais au nom de nostre Amitie, ne laissez pas abaisser vostre Courage. Lutez contre les travers de la fortune; c'est digne de vostre Esprit de vaincre ces obstacles

[1] Antonio (Alvise V) Mocenigo (1672–1763).

[2] Lucrezia, da. of Girolamo Basadonna and widow of Gerolamo Mocenigo, m. (1714) Antonio Mocenigo (Archivio di Stato, Venice). LM owned a portrait miniature of her (see below, pp. 174–5).

qu'empoisonnent vostre vie. Croiez moi, vous avez un temperament admirable, capable de resister a tout; mais il faut l'aider par vostre raison. Riez des sottisses que vous voyez, et ne vous laisser pas entrainer par des Idées noirs qui se fortifiront si vous ne les detruisez en leur naissance. Je vous donne des Leçons que je mets tous les jours en pratique, et m'en trouve bien. M. Mackensie est sans doute parti de Londres. Je craigne qu'il prends la route de la Suisse, et nous ne le verrons pas a Venise.[1]

Je vous suis tres obligée (mia Carissima) d'avoir entrepris ma defense; si je devine la personne contre qui vous avez disputée, elle doit (moins qu'une autre) justifier Palazzi. Il est Menteur, ou elle est——ce que se nomme point.[2]

Il est vraie, chere amie, le monde est un vilain chose; il faut pourtant s'y accomoder. Nous y sommes, et peutestre nous nous trouverons encore pis en le quittant. Banissons les regrets inutiles; cherchons les plaisirs faciles et meprisons ceux que la Fortune a éloignée de nous. Je ne m'estimerois jamais malheureuse tant que je puis me flatter d'avoir part dans un Cœur aussi precieux que le vostre; le mien est tout a vous.

M. W. M.

Padoue, ce 11 d'Août

Text Bute MS   *Address* A S. E. La Signora Signora Chiara Michielli Bragadini Venezia   *End. by Mme Michiel* Risposto li 2. 7bre

---

[1] Mackensie did not leave London until Oct., and—protected by diplomatic immunity—travelled through France (Louis Dutens, *Mémoires d'un voyageur qui se repose*, 3rd ed., 1807, i. 102).

[2] The last known facts of Count Palazzi's history clearly prove his villainy. On 5 Jan. 1760 he and his brothers were brought to trial before the Senate Council of Ten on accusations by their tenants that they had repeatedly committed violence, outrages, and homicide (Consiglio dei X, Criminal Reg. 177, cc. 63–73t, Archivio di Stato, Venice). He was convicted, and imprisoned until March 1766, when he was released through the intercession of the King of Poland (MS Cicogna 3426/III, Museo Correr, Venice).

To Mme Marie Anne du Boccage[1] [*Aug. 1758*][2]

War.

Text CB MS, f. 15 (summary)

To Lady Bute *21 Aug.* [*1758*]

I am much oblig'd to you (my dear child) for the concern
you express for me in yours of July 10th, which I receiv'd
yesterday, Aug't 20th, but I can assure you I lose very little
in not being visited by the English, Boys and Governors
being commonly (not always) the worst company in the
World. I am no otherwaies affected by it, that [*sic*] as it has
an ill Appearance in a Strange Country, thô hitherto I have
not found any bad Effect from it amongst my Venetian
Acquaintance.

I was visited two days ago by my good Freind Cavalier
Antonio Mocenigo, who came from Venice to present to me
the Elected Husband of his Brother's great Grand Daughter,
who is a noble Venetian (Signor Zeno)[3] just of Age, heir
to a large Fortune, and is one of the most agreable Figures
I ever saw: not beautifull, but has an Air of so much modesty
and good sense, I could easily beleive all the good Signor
Antonio said of him. They came to invite me to the Wedding.
I could not refuse such a distinction, but hope to find some
excuse before the Solemnity, being unwilling to throw away

---

[1] Marie Anne Le Page (1710–1802)
m. Fiquet du Boccage; she was a poet
and blue-stocking. She called on LM
in Venice in May–June 1757, and talked
with her several times. After reporting
LM's conversation, with its customary
display of paradox, Mme du Boccage
continued: 'Les caresses dont cette
Lady m'honora, finirent par m'assurer
que dix ans de trop arrêtoient son envie
de m'accompagner jusqu'à Naples
dont la situation la charme. Constantinople lui semble aussi une demeure
très agréable, pour quiconque peut se
passer de l'opéra & des Thuilleries . . .'
(*Lettres sur l'Angleterre . . . et l'Italie*
in *Recueil des œuvres*, 1762, iii. 177–8).

[2] Dated from its position among the
other summaries.

[3] Not identified.

money on fine cloaths, which are as improper for me as an embrodier'd Pall for a Coffin, but I durst not mention age before my Freind, who told me he is 86. I thought him 4 years younger. He has all his senses perfect and is as lively as a man of Thirty. It was very pleasing to see the affectionate respect of the young Man, and the fond Joy that the old one took in praising him. They would have persuaded me to return with them to Venice. I objected that my House was not ready to receive me. Signor Antonio laugh'd, and ask'd me if I did not think he could give me an Apartment (in truth it was very easy, having 5 palaces on a row on the great Canal, his own being the center, and the others inhabited by his Relations). I was reduce'd to tell a Fib (God Forgive me) and pretend a pain in my Head, promising to come to Venice before the marriage, which I realy intend. They din'd here; your Health was the first drank. You may imagine I did not fail to toast the Bride. She is yet in a Convent, but is to be immediately releas'd, and receive visits of Congratulation on the contract till the celebration of the Church Ceremony, which perhaps may not be this two months, during which time the Lover makes a daily visit, and never comes without a present, which custom (at least sometimes) adds to the impatience of the Bridegroom and very much qualifys that of the Lady.

You would find it hard to beleive a Relation of the Magnificence, not to say Extravagance, on these occasions. Indeed, it is the only one they are gui⟨lty⟩ of, their lives in general being spent in a regular handsome Oeconomy, the weddings and the creation of a Procurator being the only occasions they have of displaying their Wealth, which is very great in many Houses, particularly this of Mocenigo, of which my Freind is the present Head. I may justly call him so, giving me proofes of an attachment quite uncommon at London, and certainly disinterested, since I can no way possibly be of use to him. I could tell you some strong instances of it if I did not remember you have not time to listen to my storys; and there is scarce room on my paper to assure you I am (my dear child) your most affectionate Mother,

M. Wortley.

Complements to Lord Bute and blessing to all yours.
Padoua, Aug't 21.[1]

Text W MS iii. 76–77   *Address* To The Rt Honble the Countess of Bute recommended to Fran: Child Esqr near Temple Bar London Angleterre par Amsterdam   *Postmark* SE 11

To Mme Chiara Michiel *30 Aug.* [*1758*]

Carissima Padrona mia,

Je meure d'envie de causer avec vous. Le Diable s'en mesle; dans le moment que je me prepare pour venir à Venise, il faut que les Rives de la Riviere se rompent, et me voici Prisoniere jusqu'ils sont ajustez. Je suis seurement talonée de quelque lutin pis qu'un Vampire.

Je vous envoye les premices de mon Laboratoire; je souhaitte pourtant que vous n'en avez jamais besoin.

Padoue, ce 30 d'Août.

J'ai reçeu des compliments pour vous D'Angleterre;[2] vous n'est pas faitte pour estre oubliée.

Text Bute MS   *End. by Mme Michiel* Risposto li 2. 7bre.

To Lady Frances Steuart[3] *4 Sept.* [*1758*]

My dear Lady Fanny,

I have been some time in pain for your silence, and at last begun to fear that either some accident had befallen you, or you had been so surfeited with my dullness at Padua you resolved not to be plagued with it when at a distance. These melancholy ideas growing strong upon me, I wrote to Mr.

---

[1] Under the date of 26 Aug. LM summarized a letter to Lady Bute, presumably this one, as 'Signor Mocenigo' (CB MS, f. 15).

[2] From Mackenzie (see above, p. 155, n. 2).

[3] LM's summary is addressed to Sir James (CB MS, f. 15).

Duff to inquire after your health.[1] I have received his answer this morning: he tells me you are both well and safely arrived at Tubingen; and I take the liberty to put you in mind of one that can never forget you and the chearful hours we have passed together. The weather favoured you according to your prayers; since that time we have had storms, tempests, pestilential blasts, and at this moment such suffocating heat the Doctor[2] is sick in bed, and nobody in health in my family excepting myselfe and my Swiss servants, who support our constitutions by hearty eating and drinking, while the poor Italians are languishing on their salads and limonade. I confess I am in high spirits, having succeeded in my endeavor to get a promise of assisting some very worthy people whom I am fond of.[3] You know I am enthusiastic in my friendships.

I also hear from all hands of my daughter's prosperity; you, Madam, that are a mother, may judge of my pleasure in her happiness, tho' I have no taste for that sort of felicity. I could never endure with tolerable patience the austerities of a court life. I was saying every day from my heart (while I was condemned to it), 'the things that I would do, those do I not, and the things I would not do, those do I daily';[4] and I had rather be a Sister of Saint Clara[5] than Lady of the Bedchamber to any Queen in Europe.[6] It is not age and disappointment that has given me these sentiments; you may see them in a copy of verses sent from Constantinople in my early youth to my uncle Fielding and by his (well intended) indiscretion shewn about, copies taken, and at length miserably printed.[7] I own myselfe such a rake, I

---

[1] A letter to Lady Frances from J. Duff (not identified) accompanied this letter (1818, pp. 13–14).

[2] Her secretary, Moro.

[3] LM had begun her campaign, which she pursued for the rest of her life, to assist the Steuart family by having Sir James pardoned. In 1756 Lady Frances had appealed, in vain, to the Duke of Newcastle (Add MS 32,862, ff. 287–8).

[4] LM here echoes Romans vii. 15, 19.

[5] A particularly austere order of nuns founded by St. Clare in the thirteenth century.

[6] LM had never held any Court appointment.

[7] By Anthony Hammond in *A New Miscellany of Original Poems, Translations and Imitations* (1720) as 'Verses Written in the Chiask [*sic*] at Pera overlooking Constantinople . . . By a Lady' (pp. 95–101), and identified in the table of contents as by 'Lady M. W. M.' Her uncle was William Feilding (see i. 353). In 1736 Voltaire quoted (with slight variants) three lines from the verse (*Corr.*, ed. T. Besterman, 1953-64, v. 67). It is printed in 1861, ii. 449–51.

prefer liberty to chains of diamonds, and when I hold my peace (like King David) it is pain and griefe to me.

> No fraud the Poet's sacred breast can bear,
> Mild are our manners and our hearts sincere.
> Rude and unpolished in the courtier's school,
> I loathe a knave and tremble at a fool.[1]

With this rusticity of manners I do not wonder to see my company avoided by all great men and fine ladies. I could tell your ladyship such a history of my calamities since we parted, you will be surprised to hear I have not despaired and dy'd like the sick lyon in Æsop's fables, who so pathetically crys out—Bis videor mori[2]—when he was kicked by a certain animal I will not name because it is very like a paw word. Vale.

Padoua, Sept. 4
San Massimo[3]

I desire this letter (innocent as it is) may be burnt. All my works are consecrated to the fire for fear of being put to more ignoble uses, as their betters have been before them. I beg an immediate answer.

Text Wh MS 509 (transcript)   *Address [from 1818, p. 10]* To Lady Frances Steuart, at Tubingen, in Suabia. *End. by Lady Frances* Padua Septr 7th 1758 the first letter after leaving her at Padua to go back to Tubingen.

To Sir James Steuart [*5 Sept. 1758*][4]

Sir,

On the information of Mr. Duff that you had certainly wrote, tho' I had not been so happy to receive your letter,

---

[1] The first couplet is quoted from Congreve's translation of Ovid's *Art of Love*, Book III (*Complete Works*, ed. M. Summers, 1923, iv. 106); the second is adapted from verse by George Granville (Lord Lansdown) in *Poems upon Several Occasions* (4th ed., 1726, p. 69), of which LM owned a copy (3rd ed., 1721: Sotheby Catalogue, 1 Aug. 1928,

p. 87).

[2] 'I seem to die twice': in Fable xiv, called by Roger L'Estrange 'An old Lion kicked by an Asse' (8th ed., 1738).

[3] A church in Padua; LM's house may have been in the parish.

[4] Summary dated 6 Sept. (CB MS, f. 15).

I thought (God forgive the vanity!) that perhaps I was important enough to have my letters stopped, and immediately sent you a long scrawl without head or tail, which I am afraid is scarce intelligible, if ever it arrives. This day, Sept'r 5th, I have had the pleasure of a most agreeable and obliging mark of your remembrance, but as it has no date I neither know when nor from whence it was written.

I am extremely sorry for dear Lady Fanny's disorder. I could repeat to her many wise sayings of Ancients and Moderns, which would be of as much service to her as a present of embroidered slippers to you when you have a fit of the gout. I have seen so much of hysterical complaints, tho' Heaven be praised I never felt them, I know it is an obstinate and very uneasy distemper, tho' never fatal unless when Quacks undertake to cure it. I have even observed that those who are troubled with it commonly live to old age. Lady Stair[1] is one instance; I remember her screaming and crying when Miss Primrose,[2] my selfe, and other girls were dancing 2 rooms distant. Lady Fanny has but a slight touch of this distemper: read Dr. Sydenham; you will find the analyse of that and many other diseases, with a candor I never found in any other author.[3] I confess I never had faith in any other physician, living or dead. Mr. Locke places him in the same rank with Sir Isaac Newton,[4] and the Italians call him the English Hipocrates. I own I am charmed with his taking off the reproach which you men so saucily throw on our sex, as if we alone were subject to vapours. He clearly proves that your wise honourable spleen is the same disorder and arises from the same cause; but you vile usurpers do not only engross learning, power, and authority to yourselves, but will be our superiors even in constitution

[1] Elizabeth Dundas (d. 1731), who m. (1669) the future 1st Earl of Stair.

[2] Margaret (d. 1771), da. of 1st Viscount Primrose. Her mother remarried (1708) 2nd Earl of Stair.

[3] Thomas Sydenham published his work on hysteric diseases in 1680. LM had already expressed her admiration for him to Lady Oxford (see ii. 442); and in her Commonplace Book she wrote: 'Dr. Sydenham the honestest

Author I know, recommends to avoid Knaves' (MS, f. 21).

[4] '. . . every one must not hope to be a Boyle or a Sydenham; and in an age that produces such masters as the great Huygenius and the incomparable Mr. Newton . . . it is ambition enough to be employed as an under-labourer in clearing the ground a little . . .' (*An Essay Concerning Human Understanding*, ed. A. C. Fraser, 1894, i. 14).

of mind, and fancy you are incapable of the woman's weakness of fear and tenderness. Ignorance! I could produce such examples—

> Show me that man of wit in all your roll
> Whom some one woman has not made a fool.

I beg your pardon for these verses, but I have a right to scribble all that comes at my pen's end, being in high spirits on an occasion more interesting to me than the election of Popes or Emperors. His present Holiness is not much my acquaintance, but his family have been so since my first arrival at Venice, 1740. His father dy'd only last winter, and was a very agreeable worthy man, killed by a doctor. His mother rather suffered life than enjoyed it after the death of her husband, and was little sensible of the advancement of her son, tho' I believe it made a greater impression on her than appeared, and, it may be, hastened her death, which happened a fortnight after his elevation, in the midst of the extraordinary rejoycings at Venice on that occasion. The honours bestowed on his brother,[1] the balls, [fireworks, etc. with the magnificent Embassy of congratulation]: are they not written in the daily books [vulgarly][2] called Newspapers? I resisted all invitations and am still at Padoua, where reading, writing, riding and walking find me full employment.

I accept the compliments of the fine young gentleman[3] with the joy of an old woman who does not expect to be taken notice of; pray don't tell him I am an old woman. He shall be my toast from this forward, and (provided he never sees me as long as he lives) I may be his. A propos of toasting, upon my honour I have not tasted a drop of punch since we parted. I cannot bear the sight of it; it would recall too tender ideas, and I should be quarrelling with Fortune for our separation, when I ought to thank her divinity for having brought us together. I could tell a long story of Princes and Potentates, but I am so little versed in State affairs I will not so much as answer your ensnaring question concerning the Jesuits, which is meddling at once with Church and State.

[1] For Clement XIII, see above, p. 161. His brother was Aurelio Rezzonico.
[2] Restored from 1818, p. 18.
[3] James Steuart (1744–1839), Sir James's only child. He attended the University of Tübingen 1757–61.

This letter is of a horrible length, and what is worse (if any worse can be) such a rhapsody of nonsense as may kill poor Lady Fanny, now she is low-spirited, tho' I am persuaded she has good nature enough to be glad to hear I am happy, which I could not be if I had not a view of seeing my friends so. As to you, Sir, I make no excuses; you are bound to have indulgence for me, as for a sister of the quill. I have heard Mr. Addison say he always listened to poets with patience, to keep up the dignity of the fraternity. Let me have an answer as soon as possible. Si valeas [*sic*], bene est; valeo.[1]

P.S. Do not be offended at the word Poet; it slip'd out unawares. I know you scorn it, tho' it has been dignify'd by Lord Sommers, Lord Godolphin, and Dr. Atterbury.[2]

Text Wh MS 509 (transcript)   *Address* A Monsieur Monsieur le Chevalier Stuart à Tubingen en Suabe   *End.* Septr 5, 1758 the 2nd to Tubingen from Padua

To Lady Bute 5 *Sept.* [*1758*]

Padoua, Sept. 5.

I wrote to you very lately[3] (my Dear child) in Answer to that Letter Mr. Hamilton brought me. He was so obliging to come on purpose from Venice to deliver it, as I beleive I told you. But I am so highly delighted with this, dated Aug't 4, giving an Account of your little Colony, I cannot help setting pen to paper to tell you the melancholy joy I had in reading it. You would have laugh'd to see the old Fool weep over it.

I now find that Age, when it does not harden the Heart and

---

[1] 'If you're well, that's good; I'm well': very commonly used at the beginning of letters by Cicero and others.

[2] John Somers (1651–1716), 1st Baron, Lord Chancellor of England, wrote verse on classical themes (Walpole, *Cat. of Royal and Noble Authors* in *Works*, 1798, i. 432–3); Sidney Godolphin (1645–1712), 1st Earl, politician and statesman, wrote three fables in verse; and Bishop Atterbury wrote Latin verse.

[3] On 10 Aug. [1758].

sower the Temper, naturally returns to the milky disposition
of Infancy. Time has the same Effect on the mind as on the
Face; the predominant Passion and the strongest Feature
become more Conspicuous from the others' retiring. The
various views of Life are abandonn'd from want of Abillity
to persue them, as the fine Complexion is lost in wrinkles;
but as surely as a large Nose grows larger and a wide mouth
wider, the tender child in your Nursery will be a tender old
Woman, thô perhaps reason may have restrain'd the Appearance of it, till the mind relax'd is no longer capable of
concealing its weakness. For weakness it is to indulge any
attachment at a Period of Life when we are sure to part with
Life it selfe at a very short warning; according to the good
English Proverb, young people may die, but old must. You
see I am very industrious in finding comfort to my selfe in
my Exile, and to guard as long as I can against the peevishness which makes age miserable in its selfe and contemptible
to others. 'Tis surprizing to me that with the most inoffen-
sive Conduct I should meet Enemys, when I cannot be envy'd
for any thing, and have pretentions to nothing.

Is it possible the old Colonel Duncomb I knew should
be Lord Feversham and marry'd to a young Wife?[1] As to
Lord Ranelagh, I confess it must be a very bitter draught
to submit to take his Name, but his Lady has had a short
Purgatory and now enjoys Affluence with a Man she likes
and who, I am told, is a Man of Merit, which I suppose
she thinks preferable to Lady Selina's Nursery.[2]

Here are no old people in this country, neither in Dress
or Galantry. I know only my Freind Antonio who is true to
the Memory of his Ador'd Lady.[3] Her picture is allways in
his sight and he talks of her in the Style of Pastor Fido.[4] I
beleive I owe his favor to having shewn him her Miniature

---

[1] Anthony Duncombe (*c.* 1695–
1763), cr. Lord Feversham (1747),
a widower in 1755, m. (Nov. 1756)
Frances, da. of Peter Bathurst. She
died almost exactly a year later, and
he m. (10 Aug. 1758) Anne (1736–
95), da. of Sir Thomas Hales.

[2] Arthur Cole (*c.* 1669–1754), 1st
Baron Ranelagh, a widower in 1746,
m. (1748) Selina (1721–81), another da.

of Peter Bathurst and Lady Selina
Shirley. She remarried (1755) Sir John
Elwill (d. 1778). In 1738 Ranelagh had
bought from the Duke of Kingston the
Evelyn estate at West Dean, Wilts.,
where LM had passed her childhood
(Eg MS 3660A).

[3] See above, p. 164.

[4] As a girl LM had quoted from this
pastoral play by Guarini (i. 49).

by Rosalba[1] which I bought at London; perhaps you remember it in my little collection.[2] He is realy a Man of Worth and sense. Hearing it reported (I need not say by whom) that my retirement was owing to having lost all my money at play at Avignon, he sent privately for my cheife Servant and desir'd him to tell him naturally if I was in any distress, and not only offer'd, but press'd him to lay 3,000 sequins on my Toilet. I don't beleive I could borrow that Sumn without good Security amongst my great Relations. I thank God I had no occasion to make use of this Generosity, but I am sure you will agree with me that I ought never to forget the obligation. I could give some other Instances in which he has shewn his Freindship in protecting me from mortifications invented by those that ought to have assisted me, but tis a long tiresome story.

You will be surpriz'd to hear the General does not yet know these circumstances. He arriv'd at Venice[3] but few days before I left it, and promising me to come to Padoua at the Fair,[4] I thought I should have time sufficient to tell him my History. Indeed, I was in hopes he would have accepted my Invitation of lodging in my House, but his multiplicity of Affairs hinder'd him from coming at all; and tis only a few days since that he made me a visit, in Company with Mr. Hamilton, before whom I did not think it proper to speak my Complaints. They are now gone to drink the waters at Vicenza. When they return, I intend removing to Venice, and then shall relate my Greivances, which I have more reason to do than ever. I have tir'd you with this disagreable Subject. I will release you and please my selfe in repeating the assurance of my being ever (while I have a Being) your most affectionate Mother.

M. Wortley

My Dear Child, do not think of reverseing Nature by making me presents. I would send you all my Jewells and my Toilet if I knew how to convey them, thô they are in

---

1 Rosalba Carriera (1675–1757), famous woman painter.

2 The miniature may be the portrait of an Italianate lady clearly not LM, on vellum, inscribed 'Lady Wortley Montague by Rosalba' (Daphne Foskett, *British Portrait Miniatures*, 1963, p. 93 and plate 70).

3 In May (see above, p. 144).

4 Fiera della Santa, 13 June.

some measure necessary in this country, where it would be (perhaps) reported I had pawn'd them if they did not sometimes make their appearance.[1] I know not how to send commissions for things I never saw; nothing of price I would have. As I would not new furnish an Inn I was on the point of leaving, such is this world to me. Thô china is in such high Estimation here I have sometimes an Inclination to desire your Father to send me the 2 large Jars that stood in the Windows in Cavendish Square. I am sure he don't value them and beleive they would be of no use to you. I bought them at an Auction for 2 Guineas before the Duke of Argyle's example had made all china (more or less) Fashionable. My complements to Lord Bute and blessing to our Dear Children.

Text W MS iii. 150–1[2]

To Mme Chiara Michiel 7 *Sept.* [*1758*]

Je vous jure (ma chere Amie) que vostre Lettre m'a percée l'ame. Prenez Courage; il est impossible d'avoir l'esprit aussi vif que vous l'avez, sans un fonds de vigeur capable de vaincre toutes les maladies; vous n'est pas d'Age a succomber. Ayez soin de vous, pour la Consolation de vos Amis. Le premier jour que les chemins sont passable, je coure vous embrasser, étant toute a vous.

M. W. M.

Padoue, Sept. 7.

Vous brillez de toutes les façons, mais vous rencherissez trop sur la reconnoisance. Plût a Dieu que je pourrois vous rendre quelque service essentielle.

Text Bute MS

[1] Graeme reported to Bute: 'I saw her jwels once befor I went to Dalmatia etc. and to me they did not apear worth two thousand pounds. Mr. Smith the Consul, who had seen them since, assures me they are not worth 1,500. She talks no more to me of sending them over. . . .' (8 Sept. 1758, Bute MS). Later in the year (31 Dec.) Graeme amended his estimate: 'I belive I under valued her juels in my last by about five hundred pounds besides her plate and trinkets' (ibid.).

[2] Summary in CB MS, f. 15.

To Lady Bute [*16 Sept. 1758*]

I have this minute, Sept. 16, had the pleasure of yours of Aug't 28. I had yours that came by Mr. Pitt's Packet some days ago. I can easily account for the Delay, but of that another time. I hope you have receiv'd mine in which I gave you an account of the agreable visit I had from General Graham and Mr. Hamilton. I cannot recapitulate any thing, having scarce time to write a few lines if I would have my Letter go this post, which you say is necessary if I would have any thing come by Mr. Mackensie.[1] I beg you would make him my very sincere Complements. I wrote him a Congratulation on his marriage, to which I never had any Answer. Perhaps it never went, being then at Avignon[2] and my Letters often stopp'd by the profound she and He statesmen of that Town, who are perhaps to this Day decyphering to discover what can never be found, having never medled where I had no vocation.

I would give as little trouble as possible, but since the occasion is so fair, perhaps Mr. Mackensie can order to be put up with his china a few dishes in the shape of leaves, a salad dish, and a dozen of plates of English china, and any other new fashion'd Triffle. I beg you to send the Price, which shall be immediately transmitted. My dear Child, I am highly sensible of your Attention to what may amuse an old decaid Parent, who has no wish on Earth but ⟨in⟩ regard to you, being with a warm Heart your most affectionate Mother,

M. Wortley.

My complements and thanks to Lord Bute, with a hearty blessing to all yours.

I set out for Venice to morrow, cheiffly to see a very deserving Freind of Mr. Mackensie, Signora Chiara Michielli, who has sent me a very pressing invitation. She is a Lady of the first Quality and Merit in this Country.

---

[1] Mackenzie did not receive his credentials as envoy to Turin until 13 Oct. (D. B. Horn, p. 125).

[2] Mackenzie had actually married in 1749, three years after LM left Avignon.

Our Freindship is now 18 years old, and has never been discontinu'd.

Padoua.

I hope H[orace] W[alpole]'s works are amongst the Books.[1]

Text W MS iii. 292–3   *Address* To The Rt Honble the Countess of Bute recommended to Fran: Child Esqr near Temple Bar London par Amsterdam   *Postmark* oc 4

To Wortley *16 Sept.* [*1758*]

I am inform'd that your Health and sight are perfectly good, which gives me courrage to trouble you with a Letter of Congratulation on a Blessing that is equal to us both; I mean the great and good Character I hear from every body of Lord Bute. It is a Satisfaction I never hop'd, to have a Son that does Honor to his Family. I am persuaded you are of my Opinion, and had rather be related to him than to any silly Duke[2] in Christendom. Indeed, Money (however considerable the Sumn) in the hands of a Fool is as useless as if presented to a Monkey and will as surely be scatter'd in the Street. I need not quote Examples. My Daughter is also generally esteem'd, and I cannot help communicateing to you the pleasure I receive whenever I hear her commended. I am afraid my Letter is too long; this subject runs away with me.

I wish you many years continuance of the Health and Spirits I am told you now enjoy.

Padoua, Sept. 16.

Text W MS ii. 249–50   *Address* To Edwd Wortley Esqr recommended to Fran: Child Esqr near Temple Bar London Angleterre par Amsterdam   *Postmark* oc 4   *End. by W* L.M. 16 Sept. 1758. Ad 5 Jan. 1759 Recd in London 7 Oct.

---

[1] On 14 July [1758] she had asked Lady Bute to send his *Catalogue of Royal and Noble Authors*.   [2] Referring to her nephew Kingston.

To Lady Bute 3 *Oct.* [*1758*]

My Dear Child,

I am under a sort of Necessity of troubling you with an Impertinent Letter. Three fine Ladys (I should say 4 includeing the Signora Madre) set out for London a few days ago. As they have no Acquaintance there, I think it very possible (knowing their assurance) that some of them may try to make some by visiting you, perhaps in my Name. Upon my Word I never saw them except in Public and at the Resident's, who being one of their numerous passionate Admirers, oblig'd his Wife[1] to receive them. The Father's name was Wynne. Some say he had £1,200 per Annum, others £2,000. He came several years since to Venice to disipate his affliction for the loss of his Lady. He was introduc'd by his Gondolier (who are as industrious as the Drawers at London) to this Greek, who I beleive was then remarkably handsome, having still great remains of Beauty. He lik'd her well enough to take her into keeping, and had 3 daughters by her before her artifices prevail'd on him to marry her. Since that she produce'd two Boys.[2]

Mr. Wynne dy'd here leaving all his children infants. He left the Girls £1,500 each. The Mother carry'd them all to England, I suppose being told it was necessary to prove her marriage. She staid there one Year, but being tir'd of a Place where she knew no body nor one word of the Language, she return'd hither, where she has flourish'd exceedingly and receiv'd the Homage of all the young fellows in the Town, Strangers and Natives. They kept a constant assembly but had no female visitors of any Distinction. The eldest Daughter speaks English.[3] I have said enough of them to hinder your being deceiv'd by them, but should

---

[1] Lady Wentworth (see above, p. 147, n. 3).

[2] Richard Wynne of Folkingham (d. 1751), a childless widower, arrived in Venice 1735. He m. (1740) Anna Gazzini, by whom he had four daughters (one died 1750) and two sons (*The Wynne Diaries*, ed. A. Freemantle, 1935, i. 309–10).

[3] Giustiniana Wynne (b. 1737, legitimated 1745, d. 1791) became the most famous of the family, as a writer and as a mistress of Casanova (Bruno Brunelli, *Casanova Loved Her*, transl. A. McKechnie, 1929). For her marriage, see below, p. 288, n. 1.

have said much more if you had been at Cane Wood, in full Leisure to read Novels. The story deserves the Pen of my dear Smollot, who I am sorry disgraces his Talent by writeing those Stupid Romances commonly call'd History.¹ Sheabeare does yet worse and dabbles in filthy Politics instead of making more Lydias for my Entertainment.²

Lord Brudenalle³ has been here a fortnight and been several times to see me. He ⟨has⟩ a general good character and some ressemblance of ⟨the Duke of M⟩ontagu.⁴

I am sorry your Father has parted with Twictnam.⁵ I am afraid 'tis with an Intention of passing much of his Time at a Distance from London. I wish, both for his sake and yours, he was often with you.

General Graham and Collonel Hamilton (who alwaies toasts Lady Anne Stuart)⁶ din'd with me yesterday. I am ever, my Dearest Child, Your most affectionate Mother,

M. Wortley.

Venice, Oct. 3rd

My Complements to Lord Bute and blessing to all yours.

Text W MS iii. 199–200   *Address* To The Rt Honble the Countess of Bute recommended to Fran: Child Esqr near Temple Bar London par Amsterdam   *Postmark* OC 21

To Sir James and Lady Frances Steuart [*5 Oct. 1758*]

I am exceedingly delighted, my dear Lady Fanny, to hear of the recovery of your health and spirits; if my prayers

---

¹ *A Complete History of England* in 4 vols. (1757–8) by Tobias Smollett.

² John Shebbeare (1709-88); his novel *Lydia* (1755) was called by LM 'charming' (Sotheby Catalogue, 1 Aug. 1928, p. 96). In June 1758 he was tried for libellous political writings, and in Nov. was sentenced to three years' imprisonment.

³ John Brudenell (1735–70), son and heir of 4th Earl of Cardigan. For an account of his Grand Tour, see John Fleming, 'Lord Brudenell and his

Bear-Leader', *English Miscellany*, 1958, pp. 127–41.

⁴ In her summary of this letter LM wrote: '. . . a good character. Like the D. of M.' (CB MS, f. 15)—meaning the 2nd Duke of Montagu, Brudenell's maternal grandfather.

⁵ The house he had bought in 1722. On 22 July 1758 Lady Frances Shirley, W's neighbour at Twickenham, mentioned his having sold his 'pretty little house' (W MS v. 48).

⁶ Lady Bute's third daughter.

or endeavors prevail, you will never have any thing to displease you. 'Tis the height of my ambition to serve my friends, and their number is so very small I may hope to succeed without aiming at any great degree of power. My daughter shall be informed of your favorable opinion; she has already all the esteem for your Ladyship that your merit exacts from all that know you. Alas Madam! You talk at your ease of two or three years hence; I hardly extend my views to so many weeks, and cannot flatter myself with the hopes of seeing you again. I have not your satisfaction less at heart, and am persuaded that I shall be succeeded [*sic*] in my desire to serve you, when I shall no longer be capable of giving thanks for it. I am very sorry for Lord G[arlie]'s[1] loss of his brother,[2] and heartily wish 7 or 8 more might arise from his ashes.

The magnificent rejoycings for the Pope's elevation are not yet over: there was last night very fine fire-works before the Palace Rezzonico; I suppose the newspapers have given an account of the Regatta etc. You may be sure I have very little share in the night diversions, which generally begin at the hour I undress for bed. Here are few English this Carnival, and those few extremely engaged in partys of pleasure which, ten to one, they will never forget to their dying day.

Permit me, dear Madam, to address myself to Sir James. I can assure you, Sir, I am sincerely grieved at the return of your disorder. You would think me too interested if I recommended a warm climate. I confess selfe love will mix even imperceptibly in all our sentiments, yet I verily believe a northern air cannot be good either for you or Lord Marischall.[3] I am very much obliged to him for remembering a useless friend and servant; my good wishes, with a grateful sense of his civilities, always attend him. I expect with impatience the present you have promised me;[4] it

---

[1] 'Garlies, I think' (note by Lady Frances)—meaning John Stewart (1736–1806), son and heir of 6th Earl of Galloway.

[2] George, Galloway's 2nd surviving son, a lieutenant, was killed in the disastrous battle of Ticonderoga on 8 July 1758.

[3] LM had last seen him in Avignon (see ii. 333); in the service of Frederick of Prussia, he was from 1754 to 1763 Governor of Neuchatel.

[4] 'Part of the Political Oeconomy' (note, 1818 ed.), referring to Sir

would have been always agreeable but is particularly so now, when I am in a great town almost as solitary as in a desert. All my pleasures are recollections of those past. There are (I think) some refined metaphysicians that assert they are the only realitys. I agree they are highly pleasing with a dash of hope to enliven them; but in my melancholy case, when all my prospects are as bounded as those from a window against a dead wall——I will not go on in this dismal strain. I wish the post would suffer me to entertain you with some ridiculous farces exhibited by my loving countrymen; even that is denied me from prudential considerations. Nothing can hinder my being to my last moment faithfully attached to Lady F[anny] and your selfe.

Text Wh MS 509 (transcript)[1]   *Address* [*see 1818, p. 21*] A Monsieur Monsieur le Chevalier Stuart à Tubingen en Suabe   *End.* from Venice October 5 [*1818*] 1758

To Sir James Steuart *18 Oct.* [*1758*][2]

Venice, October ⟨18⟩, 1759 [*sic*]

You have made (what I did not think possible) writing to you uneasy to me. After confessing that you barbarously criticize on my letters, I have much ado to summon up courage enough to set pen to paper. Can you answer this to your conscience, to sit gravely and maliciously to examine lines written with rapidity and sent without reading over? This is worse than surprising a fine lady just sat down to her toilet. I am content to let you see my mind undressed, but I will not have you so curiously remark the defects in it. To carry on the simile, when a Beauty appears with all her graces and airs adorned for a ball, it is lawful to censure whatever you see amiss in her ornaments, but when you are

---

James's *Inquiry into the Principles of Political Economy,* not published until 1767.

[1] Summary in CB MS, f. 15.
[2] Summary dated 17 Oct. 1758 (CB MS, f. 15).

received to a friendly breakfast, 'tis downright cruelty or (something worse) ingratitude to view too nicely all the disorder you may see. I desire you would sink the critic in the friend, and never forget that I do not write to you and dear Lady Fanny from my head but from my heart.

I wish her joy on the continuance of her taste for punch, but I am sure she will agree with me that the zest of good company is very necessary to give it a flavour; to her it is a vivifying nectar, to me it would be insipid river-water, and chill the spirits it should raise, by reflecting on the chearful moments we once passed together, which can no more return. This thought is so disagreeable, I will put it as far from me as possible. My chiefe study all my life has been to lighten misfortunes and multiply pleasures as far as human nature can; when I have nothing to find in myselfe from which I can extract any kind of delight, I think on the happiness of my friends, and rejoyce in the joy with which you converse together and look on the beautiful young plant from which you may so reasonably expect honour and felicity.

In other days I think over the comic scenes that are daily exhibited on the great stage of the world for my entertainment. I am charmed with the account of the Moravians, who certainly exceed all mankind in absurdity of principles and madness of practice; yet this people walk erect and are numbered amongst rational beings. I imagined after three thousand years working at creeds and theological whimsies there remained nothing new to be invented; I see the fund is inexhaustible, and we may say of folly what Horace has said of vice—

> Ætas parentum, pejor avis, tulit
> Nos nequiores, mox daturos
> Progeniem vitiosiorem.[1]

I will not ask pardon for this quotation; it is God's mercy I did not put it into English: when one is haunted (as I am) by the Dæmon of Poesie, it must come out in one shape or another, and you will own that nobody shows it to more advantage than the author I have mentioned.

---

[1] 'Our parents' age, worse than our grandsires', has brought forth us less worthy and destined soon to yield an offspring still more wicked' (*Odes*, III. vi. 46–48; transl. Loeb Library).

Adieu Sir, read with candor, forgive what you can't excuse, in favor of the real esteem and affection with which I am Lady Fanny's and your most humble servant,

M. W. M.

Permit my compliments to Mr. Stewart.

Text Wh MS 509 (transcript)   *Address* A Monsieur, Monsieur le Chevalier Stuart a Tubingen en Suabe

To Lady Bute [*31 Oct. 1758*]

My Dear Child,

I receiv'd yours of October 2nd this day, the 31st Instant.

The Death of the two great Ladies you mention, I beleive does not occasion much sorrow. They have long been burdens (not to say nusances) on the face of the Earth.¹ I am sorry for Lord Carlisle. He was my Freind as well as Acquaintance, and a Man of uncommon Probity and good nature. I think he has shew'd it by the disposition of his Will in the favor of a Lady he had no reason to esteem. It is certainly the kindest thing he could do for her, to endeavor to save her from her own Folly, which would have probably have [*sic*] precipitately hurry'd her into a second marriage, which would most surely have reveng'd all her misdemeanors.²

I was well acquainted with Mr. Walpole at Florence³ and indeed he was particularly civil to me. I have great encourragment to ask a favor of him, if I did not know that few

¹ Anna Maria Pulteney, Countess of Bath (see ii. 122), died on 14 Sept., and the Countess of Burlington (see ii. 87) on 21 Sept. 1758. Walpole's comment was: 'You know that the wife of Bath is gone to maunder at St Peter, and before he could hobble to the gate, my Lady Burlington, cursing and blaspheming, overtook t'other Countess, and both together made such an uproar, that the cock flew up into the tree of life for safety, and St Peter himself turned the key and hid himself . . .' (*Corr.* ix. 226).

² The 4th Earl of Carlisle died on 3 Sept. 1758; for his widow, see ii. 312. In his will, after leaving her £1,000, silver, and the jewels she usually wore, he specified that if she remarried she would have only what her marriage settlement allowed and would lose custody of their children and executorship of the estate (P.C.C. Arran, f. 50). Lady Carlisle remarried in 1759, and separated from her husband a few years later.

³ In the summer of 1740.

people have so good memorys to remember so many years backwards as have past since I have seen him.[1] If he has treated the character of Queen Elizabeth with disrespect, all the Women should tear him to pieces for abusing the Glory of their Sex. Neither is it Just to put her in the list of Authors, having never publish'd any thing, thô we have Mr. Cambden's Authority that she wrote many valuable Pieces, cheiffly Greek Translations.[2] I wish all Monarchs would bestow their Leisure hours on such studys. Perhaps they would not be very usefull to Mankind, but it may ⟨be⟩ asserted for a certain Truth, their own Minds would be more improv'd than by the Amusements of Quadrille or Cavagnole.

I desire you would thank your Father for the China Jars. If they arrive safe, they will do me great Honor in this Country. The Patriarch dy'd here a few days ago.[3] He had a large Temporal Estate, and by long Life and extream parcimony has left 400 thousand sequins in his Coffers, which is inherited by two nephews, and I suppose will be disipated as scandalously as it has been accumulated. The Town is at present full of Factions for the Election of his Successor.[4] The Ladies are alwaies very active on these Occasions. I have observ'd that they ever have more Influence in Republics than Monarchy. 'Tis true a King has often a powerfull Mistriss, but she is govern'd by some Male Favorite. In Common wealths, votes are easily acquir'd by the Fair, and she who has most Beauty or Art has a great sway in a Senate.

I run on troubling you with storys very insignificant to you, and taking up your time which I am sensible is fully employ'd in matters of more Importance than my old Wives' Tales. My Dear child, God bless you and yours. I

---

[1] LM wanted a copy of Walpole's *Cat. of the Royal and Noble Authors.*

[2] Except for a note about her foibles, Walpole treated 'this great princess' with respect, and listed her many writings, including translations from Greek (*Works*, 1798, i. 266–72). William Camden, in *Annales Rerum . . . Regnante Elizabetha,* mentions only her translations from Latin (ed. T. Hearne, 1717, iii. 782–8).

[3] Alvise Foscari (1679–28 Oct. 1758),

Patriarch since 1741. The Abbé de Bernis, French Ambassador, described him as 'le meilleur et le plus saint vieillard que j'aie connu' (*Mémoires et lettres*, ed. F. Masson, 1878, i. 193).

[4] After reporting the Patriarch's death, John Murray added: 'The Senate will be assembled to elect a new Patriarch in a few Days' (to Pitt, 3 Nov. 1758, SP 99/67). Giovanni Bragadin (d. 1775) was chosen, and consecrated 27 Nov. 1758.

am, with the warmest sentiments of my Heart, your most affectionate Mother,

M. Wortley.

My Complements to Lord Bute and blessing to my Grand children.

Text W MS iii. 174–5[1]   *Address* To The Rt Honble the Countess of Bute recommended to Fran: Child Esqr near Temple Bar London Angleterre par Amsterdam   *Postmark* NO 22

To Lady Bute *8 Nov.* [*1758*]

My Dear Child,
 You are extremely good to take so much care of my triffling Commissions in the midst of so many important occupations.
 You judge very right on the subject of Mr. W[alpole]. I saw him often both at Florence and Genoa, and you may beleive I know him. I am not surp⟨riz'd⟩ at the character of poor Ch[arles] Fielding's Sons. The Epithet of Fair and Foolish belong'd to the whole Family, and as he was over persuaded to marry an ugly Woman, I suppose his offspring may have lost the Beauty and retain'd the Folly in full Bloom.[2] Collonel Otway, younger Brother to Lady Bridget's Spouse, came hither with Lord Mandevile.[3] He told me that she has a Daughter with the perfect figure of Lady Winchelsea. I wish she may meet with as good Freinds as I was to her Aunt;[4] but I won't trouble you with old storys. I have indeed my Head so full of one new one that I hardly know what I say.

[1] Summary in CB MS, f. 15.

[2] Charles Feilding (d. 1746), a lieutenant and one of the King's equerries, son of 4th Earl of Denbigh, and a cousin of LM's, m. (1737) Anne (1714–43), da. of Sir Thomas Palmer, widow of Sir Brook Bridges. Their two sons were William, who entered the army, and Charles (d. 1783), who distinguished himself in the navy (John Charnock,

Biographia Navalis, 1795, vi. 391–3).

[3] Lady Bridget Feilding, da. of 4th Earl of Denbigh, m. James Otway, Colonel of the 9th Regiment of Foot. For Mandeville and the younger Colonel Otway, see above, p. 151.

[4] Miss Otway's aunt was Lady Frances Feilding (d. 1734), 1st wife of 8th Earl of Winchilsea. For LM's high opinion of her, see ii. 74.

I am advis'd to tell it you, thô I had resolv'd not to do it.
I leave it to your prudence to act as you think proper.
Commonly speaking, silence and neglect is the best Answer
to defamation, but this is a case so peculiar that I am persuaded it never happen'd to any one but my selfe.

Some few months before Lord W. Hamilton marry'd[1]
there appear'd a foolish Song said to be wrote by a Poetical
Great Lady who I realy think was the character of Lady
Arabella in the Female Quixote (without the Beauty).[2] You
may imagine such a conduct at Court made her superlatively
ridiculous. Lady Delawar, a Woman of great merit with
whom I liv'd in much Intimacy, shew'd this fine performance
to me.[3] We were very merry in supposing what Answer
Lord William would make to these passionate addresses.
She begg'd me to say something for a poor man who had
nothing to say for himselfe. I wrote extempore on the back
of the Song some stanzas that went perfectly well to the
Tune. She promis'd they should never appear as mine, and
faithfully kept her word. By what accident they have fallen
into the hands of that thing Dodsley I know not, but he has
printed them as address'd by me to a very contemptible
Puppy, and my own words as his Answer.[4]

I do not beleive either Job or Socrates ever had such a
provocation. You will tell me it cannot hurt me with any
Acquaintance I ever had. It is true, but 'tis an excellent
piece of Scandal for the same sort of people[5] that propagate
with Success that your Nurse left her estate, Husband, and
Family to go with me to England, and then I turn'd her to
starve after defrauding her of God knows what. I thank God

[1] Lord William Hamilton m. (May
1733) the future Lady Vane, who
describes him in rapturous terms early
in her 'Memoirs of a Lady of Quality'
(see above, pp. 2–3).

[2] Frances (1699–1754), da. of Henry
Thynne, m. (1715) Earl of Hertford,
later 7th Duke of Somerset. In *The
Female Quixote* by Charlotte Lennox,
Arabella lives in a fantasy world derived
from her reading of romances, and
imagines every man she meets is in love
with her.

[3] For Lady De La Warr, see ii. 113.

[4] The poem in LM's own album is
entitled 'Answered (Song by the Countess of Hartfort) by Me. M. W. M.'
(Harrowby MS, vol. 255). Robert
Dodsley included it in his *Collection of
Poems*, vol. vi (published in March
1758), entitled 'Lady Mary W***, to
Sir W[illiam] Y[onge]', and under it
'Sir W***** Y*****'s Answer' (pp. 230–
1). LM had known Sir William Yonge
(d. 1755), the Whig politician. The poem
is printed among her verse (1861,
ii. 477) with four lines omitted.

[5] John Murray and his 'Court'.

Witches are out of Fashion, or I should expect to have it depos'd by several credible wittnesses that I had been seen flying through the Air on a broomstick etc.

I am realy sick with vexation, but ever your most affectionate Mother.

M. Wortley

Nov. 8, Venice

Text W MS iii. 144–5[1] *Address* To The Rt Honble the Countess of Bute recommended to Fran: Child Esqr near Temple Bar London Angleterre par Amsterdam *Postmark* NO 27

To Sir James Steuart [*14 Nov. 1758*][2]

This letter will be solely to you, and I desire you would not communicate it to Lady Fanny. She is the best woman in the world, and I would by no means make her uneasy; but there will be such strange things in it that the Talmud or the Revelations are not half so mysterious. What these prodigys portend, God knows; but I never should have suspected halfe the wonders I see before my eyes, and am convinced of the necessity of the repeal of the Witch-act (as it is commonly called),[3] I mean, to speak correctly, the tacit permission given to Witches, so scandalous to all good Christians, tho' I tremble to think of it for my own interests. It is certain the British islands have allwaies been strangely addicted to this diabolical intercourse, of which I dare swear you know many instances;[4] but since this public encouragement given to it, I am afraid there will not be an old woman in the nation intirely free from suspicion. The Devil rages

[1] Brief summary in CB MS, f. 15.

[2] Date from (brief) summary (CB MS, f. 15).

[3] The 'Witch Act'—milder than the previous one under James I—punished persons convicted of witchcraft and conjuration with one year's imprison-

ment, and standing in the pillory (Giles Jacob, *New Law-Dict.*, 1739, *sub* Conjuration).

[4] Sir James was interested in the supernatural ('Memoirs of Sir James and Lady Frances Steuart,' *Original Letters*, 1818, pp. 95–96, 124).

more powerfully than ever: you will believe me when I
assure you the great and learned English minister is turned
Methodist, several duels have been fought in the Place of
Saint Marc for the charms of his excellent lady, and I have
been seen flying in the air in the figure of Julian Cox, whose
history is related with so much candour and truth by the
pious pen of Joseph Glanville, chaplain to King Charles.[1]
I know you young rakes make a jest of all those things,[2]
but I think no good body can doubt of a relation so well
attested. She was about 70 years old (very near my age), and
the whole sworn to before Judge Archer,[3] 1663: very well
worth reading but rather too long for a letter.

You know (wretch that I am), 'tis one of my wicked
maxims to make the best of a bad bargain; and I have said
publicly that every period of life has its privileges, and that
even the most despicable creatures alive may find some pleasures. Now observe this comment: who are the most despicable creatures? Certainly, Old women. What pleasure can
an old woman take?—Only Witchcraft. I think this argument as clear as any of the devout Bishop of Cloyne's[4]
metaphysics; this being decided in a full congregation of
saints, only such atheists as you and Lady Fanny can deny it.
I own all the facts, as many witches have done before me,
and go every night in a public manner astride upon a black
cat to a meeting where you are suspected to appear. This
last article is not sworn to, it being doubtfull in what manner
our clandestine midnight correspondance is carried on. Some
think it treasonable, others lewd (don't tell Lady Fanny),
but all agree there was something very odd and unaccoun-
table in such sudden likings. I confess, as I said before, it is
witchcraft. You won't wonder I do not sign (notwithstanding all my impudence) such dangerous truths. Who knows
the consequence? The Devil is said to desert his votaries.

P.S. Fribourg,[5] who you enquire after so kindly, is turned

---

[1] Glanvill tells the story of Julian
Cox, a woman accused of being a
witch, who was executed (*Sadducismus
Triumphatus*, ed. 1726, pp. 326–30).
He was appointed chaplain to Charles II
in 1672.

[2] A draft of the letter in LM's hand

ends here (W MS iii. 252).

[3] John Archer (1598–1682).

[4] George Berkeley (1685–1753).

[5] Jean-François Gremaud *dit* Fribourg was LM's servant. By 1761 he
had retired to Avignon, with a pension
from her (W MS iv. 231–4).

Beau Garçon and actually kept by the finest lady in Venice, Doctor Moro[1] robs on the highway, and Antonio sings at the opera. Would you desire better witchcraft?[2]

This to be continued.

Nota bene. You have dispossessed me of the real Devils who haunted me; I mean the 9 Muses.

Text Wh MS 509 (transcript)   *End. by Lady Frances* Venice where we made acquaintance with her ladyship

To Sir James and Lady Frances Steuart [*27 Nov. 1758*][3]

I flatter myself my last rhapsody has revenged me of all your criticisms and railleries (however finely spread). I defy you to decypher the true meaning, yet it is truth at the bottom; but not to teize you too much with the marvelous adventures of a town with which you are yet little acquainted and perhaps not very curious to examine, at least that part of it called—gli forastieri e ministri dei grandi——Basta——.

I read the news of the Duke of Marlbro's death with all the sentiments of a true Briton touched with the misfortunes of his country.[4] I confess the writer of the English news paper (which I have seen by making interest with the Secretary of his Excellency) has taken all laudable pains to soften the affliction of his readers, by making such a panygeric as [would] force a smile from Heraclitus himselfe; he assures us that his dowager and children have cried bitterly, and that both his sons in law and many other people of the first quality will wear mourning on this sad occasion.[5] Had

---

[1] LM's secretary.

[2] Note by Lady Louisa Stuart: 'It seems almost needless to observe that this letter is written in a spirit of jesting, or, to use a lower word, of *fun. Antonio,* or Signor Antonio Mocenigo, being mentioned elsewhere as eighty-six years of age and the head of a great Venetian family, we may conclude that what is said of the two other persons named was as ludicrously improbable as his singing at the opera. . . .'

[3] Date from summary, addressed to Sir James (CB MS, f. 15).

[4] Charles Spencer (1706–20 Oct. 1758), 3rd Duke of Marlborough, died in Germany, where he was Commander-in-Chief of the British forces.

[5] For the Dowager and their daughters, see above, p. 51. Besides his heir,

I been worthy to have been consulted by this well-pensioned author, I would have added with great truth that more sincere tears have been shed for his loss than for all the Heroes departed for this last century. God knows how many breaking tradespeople and honest scriveners and usurers are breaking their hearts for this untimely fall—

> They may be false who languish and complain,
> But they who sigh for money never feign.[1]

I beg pardon for this verse, but the subject is too elevated for prose; I dare swear there are at least 50 elegies (besides the bellman's) already presented to his wretched consort and mourning heir. The younger sons, I am sure, grieve from their souls, unless their brother will generously, I don't say promise (a promise is cold comfort), solidly settle such a provision as he is no way obliged to, and may possibly forget.

I adore the conduct of the heroic Countess;[2] her amusements are worthy the generosity of a great soul; she knows how to put men to the right use—

> Their thanks she neither asks nor needs,
> For all the favours done;
> From her Love flows, as Light proceeds
> Spontaneous from the Sun.

—If I really was so skilled in Magic as I am generally supposed, I would immediately follow her footsteps in the figure of fair Fifteen, acknowledge the errors of my past life, and beg her instructions how to behave to that tyrannical sex, who with absurd cruelty[3] first put the invaluable deposite of their precious honor in our hands, and then oblige us to prove a negative for the preservation of it. I hate

Lord George Spencer (1739–1817), the Duke left two sons: Charles (1740–1820) and Robert (1747–1831). His sons-in-law were Frederick St. John (1734–87), 2nd Viscount Bolingbroke, and Henry Herbert (1734–94), 10th Earl of Pembroke.

　[1] 'He had been . . . at law with his grandmother the Dutchess Sarah, who amongst other things contested the possession of the famous diamond-hilted sword, and to give her wrath full vent,

insisted upon pleading her own cause in the court of Chancery, which she did in these words—"Consider that sword—my Lord would have carried it to the gates of Paris.—Must I live to see the diamonds picked off one by one, and sent to the pawn-broker's?"' (Lady Louisa Stuart's note on transcript).
　[2] The summary calls her 'Countess of B'. She is not identified.
　[3] '(all cruelty is absurd)' added from 1818, p. 45.

Mankind with all the fury of an old maid (indeed most women of my age do), and have no real esteem but for those heroines who give them as good as they bring.

I have serious thoughts of coming to Tubingen this spring. I shall have the pleasure of seeing friends I truly esteem, and enjoying conversation that I both respect and love, Beside the advantage of being casually admitted in the train of Madame de *B.*, *née O.*[1] I confess I don't deserve it after the stupid English way in which I received her advances; I own my sins of omission, but am a true convert to her merit, for reasons that I believe you will think good if I am so happy to see you again.— This minute brings me a long letter from my little gentlewoman at Court. She gives me such an account of the late Duke of M[arlborough]'s affairs as takes away all doubt of his well-being in the next world. He is certainly eminently distinguished amongst the[2] babes and sucklings: to say truth I never could perceive (tho' I was well acquainted with him) that he had the least tincture of the original sin; you know that was the distinction of good and evil, of which whole crouds are entirely clear, and it has been water thrown away to christen them. I have been tempted formerly to turn Quaker on this sole argument.

I am extremely sorry for any affliction that has befallen Lord M.[3]; both he and my selfe have had disappointments enough in life to be hardened against most sensations. I own the loss of a beloved deserving friend is the hardest tryal of philosophy. But—we are soon to lose our selves, a melancholy consolation, yet not so melancholy as it may appear, to people who have more extensive views in prospect.

Dear Lady Fanny, this letter is to you both, designed to make you smile, laugh if you will; but be so just to believe me, with warm affection and sincere esteem, ever yours,

M. W. M.

N.B. You are obliged to me for the shortness of this epistle. When I write to you, I could write all day with pleasure, but I will not indulge even a pleasure at the expence of giving you trouble.

---

[1] Probably the same Countess of B.

[2] 'baptized' given in 1818.

[3] Possibly Lord Marischal, whose brother, Marshal James Keith (1696–1758), had been killed in the battle of Hochkirch on 14 Oct.

If my paper and your patience was not at an end, I would say something to Mr. Stewart.

Text Wh MS 509 (transcript)   *Address [from 1818, p. 44]* To Sir James Steuart, Tubingen, Suabia.   *End.* 4th Letter from Venice to Tubingen Novr 27 1759

To Lady Bute 5 *Dec. 1758*

My Dear Child,

I have now been two posts without answering yours of Nov. 6, having my Head too muddled to write (don't laugh at me if you can help it), but it realy has been occasion'd by the vexation arising from the Impudence of Dodsley,[1] who I never saw and never mention'd or thought of in my Life. I know you will tell me that in my Situation I ought to be as indifferent to what is said of me at London as in Pekin, But—I will talk no more on this disagreable Subject.

The fine Ladys I spoke of, I hear are at Paris and perhaps may find reasons for staying there.[2] We have lately a very agreable English Family here, a Mr. Wright,[3] many of whose relations I know and esteem in England. His Lady is Niece to Lord Westmorland.[4] She is a very pretty, sensible young Woman. The union between her and her Spouse put me in mind of yours with Lord Bute. They have been stop'd here by her Lying in, unfortunately of a Dead child, But are preparing for Rome and Naples, and from thence design to return home. I think I may recommend her Acquaintance to you as one that you will be pleas'd with and need not fear repenting. Their Conversation is the greatest pleasure I have here. I have reason to applaud their good Nature, who seem to forget I am an old Woman. The Tour

---

[1] See above, p. 187.
[2] The notorious Wynne family (see above, p. 179) had arrived in Paris at the end of Nov. (Bruno Brunelli, *Casanova Loved Her*, transl. A. McKechnie, 1929, p. 76).
[3] James Wright (d. 1803), Baronet (1772) and Resident in Venice from 1766 to 1774.
[4] Catherine (1733–1802), da. of Sir William Stapleton, was a grand-niece of both the 6th and 7th Earls of Westmorland. She later corresponded with LM.

they propose is so long you may possibly not seem [*sic*] them this two year.

I am told Mr. Mackensie is arriv'd at Turin[1] with Lady Betty. I wish heartily to see them but am afraid it is impossible; they cannot quit that Capital, and the Journey is too long for me to undertake. Neither do I desire to visit a Town where I have so many Acquaintance and have been so well receiv'd I could not decently refuse Civillitys that would draw me into a Croud, as displeasing to me at present as it would have been Delightfull at fiveteen. Indeed there is no great City so proper for the retreat of Old Age as Venice, where we have not the Embarras of a Court, no Devoirs to force us into Public, and yet (which you'l think extraordinary) we may appear there without being ridiculous. This is a privilege I do not often make use of, But am not sorry to have it in my power to hear an Opera with⟨out⟩ the Mortification of shewing a wrinkled face.

I hope you will not forget to send me the bill of loading, without which I run a risque of loseing whatever is sent by Sea. I am very fond of the Jars, which I look upon as a present from your Father. I am ever, my Dearest child, Your most Affectionate Mother,

M. Wortley.

Dec. 5, 1758

My Blessing to all yours and complements to Lord Bute.

Text W MS iii. 211–12[2]   *Address* To The Rt Honble the Countess of Bute recommended to Fran: Child Esqr near Temple Bar London Angleterre par Amsterdam   *Postmark* DE 25

To Lady Bute *31 Dec.* [*1758*]

My Dear Child,

I am very sorry for the pain you have suffer'd from Lady Jane's indisposition.[3] That Distemper is seldom fatal to

---

[1] On 14 Nov. (D. B. Horn, p. 125).
[2] Summary in CB MS, f. 15.
[3] Measles; Lady Bute also caught it

(*Letters from George III to Lord Bute 1756–1766*, ed. R. Sedgwick, 1939, p. 21, n. 3).

children or very young people; I have sometimes known
it to be so to grown Persons. I hope you take all proper care
to preserve your selfe.

The young Earl of Northampton is now at Florence, and
was here the last year. He is lively and good natur'd, with
(what is call'd) a pretty Figure.[1] I beleive he is of a humour
likely to marry the first agreable Girl he gets acquainted with
at London.[2]

I send this by a Gentleman[3] who is just return'd from a
very extraordinary Journey. I din'd with him yesterday at
General Graham's. He is a sensible Man and gives a good
account of his voiage, of which he has drawn a very exact
plan. I think Lord Bute will be entertain'd by his Conversation. Almost all Books are either deffective or Fabulous.
I have observ'd the only true Intteligence of distant Coun-
tries is to be had amongst those who have pass'd them without
the Design of publishing their Remarks. Lord Brudenalle
is still here,[4] and appears to be in a very bad state of Health,
and extreme unwilling to return to England, being appre-
hensive of the Air. I fear his Parents[5] will have the affliction
of loseing him if they resolve to keep him with them.
He seems highly dispos'd to, if not actually fallen into, a
Consumption.

We are now in the Carnival, and all (but my selfe) in
eager persuit of the pleasures of the Season. I have had a
Letter from Mr. Mackensie, who is excessively lik'd at
Turin. I cannot be persuaded to go thither, but heartily
wish I could contrive some other place to see him and Lady
Betty. I am determin'd on account of my Health to take some
little jaunt this Spring, perhaps on the side of the Tirol
which I have never seen, but hear it is an exceeding fine

---

[1] Charles Compton (1737–63) had
succeeded his uncle as 7th Earl of
Northampton on 6 Dec. 1758. To
Walpole he seemed 'to have too much
of the coldness and dignity of the
Comptons' (*Corr.* xxi. 294).

[2] Soon after he returned to England
the following spring he became engaged
to the Duke of Beaufort's sister ('rather
handsome', in Walpole's opinion), but
refused to marry her unless she had

£18,000, and 8,000 were wanting—
which her uncle nobly provided (*Corr.*
xxi. 294, 313).

[3] Not identified.

[4] See above, p. 180.

[5] George Brudenell (1712–90), later
4th Earl of Cardigan, m. (1730) Mary
(1711–75), da. of 2nd Duke of Montagu,
at whose death (1749) he took the name
of Montagu.

Country. To say truth, I am tempted by the Letters of Lady F[rances] Stewart and Sir James. I never knew People more to my taste. They reside in a little Town but two days from Padoua,[1] where it will [be] easy to find a Convenient Lodging for the Summer Months, and I am sure of being pleas'd in their Company. I have found where ever I have travell'd the pleasantest spots of Ground have been in the valleys that are encompass'd with high Mountains.—My Letter must end here or not go, the Gentleman being come to demand it; he sets out to morrow early. I am ever, my Dear child, your most affectionate Mother,

M. Wortley.

My Complements to Lord Bute, and blessing to all yours. I would send you my Token but I perceive he does not care to be charg'd with it.

Dec. 31. 1759[2]

Text W MS iii. 217–18   *Address* To The Rt Honble The Countess of Bute

To James Stuart Mackenzie *11* [*Jan. 1759*]

I am extreamly oblig'd to you for your kind Letter, tho not altogether so sanguine as your selfe in regard to our meeting. I hope you cannot doubt of my earnest Desire to see you and Lady Betty, but I doe not yet see any certainty of it. When Summer approaches I shall be inventing Schemes for that purpose.[3]

The greatest pleasure I have here is in the conversation

---

[1] Tübingen, where the Steuarts lived, was certainly more than a two-day journey.

[2] Correct year from summary (CB MS, f. 15).

[3] On 13 Jan., a few days before receiving this letter, Mackenzie wrote to his brother: 'Since I have been here I have had a letter from a friend of Ours on this side of the Alps, which I answer'd directly; I learn from a Correspondent [?Gen. Graeme] in the same quarter, that that friend intends to make us a visit here in the spring, that a Berlin is bought for the purpose and that Hamilton, who you know was lately in England, is to serve as Ecuyer on the occasion. . . .' But on 17 March he added: 'As to the visit . . . I have heard nothing of it yet from the Person in question; whether or not it will ever take place Lord knows . . .' (Bute MS).

of General Graham. We talk'd over all your Nephews and Nieces last night. I find him a little disatisfy'd with the slow proceedings of this R[epublic] in relation to Mr. Hamilton, not having yet fix'd him in a suitable Pension with the Rank of Collonel, which they offer'd him above a year ago[1] by their Resident at London.[2] The General has often assur'd me that any Prince in Europe that knew him would be glad of such an Acquisition, and that he was not ten days in the King of Prussia's army before he was offer'd a Mayorality. I can be no Judge of his military Merit; I am persuaded you will think the General's recommendation sufficient. He appears to me a lively, good natur'd young Man, with great principles of Honor and probity, joyn'd to the sincerest attachment to your Brother. He would willingly enter the King of Sardinia's service, if he can do it in the Rank he now holds. I fancy you may easily sound the Disposition of the Court on that subject. I am sure you will oblige Lord Bute by any service you can do him, my Daughter having wrote to me very much in his favor; and I know your good Heart so well, I imagine I do you a pleasure in giving you an opportunity of serving a deserving Gentleman.

I am going to pass the Evening with Signora Chiara.[3] We shall wish you with us; we never meet without recollecting many Gay Scenes.—But I forget I am now talking to a Minister and a Courtier, who has no time to listen to the old Wives' Tales of Your most faithfull and obedient Humble Servant,

                                        M. W. Montagu.

Venice, Dec. [*sic*] 11

    My complements to Lady Betty.

Text Bute MS   *Address* A S. E. Monsieur Monsieur Mackensie Ministre de S.M. Brittanique a la Cour de Turin.   *End. by Mackenzie* Lady M. W. Montagu Dated [De *struck out*] Janr. 11. 1759 recd 16. Answd Febr. 3.

1 'He putt himself up upon so high a Footing here and sett so great a Value upon his military Merritt that thô they offered him double of what they paid their other Colonels, it would not Content him . . .' (John Murray to Andrew Mitchell, Add MS 6830, f. 30).
2 The Venetian Resident in London from 1754 to 30 March 1758 was Giovanni Francesco Zon (*Repertorium,* ii. 414).
3 Mme Michiel.

To Sir James Steuart *13 Jan.* [*1759*][1]

Venice, January 13th 1761 [*sic*]

I have indulged myself some time with day-dreams of the happiness I hoped to enjoy this summer in the conversation of Lady Fanny and Sir James S[teuart]; but I hear such frightful stories of precipices and hovels during the whole journey, I begin to fear there is no such pleasure allotted me in the book of fate. The Alps were once mole-hills in my sight when they interposed between me and the slightest inclination; now age begins to freeze, and brings with it the usual train of melancholy apprehensions. Poor human-kind! We always march blindly on; the fire of youth represents to us all our wishes possible; and, that over, we fall into despondency that prevents even easy enterprises: a stove in winter, a garden in summer bounds all our desires, or at least our undertakings. If Mr. Stewart would disclose all his imaginations I dare swear he has some thoughts of emulating Alexander or Demosthenes, perhaps both; nothing seems difficult at his time of life, everything at mine. I am very unwilling, but am afraid I must submit to the confinement of my boat and my easy chair, and go no farther than they can carry me. Why are our views so extensive and our power so miserably limited? This is among the mysteries which (as you justly say) will remain ever unfolded to our shallow capacities. I am much inclined to think we are no more free agents than the queen of clubs when she victoriously takes prisoner the knave of hearts, and all our efforts (when we rebel against destiny) as weak as a card that sticks to a glove when the gamester is determined to throw it on the table. Let us then (which is the only true philosophy) be contented with our chance, and make the best of that very bad bargain of being born in this vile planet, where we may find however (God be thanked!) much to laugh at, tho' little to approve.

I confess I delight extremely in looking on men in that light. How many thousands trample under foot honor, ease

[1] Summary dated 3 Jan. 1759 (CB MS, f. 15).

and pleasure, in pursuit of ribands of certain colours, dabs of embroidery on their cloaths, and gilt wood carved behind their coaches in a particular figure! others breaking their hearts till they are distinguished by the shape and color of their hats; and, in general, all people earnestly seeking what they do not want, while they neglect the real blessings in their possession: I mean the innocent gratification of their senses, which is all we can properly call our own. For my part, I will endeavour to comfort my selfe for the cruel disappointment I find in renouncing Tubingen, by eating some fresh oysters on the table. I hope you are sitting down with dear Lady F[anny] to some admirable red partridges, which I think are the growth of that country. Adieu! Live happy, and be not unmindful of your sincere distant friend, who will remember you in the tenderest manner while there is any such faculty as memory in the machine called
M. W. Montagu.

Text Wh MS 509 (transcript)   *Address* [*from 1818, p. 57*] To Sir James Steuart, Tubingen, Suabia.

To Wortley 24 *Jan.* [*1759*]

January 24, Venice

I return you many thanks for yours of the 5th Instant.[1] I never have receiv'd any in so short a time from England. I am very sincerely, heartily glad to hear of your Health, but will not trouble you with reading a long letter, which may be uneasy to you, when I write so often and fully to our Daughter. I have not heard from her of some time. I hope her silence is not occasion'd by any Indisposition. I hear her and her Family prais'd very much by every Briton that arrives here; I need not say what Comfort I receive from it.

It is now finer weather than I ever saw in the Season (Naples excepted). The Sun shines with as much warmth as in May. I walk in my little Garden every Morning; I hope

[1] W MS i. 143.

you do the same at Bath. May you long continue a Blessing
to your Family and those who know you.

Text W MS ii. 252   *End. by W* [*Summary*] Recd in London 13 Feb.

To Lady Bute 9 *Feb.* [*1759*]

Feb. 9
My Dear Child,
    This Letter will be very short (to your Comfort), having
not time to write a long one. Last night late I receiv'd
inttelligence by a Country man of yours that a ship was now
in port intending for London. The Master,[1] a man of Credit,
who hop'd arriving there in April, having no design to stop
at any other Port, I was very glad of an opportunity of
sending you something, thô perhaps you will think it hardly
worth your acceptance. I send you the Bill of Loading
enclos'd. I wish you would be as exact in sending those of
my Books and china Jars; I neither know by whom you have
sent them, or whither you have sent them at all. I had a
Letter from your Father at Bath which gave me the satisfaction of knowing he is in good Health. That you and
yours may long continue so is the most fervent Praier of your
most affectionate Mother.

                                            M. Wortley

    I beleive I need not tell you the ⟨us⟩e of the machine
I have sent you, which they call here a scaldapiedi.[2] All the
Ladys carry them to the Opera and in their Gondolas all
Winter. I find the Fashion not only convenient but necessary for my selfe; it may not be equally so to you. At least I
fancy it will be a novelty and consequently in some measure
agreable. The loss will not be great if it has the same Fate
as Lady Augusta's play things.

Text W MS iii. 275–6   *Address* To The Rt Honble the Countess
of Bute recommended to Fran: Child Esqr near Temple Bar London
Angleterre par Amsterdam   *Postmark* FE ⟨?⟩

    [1] Capt. Munden (p. 202 below).   [2] A footwarmer.

To James Stuart Mackenzie *17 Feb.* [*1759*]

I am extreamly glad to hear of your Health, and return you many thanks for interesting your selfe in the affairs of Mr. Hamilton, which you may well imagine touch me no farther than as he is a Relation of yours. These Complements being past, you must give me leave to find fault with the formal Style of your Letter, the great number of *Ladiships* that are repeated over and over; and then you mention my calling you Minister and Courtier with an Air of Resentment, as if I had call'd you all to Naught, when, God knows, I only meant an excuse for shortening a dull Epistle. You must have a very ill Opinion both of my Heart and my Head if you fancy that I am capable of supposing any change of Title will make any in your character. You will be allwaies to me the Aimable Mr. Mackensie, however dignify'd or distinguish'd; and if you was elected Pope, I am persuaded your Freinds would find no Alteration in your Behaviour to them.

If I could only call back a Triffle of twenty years I would immediately come in person to say this and a great deal more to you, but alas-a-day, my power in this, and many other things, is far short of my Will. I must content my selfe with these distant assurances of my sincerest Freindship and Esteem.[1] I din'd yesterday Tête à tête with Signora Chiara Michielli. We toasted you with great Devotion. She is mended in her Health, and ever an Agreable Companion. We talk'd over many expedients of meeting you. I am afraid there is not so much pleasure reserv'd for, Sir, Your faithfull Humble Servant,

M. W. Montagu.

Venice, Feb. 17.

[1] On 17 March Mackenzie wrote to Bute about LM: 'I am glad You have acquainted me with Your Sentiments as to that Person's return home, because the subject may in a variety of ways be brought upon the tapis, and I shall now be so much upon my guard as to suit my language to what I know is your Inclination. . . . by what I learn from a well informed Correspondent in those parts, I fancy You need not be under great apprehension of such an Event taking place, for I am assured that the Person is much failed within these two or three last years and that at times the visible signs of dotage appear; my Correspondent has been intimately acquainted with that person these many years past, and is positive of that fact—' (Bute MS).

I desire to be remember'd by Lady Betty as her most Obedient Servant.

Text Bute MS   *Address* A Monsieur Monsieur Mackensie Ministre de S.M. Brittainique a la Cour de Turin.   *End. by Mackenzie* Lady M. W. Montagu dated Febr. 12 [*sic*]. 1759. Recd 22d. answd 24.

To Lady Bute *13 March* [*1759*]

I cannot help being uneasy (I hope unreasonably) at the silence of my Dear child, from whom I have not heard of some time. I endeavor to think either mine have miscarry'd, or some pleasurable occupation has hinder'd your writeing. I hope the triffle I sent you by Captain Munden is arriv'd. I had not time to write by him, knowing nothing of his setting out till halfe an hour before his sailing, and that accidentally, being at Mrs. Wright's, whose Lodging is in the Mouth of the Port. Another accident has inform'd me of this Gentleman (Mr. Gregory)[1] being at Venice and design-ing for England. I took the Liberty of sending to ask the favor of him to convey this Letter, which he very readily agreed to, and is now in the room to receive, leaving the Town to morrow. I beleive you will think it very odd that he has been here this fortnight without my Hearing of it, but our Politic Resident is so very ministerial that he makes it a point to hinder all commerce (as far as he can) amongst the English, excepting in his own House. I could tell you several very pleasant storys if the subject was not too low for Entertainment.

Your Description of London, January 25, gives me no Envy of the Young and Gay, who seem undistinguish'd from old Women. Cards was formerly the refuge of Age and wrinkles, and it was the mark of a Prude when a young Lady pass'd her time at Quadrille. I am very happy in Mrs. Wright's Conversation, who (notwithstanding her Youth) seems pleas'd with mine. I have some Venetian Acquaintance very agreable, and in general make a shift to slide along the

---

[1] Not identified.

Day without the necessity of paying for a seat in assemblys. This Carnival has been particularly brilliant from the promotion of Procurators and Cardinals, which are allways accompany'd with much Pageantry and very fine Balls. You will wonder to hear I have had my Share of them, but I could not well avoid the Invitations of my Freinds, and the privelege of masking made it not disagreable to me. The magnificence has been beyond any thing you ever saw. I know no people exceed the Venetians when they think it necessary to appear with Splendor. The Entry of the new Patriarch[1] made me wish extreamly that my Grand Daughters had been amongst the Spectators.—I must conclude. I have already trespass'd on Mr. Gregory's Time and Patience. If I could have foreseen this opportunity I would have had something better to send Lady Mary.

I have heard nothing from you relateing to my Books or china Jars.

Venice, March 13.

Text W MS iii. 215–16

To James Stuart Mackenzie *17 March 1759*

I beg your pardon for suspecting you of an Absurdity; I confess I ought to have known you better. You must forgive me in your turn, in consideration of a time of Life that is on the verge of Dotage. Horace will tell you that suspicion is the natural vice of Age.[2] I guard as well as I can against my Infirmitys, and may boast that I am not superstitious, peevish, or censorious; and to say truth, this is the first Symptom I have found of being grown Suspicious. I hope you will be so just to think it a proofe of the value I have for your Freindship, thô an Impertinent one. I can only make the excuse that Lady Carolina Stuart[3] would do, if she had thrown down your Snuff box: Indeed I will do so no more.

---

[1] See above, p. 185.
[2] LM probably refers to *Ars Poetica*, lines 169–76.

[3] Her granddaughter, aged nearly nine.

I am too sensible of your Hurry of Busyness to take up your time by a long dull Letter. If you have commerce with the Chevalier Osorio, with whom I was well acquainted at London, I wish you would make him my complements,[1] as also to Lady Betty, who I hope to see one time or other, if my projects are not cut short by a Trip to the other World.

Adieu, may every Happiness be yours; it is the sincere wish of your faithfull Freind and Servant.

M. W. Montagu

Venice, March 17. 1759.

Text Bute MS[2]   *Address* A S. E. Monsieur Monsieur Mackensie Ministre de S.M. Brittanique a la Cour de Turin.   *End. by Mackenzie* L. M. W. Montagu dated March 17. 1759 Recd 22d. answd April 14.

To Wilhelmina Tichborne[3] *23 March* [*1759*]

March 23

Our correspondance[4] Angelical, yet I expect reward, as other spiritual beings do also.

Text CB MS, f. 16 (summary)

To Lady Bute [*?March 1759*]

My Dear Child,

I am afraid many of my Letters or yours miscarry, having receiv'd no Answer to Questions I have ask'd over and over, which thô triffling in themselves are of Importance

---

[1] Giuseppe Osorio-Alarcon (*c.* 1697–1763) had been Sardinian Ambassador in London from 1730 to 1743 (*Repertorium*, ii. 364; Walpole, *Corr.* xvii. 186, n. 20).

[2] Summary in CB MS, f. 16.

[3] Here begins a new correspondence; LM's summaries of nine letters survive. Wilhelmina (1717–90) was daughter of Capt. William Tichborne and of Charlotte-Amelia (d. 1743), da. of 1st Viscount Molesworth, and from 1714 to 1737 Woman of the Bedchamber to

Princess, later Queen, Caroline (Archives, Windsor Castle Library).

[4] One of Miss Tichborne's letters to LM, dated 25 July 1757, is W MS iv. 258–9; printed in George Paston [E. M. Symonds], *Lady Mary Wortley Montagu and Her Times*, 1907, pp. 500–2. Part of it was conflated by Dallaway with a letter by LM (1803, v. 42–43); and Moy Thomas, in reprinting Dallaway's falsification, accuses LM of plagiary (1861, ii. 315, n. 1). Byron used the same letter for *Don Juan*, III. xviii.

to me. I have never receiv'd any account of the Books you have put up for me so long ago as Aug't 28th, nor the bill of Loading, without which I am inform'd they will not be deliver'd to me. The china Jars are highly valuable to me as your Father's present, and it will vex me very much to lose them, thô I, who am to expect (by my time of Life) to lose my selfe soon, ought to be vex'd at nothing.

I have twenty people talking round me, and would not write in this Confusion if I had not heard that the Household of the P[rince] is to be settled, and I could not forgive my negligence if I did not put you in mind of Mr. A[nderson].[1] You need not fear my troubling you with solicitations; I can assure you I think there are few people that deserve any thing.

I saw your worthy Freind General Graham last night. He is in pain for a Letter he has sent to Lord Bute by the same hand that I sent a pacquet.

I am ever, my Dear child, your most affectionate Mother,

M. Wortley.

My Complements to your Lord and blessing to all our dear children.

Text W MS iii. 305–6

To Lady Bute *11 April* [*1759*]

April 11.

My Dear Child,

I desire you would make my sincere Congratulations to the D[uke] and D[uche]ss of Portland on the happy disposal of Lady Betty, with my real wishes for her future Felicity.[2] I send no complement to her, who was too much an Infant to

---

[1] In Feb. 1759 the King began to arrange a marriage between the Prince of Wales and Princess Caroline of Brunswick-Wolfenbüttel (*Letters from George III to Lord Bute 1756–1766*, ed. R. Sedgwick, 1939, pp. 22–23); and perhaps LM hoped that the expanded Household could include her son's former tutor.

[2] Lady Elizabeth Cavendish Bentinck (1735–1825), da. of 2nd Duke of Portland, m. (22 May 1759) Thomas Thynne, 3rd Viscount Weymouth, later 1st Marquess of Bath. Thomas Gray gossiped that she was 'homely' but that her dowry was £35,000 (*Corr.*, ed. P. Toynbee and L. Whibley, 1935, ii. 619).

remember me; neither do I write to either of her Parents, to avoid giveing them the trouble of answering a stupid Letter. They have busyness enough on this occasion, and I hope they both know me enough to beleive that any Descendant from Lady Oxford (could I live so long as to see the 3rd and 4th Generation) has a right to my Desires (however insignificant my endeavors) to serve them. I once wish'd much to see Lord Titchfield, he having been the principal favorite of my ever-honnor'd Friend,[1] but as things are manag'd here, am realy glad he does not pass by Venice.

Sir Wyndham K[natchbull] and a worthy Clergyman, his Governor, are under such ridiculous persecutions meerly for their Civillities to me,[2] that I heartily pray none of my Friends or Relations may travel hither. I should be asham'd (in regard to the Venetians, who are many of them particularly obliging to me) to be slighted, and very sorry to expose those I wish well entertain'd to disagreable Treatment, either in their own persons or that of the Gentlemen who are chose by their Guardians to accompany them. You will be so astonish'd at this Account, I am afraid you should (as well you may) suspect me of Doatage. I confess it is highly incredible, yet litteral, simple Truth, without the least provocation given by Sir W[yndham], who is (as I have already told you), apart from the partiality it is natural for me to have for him, one of the most modest, well dispos'd young Men I have known abroad, and generally belov'd by all that know him. Even those that do not imitate his Sobriety applaud his Conduct and that of his Governor, whose only crime is endeavoring to preserve the Health and good Principles of his Pupil.

Your worthy Friend the General is fully sensible of the ill behavior of these great people (who fancy they represent their Patrons) and has made what remonstrances he could, which were coldly receiv'd; and instead of Reformation, an encrease of ill manners succeeded.[3] I suppose these

---

[1] Titchfield, Lady Betty's brother, had been Lady Oxford's favourite grandchild; he was abroad on the Grand Tour 1758–61 (A. S. Turberville, *Hist. of Welbeck Abbey and Its Owners*, 1938–9, ii. 37–40).

[2] See above, pp. 158–9.

[3] Graeme had told Bute: 'I do think the resident ought to show some more respect than he has done of late to a woman of her birth and country' (31 Dec. [1758], Bute MS).

deep Politicians intend to drive me out of the Town in a
pique, or more refinedly expect I should desire their recall,
being every day complaining of this odious Country and
wishing a more advantageous Situation. They do not know
me. I cannot be provok'd either to misbehave my selfe to
oblige my Enemys, or ministerially to reward those that
rail against me. I have throughout my long Life persisted in
non-compliance with Hush money. While I knew I did not
want any Excuse for my Actions, perhaps I have suffer'd by
it, yet such have ever been ⟨my⟩ Sentiments, which it may be
you will call wrong headed.

I am exceeding Glad of your Father's good Health. He
owes it to his uncommon Abstinence and Resolution. I wish
I could boast the same. I own I have too much Indulg'd my
Sedentary Humour and have been a Rake in Reading. You
will laugh at the Expression, but I think the litteral meaning of the ugly word Rake is one that follows his Pleasures
in Contradiction to his Reason. I thought mine so Innocent
I might persue them with Impunity; I now find I was mistaken, and that all excesses are (thô not equally) Blameable.
My Spirits in Company are false Fire; I have a Damp within,
⟨as⟩ from marshy Grounds frequently arise an Appearance
of Light.—I grow Spleenatic and consequently ought to
stop my Pen for fear of conveying the Infection. I would
only communicate Happiness to my Dear child, being ever
Your most affectionate Mother,

M. Wortley.

My blessing to all yours. I have sent Lady Mary a small
miniature with a Letter to you, by one Mr. Bailey,[1] an East
India Merchant. I ⟨can⟩ find no picture worthy Lord Bute,
whose humble servant I am. I hope you will remember poor
Anderson on the establishment of the Household.

Text W MS iii. 273–4[2]   *Address* To The Rt Honble the Countess
of Bute South Audley Street near Hide Park London   *End.* from her
Ladyship's most obedt hble Servt. Motteux.

---

[1] John Bailey (d. 1789) (*Gentleman's Mag.*, p. 372).   [2] Summary in CB MS, f. 16.

To Wilhelmina Tichborne *13 April* [*1759*]

April 13

The World the same in all Climates and generations, perhaps we are all of one past. Knowledge out of reach. We are condemn'd to stay below ever since the Tower of Babel.

Text CB MS, f. 16 (summary)

To Sir James Steuart *4 May* [*1759*]

Venice, May 4th

You will not be surprised, Sir, that after having promised so valuable and so agreeable a present, I am a little impatient to receive it; there is no situation in which it would not be highly welcome, but it is doubly so in a town where I am almost as solitary as in a desert. I am extremely concerned at the continuation of Lady Fanny's disorder; the juvenile dissipations of Mr. Steuart I do not put into the list of misfortunes. Application is not to be expected at his age, perhaps not to be wished; the judgement must have time to ripen, and when the gaieties of early youth are over, you will see that solidity more firm than if it had appeared prematurely. I am persuaded that you will find him turn out every thing you wish, and that he will repay the care of his education by a conduct worthy of such parents.

Here is a fashion sprung up entirely new in this part of the world: I mean Suicide.[1] A rich Parish-priest and a young Celestine monk have disposed of themselves last week in that manner without any visible reason for their precipitation. The priest indeed left a paper in his hat to signify his desire of imitating the indifference of Socrates and magnanimity of Cato; the friar swung out of the world without giving any account of his design. You see it is not in Britain alone that the Spleen spreads his dominion. I look on all

[1] According to Pompeo Molmenti, suicides were very rare (*Venice,* transl. H. F. Brown, 1908, II. ii. 200).

excursions of this kind to be owing to that distemper, which shews the necessity of seeking employment for the mind and exercise for the body; the spirits and the blood stagnate without motion.[1] You are to be envied, whose studies are not only usefull to your selfe but beneficial to mankind; even mine (good for nothing as they are) contribute to my health and serve at least to lull asleep those corroding reflections that embitter life, and wear out the frail machine in which we inhabit.

I inclose a letter from Mr. Duff in which (he tells me) he has directed in what manner I may receive your enquiry into the Principles of Political Œconomy.[2] I do not doubt enjoying great pleasure and instruction in the reading of it, tho' I want no fresh inducement to bind me ever, Sir, Your most obliged and affectionate servant,

M. W. M.

Text Wh MS 509 (transcript)   *Address* [*from 1818, p. 25*] To Sir James Steuart, Tubingen, Suabia.   *End. by Lady Frances* [*1818*] 1759

To Wortley *18 May* [*1759*]

Venice, May 18

I have receiv'd yours much sooner than any I have had of a long time. You are very much in the right to take care of your Eyes, which are certainly more precious than Life to every thinking Man. I could wish I had us'd my selfe to dictateing much earlier in Life; 'tis now hard to Learn.

This Winter has been a Wonder even in this Country. I will not say more not to offend your Sight. I always write long Letters to our Daughter, and am much delighted with her prosperity.

Text W MS ii. 253   *End. by W* Ad 29 Dec. [*Summary*] Recd at Wortley 12 July.

---

1 In her Commonplace Book LM noted a different aspect of suicide: 'Self M[urder], throwing up the Cards of a Game that must be lost' (MS, f. 7).

2 The previous autumn she had asked for it (see above, p. 181.).

To Wilhelmina Tichborne *20 May* [*1759*]

May 20

Lord Montf[or]t.¹ The E[nglish] quarrel as naturally as cocks and mastives. Lord W[alde]g[ra]ve.² I wish to see nothing in L[ondon] but her selfe and the musæum.³ It[alian] Inclinations masked as much as their faces. Fig leaves as necessary for minds as Bodys.

Text CB MS, f. 16 (summary)

To Lady Bute *22 May* [*1759*]

Venice, May 22

My Dear Child,

I am always pleas'd to hear from you but particularly so when I have any occasion of Congratulation. I sincerely wish you Joy of your Infant's having gone happily through the small Pox.

I had a Letter from your Father before he left London. He does not give so good an Account of his Spirits as you do, but I hope his Journeys will restore them. I am convince'd nothing is so conducive to Health and absolutely necessary to some Constitutions. I am not surpriz'd, as I beleive you think I ought to be, at Lord Leicester's leaving his large estate to his Lady, notwithstanding the contempt with which he always treated her, and her real Inability of mannaging it.⁴ I expect you should laugh at me for the exploded notion

---

¹ Thomas Bromley (1733–99), 2nd Baron, succeeded in 1755 after his father's suicide; he inherited debts and a ruined estate.

² James, 2nd Earl; he was soon to marry (see below, p. 213, n. 1).

³ The British Museum, established in 1753, was opened to the public in Jan. 1759.

⁴ Thomas Coke (1697–20 April 1759),

1st Earl of Leicester, m. (1718) Lady Margaret Tufton (1700–75), da. of 6th Earl of Thanet. For an example of his 'contempt', see ii. 18; but the biographer of the Coke family regarded the marriage as happy (Charles W. James, *Chief Justice Coke: His Family & Descendants at Holkham*, 1929, pp. 238, 281).

of Predestination, yet I confess I am inclin'd to be of the
Opinion that no body makes their own Marriage or their own
Will. It is what I have often said to the D[uchess] of Marlbrô when she has been telling me her last Intentions, none of
which she has perform'd, chusing Lord Ch[esterfiel]d for
her Executor, whose true Character she has many times
enlarg'd upon.[1] I could say much more to support this
Doctrine if it would not lengthen my Letter beyond a
readable size.

Building is the general weakness of old people. I have had
a twitch of it my selfe, thô certainly 'tis the highest Absurdity,
and as sure a proofe of Doatage as pink colour'd Ribands,
or even Matrimony. Nay, perhaps there is more to be said
in defence of the last, I mean in a childless old Man; he may
prefer a Boy born in his own House, thô he knows it is not
his own, to disrespectfull or worthless Nephews or Nieces.
But there is no Excuse for beginning an Edifice he can never
inhabit or probably see finish'd. The D[uches]s of Marlbrô
us'd to ridicule the vanity of it by saying one might always
live upon other people's Follies, yet you see she built the
most ridiculous House I ever saw,[2] since it realy is not habitable from the excessive damps.

So true it is, the Things that we would do, those do we
not, and the Things we would not do, those do we daily.[3] I feel
in my selfe a proofe of this assertion, being much against my
Will at Venice. Thô I own it is the only great Town where
I can properly reside, yet here I find so many vexations that
in spite of all my Philosophy and (what is more powerfull)
my Phlegm, I am oftner out of Humour than amongst my
plants and Poultry in the Country. I cannot help being concern'd at the success of iniquitous Schemes, and grieve for
oppress'd Merit. You, who see these things every day,
think me as unreasonable in making them matter of
Complaint as ⟨if I seriously⟩ lamented the change of Seasons. You should consider ⟨I have lived almost⟩ a Hermit
ten years, and the world is as new ⟨to me as to a co⟩untry

[1] Sarah, Duchess of Marlborough
(d. 1744), left to Chesterfield £20,000
and the possible reversion of valuable
property; it was notorious that she
wished to reward him for his opposition

to Walpole, whom she detested (Chesterfield, *Letters*, ed. B. Dobrée, 1932, i. 89).
[2] Blenheim Palace, the extravagant
baroque creation of Vanbrugh.
[3] Quoted by LM earlier (p. 169).

Girl transported from Wales to Cove⟨nt Garden. I⟩[1] know
I ought to think my Lot very good, that can boast of some
sincere Friends amongst Strangers.

Sir W[yndham] K[natchbull] and his Governor, Mr. De
Vismes, are at length parted. I am very sorry for them both.
I cannot help wishing well to the Young Man, who realy
has merit and would have been happy in a Companion that
sincerely lov'd him and study'd his Interest.—My Letter is
so long I am frighted at it my selfe. I never know when to
end when I write to you. Forgive it, amongst the other
Infirmitys of your affectionate Mother,

M. Wortley.

If my things are at Sea, I am afraid they are lost. Here has
been such Storms these 3 days as never were known at this
Season. I shall regret nothing so much as your Father's
present. Perhaps my Token to you is also at the bottom of
the Ocean. That I sent by Land to Lady Mary is fallen
into the French Hands, as I am told.

Text W MS iii. 182–3[2] *Address* To The Rt Honble the Countess
of Bute recommended to Fran: Child Esqr near Temple Bar London
Angleterre par Amsterdam *Postmark* IV 11

To Wilhelmina Tichborne *15 June* [*1759*]

June 15

I am at P[adua] like a Mouse in a Parmasan che⟨ese⟩.
Her Correspondance my highest pleasure, having lost almost
the taste of all others, grown unfit for L[ondon] or Paris.
Railery on the English here;[3] I wish I could send their
Pictures at length. My Theft from Mr. B. Queen, Nebuchad-
nessar. I have the Spirit of Martyrdom or contradiction.
A chaplain wanted here. My stoicism not proof to the loss
of her Letters. I will send the papers she desires.

Text CB MS, f. 16 (summary)

[1] MS torn; insertions, except the last,
from 1803, v. 79.
[2] Summary in CB MS, f. 16.
[3] Elsewhere in her Commonplace

Book, among miscellaneous jottings,
LM wrote: 'English like the Hoggs in
the Gospel', and then added: 'to Miss
Tich' (MS, f. 6).

To Lady Bute *24 June* [*1759*]

Padoua, June 24

My Dear Child,

I have this minute receiv'd yours of May 24th. I am glad
the little picture pleases Lady Mary. It is a true representation of the Summer Dishabille of the Venetian Ladies. You
have taken no Notice of the Box I sent by Captain Munden.
If it is lost I will venture nothing more at Sea.

I have had a Letter from Mr. Mackensie informing me
that he has sent my Books. I have not yet receiv'd them but
hope to have that pleasure in a short time. I could heartily
wish to see Lady Betty and your Brother in law; I fancy I
have a thousand Questions to ask in Relation to their Nephews
and Nieces. What ever touches you is important to me. I
fear I must not expect that Satisfaction; they are oblig'd
to reside at Turin, and I cannot resolve to appear in a
Court, where Old People always make an ill Figure even when
they have business there.

I am not surpriz'd at Lady Waldegrave's good Fortune;[1]
Beauty has a large Prerogative. Her Mother's[2] was the most
remarkable I have ever heard of. Being taken notice of by
Mrs. Seckar[3] (who told it me) when she was in the humble
position of siting on a Dust Cart before the Bishop's door,
that Lady had the Curiosity to call her in, meerly to see her
nearer, and assur'd me that, in all her rags and Dirt, she never
saw a more lovely Creature. Some time after, she heard she
was in the hands of a Covent Garden Milliner, who trans-
ferr'd her to Neddy W[alpole], who doated on her till the
Day of her Death.

[1] Maria Walpole (1736–1807),
illegitimate daughter of Sir Edward
(1706–84), second son of Sir Robert,
m. (15 May 1759) 2nd Earl Waldegrave. Her uncle Horace, who had
'jumbled them together', wrote: 'For
character and credit, he is the first match
in England—for beauty, I think she is'
(*Corr.* xxi. 285).

[2] Dorothy Clement (*c*. 1715–*c*. 1739),
Sir Edward's mistress, da. of a post-

master in Co. Durham; about 1730,
while working in a second-hand clothes
shop in Pall Mall, she had been taken
up by Sir Edward (Violet Biddulph,
The Three Ladies Waldegrave, [1938],
pp. 13–15; Walpole, *Corr.* ix. 13).

[3] Catherine Benson (d. 1748) m.
(1725) Thomas Secker (1693–1768),
ultimately Archbishop of Canterbury.
From 1727 to 1732 he was a prebendary
of Durham.

Lord Fordwich[1] arriv'd here three days ago. He made me a visit yesterday, and appears a well dispos'd Youth. Lord Brudenalle continues here, and seems to have no Desire of seeing his Native Land. Here are beside a large Groupe of English Gentlemen who will all disperse in a short time. General Graham has promis'd to oblige me with his Company a few Days, thô his charge finds him so much employment it may (perhaps) be impossible for him to leave Venice. I suppose you are now at Kew,[2] with all your rising Family about you. May they ever be Blessings to you. I beleive you that see them every day scarce think of them oftener than I do.

This Town is at present very full of Company. Thô the Opera is not much aplauded, I have not yet seen it, nor intend to break my rest for its sake; it begins about the Hour I go to sleep. I continue my College Hours, by which I am excluded many Fashionable Amusements. In ⟨recomp⟩ence I have better Health and Spirits than many younger Ladies, who pass their Nights at the Ridotto, and ⟨their⟩ Days in Spleen for their losses there. Play is the general Plague of Europe. I know no Corner of it entirely free from the Infection. I do not doubt the Familiarities of ⟨the⟩ Gameing Table contribute very much to that decay of Politeness of which you complain. The pouts and Quarrels that naturally rise from Disputes must put an end to all Complaisance or even good will towards one another.

I am interupted by a visit from Mr. Hamilton. He desires me to make his Complements to you and Lord Bute. I am to you both a most Affectionate Mother,

M. Wortley.

My hearty blessing to all yours.

Text W MS iii. 184–5   *Address* To The Rt Honble the Countess of Bute recommended to Fran: Child Esqr near Temple Bar London Angleterre par Amsterdam   *Postmark* IY 16

[1] George Nassau Cowper (1738–89), Viscount Fordwich, son and heir to 2nd Earl Cowper.

[2] The Prince of Wales, to whom Lord Bute was Groom of the Stole, lived at Kew during the summer.

To Sir James Steuart *19 July 1759*[1]

July 19, 1759, Padua

Your letters always give me a great deal of pleasure, but particularly this, which has relieved me from the pain I was in from your silence. I have seen the Margrave of Baden Dourlach; but I hope he has forgot he has ever seen me, being at that time in a very odd situation,[2] of which I will not give you the history at present, being a long story, and you know life is too short for a long story. I am extremely obliged for the valuable present you intend me. I believe you criticize yourself too severely on your style; I do not think that very smooth harmony is necessary in a work which has a merit of a nobler kind. I think it rather a defect, as when a Roman Emperor (as we see him sometimes represented on a French stage) is dressed like a Petit-maitre. I confess the croud of readers look no farther; the tittle-tattle of Madame de Sevigné and the *clinquant* of Telemachus[3] have found admirers from that very reason.—Whatever is clearly expressed is well wrote in a book of reasoning. However, I shall obey your commands in telling you my opinion with the greatest sincerity.

I am extremely glad to hear Lady F[anny] has overcome her disorder; I wish I had no apprehensions of falling into it. Solitude begets whimsies; at my time of life one usually falls into those that are melancholy, tho' I endeavor to keep up a certain sprightly folly that (I thank God) I was born with. But alas! What can we do with all our endeavours? I am afraid we are little better than straws upon the water;

---

1 Summary dated 8 Aug. (CB MS, f. 16).

2 In her summary LM wrote: 'P[rince] of Baden D.', whom she had met in 1746, when she was travelling across northern Italy and he was a commander of the Imperial army there (see ii. 377). Steuart's friend was the Margrave, Karl Friedrich (1728–1811), to whom he presented the second MS volume of his *Political Economy* (Paul Chamley, *Documents relatifs à Sir James Steuart*, 1965, pp. 138–9). Steuart wrote a dedication of the book to LM (see below, pp. 236–7).

3 *Télémaque* (1699) by Fénelon. It was in LM's library in 1739 (Wh MS 139).

we may flatter ourselves that we swim when the current carries us along.

———

Thus far I have dictated for the first time of my life, and perhaps it will be the last, for my amanuensis is not to be hired, and I despair of ever meeting with another. He is the first that could write as fast as I talk, and yet you see there are so many mistakes, it wants a comment longer than my letter to explain my insignificant meaning, and I have fatigued my poor eyes more with correcting it than I should have done in scribbling two sheets of paper. You will think perhaps from this idle attempt that I have some fluxion on my sight. No such matter; I have suffered my selfe to be persuaded by such sort of arguments as those by which people are induced to strict abstinence or to take physic—Fear, paltry fear, founded on vapours rising from the heat, which is now excessive and has so far debilitated my miserable nerves that I submit to a present displeasure by way of precaution against a future evil that possibly may never happen. I have this to say in my excuse, that the evil is of so horrid a nature, I own I feel no philosophy that could support me under it, and no mountain-girl ever trembled more at one of Whitfield's[1] pathetic lectures than I do at the word Blindness, tho' I know all the fine things that may be said for consolation in such a case; but I know also they would not operate on my constitution.

'Why then (say my wise monitors) will you persist in reading or writing seven hours in a day?'[2]—I am happy while I read and write.—'Indeed one would suffer a great deal to be happy,' say the men sneering; and the ladies wink at each other and hold up their fans. A fine lady of threescore had the goodness to add—'At least, Madam, you should use spectacles; I have used them my selfe these twenty years. I was advised to it by a famous oculist when I was fifteen. I am really of opinion they have preserved my sight, notwithstanding the passion I always had both for reading and drawing.'—This good woman, you must know, is halfe blind, and never read a larger volume than a newspaper. I will not trouble you with the whole conversation,

---

[1] See above, p. 23.   [2] 'Dialogue at the Resident's' in LM's summary.

tho' it would make an excellent scene in a farce. But after they had, in the best-bred way in the world, convinced me that they thought I lyed when I talked of reading without glasses, the foresaid matron obligingly said she should be very proud to see the writing I talked of, having heard me say formerly I had no correspondants but my daughter and Mr. W[ortley]. She was interrupted by her sister, who said, simpering, 'You forget Sir J[ames] S[teuart]'. I took her up something short, I confess, and said in a dry stern tone—'Madam, I do write to Sir J[ames] S[teuart], and will do it as long as he will permit that honor'.

This rudeness of mine occasioned a profound silence for some minutes, and they fell into a good-natured discourse of the ill consequences of too much application, and remembered how many apoplexies, gouts and dropsies had happened amongst the hard students of their acquaintance. As I never studied any thing in my life, and have always (at least from 15) thought the reputation of learning a misfortune to a woman, I was resolve[d] to believe these stories were not meant at me. I grew silent in my turn, and took up a card that lay on a table, and amused myself with smoking it over a candle. In the mean time (as the song says)

> Their tattles all run, as swift as the sun,
> Of who had won, and who was undone,
> By their gaming and sitting up late.

When it was observed I entered into none of these topics, I was addressed by an obliging lady who pitied my stupidity.— 'Indeed, Madam, you should buy horses to that fine machine you have at Padoua; of what use is it standing in the portico?'—'Perhaps', said another wittily, 'of as much use as a standing dish.'—A gaping school-boy added with still more wit,—'I have seen at a country-gentleman's table a venison-pasty made of wood'.—I was not at all vexed by said school-boy, not because he was (in more senses than one) the highest of the company, but knowing he did not mean to offend me. I confess (to my shame be it spoken), I was grieved[1] at the triumph that appeared in the eyes of the King and Queen of the company,[2] the court being tolerably full.

---

[1] 'piqued' (1818).   [2] John Murray and his wife Lady Wentworth.

His majesty walked off early with the air befitting his dignity, followed by his train of courtiers, who, like courtiers, were laughing amongst themselves as they followed him; and I was left with the two Queens, one of whom[1] was making ruffles for the man she loved, and the other slopping tea for the good of her country. They renewed their generous endeavors to set me right, and I (graceless beast that I am) take up the smoked card which lay before me, and with the corner of another write—

> If ever I one thought bestow
>   On what such fools advise,
> May I be dull enough to grow
>   Most miserably wise—[2]

and flung down the card on the table, and myselfe out of the room in the most indecent fury. A few minutes on the cold water convinced me of my folly, and I went home as much mortified as my Lord E[dgecumbe] when he has lost his last stake at Hazard.[3] Pray don't think (if you can help it) this is an affectation of mine to enhance the value of a talent I would be thought to despise, as celebrated beauties often talk of the charms of good sense, having some reason to fear their mental qualities are not quite so conspicuous as their outside lovely form.

Apropos of beauties:

> I know not why, but Heaven has sent this way
> A nymph fair, kind, poetical and gay;
> And what is more (tho' I express it dully),
> A noble, wise, right honorable cully;
> A soldier worthy of the name he bears,
> As brave and senseless as the sword he wears.[4]

You will not doubt I am talking of a puppet-shew, and indeed so I am, but the figures (some of them) bigger than the life, and not stuffed with straw like those commonly shewn at fairs. I will allow you to think me madder than Don Quixote when I confess I am governed by the Que dira-t-on

---

[1] Consul Smith's wife, *née* Murray.

[2] Adapted from 'Song' by 6th Earl of Dorset.

[3] LM's summary identifies him; he was the 2nd Baron (see ii. 186).

[4] LM's summary names the persons in the verse: 'Mrs. W[righ]t, Lord B[rudene]lle, Col. Hamil[to]n.'

of these things, tho' I remember whereof they are made and know they are but dust. Nothing vexes me so much as that they are below satyre. (Between you and me) I think there are but two pleasures permitted to mortal man, Love and Vengeance, both which are, in a peculiar manner, forbidden to us wretches who are condemned to petticoats. Even vanity it selfe, of which you daily accuse us, is the sin against the Holy Ghost, not to be forgiven in this world or the next.

> Our sex's weakness you expose and blame,
> Of every prating fop the common theme;
> Yet from this weakness you suppose is due
> Sublimer virtue than your Cato knew.
> From whence is this unjust distinction shewn?
> Are we not formed with passions like your own?
> Nature with equal fire our souls endued,
> Our minds as lofty and as warm our blood.
> O'er the wide world your wishes you pursue,
> The change is justified by something new;
> But we must sigh in silence and be true.

How the great Dr. Swift would stare at this vile triplet!—[1]
And then what business have I to make apologies for Lady Vane, who I never spoke to, because her life is writ by Dr. Smollett,[2] who I never saw? Because my daughter fell in love with Lord B[ute] am I obliged to fall in love with the whole Scots nation? 'Tis certain I take their quarrels upon myself in a very odd way; and I cannot deny that (two or three dozen excepted), I think they make the first figure in all arts and sciences, even in gallantry, in spite of the finest gentlemen that have finished their education at Paris.

You will ask me what I mean by all this nonsense, after having declared my selfe an enemy to obscurity to such a degree that I do not forgive it to the great Lord Viscount Bolingbroke, who professes he studied it. I dare swear you will sincerely believe him when you read his celebrated works. I have got them for you and intended to bring them. —Oime! l'huomo propone, Dio dispone.—I hope you won't

---

[1] 'One of his strictest rules in poetry was to avoid *triplets*' (Orrery, *Remarks on the Life and Writings of Swift*, 3rd ed., 1752, p. 188).
[2] See above, pp. 2–3.

think this dab of Italian that slid involuntarily from my pen an affectation like his gallicisms, or a rebellion against Providence in imitation of his Lordship, who I never saw but once in my life:[1] he then appeared in a corner of the Drawing-room in the exact similitude of Satan when he was soliciting the Court of Heaven for leave to torment an honest man.[2]

There is one honest man lately gone off of the stage, which (considering the great scarcity of them) I am heartily sorry for: Dr. J[?]r,[3] who dy'd at Rome with as much stoicism as Cato at Utica, and less desperation, leaving a world he was weary of with the cool indifference you quit a dirty inn to continue your journey to a place where you hope for better accomodation. He took part of a bowl of punch with some Englishmen of my acquaintance the day before his death, and told them with a firm tone of Voice: 'by G[od] he was going'. I am afraid neither Algarotti nor Valsinura[4] will make their exit with so good a grace;[5] I shall rejoyce them both by letting them know you honour them with a place in your memory, when I see them, which I have not done since you left Padoua. Algarotti is at Bologna, I believe, composing panegyrics on whoever is victor in this uncertain war;[6] and Valsinura gone to make a tour to add to his collection. Which do you think the best employed? I confess I am woman enough to think the naturalist who searches after variegated butterflies, or even the lady who adorns her grotto with shades of shells, nay, even the devout people who spend 20 years in making a magnificent presepia at Naples,[7] throw away time in a more rational manner than any hero, ancient or modern. The lofty Pindar who celebrated

[1] In 1741 LM told Joseph Spence: 'I would never be acquainted with Lord Bolingbroke, because I always looked upon him as a vile man' (*Anecdotes*, ed. J. M. Osborn, 1966, § LM 13).

[2] Job i and ii.

[3] Not identified.

[4] Antonio Vallisnieri the younger (1708–77) held the chair of Natural History at Padua University, to which he bequeathed his great collection (Girolamo Tiraboschi, *Biblioteca Modenese*, 1781–6, v. 336).

[5] At his exit, in 1764, Algarotti's last words were less stoic: 'Mourir, c'est bien, mais souffrir tant!' (Ida Treat, *Francesco Algarotti*, 1913, p. 209).

[6] Algarotti had taken upon himself the defence of his former patron Frederick II, who was unpopular in Italy during the Seven Years War (Treat, pp. 166, 170–1).

[7] Naples was famous for models of Christ's nativity, especially in the eighteenth century (Rudolf Berliner, *Die Weihnachtskrippe*, 1955, pp. 96–117).

the Newmarket of those days, or the divine Homer who re-
corded the bloody battles the most in fashion, appear to me
either to have been extremely mistaken or extremely mercenary.

This paragraph is to be dead secret between Lady
F[anny] and your selfe. You see I dare trust you with the
knowledge of all my defects in understanding. Mine is so
stupified by age and disappointment, I own I have lost all
taste for worldly glory. This is partly your fault: I experienced
last year how much happiness may be found with two
amiable friends at a *leger repas*, and 'tis as hard to return to
political or galant conversations as it would be for a fat prelate to content himselfe with the small beer he drank at
college. You have furnished me with a new set of notions;
you ought to be punished for it, and I fancy you will (at
least in your heart) be of opinion that I have very well revenged my selfe by this tedious unconnected letter. Indeed
I intend no such thing, and have only indulged the pleasure
every body naturally feels when they talk to those they love;
as I sincerely do your selfe and dear Lady F[anny], and
your young man because he is yours.

Text Wh MS 509 (transcript) *Address* [*from 1818, p. 28*] To Sir
James Steuart, Tubingen, Suabia.

To Lady Bute *3 Aug.* [*1759*]

                                                    Aug't 3, Padoua
My Dear Child,
   I have been longer your Debtor for a kind Letter than
I ever was in my Life. I confess you in the right to advise
me to Society, which is highly necessary when reading and
writing becomes troublesome, especially to me who am of
an age to expect all sort of Infirmitys. I think my Eyes suffer
by the solitude I have condemn'd my selfe to, but I confess
(to my shame) I have the weakness to fret at the Impertinen-
cies I meet with—but let that pass—.
   I saw last night your worthy Friend the General. He is
in pain for a deserving Brother of his who, having been

unfortunate in the World, would willingly go to the West Indies, even to Guadaloup, to serve his Country.[1] These are sentiments worthy an Old British Hero, which I am sure you will approve if your interest can prevail with Mr. Pitt to serve him. I know you take pleasure in doing Good, and you will truly and infinitely Oblige (my Dear Child) Your ever affectionate mother,

M. Wortley.

I hope to send a longer Letter when my Eyes are recover'd, which I hope they will be when this immoderate Heat is over.

My Complements to your good Lord and all our young people. Both they and you are too gratefull for Triffles. I sent some of more value by the hands of Mr. Dalton.[2] I reserve a present for the first Bride in your Family. 'Tis now my Daughter's Daughters' turn to shine.

I forgot to mention, the Gentleman's name is Hugh Græme.

Text W MS iii. 213–14   *Address* To The Rt Honble the Countess of Bute recommended to Sam: [*sic*] Child Esqr near Temple Bar London Angleterre par Amsterdam

To Wilhelmina Tichborne *12 Aug.* [*1759*]

Aug't 12

Charm'd with hers; pity and contemn Lady Littleton, her Education consider'd.[3] Tasso says old Women are despicable,

---

[1] Hugh Graeme (mentioned by name at the end of the letter) did become a naval officer at Guadeloupe; when he died abroad in the 1760's he was heavily in debt (£1,775) to another brother (Louisa G. Græme, *Or and Sable: A Book of the Græmes and Grahams,* 1903, pp. 427–8).

[2] Richard Dalton (*c.* 1715–91), who had painted and travelled in Italy, corresponded with Bute 1758–9. In May 1759 he left Rome for England (*Walpole Society,* xxxvi, 1960, p. 66);

and the following year through Bute's patronage he was appointed Librarian to George III.

[3] For Lady Lyttelton, see ii. 422; her mother, Lady Rich, was frivolous and immoral—by reputation at least (see i. 269). In 1757 she and her husband quarrelled, and separated in the summer of 1759 (Rose M. Davis, *The Good Lord Lyttelton,* 1939, pp. 250, 253–4). Lady Hervey praised her for her 'very good sense' (*Letters,* 1821, p. 162).

Sir J[ohn] Van[brugh] they are amusing to themselves.[1]
I would part with all the Palaces of Palladio for a Pavillion
near Hers, and avoid being troublesome. Cowley of Mrs.
Evelyn, apologyz'd to her.[2] Must not indulge such day
dreams, my Castles in the next World. It would become me
to turn Enthusiast like poor Lady Kilm[orey].[3] I hate Hipo-
crits, formerly made War on them. Heroism not fit for our
Sex in England. My comfort here to see our sex despotic
and the mob Quiet. I am oblig'd to D[on] Phil[lip], want
Humility to appear in his court.[4] The fair brilliant here;
did not go to the Opera, had conserts at Home. Vanity, what
Rochester said of Love.[5] L[ady] Sandwich honord in
F[rance] when despis'd in E[ngland].[6] Messalina, Susanna,
Daniel.

Text CB MS, ff. 16–17 (summary)

To Lady Bute *26 Sept.* 1759

My Dear Child,
    I am very glad to find by yours of Sept. 3 that your selfe
and Family are all in good Health. I cannot complain of

[1] In his comedy *Aesop*, Part I (1697),
Act iv.

[2] In the first stanza of his verse 'The
Garden', Abraham Cowley praised the
diarist John Evelyn's 'virtuous Wife'
for her beauty and wisdom—perhaps
in apology for his prose compliment on
Evelyn's choosing gardening as his
'Wife' (*The Literary Remains of John
Evelyn*, ed. W. Upcott, 1834, p. 436).
Mary (*c.* 1635–1709), da. of Sir Richard
Browne, m. (1647) Evelyn.

[3] Mary Shirley (1712–84), da. of 2nd
Earl Ferrers, m. (1730) 9th Viscount
Kilmorey. Walpole remarked of her (in
1751): 'My Lady is almost a Methodist
though not quite a convert to her sister
Lady Huntington' (*Corr.* xx. 271)—
referring to her sister famous for evan-
gelical activities. When she was in Naples
with her husband in 1752 they held
prayers in their apartment every Sunday

(Mann to Holdernesse, 25 Aug. 1752,
Eg MS 3464).

[4] Don Philip of Spain had ruled the
Duchy of Parma since 1748.

[5] LM may have had in mind the passage from the Earl of Rochester's well-
known poem 'A Letter fancy'd from
Artemisia in the Town, to Chloe in the
Country', which complains that true love
has degenerated in modern times (*Poems
on Several Occasions*, ed. J. Thorpe,
1950, pp. 20–21).

[6] Lady Sandwich was Rochester's
daughter (see ii. 447), and even before
her widowhood had settled in Paris.
Saint-Simon commented on her prefer-
ring that city to London (*Mémoires*, ed.
G. Truc, 1954–61, v. 156); and Chesterfield (in 1751) advised his son to attend
her salon 'for the sake of the people of
wit and learning who frequent her'
(*Letters*, ed. B. Dobrée, 1932, iv. 1763).

mine, thô the Season is more sickly than has been known of
many years past, occasion'd by the excessive Heat. We have
had no Rain of three months, and if the Drougth continues
the most fatal Consequences may be expected. There is already a mortality amongst the Cattle which frightens every
body.

I am invited to a great Wedding to morrow, which will
be in the most Splendid manner, to the Contentment of both
the Familys, every thing being equal, even the Indifference
of the Bride and Bridegroom, thô each of them is extreamly
pleas'd with being set free from Governors and Governesses.
To say truth, I think they are less likely to be disapointed in
the plan they have form'd than any of our Romantic Couples
who have their Heads full of Love and Constancy.

I have not yet receiv'd my Books from Mr. Mackensie,
thô he has sent them sometime ago. I beleive you will soon
see a Mr. Ferguson,[1] who (between you and I) is in my
opinion the prettiest Man I have seen since I left England.
A propos of Men, here is lately arriv'd a Tall, fair, well
shap'd young Fellow, with a good character, the reputation
of a good understanding, and in present possession of 12
thousand pound per Annum. His name is Southwell. I
charge you not to look upon him, and to lock up your
Daughters if he should visit Lord Bute. He honor'd me with
a visit, which hinder'd my sleeping all night. You will [be]
surpriz'd to hear he has neither visible Nose nor Mouth,
yet he speaks with a clear audible voice. You may imagine
such a figure should not be seen by any Woman in a possibillity of Breeding. He appears insensible of his misfortune
and shews him selfe every day on the Piazza to the astonish-
ment of all the Spectators. I never saw ⟨so⟩ shocking a
sight.[2]

1 Not identified.

2 At Turin he was observed by
Mackenzie, who besides noting his admirable qualities of mind and character,
added: 'The misfortune He has in
being disfigur'd by the terrible fever he
had when a Boy, is a great disadvantage
to Him at his first appearance, but his
good qualities make one soon forget it.
This misfortune was not oweing to the
distemper which I remember at the
time people attributed it to; it was a
violent rash He had, which by a youthfull imprudence He struck in; *that* produced a very violent fever, and all his
lower teeth came out as well as some
of the upper Row' (to Bute, 2 April
1760, Bute MS in Cardiff Public
Library).

My Dear child, God bless you and yours; it is the Zealous and daily prayer of your most affectionate Mother,

M. Wortley.

Sept. 26, 1759

My Complements to Lord Bute and hearty blessing to all our children.

Text W MS iii. 162–3   *Address* To The Rt Honble the Countess of Bute recommended to Fran: Child Esqr near Temple Bar London Angleterre par Amsterdam   *Postmark* OC 22

To Francis Child and Company *29 Sept.* [*1759*]

Venice, September 29

Sir,

Pray pay to Mrs. Elizabeth Brown[1] or order the sumn of three hundred and fifty pounds sterling for value receiv'd and place it to the account of, Sir, your Humble Servant,

Mary Wortley Montagu.

To Fran: Child, Esq. and Comp.
London

Text MS owned by M. C. A. Lyell   *End.* 1759   October 4
C 123–200
651–100
251– 50

To Lady Bute [*9 Nov. 1759*]

My Dear Child,

I receiv'd yours of Oct. 18 this day, Nov. 9th. I am afraid some Letters both of yours and mine are lost, nor am I much

[1] Except for her being a friend of LM and of Mme Michiel, Miss Brown and the nature of her transactions with LM are unidentified. This was not the first of such transactions; the ledgers of Child and Company have the following entry: '1758 Dec. 25, Venice, pay to Mrs. Eliz. Brown £150 and charge it to account of Ma. Wortley Montagu' (MS).

surpriz'd at it, seeing the mannagements here. In this World much must be suffer'd, and we ought all to follow the rule of Epicte[t]us, bear and forbear.[1]

General Wolfe is to be lamented but not pity'd. I am of your opinion, Compassion is only owing to his Mother and intended Bride, who I think the greatest Sufferer (however sensible I am of a Parent's tenderness).[2] Disapointments in Youth are those that are felt with the greatest Anguish, when we are all in expectation of Happiness, perhaps not to be found in this Life.

I am very sorry Lady F. Erkeskine [*sic*] has remov'd my poor Sister to London, where she will only be more expos'd.[3] I would write again to her if I thought it could be any Comfort in her deplorable Condition. I say nothing to her Daughter, who [is] too like her Father for me to correspond with.

I am very much diverted with the Adventures of the three Graces[4] lately arriv'd in London and am heartily sorry their Mother has not learning enough to write memoirs; she might make the fortune of halfe a dozen Dodsleys. The youngest Girl (call'd here Bettina)[5] is taller than the Dutchess of Montagu and as red and white as any German alive. If she has sense enough to follow good Instructions she will be irresistable, and may produce very glorious Noveltys. [I know nothing of her except her figure.][6] Our Great minister[7] has her Picture amongst his Collection of *Ladies*. Basta—

My Health is better than I can reasonably expect at my Age, thô I have at present a great cold in my Head, which makes writeing uneasy to me, and forces me to shorten my Letter to my dear child. I have receiv'd the

---

[1] The theme of the *Enchiridion*, which LM had translated in 1710 (see i. 44).

[2] James Wolfe (1726–59) died on 13 Sept. at the storming of Quebec. His mother was Henrietta (d. 1764); and his fiancée, Katharine Lowther (1736–1809), m. (1765) 6th Duke of Bolton.

[3] At her death two years later Lady Mar—in the custody of her daughter Lady Frances Erskine—had a house in Newcastle Street, Cavendish Square (*London Evening Post*, 3–5 March 1761).

[4] LM's summary (CB MS, f. 17) provides their name—Wynne (see above, p. 179).

[5] Marie-Elisabeth (b. 1741) was actually the next to youngest surviving daughter.

[6] Inserted from LM's draft of part of the letter (W MS iii. 196).

[7] Murray, British Resident.

Books from Mr. Mackensie. Mr. Walpole's is not amongst them.[1]

Make my best Complements to Lord Bute, and Give my blessing to all your children. Your Happiness in e⟨very⟩ circumstance is zealously wish'd by (Dear child) Y⟨our⟩ most affectionate Mother,

                           M. Wortley.

Text W MS iii. 194–5   *Address* To The Rt Honble the Countess of Bute recommended to Fran: Child Esqr near Temple Bar London Angleterre par Amsterdam   *Postmark* DE 5

To Wilhelmina Tichborne *17 Nov.* [*1759*]

                           Nov. 17

I should be troublesome if at London. Carneades.[2] Bad Consequence of Victory.[3] Pl[easure] and debauchry, L[ight] and Darkness. Never was nor lov'd a Rake. Perhaps the view of Convents has given me too much fondness for Indolence. Hope that L. Stanh[ope] will divert us.[4]

Text CB MS, f. 17 (summary)

To Wortley *23 Nov.* [*1759*]

                     Nov. 23, Venice

I do not write to you often, being afraid of being trouble-some and supposing that my Daughter communicates my

---

[1] LM appealed to Horace Mann for the *Cat. of Royal and Noble Authors*; and he wrote to Walpole on 1 Nov. 1760 that she had 'employed all the means she could think of to induce me to send them to her'. In Jan. 1761 Walpole finally sent them to Mann, who transmitted them in Sept. (*Corr.* xxi. 447 and n. 9, 472).

[2] Carneades of Cyrene (214–129 B.C.), Greek sceptic philosopher, opposed to dogmatism.

[3] Possibly that of Quebec.

[4] Philip (1714–86), 2nd Earl Stanhope, immensely learned in Greek, mathematics, science, philosophy; or his wife. He m. (1745) Lady Grisell Hamilton (1719–1811), niece of LM's old enemy Lady Murray, who had died in June 1759.

Letters to you. I have the pleasure of hearing from her that you have good Health and Spirits, which I heartily wish the Continuance of.

I have seen lately a History of the Last Years of Queen Anne by Swift.[1] I should be very glad to know your Opinion of it.[2] Some facts are apparently False, and I beleive others partialy represented.

The Winter is begun here severely but we have had a most delightfull Autumn. I hope every thing is to your satisfaction in England.

Text W MS ii. 254   *End. by W* Ad 29 Dec. [*Summary*] recd at Bath 27 Dec.

To Lady Bute [*Dec. 1759*]

I am allways glad to hear of my dear child's Health. I daily pray for the continuance of it, and all other blessings on you and your Family. The Carnival hitherto has been clouded by extreme wet Weather, but we are in hopes the sun shine is reserv'd for the second part of it, after Xmas, when the morning Masquerades give all the Ladies an Opportunity of displaying both their Magnificence and their Taste in the various habits that appear at that time. I was very well diverted by them last year.

Mr. Southwell has left us some time. I was almost reconcil'd to his figure by his good behaviour and polite Conversation. Here are at present few English. Lord Brudenalle ought to be at London. I think I have already told you[3] he ressembles his Grand Father, but 'tis a strong Caricatura. I hear Rome is cramm'd with Britons. In their turns I

[1] *The History of the Four Last Years of the Queen,* first published in 1758.

[2] In his reply W gave his opinion: 'I dont remember particularly at present what Swift, whom you mention, has written about the 4 last years of Queen Anne, but I know that I thought it not worth remembring and filled with false facts as well as my Lord Bolingbrook's works. Probably Swift was not thought of Consequence enough to be let into the true account of things, but only such as my Lord Oxford desired to have published' (29 Dec. 1759, W MS i. 144: draft).

[3] On 3 Oct. [1758] (p. 180).

suppose we shall see them all. I cannot say the rising Generation gives any great prospect of improvement either ⟨in⟩ the Arts and Sciences or in any thing else. I am exceedingly pleas'd that the Dutchess of Portland is happy in her Son in law.[1] I must ever interest my selfe in whatever happens to any Descendant of Lady Oxford. I expect that my Books and china should set out; since the defeat of the French Fleet I should imagine there can be no danger on the Sea.[2] They will be a great Amusement to me. I mix so little in the gay World I have many Idle hours, and at present my Garden is quite useless. I wrote lately to your Father, who I guess to be return'd to London. I am inform'd Mr. Mackensie makes a very good Figure at Turin. General Graham has bad Health,[3] and Mr. Hamilton is the Lord knows where, which occasions much Speculation. Venice is not a place to make a Man's fortune. For those who have money to throw away, they may do it here more agreably than in any Town I know, strangers being receiv'd with great Civillity and admitted into all their partys of pl⟨easure⟩; but it requires a good Estate and a good C⟨onstitution⟩ to play deep and pass so many sleepless Nights as is Customary in the best Company.

Adieu, my dear child. You see I am profoundly Dull. I desire you would be so good to attribute it to the gloominess of the Weather; it is now almost Night, tho at noon day. I am in all Humors your most affectionate Mother,

M. Wortley.

My Complements to Lord Bute and blessing to all Yours.

Text W MS iii. 160–1   *Address* To The Rt Honble the Countess of Bute recommended to Fran: Child Esqr near Temple Bar London Angleterre par Amsterdam   *Postmark* FE 4

---

[1] Lord Weymouth (see above, p. 205).

[2] In Nov. 1759 Admiral Edward Hawke defeated the French fleet in the battle of Quiberon Bay, the greatest English sea victory since the Spanish Armada.

[3] On 1 Aug. 1759 Murray had reported: 'General Graeme seems to be in perfect Health, tho he is always complaining of it' (to A. Mitchell, Add MS 6830, f. 25).

To Lady Bute *12 Feb.* [*1760*]

My Dear Child,

I beleive I shall not write you many more Letters. The vexations I have here will hasten the end of all vexations, and I shall have no regret in leaving a World I have long been weary of but the Apprehension that it will be a real misfortune to you. I receiv'd a Letter[1] from your Father last post that cuts my Heart. He says he has great reason to fear Blindness. A few days before, I receiv'd from an unknown hand, without any Letter of advice, a very Nonsensical book printed with your Brother's name to it, which only serves to prove to me that he has private Correspondancies here and that he is still a knavish Fool.[2] This is no news to me. I have long wept the misfortune of being Mother to such an Animal.

This is a nice subject to speak of to you and what I never touch'd before, but I think I ought now to explain all my thoughts to you. You are now of an age more able to give me Advice than I am to direct, being in that time of Life when the mind is in its greatest vigour. If your Father should fall into the Hands of Servants (as all blind people must necessarily do), how far he may be impos'd on I tremble to think. I know by experience how magnificent your Brother can be in his promises, and thô I was never mov'd by them, you may see daily examples of mercenary tempers in those of much higher rank than Domestics. I dare not say more; I hope I say enough to be understood. I have the most perfect Confidence in Mr. W.'s[3] probity and the highest opinion of his understanding—Yet—tis possible——

I have no view of my own in what I am saying. My Life is so near a Conclusion that where or how I pass it (if innocently) is almost indifferent to me. I have outliv'd the greatest part of my Acquaintance; and to say truth, a return to Croud and Bustle after my long Retirement would

<hr/>

[1] Dated 29 Dec. 1759 (W MS i. 144).

[2] *Reflections on the Rise and Fall of the Antient Republicks* was published on 13 March 1759 (*Daily Advertiser*). The Revd. John Forster, Montagu's former tutor, may have had some part in writing it (Jonathan Curling, *Edward Wortley Montagu*, 1954, pp. 147–9).

[3] Possibly Alexander Wedderburn (see below, p. 255).

be disagreable to me,[1] yet if I could be of use either to your Father or your Family I would venture shortening the insignificant days of your most affectionate Mother,

M. Wortley.

Feb. 12.

I have wrote the enclos'd to your Father. You are more able to judge than my selfe if it is proper to be given him. I only mean what appears to me right. ⟨?⟩ should misunderstand it, it would [be] the highest afflic⟨tion to⟩ me and a real Injury to your selfe.

Text W MS iii. 271–2   *Address* To The Rt Honble The Countess of Bute

To Wortley [*12 Feb. 1760*]

Having had no opportunity of writeing by a private Hand till now, I have delaid sometime answering your last letter, which touch'd me more than I am either able or willing to express. I hope your apprehensions of Blindness are not confirm'd by any fresh symptoms of that terrible misfortune.

If I could be of any Service to you on that or any other occasion, I shall think my last remains of Life well employ'd.

I am sorry to mention a person that we can neither of us remember with pleasure. He sent me lately a very sorry Book printed in his Name, but no letter or direction to write to him, which I am very glad excuses me from that trouble.

Text W MS ii. 255–6   *Address* To Edwd Wortley Esqr   *End. by W* L.M. no Date   by Gen. Graham.[2] recd from La. Bute 14 Apr. 1760 Ad 28 Apr.

---

[1] In 1758 LM had considered returning home but then 'asked how she would get back in case the climat[e] and air of England did not agree with her' (Graeme to Bute, 31 Dec. [1758], Bute MS).

[2] On 29 Feb. John Murray reported that Gen. Graeme had set out for England 'a few days ago' on a fourmonths leave of absence from his post in Venice (to Pitt, SP 99/68).

To James Stuart Mackenzie *12 Feb.* [*1760*]

This is the first opportunity I have had of writing by a private hand since I had the pleasure of hearing from you. The conveyance of the post is so uncertain, nothing of value can be trusted to it. I fancy I see you laugh (or at least smile) at the vanity of my supposing any thing valuable in my scribble scrabbles. I can assure you it proceeds from the knowledge I have of your good heart; I am firmly persuaded you are better pleas'd with the repetition of even Insignificant good wishes from an old Freind, than all the fine things wrote by Lord Lyttleton for the good of Mankind.[1]

I need say nothing of the Merit of the Bearer of this Letter,[2] beleiving you are better acquainted with him than I am. I would willingly have accompany'd him to Turin, but the Weather (thô delightfully clear) is now so cold I dare not venture the Journey.

I am very uneasy at a report spread here, I hope without Foundation (as you know many reports are), that there is some disgust between you and Lord Bute. I am inclin'd to think him well dispos'd towards you, and I am sure you have a sincere affection for him,[3] which I have often told my Daughter.

Here is a good natur'd sensible young Gentleman of your Name;[4] we never meet without speaking of you in the manner we ought.

While there remains a parcel of attoms call'd Me, you will allwaies have a sincere and faithfull (thô I fear an insignificant) Humble servant.

M. W. M.

Feb. 12.

I shall sup to night with Signora Chiara Michielli, where your Health will be drank.

[1] LM may have had in mind Lyttelton's *Observations on the Conversion and Apostleship of St. Paul* (1747), in which he stated his religious beliefs; or she may have meant his works in general.
[2] Graeme.
[3] Mackenzie quoted to Bute this passage from LM's letter, and added: 'I shall soon acquaint her that the report is very far from being founded; I cant guess how such a thing should come into people's heads' (22 Feb. 1760, Bute MS in Cardiff Public Library).
[4] Stuart (p. 235).

Text Bute MS   *Address* A Monsieur Monsieur Mackensie Ministre
de Sa Maiestie Brittanique a la Cour de Turin.   *End. by Mackenzie*
Lady M. W. Montagu 12 Febr. 1760 Rd by General Græme 21
Febr. ansd 22 Mar.

To Sir James Steuart *13 Feb. 1760*

Sir,

I have waited (in my opinion) with very exemplary
patience for your manuscripts;[1] I have not yet received them,
but will not longer delay my thanks for your obliging and
agreeable letter. I am apt to believe Lord H[oldernesse]
may be sincere in saying he is willing to serve you: how far
he can be usefull is, I think, dubious; you know he is only
a subaltern officer.[2] I wish I knew any probable method of
insuring success to your wishes; you may certainly depend
on every thing that can be done towards it, either by my
own or the interest of those whom I can influence.

If I considered merely my own inclinations I should
advise the air of this town, since the physicians are of
opinion that the sea would be salutary to your constitution.
I dare not press this earnestly, finding my selfe highly pre-
judiced where my own happiness is so nearly concerned; yet
I can with truth assure you that yours shall always have the
first place, and was it in my power (notwithstanding the
real pleasure of such excellent conversation) I would give
up all hopes of it, and immediately transport you and Lady
Fanny to your native country, where I am persuaded the
pleasure of seeing your Household Lares and having
your friends round you would certainly contribute to your
health, if not totally restore it.

I heartily congratulate you on your happiness in the growing improvements of Mr. Stewart: it is perhaps the most
pleasing employment in life to form a young mind well
disposed to receive instruction. When a parent's care is

[1] His *Political Economy*, which he had
promised to send her (see above, p. 181).
[2] Holdernesse, Secretary of State for
the Northern Department, was 'subaltern' to Pitt, the other Secretary.

returned with gratitude and compliance, there is no conqueror or legislator that receives such sincere satisfaction. I have not seen the histories you mention, nor have had for this last twelvemonth any books from England. It is difficult to send any thing from thence, as my daughter informs me; and our travelling young gentlemen very seldom burden themselves with such unnecessary baggage as works of literature.

Give me leave to send my warmest thanks to Lady Fanny for her kind remembrance, and compliments to the young gentleman, who I hope will always be a blessing to you both. It is extreme mortifying to me that I have no better way of expressing how much I am, Sir, Your most obliged and very humble servant,

M. W. Montagu.

Venice, Feb. 13, 1760

Text Wh MS 509 (transcript)   *Address* [*from 1818, p. 48*] To Sir James Steuart, Tubingen, Suabia.   *End.* February 1760

To Lady Bute *24 Feb.* [*1760*]

Venice, Feb. 24.

My Dear Child,

I wrote to you some days ago a Letter by General Graham, but as many accidents may delay his arrival, I will not omit to thank you for yours of Jan. 18th.

I am not so much surpriz'd at Lady Louisa Ker's flight as you seem to be. Six or 7 months is a great while to wait, in the opinion of a young Lover, and I do not think Lord George much in the wrong to fear the effect of Artifices, Absence, and new proposals that could not fail of being made to her in that time.[1]

The Carnival is now over. We have no more Ridotto or

---

[1] Lady Louisa (1739–1830), da. of Earl of Ancram, eloped to Scotland in Dec. 1759 with Lord George Henry Lennox (1737–1805), son of 2nd Duke of Richmond. Her father had wanted her to wait until she was of age, in less than a year (Walpole, *Corr.* ix. 263 and n. 8).

Theatrical entertainments. Diversions have taken a more private, perhaps a more agreable, Turn. Tis the Fashion here to have little houses of retreat where the Lady retires every evening at 7 or 8 o' the Clock, and is visited ⟨by⟩ all her Intimates of both Sexes, which commonly amount to 70 or 80 persons, where they have play, concerts of Music, sometimes danceing and always a handsome Collation. I beleive you will think these little assemblys very agreable; they realy are so. Whoever is well acquainted with Venice must own it is the center of Pleasure, not so noisy, and in my opinion more refin'd than Paris.

I am extreamly glad Lady Jane turns out so much to your satisfaction, thô I am told Lady Anne is the Beauty. We have now no English here. Mr. Wright and his Lady,[1] Mr. Stuart[2] and Mr. Panton[3] set out together a few days ago intending for Rome and Naples. I suppose the Ascention will bring us a fresh Cargo, as I hear there are many dispers'd about Italy. Lord Brudenalle seem'd to leave it with great Reluctance. He is singular both in his manner and Sentiments, yet I am apt to beleive if he meets with a sensible Wife, she may be very happy with him. Whoever leaves him at his liberty will certainly meet no Contradiction from him, who is too Indolent to dispute with any body and appears ⟨?⟩ indifferent to our Se⟨x.[4] I a⟩m persuaded he will ⟨? lik⟩e any ⟨? r⟩ecommended by ⟨? p⟩arents without Hesitation.

I have had lately a Letter from poor Lady Blount.[5] She is now in easy Circumstances if she can mannage discreetly. I have a great regard for the uncommon sincerity of her character, but am afraid she will be always too open to the attacks of Flattery.

Adieu, my Dear child. God bless you and yours, which

---

1 See above, p. 193.

2 Not identified.

3 Thomas Panton (1731–1808), whom Robert Adam had met in Rome in 1756 (John Fleming, *Robert Adam and His Circle*, 1962, pp. 195, 358).

4 In 1755 Adam had taken an instant dislike to Brudenell: 'a stupid, meaning-less creature and has not the mein of a tailor nor the spirit of a louse' (Fleming, pp. 123–4). He never married.

5 Anne Cornwallis (1704–61), with a dowry of £10,000, m. (1728) Harry Pope Blount (1702–57), later Baronet, who had a house in Twickenham. A year after their marriage she separated from her husband, whose friends thought she was 'a fury'; but six years later she returned to him promising submission (Pope, *Corr.*, ed. G. Sherburn, 1956, ii. 519; iii. 55, 510).

[is] the most zealous prayer of Your truly affectionate Mother.

M. Wortley

My Complements to Lord Bute.

Text W MS iii. 241–2   *Address* ⟨To⟩ The Rt Honble the Countess of Bute recommended to Fran: Child Esqr near Temple Bar London Angleterre par Amsterdam   *Postmark* MR 20

To Sir James Steuart *1 March 1760*

I have at length received your valuable and magnificent present.[1] You will have me give my opinion; I know not how to do it without your accusing me of flattery (tho' I am sure no other person would suspect it). It is hard to forbear praising where there is so much due, yet I would rather talk of your performance to any other than yourselfe. If I durst speak out I would say that you have explained in the best manner the most difficult subject, and struck out new lights that [are] necessary to enforce conviction even to those who have studied the points you treat, and who are often misled by prejudices which fall away; while your instructions take place in every mind capable of distinguishing truth from falsehood. Upon the whole permit me to say I never saw a treatise which gave me so much pleasure and information. You shew your selfe qualified by Nature for the charge of first minister; how far that would recommend you to a minister I think problematic.

I am beginning to read over your work a second time; my approbation increases as I go on. The solidity of your reflections would over[ba]lance a defect in style, if there was any; but I sincerely find none. The nervous manner in which you write is infinitely preferable to the florid phrases which are always improper in a book of this nature, which is not designed to move the passions but to convince the reason.

I ought to say a great deal for the honour you have done

---

[1] *Political Economy* in MS (see endorsement). This fair copy has only recently been rediscovered (Paul Cham- ley, *Documents relatifs à Sir James Steuart*, 1965, p. 20). It is now among the Bute MS.

me in your dedication.[1] Lord Burleigh[2] or even Julius Cæsar would have been proud of it. I can have no pretence to deserve it, yet I may truly say nobody can be more sensible of the value of your present. It is pity the world should be deprived of the advantage of so useful a performance; yet perhaps it may be necessary to wait some time before you publish certain truths that are not yet popularly received.

I hope our dear Lady Fanny is in good health and your young gentleman daily improving both by nature and instruction. I flatter my selfe that your affairs will soon take a more agreeable turn. Wherever you are, I wish you every happiness, and where ever I am, you will ever have a faithful humble servant engaged both by inclination and obligation to be always at your command,

M. W. Montagu.

Venice, March 1, 1760

Text Wh MS 509 (transcript) *Address* [*from 1818, p. 51*] To Sir James Steuart, Tubingen, Suabia. *End. by Sir James* On receiving a M.S. neatly bound and gilt of the two first books of my Pol: Oeconomy with a dedication to her Ladyship

To Wilhelmina Tichborne 6 *March* [*1760*]

March 6

She in the great World, me retir'd. Venetian Weddings and Galantry. Time and Place if they do not regulate morals determine Reputation. Lord Chesterf[iel]d popular aplause.

Text CB MS, f. 17 (summary)

To Sir James Steuart 7 *April 1760*

I have now with great pleasure and, I flatter my selfe, with some improvement read over again your delightful

---

[1] When published in 1767, after LM's death, the book bore no dedication. That to LM, which is dated 11 Aug.

1759, is printed in Chamley, pp. 130–7.
[2] Queen Elizabeth's chief minister.

and instructive treatise; you have opened to me several truths of which I had before only a confused idea. I confess I cannot help being a little vain of comprehending a system that is calculated only for a thinking mind and cannot be tasted without a willingness to lay aside many prejudices which arise from education and the conversation of people no wiser than our selves. I do not only mean my own sex when I speak of our confined way of reasoning; there are very many of yours as incapable of judging otherwise than they have been early taught, as the most ignorant milk maid. Nay, I believe a girl out of a village or a nursery more capable of receiving instruction than a lad just set free from the university. It is not difficult to write on blank paper, but 'tis a tedious if not an impossible task to scrape out nonsense already written, and put better sense in the place of it. Mr. Stewart is very happy to be under the direction of a father who will not suffer him to entertain errors at an age when 'tis hard to distinguish them. I often look back on my past life in the light in which old Montaigne considered it;[1] it is perhaps a more useful study than it is generally imagined. Mr. Locke, who has made the best dissection of the human mind of any author I have ever read, declares that he has drawn all his observations from reflecting on the progression of his own ideas.[2] It is true a very small proportion of knowledge is allowed us in this world, few truths permitted, but those truths are plain; they may be overseen or artfully obscured from our sight, but when pointed out to us it is impossible to resist the conviction that accompanies them. I am persuaded your manuscript would have the same effect on every candid reader it has on me, but I am afraid their number is very small.

I think the omission you desire in the Act of Indemnity cannot fail of happening.[3] I shall take every opportunity of putting people of my acquaintance in mind of it; at present the real director (at least of home-affairs) is a countryman of yours; but you know there are certain circumstances that may

[1] 'De l'expérience' (*Œuvres complètes*, ed. A. Thibaudet and M. Rat, 1962, p. 1051).
[2] LM had cited this to Lady Bute on 1 March [1754] (p. 48 above).

[3] Steuart had been excluded by name from pardon in the Act of Indemnity following the Jacobite rebellion; now LM hopes his name will be removed from the list of those excluded.

disincline [him] from meddling in some nice matters.[1]
I am always with gratitude and the truest esteem both to
Lady Francesse and yourselfe a faithful humble servant,

M. W. Montagu.

Venice, April 7th 1760

Text Wh MS 509 (transcript)[2] *Address* A Monsieur Monsieur le
Chevalier Stuart A Tubingen en Suabe par Augsbourg

To Lady Bute *15 April* [*1760*]

My dear Child,
I am very uneasy at hearing nothing from you or General
G[raeme], being told he has been arriv'd near a Month.[3]
I do not doubt his first visit was to you, having given him a
Letter which I desir'd him ⟨to deliver⟩[4] with all speed. Perhaps I was more frighted th⟨an ?⟩ need to be, when I wrote
it; all Weaknesses appear (as they encrease) with Age. I am
afraid all Humankind are born with the seeds of them, thô
they may be totally conceal'd and consequently considerably
lessen'd by Education and Philosophy. I have endeavor'd
to study and correct my selfe, and as Courage was the
favorite Virtue in my early Youth, I study'd to seem void
of Fear, and I beleive was rather esteem'd Fool-hardy. I am
now grown Timerous and enclin'd to low Spirits. Whatever
you may hear to the contrary, my chearfullness is like the
Fire kindled in Brush wood, which makes a shew but is soon
turn'd to cold Ashes. I do not (like Madame Maintenon)
greive at the Decay which is alloted to all Mortals,[5] but
would willingly excuse to you the Heat that was in my last.

[1] LM probably alludes to William
Murray, Lord Mansfield. Although he
had great influence with Newcastle, he
might be cautious of protecting persons
like Steuart because he was himself
accused of having been a Jacobite in his
younger days (Lady Louisa Stuart, note
on transcript).

[2] Summary in CB MS, f. 17.

[3] Graeme had arrived in London
shortly before 7 April (Bruno Brunelli,
Casanova Loved Her, transl. A.
McKechnie, 1929, p. 186).

[4] From 1861, ii. 378.

[5] Françoise d'Aubigné (1635–1719),
marquise de Maintenon, pious mistress
of Louis XIV; her letters, in nine
volumes, were published in 1758.

I would by no means have you give the least uneasyness to your Father. At his time of Life the mind should be vacant and quiet—As for the rest—let Providence as it will dispose of your most affectionate Mother,

M. Wortley.

You may be surpriz'd I sent you no Token by the General. To say truth he was in so ill a state of Health I was afraid he should die on the road. I shall be more explicit in my next.

My sincere good wishes to Lord Bute and Blessing to all yours.

April 15.[1]

Text W MS iii. 25–26   *Address* To The Rt Honble the Countess of Bute recommended to Fran. Child Esqr near Temple Bar London Angleterre par Amsterdam   *Postmark* MA 14

From Edward Wortley Montagu, junior, [*April 1760*]

Madam,

The deep Sense I have of my past ill Conduct, for which I have long felt and ever shall feel the most painful Self abhorrence, deterrd me from sending a letter with my Book[2] to Your Ladyship. So bold a step, I fear'd, would tend to increase that just displeasure which I have so repeatedly incurr'd, and might have prevented You from looking into the Book, which I most ardently wish'd You would condescend to peruse. Not that I presum'd to offer it as worthy of Your Ladyship's Attention in any other light than as a proof of my turn of Mind and application to Study, and as I judg'd a proof of that Nature would carry a more convincing Evidence of a thorough change in my way of thinking, as well as way of life, than all the assurances I could make by letter. I thank God! it has in some measure had the wish'd for effect, as it has procur'd me the honour of a letter from Your Ladyship: a Blessing which I had the less reason to expect, as I was truely conscious how little I deserv'd it.

I had long reflected with Anguish of Soul that I was in a manner cut off as an Alien and an Outcast from my Parents, and what peirc'd still more deeply was the Consciousness that the blame lay wholly upon myself, and that I had nothing to plead in Mitigation of what

----

[1] Summary dated 25 April (CB MS, f. 17).   [2] On the ancient republics (see above, p. 230).

I had been guilty of. Judge then, Madam, of the Joy I must feel on the receipt of Your letter. It was a Joy too big for Utterance, and was I to inform Your Ladyship of the Effects it produc'd, the[y] would appear extravagant. I shall therefore only assure You, that no one thing ever affected me so much.

Your Ladyship will see by my preface and Introduction the true reason of my Choice of that Subject, which seem'd to me the best adapted to the State of our affairs at that time both at Home and Abroad. How I have acquitted myself in the Execution of my Plan, I beg leave to submit to Your Ladyship's greatly Superior Judgement. I have some years since bid a final Adieu to the hurry and dissipation of a Town life. My thoughts have been entirely turn'd upon the past, and I now labour to make all the atonement in my Power for my former follies, and to form such a Character as I should wish to die with. Reflections of this Nature must unavoidably lead me to weigh seriously the Duty I owe to God, to my Country, to my Parents, and to myself; and I make it my daily Study to know the extent of those Duties, and to discharge them as far as I am able.

Your Ladyship's kind wishes that my Amusements may be innocent, if not useful, seem to imply a hint that I might have been happyer in the Choice of my Subject. Would Your Ladyship but honour me so far as to point out One which You judge proper, I shall gladly exert the utmost of my poor Abilities on so pleasing an Occasion.

Accept, Madam, the sincerest Wishes and Prayers for Your Ladyship's Health which the warmest Duty and Gratitude can inspire; for I had so often abus'd Your Goodness, that 'till now I despair'd of regaining that Maternal affection which will be the cheif Happyness of my Life. Encourag'd therefore by this fresh instance of Your Goodness, I take the liberty to send the second Edition of my Book (which I have corrected)[1] as some proof of the Indulgence with which it was receiv'd by the Publick.[2]

I cannot leave off without informing Your Ladyship of the deep Sense I have of my Father's goodness, who has been pleas'd to place me in the present and assure me of a Seat in the next Parliament;[3] in which, as well as in every other Station of life, it is the highest Object of my Ambition to appear in a Character worthy of Your Son; and

---

[1] On 13 Sept. 1759 Montagu, then in Bloomsbury, had been very busy preparing the second edition (to Edward Montagu, MS Mo 2849, Huntington Library)—duly published on 23 Feb. 1760 (*Daily Advertiser*).

[2] It was favourably noticed in both the *Monthly Review* (xx. 419–27) and the *Critical Review* (vii. 249–54), 1759.

[3] In 1754 Montagu had been elected to Bossiney, a Cornish seat controlled by his father; in the next election (30 March 1761), W having died, Montagu was re-elected as Bute's nominee (History of Parliament, *House of Commons 1754–1790*, ed. L. Namier and J. Brooke, 1964, i. 223; iii. 662).

to support which, shall be the constant Study of, Madam, Your Ladyship's for evermore most dutiful Son and faithful Servant,

Ed. Wortley Montagu.

Text W MS iii. 3–4

To Lady Bute 9 *May 1760*

My dear child must forgive me if I load her with Letters. I confess I am so uneasy at the silence of General Graham[1] and yours that I have little peace of mind. I sent by him a letter of great Importance to me.[2] I am told he is arriv'd many posts ago. I have no Notice from him that he has seen you, or from you that you have receiv'd my Scrawl, which (perhaps) you think very impertinent. I cannot suppose he has not seen you, after so many promises to make you his first visit. I will not fancy you are sick, and only imagine you may misaprehend my design in writing. I thank God I can live here in a Quiet retirement. I am very far from any view beyond Tranquility; and if I have been so weak to be vex'd at the misbehaviour of a Fool,[3] I desire not his ruin, and much less that he should be preferr'd, which will subject me to the same ill usage by whatever successor is appointed. I am inform'd he gives political reasons for his conduct towards me, which (if true) I ought to pardon him by all the maxims of modern Ethics.

I am ever, my Dear ⟨Chil⟩d, your most affectionate Mother,

M. Wortley.

My complements to Lord Bute and blessing to all yours. Venice, May 9th 1760

If you have not already sent my Letter to your Father, I desire you would not do it.[4]

---

[1] On 15 May 1760, when Graeme reached the Hague on his way back to Venice, he wrote to Newcastle offering his services to England (Add MS 32,906, f. 90). He reached Turin on 13 June (Mackenzie to Bute, 18 June 1760, Bute MS in Cardiff Public Library).

[2] On 12 Feb. [1760].

[3] John Murray.

[4] She had done so (p. 231).

PLATE 4

Page of Commonplace Book by Lady Mary Wortley Montagu, [1760]

Text W MS iii. 223–4[1]   *Address* To The Rt Honble the Countess
of Bute recommended to Fran: Child Esqr near Temple Bar London
Angleterre par Amsterdam   *Postmark* MA 26

To Wilhelmina Tichborne *30 May* [*1760*]

May 30

Lord F[er]re[r]s.[2] Lord G. Sackvile.[3] No Toilet can fight
against Nature, the advantage of Masking.

Text CB MS, f. 17 (summary)

To Louis Devismes[4] *3 July* [*1760*]

July 3

Never doubted his good Intention. All instruction over
with me, the wisdom of an old Woman as much laugh'd at
as the wisdom of Solomon; I read with pleasure the delec-
table History of R[eynard] the Fox[5] etc. Q[ueen] Eliz[abeth]
bespatter'd because she was a woman, as P[ope] raild at
M[adame] Dacier[6] for understanding H[omer] better than
he did.[7] Should be glad of T[ristram] Shan[dy].[8] Our
hopefull youth, my obsolete Education, was aplauded when
I should have been whipp'd. Mr. Pant[on] a pretty Man.[9]

[1] Summary in CB MS, f. 17.
[2] Laurence Shirley (b. 1720), 4th
Earl Ferrers, murdered his steward in
Jan. 1760; he was tried by his peers,
found guilty, and hanged on 5 May.
[3] Lord George Sackville (1716–85),
later 1st Viscount, had been Commander-in-Chief of the British forces
in Germany at the battle of Minden
the year before; in April 1760 he was
found guilty by court martial of dis-
obeying orders.
[4] Tutor to Sir Wyndham Knatchbull-Wyndham (see above, p. 159).

[5] LM's library in 1739 included
'Reynard the Fox' (Wh MS 135).
[6] Anne Lefebvre (1654–1720) m.
(1683) André Dacier. She translated
into prose the *Iliad* (1711) and the
Odyssey (1716).
[7] In a letter to Buckingham in 1718,
Pope criticized her translation and notes
(*Corr.*, ed. G. Sherburn, 1956, i. 492).
[8] The first two volumes of Laurence
Sterne's *Tristram Shandy* were published Jan. 1760; a second edition
followed in April.
[9] Thomas Panton (see above, p. 235).

More afraid of Panegyric than Satyr. Lord Littlet[on], Pope's Candor,[1] a similitude between him and Sir J[ohn] Falstaffe of Venice.[2] Q[ueen] B[e]ss never thought it etc. Signor Barsia,[3] me Drunk. Mr. Frazier.[4]

Text CB MS, f. 17 (summary)

To Lady Bute 9 *Aug.* [*1760*]

Aug't 9

I seldom see a news[paper] and live quite retir'd. I will not imitate R[ichardson] by giving a long detail of triffles. Tis a sad Refflection we can neither chuse or confer Happyness, all events beyond the foresight of Prudence. My esteem for the D[uches]s of Bedf[or]d.[5] My vexation for the irrecoverable loss of my Books and china.

Text CB MS, f. 17 (summary)

To Wortley 5 *Oct.* *1760*

I receiv'd yours of Sept. 2nd two posts ago, and have been much mortify'd I could not answer it immediately. Indeed it is not easy for me to write at present, haveing a defluction on my Eyes that is very painfull to me. I ought to thank you for the china Jars that you were so obliging to send me, thô I had the ill Fortune to lose them, being taken by a French privateer. I am very uneasy at my Daughter's

---

[1] Referring to Lyttelton's *Dialogues of the Dead*, published on 17 May 1760 (*Daily Advertiser*); Boileau and Pope candidly discuss their own faults in *Dialogue* xiv.
[2] Probably John Murray, the Resi-

dent, who was fat, rubicund, and jovial.
[3] Not identified.
[4] Not identified.
[5] LM's niece, Gertrude Leveson-Gower (1719–94), m. (1737) 4th Duke.

long silence, fearing it may be occasion'd by her ill Health or that of some part of her large Family.[1]

Venice, October 5. 1760[2]

Text W MS ii. 257   *End. by W* [*Summary*] Ad 15 Dec. Recd 3 Nov. 1760.

To Lady Bute 25 *Oct. 1760*

My Dear Child,

I have receiv'd yours of the 16th of September, and should have answer'd it the very next post (as I usually do) had I not been troubled with a complaint uncommon to me; I mean a Defluction on my Eyes, which is now over, but they are still weak, and I dare not indulge the pleasure I always find in scribbling to my dear child. I must think no more of any thing from England till it pleases Heaven to send Peace upon Earth. I have some small Tokens prepar'd for some of yours. I hope you will beleive me (I confess it is scarce credible) I cannot find any one (amongst all our English noble and Gentle Travellers) to send them by. Some are too Giddy and careless to be trusted, others too cautious to undertake the charge, and the greatest Number I never see at all, M[urray] makeing it a point to hinder me from converseing with those of my own Country.

I am not surpriz'd at the long Vegetation of the D[uche]sse of Argyle;[3] her Heart has been of a stronger temper than mine. I am persuaded too much sensibillity (or, if you will, too little Philosophy) destroys the Constitution as certainly as any Consumption. I ought not to repine; mine has held out to a miracle.

[1] In the summer Lord and Lady Bute and several of their daughters suffered serious illness, fever, and sore throat (Walpole, *Corr.* xxi. 416; *Selections from Family Papers at Caldwell*, ed. W. Mure, 1854, ii. 125).

[2] On 15 Sept. Graeme had reported to Bute: 'Lady Mary is stil at Padou but returns to Venise next month' (Bute MS in Cardiff Public Library).

[3] The Duchess (1683–1767) had been since 1743 widow of the 2nd Duke, Bute's uncle. In temperament she was notably phlegmatic (Lady Louisa Stuart, *Selections from Her Manuscripts*, ed. J. Home, 1899, pp. 10, 12, 14, 36).

Your Life is far more important than mine; you owe it to your children, to your Lord, (it may be) to your Country. I am of opinion he would not be at so much trouble but to make you and his Family happy.

I hope my next Letter will be longer. I am never so agreably employ'd as when endeavoring to shew you, to the best of my power, that I am ever your most affectionate Mother,

M. Wortley.

Oct. 25. 1760

My complements to Lord Bute and hearty Blessing to all yours. You have not mention'd the receit of my ten pound bill.

Text W MS iii. 227–8   *Address* To The Rt Honble the Countess of Bute recommended to Sam: Child Esqr near Temple Bar London Angleterre par Amsterdam   *Postmark* DE 2

To Wilhelmina Tichborne *30 Oct.* [*1760*]

October 30

I write to her with more pleasure than I ever dressd for a Birth day. Lady Coventry and D[uches]s of H[amilton].[1] Time gives experience, as useless to the old[2] as the Art of painting to the blind. My Plan of Liberty visionary; description of the Salvatica.[3]

Text CB MS, f. 17 (summary)

[1] Lady Coventry, elder of the beauti-ful Gunning sisters (see above, p. 18), died on 30 Sept. 1760. Her widowed sister, the Duchess of Hamilton, m. (1759) John Campbell, later 5th Duke of Argyll. Perhaps LM knew that they planned to set out for Italy in early Nov. 1760 (Walpole, *Corr.* xxi. 450).

[2] This is the theme of LM's verse 'Written at Lovere, 1755' (1861, ii. 503).

[3] The Selvatico was an inn near San Marco (Pompeo Molmenti, *Venice*, transl. H. F. Brown, 1908, III. i. 94, n. 4).

To Lady Bute *18 Nov. 1760*

I give you thanks (my Dear child) for your Information of the death of the King.[1] You may imagine how I am affected by it. I will not trouble you in this busy time with a long Letter. I do not doubt you are sufficiently tormented by pretentions and petitions. I hope you will not forget poor Mr. Anderson; and I desire Lord Bute to take care that Sir James Stewart's name is not excluded in the Act of Indemnity. This is a very small favor, yet it will make the Happiness of a Man of great merit.

My Health is very precarious. May Yours long continue, and the Prosperity of your Family. I bless God I have liv'd to see you so well establish'd, and am ready to sing my *Nunc Dimittis* with Pleasure.

I own I could wish that we had a minister here who I had not reason to suspect would plunder my House if I die while he is in Authority. General G[raeme] is extreamly infirm, and also so easily impos'd on that whatever his Intentions may be, he is incapable of protecting any body.[2] You will (perhaps) laugh at these Apprehensions, since whatever happens in this World after our Death is certainly nothing to us. It may be thought a Fantastic satisfaction, but I confess I cannot help being earnestly desirous that what I leave may ⟨fall⟩ into your Hands. Do not so far mistake me as to think I would have the present M[inister] remov'd by Advancement, which would have the sure Consequence of my suffering (if possible) more impertinence from his Successor.

My Dear Child, I am ever Your most affectionate Mother,

M. Wortley.

Nov. 18. 1760

Text W MS iii. 229–30   *Address* To The Rt Honble the Countess of Bute recommended to Sam: Child Esqr near Temple Bar London Angleterre par Amsterdam   *Postmark* IA I

[1] George II died on 25 Oct. As the intimate adviser of the new King, Bute was immediately rewarded with posts—on 27 Oct. as member of the Privy Council, and on 15 Nov. as Groom of the Stole and First Gentleman of the Bedchamber.

[2] In her Commonplace Book LM noted: 'to tell the General [that] M[urray] ask'd me to be employ'd in my affairs; I did not ask him' (MS, f. 21).

To Sir James Steuart *20 Nov. 1760*

Sir,

I will not trouble you with a long letter; this is only to let you know that as soon as my daughter informed me of the late great event, I immediately put her in mind of your affairs in the warmest manner. I do not doubt it will have the effect I wish. Your interest is one of the most considerable to my selfe, being with the strongest tyes of esteem and gratitude, Sir, Your most obliged and faithful humble servant,

M. W. Montagu.

Venice, Nov'r 20, 1760

I hope Lady Fanny and your young gentleman are in perfect health.

Text Wh MS 509 (transcript)   *Address* [*from 1818, p. 56*] To Sir James Steuart, Tubingen, Suabia.

To Lady Bute *26 Nov.* [*1760*]

My Dear Child,

I am afraid you will think me very troublesome, and that I do not enough consider the various Duties you are now oblig'd to. Indeed I am throughly sensible you have little time to throw away, but I am (privately) solicited to mention a thing to you which in my opinion I ought not to omit.

The Senate have appointed two Procurators of St. Mark to complement his Majesty on his accession. They are of the first Familys here, Contarini and Morosini,[1] and are neither of them marry'd. Madam Capello has been so ridiculous both at London and Rome, I beleive they will not often send

[1] On 22 Nov. the Senate chose two Procurators, Angelo Contarini and Francesco Morosini (Murray to Pitt, 26 Nov. 1760, SP 99/68). But Contarini, whom LM had known in Brescia (see ii. 456), did not go. Instead Morosini was accompanied by the Procurator Tommaso Querini (1706–75), appointed Feb. 1761; they left in April 1762 (*Repertorium*, ii. 414). Horace Mann predicted that they would make 'a splendid appearance' (Walpole, *Corr*. xxi. 508–9).

Ambassadresses.[1] These Cavaliers are of such a character as will do honor to their Country. They are vastly rich, and desirous to shew their Magnificence in the Court of England. They apprehend (I know not why) that they shall be thank'd and not permitted to come.[2] I am far from a Politician, God knows, but it seems to me, both in public and private Life Civillitys should never be refus'd when they are sincerely meant as proofes of Respect. I have no personal Interest in this affair, nor can receive any advantage from their Embassy but an opportunity of sending some triffles to my Grand Daughters, which I hop'd to do by Lord Titchfield, who has been long at Turin. I am now told he will not take Venice in his road when he returns to London.

I am sorry to tell you I fear General Græme is in a declining state of Health. I suppose (you know) poor Mr. Hamilton is at Petersburgh.[3] I am ever (my Dear child) Your most affectionate Mother,

M. Wortley.

Venice, Nov. 26

Text W MS iii. 197–8   *Address* To The Rt Honble the Countess of Bute recommended to Sam: Child Esqr near Temple Bar London Angleterre par Amsterdam   *Postmark* IA I

To Lady Bute *31 Dec.* [*1760*]

December 31.

I receiv'd a Letter from you last post which gave me great Pleasure by the account of your Health and Prosperity, which I pray God continue. I am a good deal out of order

[1] Pietro Andrea Capello (*c.* 1702–63) had been ambassador at London 1744–8 and at Rome 1750–7 (*Repertorium*, ii. 414, 416). He m. (1742) Eleonora Collalto (Archivio di Stato, Venice). When she first came to London in 1744 she was little more than sixteen, and aroused amused comment by her flighty foolishness (Elizabeth Carter and Catherine Talbot, *A Series of Letters 1741–1770*, 3rd ed., 1819, i. 45; also Walpole,

Corr. xviii. 431; xx. 169).

[2] Two months later the British Resident knew that the King had 'accepted of the Venetian ambassadors to compliment him upon his Accession to the Throne' (Murray to A. Mitchell, 28 Jan. 1761, Add MS 6830, f. 28).

[3] Graeme also recommended 'poor Hamilton' at St. Petersburg to the attention of Bute (26 Feb. 1761, Bute MS).

my selfe, and not very capable of writeing a long Letter, but I would not omit sending you the Bill, which it is just I should pay, being demanded by me.

Sir,   Venice, December 31, 1760
   Pray pay to the Countess of Bute or order, this my second Bill of Exchange (the second [*sic*] not being paid) for ten pounds sterling and place it to account of, Sir, your humble Servant,
                                       Mary Wortley Montague.
To Fran: Child near Temple Bar London

Text W MS iii. 259–60   *Address* To The Rt Honble the Countess of Bute recommended to Fran: Child Esqr near Temple Bar London Angleterre par Amsterdam   *Postmark* ⟨?⟩

To Wortley *12 Jan. 1761*

                                       Jan. 12. 1761
   I receiv'd yours of Dec. 16[1] last post and had much Satisfaction by the news of your Health. Mine is very infirm, and hardly permits me to write long letters. My Daughter has so much imployment at present, I beleive she has scarce time to read, much less to write. I hear her conduct and that of Lord Bute generally applauded. May you long enjoy the Happiness of their Conversation and the prosperity of your Family.

Text W MS ii. 258–9   *Address* To Edwd Wortley Esqr recommended to Fran: Child Esqr near Temple Bar London Angleterre par Amsterdam   *Postmark* IA 31

To Sir James Steuart *25 Jan. 1761*

Sir,   Venice, 25th January 1761
   I have not returned my thanks for your obliging letter so soon as both duty and inclination prompted me, but I have

───────────
   [1] W MS i. 145 (? draft).

had so severe a cold, accompanied with a weakness in my eyes, that I have been confined to my stove for many days. This is the first use I make of my pen. I will not engage in a dispute with you, being very sure that I am unable to support it against you; yet I own I am not intirely of your opinion in relation to the Civil List. I know it has long been a custom to begin every reign with some mark of the People's love exceeding what was shown to the predecessor; I am glad to see this distinguished by the trust and affection of the King to his people, and am persu[a]ded it will have a very good effect on all our affairs, foreign and domestic.[1] It is possible my daughter may have some partiality; the character of his present Majesty needs only be halfe so perfect as she describes it to be such a monarch as has never existed but in romances.

Tho' I am preparing for my last and longest journey, and stand on the threshold of this dirty world, my several infirmities like post-horses ready to hurry me away, I cannot be insensible to the happiness of my native country, and am glad to see the prospect of a prosperity and harmony that I never was witness to. I hope my friends will be included in the public joy; and I shall always think Lady Fanny and Sir James Stewart in the first rank of those I wish to serve. Your conversation is a pleasure I would prefer to any other; but I confess even that cannot make me desire to be in London, especially at this time when the shadow of credit that I should be supposed to possess would attract daily solicitations, and gain me a number of enemies who would never forgive me the not performing impossibilities. If all people thought of power as I do, it would be avoided with as much eagerness as it is now sought. I never knew any person that had it who did not lament the load, tho' I confess (so infirm is human nature) they have all endeavoured to retain it, at the same time they complained of it.

You are above any view of that kind. I hope every post to hear news of your return to your native country, where that

---

[1] At the beginning of each reign Parliament customarily passed an Act granting a revenue to the new sovereign annually for his entire reign; from it he was expected to meet the whole cost of civil government. George III surrendered his hereditary revenues in return for a fixed annual income of £800,000 (J. Steven Watson, *The Reign of George III*, 1960, p. 61).

you may long enjoy a happiness superior to any a Court can give is the most ardent desire of, Sir, Your grateful and faithful humble servant,

M. W. Montagu.

Text Wh MS 509 (transcript)[1]   *Address* [*from 1818, p. 61*] To Sir James Steuart, Tubingen, Suabia.

To Lady Bute [*Feb. 1761*]

My Dear Child,
    I have this minute receiv'd your Letter, and am little capable of answering it.[2] I cannot help taking notice of the Brutal usage I have receiv'd from Mr. Murray on this occasion, which has exasperated even the Venetians, thô neither my Freinds nor Relations.
    I am ever your truly affectionate Mother,

M. W. Montagu.

I am not able to give any Directions at present. I do not doubt you will do what is proper.

Text W MS iii. 265–6   *Address* To The Rt Honble the Countess of Bute recommended to Fran: Child Esqr near Temple Bar London Angleterre par Amsterdam   *Postmark* ⟨?⟩

To Lady Bute [*c. 20 Feb. 1761*]

My Dear Child,
    I hardly know how to write what I do. I may truly say I have not sle⟨pt⟩ soundly since I receiv'd yours. My Eyes are al⟨so⟩ very bad. There are reports here in relation to your Brother so infamous[3] I hope they are not true.

---

[1] Summary in CB MS, f. 13.

[2] Evidently it contained the news that W had died on 22 Jan. at his house in Cavendish Square (date from various newspapers; Lady Bute's plaque in the Wortley parish church gives 21 Jan.).

[3] Regarding his opposition to W's will (see below, p. 254, n. 5).

I am sorry to tell you I fear the General is in a very bad state of Health. He has kept his Bed several days, alwaies surrounded by Murray's imps. I did not know till yesterday Mr. Udney is Consul, which it seems he has been some time.[1] I desire you would direct your next to him. All yours have been aukardly, palpaply [*sic*] open'd, and I suppose many of mine has miscarry'd by the same management. I have alwaies thought revenge a mean Sentiment. I know that in this world one must bear and forbear. I will write to my Son, having had a command from your Father in his last letter to me so to do.[2] I never disobey'd him in my Life and will not now begin.

I will set out for England as soon as the Weather and my Health permits passing through Germany.[3] I am heartily sorry to put you to any expence, but beg you would keep the Horses or dispose of them as you think proper, and take care of the other baggage. Your B[rother] has certainly correspondents here.

I desire Lord Holderness would order his Cousin to be civil to me,[4] which he says is not in his Instructions.

I am ever your most affectionate Mother.

M. W. M.

I will write a longer letter next post.

Text W MS iii. 247–8   *Address* To the Rt Honble the Countess of Bute recommend[e]d to Fran: Child Esqr near Temple Bar London Angleterre par Amsterdam   *Postmark* MR 10

To Lady Bute [*Feb. 1761*]

I own it cuts me to the Heart to be ill treated by you, and receive insults of the most outrageous kind from one that

[1] John Udney (1727–1800) had been nominated by Smith as his successor (Smith to Pitt, 29 Oct. 1760, SP 99/68). He presented his patent on 6 Feb. 1761 (Murray to Pitt, ibid.).

[2] W's last surviving letter, dated 16 Dec. 1760, does not mention their son (W MS i. 145: ? draft).

[3] It was generally assumed that LM would return to England after W's death (Eliz. Montagu, *Corr. 1720–1761*, ed. E. J. Climenson, 1906, ii. 230).

[4] Holdernesse, Secretary of State, was cousin to Murray's wife, Lady Wentworth.

was recommended to me by being, as he said and Lord
B[ute] confirm'd, your Freind and Relation.[1] I can easily
account for his narrow way of thinking; I cannot for yours.
I am now told the young People understand one another
and have a mind to get rid of an Old Woman, like J. S. and
his Brother the D[uke].[2] I never beleiv'd it of them; I confess I remember the Report.

Text W MS iii. 286–7   *Address* To The Rt Honble the Countess of
Bute recommended to Fran: Child Esqr near Temple Bar London
Angleterre par Amsterdam   *Postmark* MR ⟨?⟩

To Lady Bute [*c. 25 Feb. 1761*]

My dearest Child,
    I do not love to break the most triffling promise and would
willingly write every post, but my Eyes are now so bad I
can hardly see to read. I hope they will recover, and beg
you take care of the books and plate.[3] The fine Gentleman[4]
may defame and even break an Indulgent mother's heart,
but shall never make her Guilty of hurting an innocent
Daughter and a worthy Son[5] etc.

[1] Apparently Gen. Graeme.
[2] Probably John Spencer (1708–46),
heir to Sarah, Duchess of Marlborough,
and his brother the 3rd Duke.
[3] By W's will, drawn up in 1755, LM
was left £1,200 a year in full for 'her
dower and all Right and Title of Dower
to any of my Real Estate'; and she was
permitted to keep all her paraphernalia:
jewels, plate, and books (P.C.C.
Cheslyn, f. 198).
[4] LM's son, who was virtually dis-
inherited (see below, p. 257).
[5] Lord and Lady Bute. On 30 Jan.
1761 Robert Symmer informed Andrew
Mitchell (British Envoy in Berlin) of
what Bute's family had inherited: 'it is
said the personal Estate amounts to
7 or £800,000 and the Landed Estate,
Coal Mines included, to £20,000 per
annum. Lady Bute, after payment of
Legacies, has the whole during Life.

But young Wortley has enter'd a Caveat,
in his Mother's name; and it is thought
she will be found to be entitled to her
Thirds, there having been no marriage
settlement duely executed.' On 3 Feb.
he gave further details: 'I have it from
a pretty good Hand that £50,000 per
Annum will come into Lord Bute's
Family during the Life of My Lady.
The Thirds which Lady Mary Wortley
claims will not be any great Matter, as it
affects only the Landed Estate (which
does not exceed £7,000 per Annum). . .'
(Add MS 6839, ff. 207, 210). Elizabeth
Montagu estimated the estate as £800,000
in money, and £17,000 a year in land
and mines (*Letters 1762–1800*, ed. R.
Blunt, 1923, i. 14).
    The *London Evening Post* noted: 'We
hear that the Will of a certain rich
Commoner lately deceased, is likely to
be contested' (12–14 Feb. 1761).

You would not wonder at my writeing misteriously if you knew, or I (for your sake) darst tell you, all that passes here.

When I can get a safe conveyance you shall know my Heart as clear to you as it has ever been. God send us a happy meeting. Never make an infamous concession.

All this mischeife comes from the Villainy of M[urray] and weakness of a worthy Freind of yours.¹ I wish you joy of a L[ord] H[igh] C[hancellor]² who I beleive as strictly just [as] any every [*sic*] grac'd the B[ench], not excepting S[ir] T[homas] M[ore], who dy'd a Martyr. I would write to W.³ if my head permitted. Perhaps it is better let alone in the present circumstance. I know all will be told you of my great Avarice, etc. You ⟨ought⟩ to know me better.

Text W MS iii. 282–3   *Address* To The Rt Honble the Countess of Bute recommended to Fran: Child Esqr near Temple Bar London Angleterre par Amsterdam   *Postmark* MR 14

To [Lord Bute] [*Feb. 1761*]

My Lord,

I beg your pardon for this Liberty I take. I realy feel my Head light. I swear to you (so may my Soul find peace with God) I know nothing of those infamous libels my son has produce'd in my name. I dare be poor, I dare not be dishonest. I own I am weary of fighting with one hand ty'd behind. Do what you think fitting with the plate and Jewells etc. The General (*if he remembers it*) may be wittness; I told him sometime ago. Mr. W[ortley] was persuaded by the Agents of his Son I had sold my Daughter to you. Indeed I desir'd you might never know it.

> To dare in Fields is valour, but how few
> Dare have the real courage to be true?

Text W MS v. 1

¹ Gen. Graeme.
² Robert Henley (1708 ?–72), 1st Baron, appointed 16 Jan. 1761, would judge any litigation over W's will. A *caveat* to delay the proving of a will stood in force for three months (Giles Jacob, *New Law-Dict.*, 1739); and W's will was not proved until 4 May.
³ Probably Alexander Wedderburn (1733–1805), advocate; he later assisted Bute in his appeal to break the will (below, p. 270, n. 2).

To James Stuart Mackenzie [*28 Feb. 1761*]

I this moment receiv'd a large pacquet[1] from Mr. Mackensie worthy the honest disinterested Heart I have allwaies esteem[ed]. I am allmost mad with the minister[i]al proceedings of a manze Puffin.[2] All my Letters are open'd and stopp'd, my servants threaten'd, or spies. In this conjuncture I dare write no clearer than to say I entirely acquiesce to the Will you wot off.[3] God knows whither you will ever receive this. I am now oblig'd (a little, God knows) to Cameran.[4] In this corrupt Age you know money does every thing. I write every post to my Daughter but so distracted I hardly know what I say.[5]

I am ever your oblig'd and faithfull Humble Servant,

M. Wortley Monta[gu]

Text Bute MS   *Address* A Monsieur Monsieur Mackensie Ministre a la Cour de Turin par Milano   *End. by Mackenzie* Lady M. Wortley 28 Febr. Rd 5 March 1761. ansd 7th. *to be kept* as it contains Her acquiescence to Mr. Wortley's *Will* [6]

[1] Containing a copy of W's will which he had received from Bute on 24 Feb.

[2] I.e. Murray, who was born on the Isle of Man. The word *puffin* was applied to the Manx shearwater (a bird), and also to a person puffed up with vanity (*OED*).

[3] 'By what I have heard of the *Will*,' Mackenzie wrote to Bute, "tis certainly a most extraordinary one, especially with respect to my poor little neighbour here [Lord Mountstuart], to whom the Testator has indeed been most unkind, as well as to His worthy Father [Lord Bute]—*mais, patience!*' (25 Feb. 1761, Bute MS). The bulk of W's estate was to go to Lady Bute's second son; and she was to receive in her lifetime the income 'wherewith her present or future husband shall not intermeddle or have any power to dispose' (P.C.C. Cheslyn, f. 198).

[4] Giulio Vittorio d'Incisa, conte di Camerana, Sardinian Minister to Venice

from 1749 to 6 Sept. 1759 (*Repertorium*, ii. 367). He had forwarded the packet to LM.

[5] On this same day (28 Feb.) Joseph Smith wrote to an unnamed Italian correspondent that LM was very well, and in her widowhood behaved with philosophical calm (Epistolario Moschini, Museo Correr, Venice).

[6] On 7 March Mackenzie sent Bute a summary of LM's letter, confessing himself puzzled. He continued: 'I had another letter from Her last week (before she had received the Packet) wherein she mentions certain Reports of malicious persons relating to what young W[ortley] and Herself intended to do, which she vows and protests she knows nothing at all of, and would not be concern'd in for the wealth of the Indies; with all this, she does not give me the most distant hint of what those malicious Reports are, and as I never heard any of them, Her letter is totally

To Edward Wortley Montagu, junior, *3 March* [*1761*][1]

Son,
   I know not how to write to you and scarcely what to say.
Your present conduct is far more Infamous than the past.
It is small sign of reformation of Manners when you durst
attempt to disturb an Indulgent (too indulgent) Father's
dying pangs on mercenary Considerations, and are now
defameing a too fond Mother by the most impudent For-
gery. I think no single man deserves Bread that cannot live
decently and honorably on £1,600 sterling per Annum rent
charge.[2] I liv'd on less than halfe that summ with your
worthy Father when you was born and sometime after,
without ever borrowing or raising money on Contingencies
or even on certaintys, which was in some measure our Case.[3]
I can add no more. You have shorten'd your Father's days
and will perhaps have the Glory to break your mother's
Heart—I will not curse you—God give you a real not affected
Repentance.

                                                  M. W. Montagu

March third N.S., 1761/2 [*sic*][4]

unintelligible to me. She says nothing
of what she intends to do, and by what
I learn from those who see Her frequently, she does not seem to know
Herself what she will do; she is so un-
determin'd about everything she makes
fifty resolutions every day, and changes
them before night. I once thought of
imparting to Her that there was a possibility of my being soon where she is,
as I know that that would be an inducement to Her to remain there, which
I imagine is what you would choose she
should do, but I was afterwards afraid
of Her speaking of it, which would have
been highly improper till I am author-
ised thrô the regular channel to mention
it. However if I learn from a Correspondent of mine there that there is any like-
lyhood of Her moving from thence . . .
I beleive I shall drop Her some hints,

from the notion I entertain of your
sentiments on that subject' (Bute MS).
   [1] Sent to Lady Bute (see next letter).
   [2] Montagu, who already had an
annuity of £600 settled on him, was
left £1,000 a year, to which LM's
annuity of £1,200 would be added
after her death. By a codicil he was also
given the furniture and the use of the
house at Newbold Verdon. That summer
he sold off the pictures to pay his debts
(Eliz. Montagu, *Corr. 1720–1761*, ed.
E. J. Climenson, 1906, ii. 249).
   [3] He had borrowed from a money-
lender nearly £7,000 at 10% interest
(History of Parliament, *House of
Commons 1754–1790*, ed. L. Namier and
J. Brooke, 1964, iii. 662).
   [4] In her distraction LM's dates during this period are sometimes confused.

You say you know Venice. I am sorry to say Venice knows you, and I know all your Criminal Extravagancies.

M. W. Montagu

Text W MS iii. 9–10   *Address* To E. W. Montagu Esqr

To Lady Bute *4 March* [*1761*]

My Dear Child,

After (what I thought in the present Circumstance) a long silence, I receiv'd a large pacquet from you by the Milan post and the assistance of the Sardinian Minister here.[1] It came not to my hands till near nine at Night; at the same time an obliging Letter from Mr. Mackensie, which came too late to answer by that post, and indeed my Eyes are now so weaken'd I cannot (without great uneasyness) write by candle light. I will not trouble you with a long detail of my vexations, which may seem triffling to you, and would have been so to me thirty year ago or even five and twenty. God keep you from such severe Tryals. I will only assure you I never will fail in shewing you and yours all the proofes you can require of your most tender and affectionate Mother.

M. Wortley

The enclos'd to my unhappy and Guilty Son you may send under Cover to him. I know not where he is.

March 4th, Venice, 1760 [*sic*]

I will write to Lord Mountstuart directed to his Uncle at T[urin].[2]

Text W MS iii. 220A–B   *Address* To The Rt Honble The Countess of Bute recommended to Fran: Child Esqr near Temple Bar London Angleterre par Amsterdam.

[1] Camerana (see above, p. 256) had ceased being Minister in 1759 but had no successor.

[2] Lady Bute's eldest son evidently attended the academy there.

To Lady Bute [*5 March 1761*]

My Dear Child,

You will be surpriz'd to hear I have only finish'd the reading of the will this morning, the 5th of March 1761. I think your Brother has far more than he deserves. I wish I had been left mourning, being out of Cash at present, which if I had not been I had begun my Journey, thinking it my Duty to risk my Life if I can contribute to the due Execution of your honor'd Father's last will and Testament. You must not offer to compound with your Brother, if you take my Advice. His Grandfather, Sidney,[1] had only an Annuity for Life of £500 from his Family. He had an eldest Son, Francis Wortley Esqr., on whom I beleive the Wortley Estate (I mean only the Mannor of Wortley and woods) was entail'd. He dy'd unmarry'd and the Estate came by Law to your late respected Father.[2] All the rest are acquire'd by him by true and lawfull Purchase. My Head is too bad to be prolix. I receiv'd the will last Saturday late at night, too late either to read or answer the Letter of Lord Mountstuart.[3]

I am your afflicted and sincerely affectionate Mother.

M. Wortley

I think you would do well to visit Mrs. Wright. I have said this before or I am mistaken. I know not where to direct to her.[4]

Text W MS iii. 257–8   *Address* To The Rt Honble the Countess of Bute recommended to Fran: Child Esqr near Temple Bar London Angleterre par Amsterdam   *Postmark* MR 26

[1] Sidney Wortley (d. 1727), 2nd son of Edward Montagu, 1st Earl of Sandwich.

[2] At the death of his elder brother Francis Wortley in 1702, W became heir to the 'settled estates', including Wortley and six other manors (Jos. Hunter, *South Yorkshire*, 1831, ii. 320). By his will, drawn in 1726, Sidney Wortley left W only the coal-mines in Barnsley; and young Montagu was unmentioned (P.C.C. Farrant, f. 281).

LM's summary of this letter is: 'a sketch of the Entail to serve in her [Lady Bute's] unhappy Law suit' (CB MS, f. 13). This suggests that Montagu planned to sue for part of W's landed estate on the basis that it was entailed on him and could not be transferred to Lady Bute and her second son.

[3] The summary of her letter to Mackenzie on 6 March (CB MS, f. 13) notes that she answered Mountstuart.

[4] See below, p. 263.

To James Stuart Mackenzie 6 *March 1761*

I am still in the state of Halfe-witted, that is to say, halfe out of my Wits. I neither comprehend what my Daughter demands, nor my extravagant Son acts. I am fully persuaded of his bad Heart and of her good one. I no ways doubt Lord Bute's Honor, and beleive he would not ask me to accept the Will in such a manner as would bar me of a just demand. I do not speak of thirds[1] (which I renounce) but other affairs, the detail of which is too long to trouble you with.[2]

I am here in the midst of all the Iniquitys of a Court without any of the Amusements. Our Great (i.e. Grosse) Minister[3] is the perfect Figure of Sir R[obert] W[alpole], and his pious Lady has the Heart and manners of a Great Queen deceas'd.[4] If I was in England I would implore the assistance of the Duke of Argyle;[5] at present I know nothing but that I am unalterably your Faithfull Freind and servant,

M. Wortley Montagu.

March 6th 1761.

I beg my Complements to Lord Titchfield.

I negotii vogliono stare gran tempo à molle come i pesci salati.[6]

Text Bute MS   *Address* A Monsieur Monsieur Mackensie Ministre de S. M. Brittanique a la Cour de Turin par Milano   *End. by Mackenzie* Ly M. Wortley 7 Mar. Rd 12 Mar. 1761 ansd 14.[7] *about Mr. Wortleys Will*

[1] See above, p. 254, n. 5.

[2] Mackenzie, after quoting this paragraph in his letter of 14 March to Bute, wrote that he was puzzled as to what LM meant by the 'other affairs' (Bute MS in Cardiff Public Library). LM explained in her next letter to Lady Bute.

[3] To Casanova, John Murray 'avait l'air d'un beau Baccus peint par Rubens' (*Histoire de ma vie*, ed. F. A. Brockhaus, 1960–2, iv. 161).

[4] LM unflatteringly compares Murray and his wife to Walpole and to Queen Caroline, whom she described as having a 'low cunning, which gave her an inclination to cheat all the people she conversed with. . . ' ('Account of George I', 1861, i. 133).

[5] Mackenzie's uncle the 3rd Duke of Argyll.

[6] 'Business ought to stand a long time softening like fish in brine'. She repeated part of this sentence in her summary (CB MS, f. 13), but its meaning is not clear.

[7] He quoted his answer in a letter to Bute the same day.

To Lady Bute *11 March* [*1761*]

March 11. 1760 [*sic*]

My dear Child,

My Health is a little mended, very little, God knows. I have in a great degree lost my sleep and appetite; what I most dreaded (the greatest part of my Life) has now happen'd. I never thought to survive your (ever honor'd) Father, and was perfectly persuaded I should [never] see my Family torn to pieces and my selfe involv'd in Difficulties very hard to struggle with at my Time of Life. I desire nothing but peace and Retirement.

I have Catalogues of the Books, household stuff, and Plate given me by your Father when I left England. I had some other writeings. I beleive you would not counsel me to authen[t]icate the Will in such a manner as to deprive me of the Benefit, thô perhaps they are of little use, the Wittnesses being (it may be) all dead. Adieu, my Dear child, I conclude with Mr. Earle's[1] Toast: God bless you whatever becomes of me. Your most affectionate Mother,

M. Wortley M.

I never will joyn with your profligate Brother, and hope you will not compound with him.

Text W MS iii. 221–22[2]   *Address* To The Rt Honble the Countess of Bute recommended to Fran: Child Esqr near Temple Bar London Angleterre par Amsterdam   *Postmark* MR 30

To John Anderson[3] *13 March* [*1761*]

March 13th

To be shew'd my Son. My affliction and sorrow for his Father's Death and his past and present infamous

---

[1] Giles Earle (1678 ?–1758), politician and wit.

[2] Summary in CB MS, f. 13.

[3] Former tutor to LM's son.

Behavior, as a Tallier to Mirepoix[1] and debaucheries at Venice.

Text CB MS, f. 13 (summary)

To Humphry Morice[2] *14 March* [*1761*]

Sir:

I can assure you with great Truth that the account of your Health has given me pleasure, even now that I am in a situation where very few things can give me a pleasing Sensation. I have naturally good Spirits, but a long series of vexations, added to a long series of years, has at length wore them out, and I am realy weak both in Body and mind. If my strength permitted I would immediately set out for Naples; that Air and your Conversation would be the best Remedys for the distemper'd Head and Heart of, Sir, Your oblig'd Humble Servant,

                                   M. Wortley Montagu.

March 14. 1760 [*sic*]

I receiv'd yours last Thursday. I beg my Complements to Sir J[ames] Gray.[3]

Text Swinburne (Capheaton) MS owned by Mrs. R. G. Browne-Swinburne   *Address* A Monsieur Monsieur H. Morice recommandée a Monsieur le Chevalier James Gray Ministre de S. M. Brittainique a la Cour de Naples par Milano   *Postmark* ⟨?⟩   *End.* La. W Mountague rec'd Apr. 1761 K

---

[1] Anne-Marguerite-Gabrielle de Beau-vau-Craon (1709–91) m. (1739) the marquis, later duc, de Mirepoix, French Ambassador to London 1749–55. LM means that her son had served as 'banker' to the Duchess, whose great passion was gambling (Walpole, *Corr.* xiv. 152; xxxi. 89).

[2] In 1750 Morice (1723–85) had inherited Sir William Morice's estate (but not baronetcy), which included parlia-mentary patronage, and he sat from 1750 to 1780. He was 'puny and precious' (History of Parliament, *House of Commons 1754–1790*, ed. L. Namier and J. Brooke, 1964, iii. 166–8). In July 1760 he went abroad for his health (*Daily Advertiser*, 9 July); he reached Florence in Oct., and then went to Naples (Walpole, *Corr.* xxi. 442 and n. 15).

[3] See above, p. 128.

To Lady Frances Steuart *14 March* [*1761*]

March 14

Weak in body and mind, always a warm Freind to her and Family.

Text CB MS, f. 13 (summary)

To Mrs. Catherine Wright[1] *20 March* [*1761*]

March 20

Her letter open'd. My Spirits low. Lord Ch[olmondeley] strong in body and mind. I hope his Fatigue will not injure his Health. Great Idea of his Lady.[2] Burlesque account of Mrs. Mendez, and her Favor at Court.[3]

Text CB MS, f. 13 (summary)

To James Stuart Mackenzie *28 March 1761*

1761 March 28, 30 minutes past 4.
just dine'd; halfe asleep.

Yours of 14th Instant is this minute arriv'd, and I will not delay answering it. As to the Will, I am very sincere in acquiesceing to it, but I mean that my Father's Legacy

---

[1] A friend since 1758 (see above, p. 193).

[2] Probably George Cholmondeley (1703–70), 3rd Earl, who m. (1723) Mary Walpole (1705–31), Sir Robert's only legitimate daughter. A member of the Privy Council under George II and George III, he was in Horace Walpole's opinion a 'vain empty man, shoved up too high by his father-in-law' (*Mem. of George II*, 1822, i. 150–1).

[3] Miss Tabitha Mendez (b. 1728), a rich, witty, and extremely cultivated Catholic lady, had left England in Sept. 1760 with the Wynne family. In Nov. she was in Venice (Bruno Brunelli, *Casanova Loved Her*, transl. A. McKechnie, 1929, pp. 208, 216). In Aug. 1761, in Rome, James Adam shunned her because she was ugly, ill-dressed, and looked like a Jewess (John Fleming, *Robert Adam and His Circle*, 1962, pp. 286–7). By 'Court', LM means John Murray and his satellites.

etc. which is therein given me, being mine before, independant of any Husband, I will preserve the right of demanding.[1]

I am not surpriz'd you comprehend nothing of M[urray]'s
proceedings, it being (as you justly say) utterly impossible
there should be any Rivalry between us, which is generally
the root of all dissentions. I confess it appears a Phenomenon
to me that he has not once, either here or at Padoua (where
I pass the Summer Months), ever call'd at my door or paid
me the common Civilities due to every English Subject from
the King's minister, notwithstanding I continue my Visits
to his Excellency's Lady, and will do so. This is realy not
worth talking of; and as to the occasion of it I am entirely
ignorant, having not given the least offence either to him or
any of his Court, directly or indirectly.

I wish I could hope to see you. The continue'd Freindship
of Signora Chiara Michielli is the greatest, indeed the only
pleasure I have here. I confess my selfe overcharg'd with
Spleen, but in all Humours I am with warmth and tenderness
Your faithfull Humble Servant,

M. W. M.

I intend to make my Will this evening, where your Name
shall be inserted.[2]

Text Bute MS[3]   *Address* A Monsieur Monsieur Mackensie Ministre
de S. M. Brittanique a la Cour de Turin   *End. by Mackenzie* Ly M.
Wortley Rd 2 April ansd 9 May 1761

To Lady Bute *3 April 1761*

April 3rd, 1761.

I made my Will last wednesday, which is wittness'd by
Lord Torrington, Mr. Horton James, Mr. Mytton, and
Mr. Jennings, all the English Gentlemen who are now at

[1] W did not specifically mention the
legacy of £6,000 left to her by her
father, whose will stipulated that she
was to receive only the income, and that
after her death the principal was to go
to her daughter (see ii. 63, n. 3).
[2] For her bequest to him (in her final
will) see below, p. 295.
[3] Summary in CB MS, f. 13.

Venice.[1] I have had no Lawyer to assist me, yet as it is wrote by my own Hand,[2] I think it is so worded as to admit of no dispute. You will laugh (perhaps) at so much caution about a Triffle, yet I confess I am weak enough to be solicitous about it.—

I receive this minute your welcome Letter of March 17. I wish you joy of every thing, and pray God to continue the prosperity of your Family. I think Lord Bute behaves very generously to your Brother.[3] I fear there is little Gratitude to be expected. If I live to September I intend to set out for England. You need not apprehend my being troublesome by Solicitations. I have only two engagements: something for poor Mr. Anderson, who I think has suffer'd by his attachment to an unworthy Pupil, and the Indemnity of Sir J[ames] Stewart, who I think a very deserving Man. I can say on my Death bed I have had clean hands, never haveing taken (in any Shape) either Præmium or Gratification for any Service that I have render'd to any of my Acquaintance or suppos'd Freinds.

I congratulate you on the return of Lord Marischalle, who is (in my opinion) a truly worthy and agreable Companion.[4] I am sorry to tell you poor General Graham is in so bad a state of Health, his Life is doubted.

Mr. Mackensie has sent me the pacquet to which I imagine you have already an Answer. I receiv'd in it a Letter from our Lord Mountstewart, which I immediately answer'd.

[1] George Byng (1740–1812), 4th Viscount Torrington. The others are probably Haughton James of Jamaica (1738–1813), elected to the Society of Dilettanti 1763 (Lionel Cust, *History of the Society of Dilettanti*, 1898, p. 260); John Mytton (1737–83), elected to the Dilettanti 1764, and the Royal Society 1767; Henry Constantine Jennings (1731–1819). In Turin a year earlier, Mackenzie had reported on the characters of Torrington and Mytton (to Bute, 2 April 1760, Bute MS in Cardiff Public Library).

[2] LM made her final will on 23 June 1762 (printed below, pp. 294–5).

[3] On 30 March, Montagu was re-elected to Parliament for Bossiney, the Cornish pocket borough formerly controlled by his father and now by Lady [and Lord] Bute (History of Parliament, *House of Commons 1754–1790*, ed. L. Namier and J. Brooke, 1964, i. 224). Lady Bute also (perhaps at this time) granted him an estate in Chancery valued at £8,000 (Jonathan Curling, *Edward Wortley Montagu*, 1954, p. 159). The ledgers of Coutts and Co. show that Bute paid Montagu £300 on 15 June 1761 (MS).

[4] Lord Marischal, who had returned to London in Aug. 1760, took the Oath of Allegiance on 26 Jan. 1761 and resumed his forfeited personal estate (Edith E. Cuthell, *The Last Earl Marischall*, 1915, ii. 91, 100).

If it be possible, I will see him in my Journey, being very desirous to embrace him, of whom I hear so much good and never heard any evil. I am glad he did not come here, where I think (while M[urray] presides) it would have been impossible to preserve his Health and Innocence. This consideration may be the reason of Lord Titchfield's not comeing, and is indeed very reasonable. I hear him much commended.

I cannot help being sincerely concern'd for the Death of my unfortunate Sister.[1] I propos'd to my selfe (if it please'd God I should arrive at London) a great pleasure in giveing her some comfort. She was realy honest, and lov'd me.

Adieu my dear child, my Eyes are weak. I am ever your most affectionate Mother,

M. Wortley.

My thanks and complements to Lord Bute and blessing to all Yours.

Text W MS iii. 231–2[2]   *Address* To The Rt Honble the Countess of Bute recommended to Fran: Child Esqr near Temple Bar London Angleterre par Amsterdam   *Postmark* ⟨?⟩ 18

To Lady Bute *10 April 1761*

My Dear Child,

I hope there never will be any misunderstanding between us. I am persuaded my Late Letters (wrote with a confus'd Head and trembling hand) may want some explanation. I hardly remember what is in them. I am now (I thank God) more settled in my Mind, and (at least in some measure) resign'd to my ill Fortune.

I have read over your Father's Will with more attention than I did the first time. If I understand it, he seems to imagine I have sumns of Money conceal'd, which I have not, nor ever had any with which I did not acquaint him.[3] If he

---

[1] Lady Mar died in London on 4 March (*Daily Advertiser*, 6 March 1761).

[2] Summary in CB MS, f. 13.

[3] The section of W's will that deals with this is: 'I give to my said Wife all such sum and sums of money which she has put out on Government or other

means the £6,000 left me by my Father, it was left by his Will for my separate use during my Life, and the Reversion to you, which I suppose you know, thô I never told it to you, being forbidden by Mr. Wortley; yet you may recollect, when you once hinted to me your knowledge of it I did not contradict it. I have long known he design'd you his Heiresse, some years before your Marriage, but as he desir'd I never would speak of it, this is the first time I have mention'd it in my Life.

I acquiesce to every part of his Will that does not injure the just demand I have of what my Father left me. I do not beleive he intended I should be depriv'd of it. If it please God we meet, I hope you will be convince'd of my sincere affection to you and yours. I have put my Will in the upper drawer of that little Cabinet of decoupeures that you have seen; I will seal it up. This caution I think necessary. I may dye here suddenly, and I would leave my little affairs in such a manner that you may not be impos'd on. I have no debts, having always paid ready money. General Græme is something better, but still keeps his Bed. He begs his Complements of Congratulation to you and Lord Bute. I think him an honest Man and sincerely your Freind, but I can trust him with nothing which Murray cannot persuade him out of.

My decaid Sight will not suffer me to write more at this time. I am ever your most affectionate Mother,

M. Wortley.

My Bl⟨essing⟩ to all yours and complements to my Lord Bute.

April 10th 1761

I have this minute receiv'd a very gratefull Letter from Sir J[ames] Steuart to thank me for his son's advancement, in which I have no part, having never ask'd it. However, I return thanks to Lord Bute, who doubly deserves it from me,

Securitys in her own or any other person's name in Trust for her and such ready money and other things she has and which were reputed hers . . . I having allowed her in my lifetime to manage and keep for her separate use and advantage and to improve the several sums of money she had by her at Interest in her own Name or any other person's Name in Trust for her. . .' (P.C.C. Cheslyn, f. 198).

having done an agreable thing to me without my demand.[1]
Poor Lady Fanny is very ill; I am sorry for it, thô I (almost)
envy her happiness in domestic Life, where only true happiness is existing.

Text W MS iii. 233–4[2]   *Address* To The Rt Honble the Countess
of Bute recommended to Fran: Child Esqr near Temple Bar London
Angleterre par Amsterdam   *Postmark* AP 24

To Sir James Steuart *12 April 1761*

Venice, April 12th 1761

Sir,
I received your obliging letter yesterday and make haste
to answer it the first post. I am very sincere in assuring you
all your interests are mine, consequently I share with you the
concern you feel for Lady Fanny's disorders.

You observe justly there is no happiness without an alloy,
nor indeed any misfortune without some mixture of consolation, if our passions permitted us to perceive it. But alas!
we are too imperfect to see on all sides; our wisest reflections
(if the word wise may be given to humanity) are tainted by
our hopes and fears: we all indulge views almost as extravagant as those of Phaeton, and are angry when we do not succeed in projects that are above the reach of mortality. The
happiness of domestic life seems the most laudable as it is
certainly the most delightful of our prospects, yet even that is
denied, or at least so mixed 'we think it not sincere or fear it
cannot last'.[3] A long series of disappointments have perhaps
worn out my natural spirits and given a melancholy cast to
my way of thinking. I would not communicate this weakness
to any but your selfe, who can have compassion even where
your superior understanding condemns.

I confess that tho' I am (it may be) beyond the strict
bounds of reason pleased with my Lord Bute's and my

[1] On 17 March 1761 James Steuart
entered the army as cornet in the 1st
Dragoons. He owed the appointment to
Lord Barrington, Secretary at War
1755–61, who had met and befriended

his father in Paris ('Memoirs', *Original
Letters*, 1818, p. 126).
[2] Summary in CB MS, f. 13.
[3] Matthew Prior, *Henry and Emma*
(*Works*, 1959, i. 283).

daughter's prosperity, I am doubtful whether I will attempt to be a spectator of it. I have so many years indulged my natural inclinations to solitude and reading, I am unwilling to return to crouds and bustle, which would be unavoidable in London. The few friends I esteemed are now no more; the new set of people who fill the stage at present are too indifferent to me even to raise my curiosity.

I now begin[1] (very late, you'll say) the worst effects of Age, blindness excepted: I am grown timorous and suspicious; I fear the inconstancy of that Goddess so publickly adored in Ancient Rome and so heartily inwardly worship'd in the Modern. I retain, how[ever], such a degree of that uncommon thing called Common Sense not to trouble the felicity of my children with my foreboding dreams, which I hope will prove as idle as the croaking of ravens or the noise of that harmless animal distinguished by the odious name of screech-owl. You will say, why then do I trouble you with my old wives' prophecies? Need I tell you that it is one of the privileges of friendship to talk of our own follies and infirmities? You must then, nay you ought to, pardon my tiresome tattle in consideration of the real attachment with which I am unalterably, Sir, Your obliged and faithful humble servant,

M. W. Montagu.

My best Compliments to dear Lady Fanny and congratulation to the young gentleman. I do not doubt he is sorry to leave her, but if it be necessary for his advancement you will teach him to suffer it at least with patience.

Text Wh MS 509 (transcript)[2]   *Address* [*from 1818, p. 64*] To Sir James Steuart, Tubingen, Suabia.

To Lady Bute 29 April [1761]

My Dear Child,

I hope there never will be any misunderstanding between us. I am sure it must be a misunderstanding in every sense of that word if ever it happens. It is true I have receiv'd a

---

[1] 'to feel' (1818).   [2] Summary in CB MS, f. 13.

letter from your Brother which frighted me, and I have since been told many circumstances, either from Folly or malice (perhaps a mixture of both), which made me very uneasy on your account. As to my selfe, I have so short a time to stay in this World I can be strongly affected by nothing.

I am extremely pleas'd (that is, as far as I can be pleas'd) with the expectation of seeing Mr. Mackensie here,[1] and shall delay my Journey to England that I may put my little affairs here into his hands. General Græme is much recover'd, thô still very infirm and hardly capable of mannaging his own business, consequently not to be troubled with things that are of no concern to him. I am always sorry when I see a good Heart misled. A small degree of Prudence would have secur'd him a very high Establishment. However, I think he has no reason to Complain; he has at least £900 sterling hand pay, nothing to do, and may, if he pleases, shine in this Country for that Sumn.

I am glad that you have it not in your power to alter any part of your Father's will.[2]

The Duke of M[arlborough] is now here; I have seen him once. He ressembles both his Parents, I beleive inside and out. Lord Charles has a more Spritely look.[3] Your Countrimen preserve their preheminence. Lord Archibald Hamilton is a very pretty, Wellbred Youth.[4] I would give you my simple opinion of all the passengers if I thought it could be of any service to you, but I ought to remember that you are both encumber'd with Court attendance and loaded with Business, and cannot have much leisure to read my useless Epistles.

[1] On 18 Feb. 1761 Mackenzie had asked Pitt for an appointment as Ambassador Extraordinary to Venice; on 14 April Pitt answered that the King had granted his request (SP 92/68).

[2] On 11 March Lady Bute had assigned to Bute coal properties in Durham and Northumberland, part of W's vast estate entailed on her second son, whose trustees sued in the Court of Chancery to prevent this, and in July won their case. In Nov., Bute's appeal was denied by the Lord Chancellor, [and in Jan. 1762 by the House of Lords] (full account in *Reports of Cases . . . in the High Court of Chancery 1757 to 1766*, ed. R. H. Eden, 1818, ii. 87–107).

[3] The Duke and his brother (see above, pp. 190–1) arrived in Venice on 17 April (Murray to Pitt, 22 April 1761, SP 99/68).

[4] Lord Archibald (1740–1819), later 9th Duke. In Nov. 1760 Horace Mann reported from Florence that he 'lives in the woods of Tuscany. He is quite a wild boy, has nothing human in him but the pride of the Hamiltons. . .' (Walpole, *Corr.* xxi. 457).

I beg my complements to Lord Bute. I never hear him mention'd without praise, as you may very well think. My Blessing to all yours. I should be glad you gave me some account of Mr. J[ames] W[ortley] S[tuart].[1] I depend so much on your Sincerity, I shall beleive that you will lay aside all partiality when you talk even of him to your most affectionate Mother.

M. Wortley M.

Venice, April 29

Text W MS iii. 219–20[2]   *Address* To The Rt Honble the Countess of Bute recommended to Fran: Child Esqr near Temple Bar London Angleterre par Amsterdam   *Postmark* MA 12

To Lord Bristol[3] *2 May* [*1761*]

May 2nd

My selfe uncertain, am too insignificant to speak much of. Wish him all Satisfaction.

Text CB MS, f. 13 (summary)

To Lady Bute [*3 May 1761*][4]

My Dear and only Child,

I hope you will see by the dates of the Letters, the last I wrote to my Son was sent before I knew or had the least Suspicion of the misfortune that was impending.[5] I now give you my solemn word I never will see him, without [being] forc'd to it by some unavoidable Distress.

---

[1] Lady Bute's second surviving son (1747–1818); he took W's name in 1794, when he succeeded to his estates.

[2] Summary in CB MS, f. 13.

[3] The 2nd Earl, son of LM's old friend Lord Hervey, had probably written her a letter of condolence. Formerly envoy to Turin, he served in Madrid from 1758 to Dec. 1761.

[4] For date, see below, p. 275.

[5] The 'misfortune' was undoubtedly Montagu's *caveat* to W's will. But LM had apparently heard rumours of it in Feb. (see above, p. 254), before writing to him on 3 March.

I entirely acquiese to your Father's Will, which I am persuaded was kindly meant however mistaken in some points. I will be more explicite when I can have a safe conveyance. All my letters have been open'd since I have liv'd here. I am sorry to say I have no Friend I can depend on. I dare not sign or date.

I wish you would visit Mrs. Wright. If she tells truth she will tell you the usage I have receiv'd from Murray and his Confederates.

My Life was never dear to me till now I think it necessary for your service. My hand trembles. My complements to Lord B[ute] and blessing to all yours.

I am not to be brib'd, Flatter'd or bully'd, and have allways detested Hush money in all shapes. I will write every post. I have allwaies thought Honesty the best Policy. Poor Lady Oxford![1]

Text W MS iii. 239–40   *Address* To the Rt Honble the Countess of Bute recommended to Fran: Child Esqr near Temple Bar London Angleterre par Amsterdam

To Lady Bute *20 May 1761*

My Dear Child,

I am asham'd to trouble you so often; but I hear so many reports that surprize me, and having no one I can depend on to give me a direct answer to any thing, I am in some measure forc'd to ask you Questions that may (perhaps) appear impertinent, being oblig'd to make some reply to the Enquirys of the noble Venetians, who have always been particularly civil to me, and think it is either affectation or contempt of them when I seem (what I realy am) ignorant of the public Facts which are the Entertainment of Murray's Table.

Some days ago[2] I was told Mr. Mackensie was appointed Ambassador to this Republic, which I was very glad to hear,

[1] This allusion is unexplained, unless it refers to Lady Oxford's having been cheated by a dishonest builder in 1744 (see ii. 344, 346).

[2] Actually three weeks (see above, p. 270).

not doubting to find in him his usual politeness, and flattering my selfe I should have a Freind in Lady Betty. The immediate following post I wrote to congratulate him on the occasion, and receiv'd Saturday morning, 16th Instant, a very kind Letter from him in return. The afternoon of the same day I was inform'd that M[urra]y had advertis'd the College that he was displac'd, and already on his Road to London.[1] You will say (it may be) this is no business of mine. I confess it, yet I own that I am in some degree mortify'd when I am so much neglected by our King's Minister in a Town of such nice Observation. It is the only place in which I have been so ill us'd. Sir H[orace] Mann at Florence was ever obliging to me, and Mr. Villette at Turin both a usefull and agreable Acquaintance by a behavior worthy his good sense and good Breeding. It would be absurd to expect either from the resident here. I never desir'd any Intimacy with him, yet I am apt to think he ought not to distinguish me by ill treatment.

I have said more than enough on this low subject which, however insignificant, is sufficient to make me weary of my residence in this City, thô I cannot hastily remove from it. I intend (if God permits) to set out early in September, and pass through Germany as the easiest passage to England. I have much baggage, and beg to know of you in what manner I can convey it without disputes with Custom House officers. I seriously assure you I have nothing either intended or proper for Merchandize. A smuggler I w⟨oul⟩d never be, and all prospects of improveing my Fortune are entirely over with me.

I should be sorry to come to London without a House to go to. I know not where your Father liv'd,[2] having by his orders always directed my Letters to Child. I desire an Answer as soon as suits with your Conveniency. I am sensible of the Hurry you are in, and would ask nothing of you that

---

[1] On 21 April Mackenzie was recalled from Turin (Pitt to Mackenzie, SP 92/68) because Bute wished him to take over the political affairs in Scotland formerly managed by their uncle the Duke of Argyll, who had died on 15 April (Louis Dutens, *Mémoires d'un*

voyageur qui se repose, 3rd ed., 1807, i. 146).

[2] W, who had lived in Cavendish Square since 1731, died there. In 1746 LM thought he had moved (see ii. 361); in fact he took a small house there (W to LM, 4 March 1746, W MS i. 135).

would give you the least uneasiness, being with great Truth
Your most affectionate Mother,

M. Wortley M.

May 20th 1761

I am glad to tell you I think General G[raeme] out of
Danger, thô still confin'd to his bed chamber.
My Complements to Lord Bute and blessing to all yours.

Text W MS iii. 235–6[1]   *Address* To The Rt Honble the Countess
of Bute recommended to Fran: Child Esqr near Temple Bar London
Angleterre par Amsterdam   *Postmark* IV 10

To John Anderson 3 *June* [1761]

June 3rd

I have a letter from my Son; know not what to say to him.
I beg he would advise him to submit to Mr. W[ortley's]
will.

Text CB MS, f. 13 (summary)

To James Stuart Mackenzie [6 *June 1761*][2]

Your Excellency is dead, but as I do not doubt it is only
a removal to a better Life, I ought rather to congratulate
than condole. I wish you would take Venice in your way
when you make your Journey.[3] I almost Despair of being
able to undertake mine; the infirmitys of Age come fast
upon me, and sometimes I am inclin'd to think with
Shakespear, 'tis better to endure the Ills I have, than fly to
others that I know not of.[4]

[1] Summary in CB MS, f. 13.
[2] From Mackenzie's endorsement.
[3] Mackenzie left Turin on 8 July,
on his way to London by way of Lyons
and Paris (Dutens to Pitt, 8 July 1761,
SP 92/68).
[4] *Hamlet*, III. ii. 81–82.

I should be glad to see Lord Titchfield if he intends comeing this road when he returns to England.

I will not trouble you with a long letter; you are in a Hurry sufficient to tire any Spirits but Yours. I only beg you to be assur'd that while I exist you will have a sincere and Faithfull Freind,

M. W. Montagu.

Venice, May 28 [*sic*].

Text Bute MS   *Address* A Monsieur Monsieur Stuart Mackensie ministre de S M Brittanique a la Cour de Turin   *End. by Mackenzie* Ly M. Wortley   shd have been dated 6 June Rd 11 June. ansd 20.

To Lady Bute *17 June* [*1761*]

I have wrote 4 Letters to you, dated April 3rd, 10th, 29, and May the third. I have not had any answer, and know not what to think of your silence. I receiv'd a few days ago a very extraordinary Letter from your Brother, utterly denying that he had any part in the false caveat put to your Father's Will under the name of J. Jones.[1] There are many other things in his epistle that I do not understand, and consequently have made no return to it. I have wrote to Mr. Anderson to desire him to advise his pupil to give you no trouble, and to rest contented with the Ample provision bequeath'd him.

I hope you have no other impediment to writeing but the Hurry which is natural to your Situation. I beg you would suspend your pleasures or business one quarter of an hour to give satisfaction to an affectionate mother. I delay the preparations for my Journey till I hear from you. I would willingly put all my little affairs into your mannagement, having the most entire dependance on your discretion and good Will towards me, thô I own I am sometimes weak

[1] For the *caveat*, see above, p. 254, n. 5. W's will was proved on 4 May 1761, and letters of administration were granted to the two executors, Earl Gower and Sir Matthew Lamb (the third, Godfrey Wentworth, having renounced).

enough to be mov'd at the reports set about amongst the English here by M[urray] and Company. The Truth is, I can expect neither advice or assistance from any one. General G[raeme] has so much ill Health he is not capable of mannageing his own Business, and in no condition of giving aid to another. I seldom see the young Travellers, and if I did there are few of them that I would consult on any Subject whatever. I ought to distinguish Mr. Pitt, who appears to me a Youth of uncommon understanding, and such as I wish my Lord Mountstuart. He set out for Rome last week.[1]

I am too low spirited to write a long Letter. I will only once more repeat that I expect no comfort but from you. You have at least three Daughters that may write in your name, if your affairs allow you not time to do it with your own Hand. May you ever be happy whatever becomes of your unfortunate Mother.

M. Wortley M.

June 17.

My best Complements to my Lord Bute, and blessing to all yours.

Text W MS iii. 243–4[2]   *Address* To The Rt Honble the Countess of Bute recommended to Fran: Child Esqr near Temple Bar London Angleterre par Amsterdam   *Postmark* ⟨IY 10⟩

To Lady Bute *1 July* [*1761*]

July 1

Thanks for her Letter.

Text CB MS, f. 13 (summary)

---

[1] Thomas Pitt (1737–93), later 1st Lord Camelford, was William Pitt's nephew. He was 'a man of high honour, character, and charm' (Lord Rosebery, *Lord Chatham, His Early Life and Connections*, 1910, p. 21). Abroad since 1760 for his health, he returned to England from Italy on his father's death in July 1761 (History of Parliament, *House of Commons 1754–1790*, ed. L. Namier and J. Brooke, 1964, iii. 287).

[2] Summary in CB MS, f. 13.

To Sir James Steuart[1] *22 July 1761*

July 22nd 1761

Sir,

I expect you should wish me joy on the good fortune of a friend[2] I esteem in the highest manner. I have always preferred the interest of those I love to my own. You need not doubt of my sincere affection towards the lady and young gentleman you mention.[3] My own affairs here grow worse and worse; my indiscreet well-wishers do me as much harm, more harm than any declared enemy could do. The notable plan of our great politician is to make me surrender my little castle; I, with the true spirit of old Whiggism,[4] resolve to keep my ground tho' I starve in the maintaining it, or am eat up by the wild beasts of the wood, meaning gnats and flies. A word to the wise; you understand me. You may have heard of a facetious gentleman vulgarly called Tom Earle—i.e. Giles Earle, Esqr. His toast was always—God bless you whatever becomes of me!

> The day when hungry friar wishes
> He might eat other food than fishes,
> Or, to explain the date more fully,
> The twenty second instant July.[5]

Text Wh MS 509 (transcript)

To Lady Bute *14 Aug. 1761*

My Dear Child,

I must write you a short Letter with a trembling Hand. I was in hopes to have been now some days on my Journey,

1 Now in Antwerp, where he had moved from Tübingen (1818, p. 128).

2 Mackenzie.

3 Lady Frances Steuart was then in London to petition the King to pardon Sir James; she appealed for support to Bute twice (13 July, Bute MS in Cardiff Public Library; 31 July, Bute MS), and to Newcastle (31 July, Add MS 32,926,

f. 111).

4 LM wrote in her Commonplace Book: 'I was educated in the Principles of Old Whigism, thô born in W[illia]m's reign, when the practise was abolis'd yet [not] the proffession, as some Women regard their reputation long after they have lost their Virtu' (MS, f. 8).

5 St. Mary Magdalene's Day.

but I have so bad a Fluxion on my Eyes I dare not yet venture. You need not fear ⟨any⟩ Smugglers amongst my Servants. They are neither wise enough nor rich enough to carry on any Trade whatever. I never see the news papers and know nothing of what passes in the World. The General is (I fear) mortally ill, and excepting Mr. Pit I have seen few of the numerous English. It would be too tedious and troublesome to you to enter into particulars. I hope you are now happy in the Company of Mr. Mackensie and Lady Betty.[1]

This is a sort of Codicil to my Will and I hope will be effectual. I have no body to assist me or that I dare trust even with a Triffle. I heartily forgive my persecutors, but I think it equally my Duty to remember the few to whom I am oblig'd. Mr. Villette sav'd my Life at the entrance of Turin; I will never forget it, thô I can serve him no other way than by my Praiers,[2] as the behavior of M[urray] and company has certainly shorten'd it. My Complements to your agreable Brother.[3] I wish you Joy of having been able to oblige the Dutchess of Portland,[4] as a Venetian Lady told me last night. I am, while I exist, your most affectionate Mother,

M. W. M.

August 14. 1761

My hearty blessing attends all yours.

Poor Anderson has offer'd to come hither to assist me in my Journey, but as I am uncertain when I shall be able to undertake it, I have not accepted his kindness.

Text W MS iii. 237–8   *Address* To The Rt Honble the Countess of Bute recommended to Fran: Child Esquire near Temple Bar London Angleterre par Amsterdam   *Postmark* SE 5

---

[1] They reached London on 7 Aug. (Henrietta, Countess of Suffolk, *Letters 1712–1767*, ed. J. W. Croker, 1824, ii. 260).

[2] Her summary reads: 'recommend Villette' (CB MS, f. 14).

[3] Mackenzie.

[4] Lady Henrietta Cavendish Bentinck, daughter of Lady Bute's friend the Duchess, had been appointed to be a train-bearer of George III's bride on 8 Sept. 1761.

To Sir James and Lady Frances Steuart [*1 Oct. 1761*]

Madam and Sir,

I am now part of my way to England, where I hope to have the pleasure of seeing you: it is so long since I have heard from you I cannot guess where you are. I venture this to Tubingen, tho' I fancy two letters I have directed thither have miscarried, and am so uncertain of the fate of this I know not what to say. I think I cannot err in repeating a sincere truth, that I am, and ever shall be, faithfully your most humble servant,

M. Wortley Montagu.

Since I wrote the above, I am told I may go by Wirtemberg to Frankfort. I will then take that road in hopes of seeing you.

Text Wh MS 509 (transcript)   *End.* Octr 1st 1761 Augsbourg on her way from Venice to England received 3rd of November

To Sir James and Lady Frances Steuart *20 Nov. 1761*[1]

Rotterdam, Nov'r 20, 1761

Sir,

I received yesterday your obliging and welcome letter, by the hands of Mr. Simpson.[2] I tried in vain to find you at Amsterdam; I began to think we resembled two paralell lines, destined to be always near and never to meet. You know there is no fighting (at least no overcoming) Destiny. So far I am a confirmed Calvinist, according to the notions of the country where I now exist.

I am dragging my ragged remnant of life to England. The wind and tide are against me; how far I have strength to struggle against both I know not. That I am arrived here

---

[1] Summary dated 19 Nov. (CB MS, f. 14).   [2] Not identified.

is as much a miracle as any in the Golden Legend;[1] and if I had foreseen halfe the difficulties I have met with, I should not certainly have had courage enough to undertake it. I have scrambled through more dangers than his M[ajesty] of P[russia], or even my well-beloved cousin (not counsellor) Marquis Granby;[2] but my spirits fail me when I think of my friends risqueing either health or happiness. I will write to Lady Fanny to hinder your coming to Rotterdam, and will sooner make one jump more my selfe to wait on you at Antwerp. I am glad poor D.[3] has sold his medals; I confess I thought his buying them a very bold stroke. I supposed that he had already left London, but am told that he has been prevented by the machinations of that excellent politician and truly great man, M[urray], and his ministry.

My dear Lady Fanny, I am persuaded that you are more nearly concerned for the health of Sir James than he is himselfe; I address my selfe to you to insist on it to him not to undertake a winter progress in the beginning of a fit of the gout. I am nailed down here by a severe illness of my poor Marianne,[4] who has not been able to endure the frights and fatigues that we have passed. If I live to see Great Britain, you will have there a sincere and faithful servant that will omit no occasion of serving you; and I think it almost impossible I should not succeed. You must be loved and esteemed wherever you are know[n].

Give me leave however, dear Madam, to combat some of your notions, or, more properly speaking, your passions. Mr. Steuart is in a situation that opens the fairest prospect of honor and advancement. We mothers are all apt to regret the absence of children we love. Solomon advises the sluggard to go to the ant and be wise;[5] we should take the example of the innocent inhabitants of the air: when their young are fledged they are delighted to see them fly and peck for themselves. Forgive this freedom. I have no other receipt for maternal fondness, a distemper which has long

---

[1] The thirteenth-century collection of saints' lives.

[2] At this time in the full flush of his military exploits; for his relationship to LM, see ii. 169.

[3] Probably Duff (1818, p. 72, note).

[4] LM's maid is named in her will as Mari Anna Smith Fromenta.

[5] Proverbs vi. 6.

afflicted Your ladyship's obliged and obedient humble servant,

M. W. Montagu.

Text Wh MS 509 (transcript)   *Address* [*from 1818, p. 71*] To Sir James Steuart, at Antwerp.

To Lady Bute *20 Nov.* [*1761*]

Nov. 20.

My Dear Child,

I receiv'd your welcome Letter of the 13th instant last night. You need not doubt I shall make all the haste I can to embrace you, which has been long the desire of my Life, as you very well know. I have so far forgot Great George street,[1] I do not remember I ever saw it. I hope you have taken the House only for one Year certain, or that it is such I may easily let if the Air should not agree with me. I heartily wish you may close my Eyes, but to say truth I would not have it happen immediately, and should be glad to see my other Grand Daughters as happily marry'd as Lady Mary.[2] I hope you have my Letter in which I wish'd her and you Joy of so advantageous a Match. I am told here that Lady Jane is also dispos'd of. I may perhaps not be at her Wedding; I flatter my selfe with the view of seeing Lady Anne's.[3] Forgive this old Woman's Tattle as one of the many weaknesses you will see in your most affectionate Mother,

M. Wortley.

---

[1] Now St. George Street, running south from Hanover Square.

[2] Lady Mary Stuart m. (7 Sept. 1761) Sir James Lowther, later 1st Earl of Lonsdale. According to the bride's mother, he was 'a man of 30,000 *l.* a year, as much in love and solicitous to gain her heart as if he were a half-pay officer' (Henrietta, Countess of Suffolk, *Letters 1712–1767*, ed. J. W. Croker, 1824,

ii. 259). He was later generally abhorred for his ruthless and tyrannical behaviour.

[3] Lady Jane—described by George Selwyn as *'laide à faire peur'* (HMC *Carlisle MSS*, 1897, p. 229)—m. (1768) Sir George Macartney, later 1st Earl; and Lady Anne m. (1764) Lord Warkworth, later Earl Percy (and 2nd Duke of Northumberland), who divorced her for adultery in 1779.

I do not wonder you know nothing of the Insolence of custom house officers. I have been so frighted with them that I dread their name, thô I once more solemnly assure you neither I nor my Servants have any Contreband. I have not learnt the art of Smuggling from our worthy Minister at Venice, nor ever try'd to attempt it, yet the Duke of Devonshire can tell you from what distress he rescue'd me at the Gates of Turin,[1] where I verily beleive I had dy'd if Mr. Villette had been as little instructed in his Duty as I have since found M[urray].

I design to come up the River if I can find a Vessel that takes that Route. I repeat once more, God send us a happy meeting, not withstanding the lyes that have been told (I beleive) to us both with the pious design of setting us at variance. They have had no effect on me otherwaies than making me more impatient to see you. I think I know your Heart; I shall without reserve tell you what is in mine.

My complements and thanks to Lord Bute, and hearty blessing to all yours.

Text W MS iii. 245–6[2]   *Address* To The Rt Honble the Countess of Bute recommended to Fran: Child Esqr near Temple Bar London *Postmark* NO 28

To Lady Frances Steuart [1] *Dec. 1761*

Rotterdam, December 1761.

My dear Madam,

A great snow, weak sight, trouble of mind and a feeble body, are more than sufficient excuses for a short letter; yet I would not omit a few lines to give you thanks for yours, and repeat to you my real desire to serve you in the most zealous manner. Any relation of Sir James will find a hearty welcome from me when I am in London. I now depend on wind and weather: you know how disagreeable that is. I will not afflict your good heart with my uneasinesses. I hope

---

[1] In 1739 or 1741; he was then Marquess of Hartington (see ii. 396).   [2] Summary in CB MS, f. 14.

(and am determined to hope) the best, tho' in contradiction to appearances.

In all humours I am Your Ladyship's faithful humble servant,

M. W. Montagu.

P.S. My dear Lady Fanny, we are both low-spirited; let us talk no more of melancholy matters. I should be glad to know the adventure of Sir James with the Countess B.,[1] and am sometimes tempted to seek her out, in hopes to edify by her discourse and example.

Text Wh MS 509 (transcript)   *Address [from 1818, p. 76]* The Right Hon. Lady Frances Steuart, at Antwerp. *End. by Lady Frances* 1st Dec. 1761

To Sir James Steuart *12 Dec. 1761*

I received last post your agreeable and obliging letter. I am now on the point of setting out[2] for London, very dubious (with my precarious state of health) whether I shall arrive there. If I do, you will certainly hear from me again; if not, accept ('tis all I can offer) my sincerest wishes for the prosperity of your selfe and family. I do not at all despair of your affairs going according to your desire, tho' I am not ordained the happiness to see it. My warmest compliments to Lady F[anny], and believe me ever, Sir, Your faithful friend and humble servant,

M. W. Montagu.

Rotterdam, Dec. 12, 1761

Behold, a hard impenetrable frost has stopped my voiage, and I remain in the disagreeable state of uncertainty—I will not trouble you with my fruitless complaints; I am sure you have compassion for my present situation.

Text Wh MS 509 (transcript)

---

[1] See above, p. 191 and n.2.   [2] 'setting sail' (1818, p. 74).

To Sir James and Lady Frances Steuart *26 Dec. 1761*

26th of December 1761

Sir,

The thaw is now so far advanced I am in great hopes of moving in a few days. My first care at London will be your affairs: I think it almost impossible I should not succeed. You may assure Lady Fanny no endeavor shall be wanting on my side. If I find any material objection, I shall not fail to let you know it; I confess I do not forsee any. A young gentleman arrived here last night who is perhaps of your acquaintance, Mr. Hamilton;[1] he is hastening to London in expectation of an Act of Grace, which I believe will be granted. I flatter myself with the view of seeing you in England, and can affirm with truth it is one of the greatest pleasures I expect there. Whatever prosperity my family now enjoys, it will add much to my happiness to see my friends easy; and while you are unfortunate, I shall always think my selfe so.

This very dull weather operates on my spirits, tho' I use my utmost efforts to support them. I beg dear Lady Fanny to do the same; a melancholy state of mind should never be indulged, since it often remains even when the cause of it is removed. I have here neither amusement nor conversation, and am so infected by the climate that I verily believe was I to stay long I should take to smoking and drinking like the natives.

I should wish you the compliments of the season, a merry Christmas, but I know not how to do it while you remain in so disagreeable an uncertainty; yet if you have the company of Mr. Stewart, his bloom of life will insensibly communicate part of his gaiety. If I could have foreseen my stay in this part of the world, I would have made a trip to Antwerp to enjoy a conversation ever honored and remembered by,

[1] In the 1818 edition (p. 78) he is identified as George, elder brother of Gen. James Lockhart. This George Lockhart (b. 1726) was at Tübingen when the Steuarts were there, and died in Paris (Paul Chamley, *Documents relatifs à Sir James Steuart*, 1965, p. 109). But according to *The Lockhart Papers* (1817, ii. 425) he died in 1761.

Sir and Madam, Your most faithful and obedient humble servant,

M. W. Montagu.

Text Wh MS 509 (transcript)   *Address [from 1818, p. 78]* To Sir James Steuart, at Antwerp.   *End. by Lady Frances [1818]* Rotterdam

To Lady Frances Steuart 2 *Jan.* 1762

January 2nd 1762

I have been half way to Helvoet and was obliged to turn back by the mountains of [ice][1] that obstructed our passage;[2] the Captain, however, gives me hopes of setting out in two or three days. I have had so many disappointments I can scarce entertain the flattering thought of arriving at London. Wherever I am, you may depend upon it, dear Madam, I shall ever retain the warmest sentiments of good will for you and your family, and will use my utmost endeavors to give you better proofs of it than I can do by expressions, which will always fall short of my thoughts.

Many happy new years to you, Madam. May this atone for the ill fortune of those that are past, and all those to come be chearful. Mr. Hamilton, whom I mentioned, has I believe got a particular pardon; his case is extraordinary, having no relation to public affairs. I am sorry for poor Duff, and fear that wherever he moves there will be little difference in his situation; he carries with him such a load of indiscretion, it is hardly in the power of Fortune to serve him. We are crouded with officers of all ranks returning to England. The Peace[3] seems to be more distant than ever; it would be very indifferent to me if it did not affect my friends. My remaining time in this world is so short I have few wishes to

---

[1] From 1818.

[2] On 1 Jan. the British agent in Rotterdam reported: 'Lady Mary Wortley went down yesterday in her way to join the trader her Ladyship intended to take her passage in, but by the quantity of ice the ship was obliged to return hither.' On 15 Jan., by order of the British Ambassador at the Hague, he put a 'Paquet Boat under her Ladyship's order, to sail att her own time' (HMC *Tenth Report*, i, 1885, pp. 323, 325).

[3] To end the Seven Years War.

make for my selfe, and when I am free from pain ought to think myself happy. It is uncommon at my age to have no distemper and to retain all my senses in their first degree of perfection. I should be unworthy these blessings if I did not acknowledge them. If I am so fortunate to see Your Ladyship and Sir James in good health at London it will be a great addition to the satisfaction of, dear Madam, Your faithful and obedient humble servant,

M. W. Montagu.

Text Wh MS 509 (transcript)   *Address* [*from 1818, p. 81*] The Right Hon. Lady Frances Steuart, at Antwerp. *End. by Lady Frances* [*1818*] Rotterdam.

To Mme Chiara Michiel *29 Jan. 1762*

Londre, Great George Street, near Hannover Square[1]

January 29. 1762

Je ne suis arrivée que d'avant hier. Accablée de Fatigue des visites que je ne sçaurois refuser, des Parens, des Enfans, et qui pis est, des Affaires, pourtant je ne pense qu'a ma charmante Amie La Cavaliere Chiara Michielli. Il est vrai que c'est peu de merite; elle n'est pas oubliable (permettez cette parole de ma fabrique, mais je ne sçaurois écrire regulierment en aucune langue, ayant une Capilotade dans ma pauvre Tête des Langues anciens et modernes).—On frappe a la porte; voici ma fille avec 5 ou 6 douzaines des Satellites qu'il faut que je reçois.

Ohimé, cara Venetia! Carissima Signora Chiara! Venerata Procuratessa Bragadini![2]

O Rus, quando ego te aspiciam![3]

Vous me croira possedez. Helas, je suis excedee!

[1] Lady Louisa Stuart recalled LM's wry description of the house: 'I am most handsomely lodged. I have two very decent closets and a cupboard on each floor' (1861, i. 117).

[2] Mme Michiel's mother. Tadea Maria, da. of Ludovico Manin, m. (1707) Daniele Bragadin (d. 1755), Procurator from 1735 (Archivio di Stato, Venice).

[3] 'O rural home: when shall I behold you!' (Horace, *Satires*, II. vi. 60; transl. Loeb Library).

Text Bute MS   *Address* A S. E. La Signora Signora Chiara Michielli Bragadina San Angelo Venezia par Amsterdam   *Postmark* IR   *End.* Risposto li 12 Marzo 1762

To Mme Chiara Michiel *15 Feb. 1762*

Me voici delivrée de dix mille visites,[1] et je prens cette premiere suspension des Horreurs pour écrire a ma chere et tres respectable Amie. Vous me l'avez bien dit, ma belle Dame; je suis accablée d'impertinence en guise des Honneurs. Je n'ai pas la force d'ÿ resister; plût a Dieu que j'ai la force de retourner a Venise, et me sauver dans vostre aimable Maison. Le pauvre Mackensie est plus enragé que moi. La Cour et le Parliament le mange jusqu'aux os.[2]
Londres, Great George street, Hannover square
Feb. 15. 1762

Text Bute MS   *End.* Risposto li 18 Marzo 1762[3]

To Lady Frances Steuart *5 March 1762*

London, Great George Street, Hanover Square
March 5, 1762

Dear Madam,
I have written several letters to your Ladyship, but I perceive by that I had the honour to receive yesterday, they

[1] Among those who visited LM soon after her return were Horace Walpole, Elizabeth Montagu, Sir James Caldwell, and Lord Bristol (Halsband, *LM*, p. 281). As energetic as ever, she herself called on Lady Charlotte Finch, daughter of her old friend Lady Pomfret; and Lady Charlotte wrote in her journal for 20 Feb.: 'she staid about an hour and was Vastly entertaining, very oddly dressed, but retains a great deal of beauty especially in her eyes tho. she is 73 years old' (Pearl Finch, *History of*

Burley-on-the-Hill, 1901, i. 311).
[2] On his return from Turin, Mackenzie was awarded a pension of £2,000 a year to manage Scottish affairs, and on 4 Sept. 1761 he was appointed to the Privy Council (History of Parliament, *House of Commons 1754–1790*, ed. L. Namier and J. Brooke, 1964, iii. 504).
[3] In her answer, dated 19 March, Mme Michiel consoled LM for her unhappiness, and advised her to remain 'entre les bras de votre chere et illustre Famille' (W MS iv. 198).

have all miscarried. I can assign no reason for it but the uncertainty of the post. I am told many mails have been taken and the letters either thrown away or suppressed. We must suffer this, amongst the common calamities of war. Our correspondance is so innocent we have no reason to apprehend our secrets being discovered. I am proud to make public profession of being, Dear Madam, ever your most faithful humble servant,

M. W. Montagu.

In writing to you, I think I write to your whole family; I hope they think so too.

Text Wh MS 509 (transcript)   *Address* [*from 1818, p. 84*] To the Right Hon. Lady Frances Steuart. Recommended to the care of James Crawford, Esq. Negotiant, Rotterdam.

To Mme Chiara Michiel [*April 1762*]

Je vous jure (ma belle dame) que le plus grand plaisir que j'ai reçeu a Londres a étois vostre aimable Lettre du dix du mois passé. Cest que vous avez dit sur le beau marriage de nostre Ami R[osenberg][1] est incomparable. Il y a de la finesse, de la justesse, et de la noblesse, et je comprens tout cela;[2] il n'apartient qu'a vous de vous exprimer si bien dans une Langue étrangere. Helas, j'ai le jargon de la tour de Babel dans ma pauvre Tête,[3] et je parle avec aussi peu de

---

[1] Philipp Josef, Count von Rosenberg-Orsini (1691–1765) was Imperial Ambassador to Venice 1754–64 (*Repertorium*, ii. 88). His marriage to the eldest Miss Wynne, which took place on 5 Nov. 1761, had been talked about in Venice since July (Murray to Pitt, 10 July 1761; Murray to Egremont, 6 Nov. 1761: SP 99/68).

[2] In her letter of 10 March, Mme Michiel wrote: '...Monsieur de Rosemberg a epousé la *Justiniana Wyn*, sans pourtant la déclarer ni sa Femme, ni Ambassadrice. Un de ses amis m'ont demandé ce que j'en pense; j'ai repondu,

qu'un tel Mariage est fort au dessous de sa naissance et du caractere qu'il rapresente, mais digne de son cœur. Je me flatte que vous en penserez autant' (W MS iv. 192).

[3] As Elizabeth Montagu described LM's household: 'Her *domestick* is made up of all nations, and when you get into her drawing-room, you imagine you are in the first story of the Tower of Babel. An Hungarian servant takes your name at the door; he gives it to an Italian, who delivers it to a Frenchman; the Frenchman to a Swiss, and the Swiss to a Polander; so that, by the time you get to her ladyship's presence, you have

netteté qu'une Antidiluvienne. Mon Cœur au moins est droit, et toujours a vostre Service a vendre et engager.

Si vos Messieurs ne sont pas parti je leur prierai de permettre mes petites caisses qui sont au Couvent de venir avec leur Baggage. Vous savez que la bonne Compagnie est d'une grande Utilité dans les voiages.¹ Le Comte de Northampton est fort empressé de voir vostre belle ville; il mêne avec lui une epouse charmante, et de la première Qualité de l'Angleterre.²

Au reste, je suis sincerement affligée de la conduitte de Mme vostre belle Fille.³ Nous avons un Proverbe: my Son is my Son till he has a Wife. Vous etes heureuse d'avoir une mere vraiment digne de vous; elle l'est doublement de vivre avec une Fille aussi parfaitte que la Signora Chiara M. B. Que cette union dure a jamais! et que vos petits enfans recompense tous les chagrins que vous avez reçeu d'ailleurs!

C'est sont les veux le plus ardent de vostre chetive mais sincere, tres humble et obeissante Servante,

M. Wortley Montagu.

Text Bute MS   *Address* [*by Dr. Moro*]⁴ A Sua Eccellenza La N. D. Chiara Micheli Bragadini Cavaliera Calle delli Avvocati S. Angelo Venezia [*by LM*] par Amsterdam   *End.* Risposto li 30 Aple 1762

changed your name five times, without the expense of an act of parliament' (John Doran, *A Lady of the Last Century* (*Mrs. Elizabeth Montagu*), 1873, pp. 129–30).

¹ Before leaving Venice LM left a trunk and box in the care of Mme Michiel's step-sister (*belle-sœur*), a nun at the Convent of the Angels at Murano. On 10 March Mme Michiel reminded her of this; she then explained (on 1 May) that the Venetian ambassadors, Querini and Morosini, had already left on their journey to London (W MS iv. 192, 196).

² Northampton (see above, p. 195) m. (1759) Lady Anne Noel (1741–63), da. of 4th Duke of Beaufort. He had been appointed (in Mackenzie's place)

Ambassador Extraordinary and Plenipotentiary to Venice.

³ Mme Michiel, a widow, apparently had two sons: Francesco (1730–1801) (Archivio di Stato, Venice), and Domenico (1732–82), who m. (1759) Cornelia da Lezze (Casanova, *Histoire de ma vie*, ed. F. A. Brockhaus, 1960–2, xii. 384). After her daughter-in-law asked her to move out of her son's house, Mme Michiel's own mother offered refuge (Mme Michiel to LM, 10 March 1762).

⁴ With this letter went a brief one in Italian from Moro, LM's secretary. Mme Michiel had sent a polite note to him with her letter to LM on 10 March.

To Lord Monson[1] *13 April 1762*

My Lord,

I ask your Lordship's pardon for giving you the Trouble of this Letter, but as I find by Mr. Child's account the Interest on the money left me by my Father[2] has been long unpaid, I should be oblig'd to you if you signify'd to Mr. Lister[3] that ⟨I⟩ expect he should pay in the Money lent on his Estate, or raise the Interest to 5 per cent, which is (at present) the current rate.[4]

I am, My Lord, with a very sincere Esteem, Your Lordship's obedient Humble Servant,

April 13, 1762

M. Wortley Montagu.

Great George [Street], Hannover Square

Text Monson MS vol. xvi, letter [225]   *Address* To The Rt Honble The Lord Monson at Burton[5] near Lincoln Lincolnshire

To Lady Frances Steuart *23 April* [*1762*]

Believe me, dear Madam, I see my daughter often, and never see her without mentioning (in the warmest manner) your affairs. I hope that when the proper season arrives (it cannot now be far off) all things will be adjusted to your satisfaction. It is the greatest pleasure I expect in the wretched

---

[1] John, 2nd Baron (1727–74), son of LM's old family friend.

[2] The legacy of £6,000 (see ii. 177, n. 1).

[3] Matthew Lister (d. 1786) of Burwell Park, Lincs. (Burke, *Landed Gentry*, 1852–3, i. 732).

[4] On 10 June, Monson wrote to

Lister about the 'Money lent you by Mr. Wortley Montagu and myself now being the Property of Lady Mary Wortley Montague' and repeated her instructions (Monson MS, vol. xvi, letter [226]—copy).

[5] A Monson property since at least 1594.

remnant of life remaining to, Dear Madam, Your faithful
humble servant,

                                   M. W. Montagu.

George St. Hanover Square
April 23, 1762

My sincere best wishes to all your Ladyship's family.

Text Wh MS 509 (transcript)   *End. by Lady Frances* 1762

To Mme Chiara Michiel 8 *May 1762*

Je suis au pied de la Lettre (ma Belle Dame) au desespoir
de vostre situation. Plût a Dieu qu'il dependoit de moi de
lever tous vos inquietudes; mais a quoi sert de vains souhaits?
et de tristes Helas?—N'en parlons plus.—

Monsieur Mackensie est toujours un des plus aimable
et de plus honnête Homme du monde. Nous avons mille
projets pour vous servir. En attendant, Dieu vous donne la
Santé; veillez y vous mesme, ma chere Amie, et ne vous
laisser pas accabler par des chagrins dont chaqu'un est
suffissament partagé.

Milord Northampton dit qu'il enrage que le jour de son
depart n'est pas encore fixé.[1] Je serois bien aise que les Bagatelles que j'ai laissée au Couvent de Muran me seront
envoyé, s'il est possible, parmi l'equipage de vos Ambassa-
deurs; si non, au moins faittes les addresser a un de leurs
Excellences. J'ai honte d'entrer dans ces petits details avec
vous, mais vostre Bonté est aussi universelle que la Lumiere
du jour. Je me flatte que je ne mourirai pas ingratte.

Nostre Grand Roi (qui se peut dire, au pied de la Lettre,
le bien aimé)[2] vient d'acheter une Belle Maison au fonds du
Parc de St. James, qu'il destine, dit-on, pour estre le Marli
de Londres.[3] Il y placera des Livres et des Curiositez de

[1] His credentials were not ready until
26 Aug.; he arrived in Venice on 17
Oct. 1762 (D. B. Horn, p. 85).

[2] On 19 March Mme Michiel had
mentioned 'votre jeune Monarque,

duquel notre *imcomparable* MacKenzie
m'a fait devenir amoureuse' (W MS iv.
198).

[3] In April 1762 the King purchased
Buckingham House.

toutes especes. Il faut voir comme on courre pour regarder des Murailles qu'on a vû mille fois.[1] Ce sont des petites attentions qui marquent le Cœur; il paroist que tous ses sujets sont amoureux de lui. C'est un Spectacle que je ne crû jamais voir en Angleterre. Quel changement! Peutestre que nous verrons des Muscadiers fleurir dans nos champs; je ne serai guerre plus surprise. En attendant nous mourons de froid ce moi de Mai present. Dieu vous preserve, chere Amie. Je suis avec un attachment éternel toute a vous,

                                                    M. W. Montagu.
ce moi de Mai 8. 1762.

Great George street, Hannover Square

   On dit ici que vostre Doge se meure,[2] et que la Belle Justiniana va donner au monde du Fruit nouveau.[3]

Text Bute MS   *Address* [*by Dr. Moro*] A Sua Eccellenza La N. D. Chiara Bragadini Cavaliera Micheli In Calle delli Avvocati S. Angelo Venezia   *Postmark* IR   *End.* Risposto prima d'uscire da la Michiel

To Mme Chiara Michiel *18 May 1762*

Ma chere et tres estimable Amie,

   Pour toute autre occasion je ne toucherai pas une plume, mais quand il s'agit de vous remercier d'une Aimable Lettre et vous tirer d'une peine, je veux bien m'oublier moi même, quoi qu'il est assez difficile d'oublier un pesanteur de Tête, et des vertiges dont je suis accablée. C'est un Maladie epidemique qui regne dans cette malheureuse Isle; on dit que personne ne meure; en attendant tout le monde est incommodée. Le Duc de Kingston a été forcée de remettre un

---

[1] The King wrote to Bute in April: 'all I want for the present is to have the outward walls planted and a gravel walk round' (*Letters from George III to Lord Bute 1756–1766*, ed. R. Sedgwick, 1939, p. 93). A month later he and his Queen moved there, and—Walpole reported—stripped the other palaces to furnish it (*Corr.* x. 33).

[2] Francesco Loredan (1685–19 May 1762), Doge since 1752 (Andrea da Mosto, *I Dogi di Venezia*, 1939, p. 298).

[3] Giustiniana Wynne, recently married to the septuagenarian Count Rosenberg. The report was a joke, their union being childless.

Diner dont j'étois priée avant hier, n'ayant pas parmi sa nombreuse domestique des Valets pour servir a Table. Marianne a subi un attaque terrible, Docteur Moro a eû sa portion, et pauvre moi souffre comme une miserable. Il m'est impossible de vous envoyer par cette poste l'inventaire en question; heureusement il n'est pas trop necessaire pour le present, mais le buste est ouvert et vous avez vû les bagatelles qui y sont. C'est une caffatière d'argent, une petite scudello ditto, et un tasse de Vermeil. Si my Lord Tavistock est a Venise—il est mon Neveu; tout le monde en dit beaucoup de bien—je suis persuadée qu'il s'en chargera Volontiers.[1] Il les peut mettre entre son baggage sans s'incommoder, et pour le Buste le jetter ou il veut.[2]

Je ne scai ce que je dis; pardonnez moi toutes mes Foiblesses, mon cœur est toujours le même. J'exprime mal, mais je sens parfaittement bien, que je suis toute a vous.

M. W. Montagu

1762 May 18.

Great George street, Hannover Square

Text Bute MS   *End.* Risposto li 7 Lugo 1762

To Mme Chiara Michiel *11 June* [*1762*]

Il faut que vous ayez une Bonté d'Ange pour me pardonner tous les torts que j'ai avec vous. Quand je vous priai de remettre mes Bagatelles a milord Tavistock, il étoit deja parti de Venise.[3] Enfin il ne me reste que la Patience pour

---

[1] Francis Russell (1739–67), Marquess of Tavistock, son and heir of 7th Duke of Bedford; his maternal grandmother was LM's sister Lady Gower. Walpole praised his 'perfectly amiable and unblemished character'; his 'gentleness, generosity, and strict integrity made all the world or love or admire him' (*Mem. of George III*, 1845, ii. 440). He arrived at Venice on 13 April (Murray to Egremont, 16 April 1762, SP 99/68).

[2] In her letter of 1 May (probably the one LM is answering) Mme Michiel explained in very patient detail why the trunk and box could not be taken from the convent, where they were sealed, without a legal certified order from LM (W MS iv. 196–7).

[3] On 29 April he had left Venice for England (Murray to Egremont, 30 April 1762, SP 99/68).

me soutenir contre tous les travers de la vie; personne n'en est exempt. Foible Consolation!

Je ne veux pas vous ennuyer par une Longue Lettre que ne peut estre divertissante. Mon Cœur est toujours le même, mais mon esprit est si fort appesanti par l'air grossier de cet Païs, que j'avoue que je ne me reconnois plus.

Adieu ma Belle et digne Amie; soyez persuadée que je suis avec le plus parfait devouement tout a Vous,

M. W. Montagu.

ce 11 de Juin

Text Bute MS   *End.* Risposto li 7 Lugo 1762[1]

LM's will [*23 June 1762*]

In the Name of God, Amen.

I give and bequeath to Her Grace Margaret Dutchess of Portland a white brilliant diamond Ring with this motto enamell'd: Maria Henrietta.[2]

I give to Signora Chiara Michielli Bragadini her choice of all my Rings excepting that already bequeath'd to the Dutchess of Portland.

I give to Doctor Julio Bartholemeo Moro, who has faithfully serv'd me seven years, five hundred pounds sterling.

I give to Mari Anna Smith Fromenta all my wearing Apparel either made or not made and all my Linnen either for the Bed, Table, or my person.

I give to my Son Edw[ar]d Wortley one Guinea, his Father having amply provided for him.[3]

---

[1] Reply dated 10 July; she also wrote to Dr. Moro at the same time (W MS iv. 190–1, 194–5).

[2] LM had bought the ring with the legacy of £200 left to her by Henrietta, Lady Oxford, the Duchess's mother (see above, pp. 109–10).

[3] LM's annuity of £1,200 automatically went to Montagu, by the terms of W's will. Early in 1762 he had gone abroad, reaching Turin on 3 April (Montagu to Bute, 24 April [1762], Bute MS in Cardiff Public Library). In some way he had become reconciled to Bute, who paid him generously: £250 on 18 Jan., £500 on 21 Aug. and £225 on 13 Dec. 1762; £1,750 in 1763; and £1,000 in 1764 and again in 1765 (Coutts and Co. MS ledgers).

I give to the Honourable James Stuart Mackensie one large Gold Octogon Snuff Box.

To my dear daughter Mary Countess of Bute I give and Bequeath whatever I am possess'd of, all my Messuages Lands and Tenements and Hereditaments whether now in possession or in Reversion,[1] desiring her to see duly executed this last Will and Testament of her affectionate Mother.

I give to all the servants living with me at the time of my Decease a year's wages each; and if there is amongst them any Foreigners, their charges to their own Country; and ten guineas above the said Legacy to Mari Anna Smith Fromenta.

I here publish and declare this to be my last Will and Testament, in wittness where of I have to two parts[2] of this my Will set my Hand and seal this 23rd of June 1762.

Mary Wortley Montagu

[*Here follows the legal formula to introduce the witnesses' signatures*]

John Lane[3]
David Rees
Thomas Burch

Text P.C.C. St. Eloy, f. 349

To Lady Frances Steuart 2 *July 1762*

Dear Madam,

I have been ill a long time, and am now so bad I am little capable of writing, but I would not pass in your opinion as either stupid or ungrateful. My heart is always warm in your service and I am always told your affairs shall be taken

---

[1] Estimates of the size of her estate varied—from Walpole's 'inconsiderable' to Sir James Gray's '80 thousand pound' (*Corr.* xxii. 72 and n. 19).

[2] These two copies are headed by her No. 1 (printed here) and No. 2. Both are in her autograph; they differ slightly, only in the order of bequests and in phraseology.

[3] Identified only by an effusive letter he sent her on 1 June in which he thanked her for letting him read her verse and sent some of his own (W MS iv. 179–80; printed in George Paston [E. M. Symonds], *Lady Mary Wortley Montagu and Her Times*, 1907, pp. 530–1). The other two witnesses are not identified.

care of.[1] You may depend, dear Madam, nothing shall be wanting on the part of Your Ladyship's faithful humble servant,

                                     M. W. Montagu.

July 2nd 1762

Text Wh MS 509 (transcript)   *Address [from 1818, p. 87]* To the Right Hon. the Lady Francesse Stewart. A Anvers, Par Hollande. *End. by Lady Frances* Lady Mary's last Letter from London[2]

[1] At the beginning of 1763 Sir James received permission to return to Scotland (his son wrote), 'which he owed to his wife's solicitations, to Lady Mary Wortley's intrigues, to Lord Barrington's friendship, and, above all, to the king's goodness' (Sir James Steuart, *Works, Political, Metaphysical, and Chronological*, ed. J. Steuart, 1805, vi. 373).

[2] And her last surviving letter. On 10 July, Elizabeth Montagu reported that she was dying: 'she is very placid and easy tho' she sees her end approach' (*Letters 1762–1800*, ed. R. Blunt, 1923, i. 25); and a few days later Walpole wrote of her imminent death of cancer of the breast: 'She behaves with great fortitude, and says she has lived long enough' (*Corr.* xxii. 56). She died on 21 Aug. and was buried the next day in the vault of Grosvenor Chapel in South Audley Street (Register Book of Burials, Parish of St. George, Hanover Square, p. 13; plaque on wall of Grosvenor Chapel).

Appendix I

TRANSLATION OF FRENCH AND ITALIAN CORRESPONDENCE

To Mme Chiara Michiel [*Sept. 1756*]

My dear and very kind Madam,

I could not possibly express to what extent I am mortified at being in Venice without having the honour of seeing you; I swear to you that it was the principal object of my journey. I should be in despair if I did not flatter myself that time, which heals so many things, will also remedy this disagreeable suspension. In any case, we shall see each other again in Padua. I am returning there immediately; everywhere I shall have the same Heart, zealous for you, and filled with a respectful tenderness for her who is the glory of (my very dear and very kind Madam) your very obliged and obedient Servant,

M. W. Montagu.

Text (p. 111 above)

To Mme Chiara Michiel 4 *Nov. 1756*

Very dear and kind Madam,

I have received with inexpressible pleasure the kind Letter with which you have honoured me. I am delighted that you have done my Language the honour of taking the trouble to learn it. You are endowed with a marvellous facility to learn all that you wish. I flatter myself that we have some Books worthy of entertaining you, and perhaps my small Library may be of some use to you. I should be very proud of that.

I am hastening to Venice to embrace you, since it is permitted. As soon as I arrive, I shall not fail to pay my respects to you, and on every occasion you will find me, with an eternal devotion, Madam, your very humble and Obedient Servant,

M. W. Montagu.

Nov. 4. 1756, Padua

I have not written in English; I am very glad, in case my Letter is opened, to have people see the innocence of our Correspondence. If it were known how much I hate and scorn Politics I would never be suspected.

Text (p. 111 above)

To Mme Chiara Michiel *18 Nov.* [*1756*]

My very dear and kind Friend,

I could not possibly express to what extent I am mortified at having been forced to leave Venice without saying Goodbye to you. I am sure that you do Justice to my Heart, which is entirely yours, but I have my Ill-luck as you have yours. I flatter myself, however, that better times lie ahead. I aspire only to pass my life near you, in proving to you that I am with the most perfect devotion, my dear Madam, your very humble and very obedient Servant,

M. W. Montagu.

Padua, Nov. 18.

Text (p. 112 above)

To Mme Chiara Michiel [*23 Dec. 1756*]

I have received this morning, Dec. 23, two dear Letters from my Kind Friend, one of which is dated the 26th of last month, and the other the 13th of this. I am furious at the negligence of the post, and fear I have suffered very much in your Opinion. You had reason to accuse me of ingratitude or of insensibility, though I was wholly concerned with you, asking for news of you from all I saw, and very sad about your silence, the cause of which I could not guess—but I forget myself in writing to you in French, when you are as capable of writing in English as I. . . .

Text (p. 114 above)

To Francesco Algarotti *30 Dec. 1756*

. . . to change his heroic Madness for Rustic wisdom, and leave the diabolical Pleasures of destruction, to enjoy those of Paradise in the pleasures of a little Garden ornamented with all the delights of Nature's hand. Alcinous in Homer seems to me more of a Hero than Achilles; certainly he is more pleasing, just as Benevolence is more worthy than Cruelty. What an example of true Heroism! If one could see a Conqueror who never met defeat set limits to his Triumphs and retire like Diocletian, a thousand times greater in his retirement than in his Elevation! You see that I imitate Homer, at least in one respect, in writing in a style composed of different dialects, for in the end all our modern Languages are nothing but vernaculars of ancient Rome.

Padua, Dec. 30, 1756

Text (p. 117 above)

To Francesco Algarotti [*Feb. 1757*]

You have not yet received the insults which I sent you, and I receive from you a Letter capable of calming all my anger. Here I am mollified to the point of believing myself obliged to thank you for the precious waters, which come very much apropos, after my spending the Night at the Regina d'Inghilterra.

You see that I plunge headlong into all the debaucheries of the Carnival. I confess that I no longer have the right to make fun of monarchs who dissipate their treasures and diminish their subjects for a phantom of Ambition; I, who dissipate my Health and diminish my few remaining days pursuing a phantom of pleasure which I seek through blood and Destruction. I can say to excuse myself (you know that one always believes one can find something to say in favour of one's stupidities) that Pheasants and Partridges are hatched to be the prey of men, that they are made for our nourishment, that they may be prepared in any sauce, and that such a short space of time is curtailed by depriving them of life that it is not worth thinking about. A Hero could justify his conduct, perhaps, with more reason. He will say that the human race is born to die, and when they perish by sword or fire they escape diseases a thousand times more cruel, to which Nature has destined them, not to mention the pleasure that they ought to find in dying for the Glory of their Master, and that among a hundred thousand one will not find ten who have not deserved the noose for their Crimes. The innocent birds are created to enjoy a sweet and peaceful life, without vice or Ambition. They limit their Purposes to populating the Woods with their posterity, and it is depriving them of a true blessing to plunge them into nothingness. I am struck with this truth, and I regard Conquerors as the avengers of the Beasts which are sacrificed so ruthlessly to our caprices and our Lust. Is it right to look with horror on a Battlefield strewn with dead bodies, and with joy on a Supper for which hundreds of different species have been massacred?

If I were inclined to write, I would compose an epistle in the name of all the animals to the greatest Warrior of the Century, to encourage him to the Slaughter of these Tyrants, who imagine themselves privileged to exercise the most enormous cruelty.

You will admit that debauchery inspires me to beautiful moralizing. If anyone wanted to have the thoughts after a victory that I have on leaving Table, he would agree with me that friendship alone can bring happiness. Firm in this sentiment, judge what [friendship] I feel for you.

Text (p. 120 above)

To Francesco Algarotti *19 Feb. 1757*

It must be admitted (Sir) that you know how to take vengeance in a fine and truly apostolic way, in returning good deeds for injuries. You disarm your enemies, and you pride yourself (no doubt) on drawing upon them the fires of Heaven.

I did not fail to present your compliments to the General. He embraces you with all his Heart, he says, but (between ourselves) I believe he is a little annoyed at having laid siege for six months, without being able to boast of having made great progress, to a Place that you took by assault in less than two weeks. One must forgive the Coolness that comes from so justified a cause. In vain he gives Parties, attends at the opera, and what is worse, loses his Money at Faro. If inclination does not turn traitor, the castle is invincible. I carefully refrain from announcing that sad news to him. The hunt is often agreeable although one catches nothing.

I like Madame Barbarigo very much. She has a goodness of Heart which enchants me. If her Court were less numerous she would be more lovely. She pleases me very much, but I imagine that she will

please me even more at Padua. I should like to return there, but I am
chained here in thousands of ways. We shall meet again. What things
I shall have to tell you!

Feb. 19. 1757.

Text (p. 121 above)

From Francesco Algarotti *3 March 1757*

Bologna, 3 March 1757

From this City of learning where I am, I send a short essay on the
Ancients and Moderns to you, my Lady, who staying in Padua have
halted the Muses there. No one could be better able than you to decide
the fine dispute that is still unresolved as to which of the two can boast
of more learning and skill. Thanks to your wide reading and your
many travels, you are able to compare with the just balance of knowledge free from any bias the excellence of each century and each
country: That which is best in the writings of the Ancients you have
retained in your mind; and that which you write, my Lady, the
Moderns already regard as treasure, and much more so will those

Who will call this time ancient.

Text (p. 122 above)

To Francesco Algarotti *12 March* [*1757*]

Farewell Philosophy; here are the fine beginnings of Dotage. I gave
proof of it last night at the academy of M. Barbarigo in the
presence of three or four hundred people. I must tell you the story.
There was excellent Music. Perhaps you do not know that I love
Music to the point of Hatred. I could not listen to it with impunity;
I am as sensitive as Alexander, and another Timotheus would make
me run, Torch in hand, to set fire to the city. But since I have not
won enough Battles to make my follies respected, I have kept myself as
distant as I could from that charming seductress, and I flattered
myself that my Weakness was not known. Poor human Wisdom!
it is your last effort: you can hide the passions, never will you succeed
in exterminating them. This Reflection smells terribly of Marivaux.—
Let us return to my Story. I abandoned myself to the Pleasure of
listening to enchanting sounds which stir the soul, thinking mine

frozen enough by time to be able to resist even the Sirens. Mademoiselle Barbarigo with her Angelic face joins her voice with the Instruments, the Applause is deserved and general; her mother's eyes sparkle with joy. A certain Chevalier Sagramoso (whom I shall hate all my life) whispers to me, out of an accursed Politeness, that he had heard my Daughter sing in London. A thousand pictures present themselves at the same time to my mind, the Impression becomes too strong and, fool that I am, I burst into tears, and am obliged to leave in order not to disturb the concert by my sobs. I return home, exasperated at having drawn public scorn on myself deservedly: a sentimental old woman, what a Monster!

I feel this ridicule in all its force. Defend me, if you can, against the jokes which people will not fail to make. I should like still to keep a little corner in your esteem. If that is impossible, keep in mind at least that it is in your Interest to save me from pitiless mockers. My Friendship, which is entirely yours, would lose all value if I fall into disrepute for Stupidity. You would be as imprudent to make fun of my Weakness, as a Painter to admit the uselessness of Pictures.

Venice, 12 March.

Text (p. 123 above)

To Francesco Algarotti 5 *March* [*1758*]

You flatter me, Sir, but you know how to season flattery with so many Graces, it is impossible not to be pleased with it. Let us acknowledge the Debt: humankind is full of vanity. We are all lodged there, Saints, Heroes, Philosophers. Dear Flattery is our favourite nourishment. One need only know how to flavour it to make it tasty. You possess the Art of dressing it lightly, of putting in a piquant salt; you make it so tender, so delicate, I swallow it avidly, and I do not wish to perceive that my poor Head aches because of it.

Too fortunate are those who dare to flatter themselves! I have seen a work of Voltaire's where he pays homage to himself in the most beautiful manner. With what Fire does he sing his own praises! That is what is called a sincere Panegyric! something almost unique.—I feel violent temptations to imitate him. Imagination catches fire easily when one wishes to discuss one's own merit, but Alas! I have some glimmer of common sense, which shows me pitilessly what I am. All I can truly say is that I was young without coquetry, affectation, or giddiness; I am old without peevishness, superstition, or slander. Here

are many negatives, a miserable refuge for my self-Love! I try to protect its rights by persuading myself that I am less stupid than another, in
that I see my stupidities at the very moment when I allow myself to
be swept away by them.

March fifth, Venice

They say the Pope is dead; as a Citizeness of the World I am in
despair.

Text (p. 141 above)

To Mme Chiara Michiel *13 June* [*1758*]

I received your two charming Letters only a moment ago; I hasten
to thank you. For a long time, I have been thoroughly accustomed to
your Kindnesses, without their losing anything of their value. They
seem to me always new and precious.

You know that the House of Oldenburg is that of the King of
Denmark. The Lady in question is his relation, and sovereign of
a little state. She took it into her head (some years ago) to marry
a Younger brother of the Duke of Portland. My step-mother (who
was his Sister) spoke to me about it years ago, but I frankly confess
that I have forgotten all that she told me. All I know is that she is
a person whose appearance and conversation are worthy of being
depicted by Scudéry or La Calprenède. She was going to carry some
Letters from the Empress to the Princess of Modena, and then seek
a Retreat (she said) in Switzerland. If she does not find one to her
liking, she wants to return to Venice. She added that all Europe was
informed of her Misfortunes; I dared not confess my Ignorance after
that declaration.

I am very concerned about the Illness of the Procuratessa, esteeming
her infinitely for her Merit, and knowing how dear she is to you.

Profit from the strength of your Mind (My beautiful Lady);
believe that Heaven has never favoured anybody with so many Graces
as adorn you, without adding to them enough vexatious misfortunes to
exercise these superior Talents.

Miss Brown does not expect a visit; she would be ashamed to see
you in her small Apartment, and will think herself more than fortunate
to be received in your house. She is a good person; I am sure
that you would never have reason to repent having known her.

Here are visitors, which forces me to tell you hastily that I am always with the greatest esteem and the tenderest Sentiments (my charming Friend) entirely yours.

M.W.M.

13 June, Padua

Text (p. 152 above)

To Mme Chiara Michiel 5 *July* [*1758*]

I fear bothering you (My beautiful Lady) but I cannot resist giving you the News that Mr. Mackenzie is going to replace Lord Bristol at Turin. I flatter myself that you will be as pleased as I. For a long time he has sighed for a post in Italy. Upon this I build charming Castles in Spain, about which I will take you into my Confidence when I have the honour of seeing you. Preserve your Health, my Kind Friend, and I shall be more than happy, being yours with all my Heart.

Padua, 5 July

Text (p. 155 above)

To Mme Chiara Michiel [*c. 15 July 1758*]

My Dearest Friend,

I have received your dear Letter with great pleasure, although mixed with much Bitterness at seeing the state of your Health. In God's name, lovely lady, take care of yourself; a life as precious as yours is public property. I would come to see you were it not for fear of bothering you; the same reason forces me to conclude, by assuring you of eternal affection.

M.W.M.

Text (p. 160 above)

To Mme Chiara Michiel *11 Aug.* [*1758*]

I cannot possibly express to you (my Beautiful Lady) to what extent I am touched by the account you give me of your Sufferings, but in the

name of our Friendship, don't let your Courage droop. Fight against
the reverses of fortune; it is worthy of your Spirit to vanquish these
obstacles which poison your life. Believe me, you have an admirable
temperament, capable of resisting anything; but you must help it by
your reason. Laugh at the stupidities that you see, and do not let yourself be carried away by dark Thoughts that will grow stronger if you
do not destroy them at their birth. I give you Lessons that I put into
practice every day, and find effective.

Mr. Mackenzie has no doubt left London. I fear that he is taking
the Swiss route, and we shall not see him in Venice.

I am very much obliged to you (my Dearest) for having undertaken
my defence; if I guess the person with whom you disputed, she ought
less than anyone to excuse Palazzi. He is a Liar, or she is——what
one does not name.

It is true, dear friend, the world is a vile place; it is necessary, however, to accommodate oneself to it. We are here, and perhaps we shall
find ourselves still worse off on leaving it. Let us banish useless regrets;
let us seek ready pleasures and scorn those that Fortune has put
beyond our reach. I will never consider myself unfortunate so long
as I can flatter myself on having a place in a Heart as precious as yours;
mine is entirely yours.

M.W.M.

Padua, 11 August

Text (p. 164 above)

To Mme Chiara Michiel *30 Aug.* [*1758*]

My Dearest Mistress,

I am dying to talk with you. The Devil is in it; the very moment
that I am about to come to Venice, the Banks of the River have to
burst, and here I am a Prisoner until they are repaired. Assuredly
I am pursued by some goblin worse than a Vampire.

I am sending you the first fruits of my Laboratory; I wish, however,
that you may never need them.

Padua, 30 August.

I have received compliments for you from England; you are not
made to be forgotten.

Text (p. 168 above)

To Mme Chiara Michiel 7 *Sept.* [*1758*]

I swear to you (my dear Friend) that your Letter has pierced my soul. Take Courage; it is impossible to have a spirit as lively as yours without a fund of vigour capable of vanquishing all maladies; you are not of an Age to succumb. Take care of yourself, for the Consolation of your Friends. The first day that the roads are passable I will hasten to embrace you, being entirely yours.

M.W.M.

Padua, Sept. 7.

You shine in all ways, but you go much too far in your gratitude. Would to God that I could render you some essential service.

Text (p. 176 above)

To Mme Chiara Michiel *29 Jan. 1762*

London, Great George Street, near Hanover Square
January 29. 1762

I arrived only the day before yesterday. Crushed by the Fatigue of visits that I could not possibly refuse, from Relations, from Children, and what is worse, by business Affairs, I think, however, only of my charming Friend the Cavaliera Chiara Michiel. It is true that there is little merit in this; she is not forgettable (allow this word of my making, but I cannot write correctly in any language, having a Hodge-podge in my poor Head of ancient and modern Languages).—Someone is knocking at the door; here is my daughter with 5 or 6 dozen Satellites whom I must receive.

Woe is me, dear Venice! Dearest Signora Chiara! Esteemed Procuratessa Bragadini!

O rural home: when shall I behold you!

You will think me possessed. Alas, I am worn out!

Text (p. 286 above)

To Mme Chiara Michiel *15 Feb. 1762*

Here I am released from ten thousand visits, and I take this first suspension of Horrors to write to my dear and very revered Friend.

You told me so, my beautiful Lady; I am crushed with impertinence in the guise of Honours. I have not the strength to resist; would to God I may have the strength to return to Venice, and take refuge in your pleasant House. Poor Mackenzie is more vexed than I. The Court and Parliament devour him right to the bone.

London, Great George Street, Hanover Square

Feb. 15. 1762

Text (p. 287 above)

To Mme Chiara Michiel [*April 1762*]

I swear to you (my beautiful lady) that the greatest pleasure I have received in London has been your kind Letter of the tenth of last month. What you said about the fine marriage of our Friend R[osenberg] is incomparable. It has finesse, justice, and nobility, and all that; only you could express yourself so well in a foreign Language. Alas, I have the gibberish of the tower of Babel in my poor Head, and I speak with as little clarity as an Antediluvian. My Heart at least is sincere, and always at your service to sell and pledge.

If your Gentlemen have not left I shall beg them to allow my little coffers which are in the Convent to come with their Baggage. You know that good Company is very Useful on journeys. The Earl of Northampton is very eager to see your beautiful city; he is bringing with him a charming wife, of the first Rank in England.

I am, besides, sincerely grieved at the conduct of Madam your Daughter-in-law. We have a Proverb: My Son is my Son till he has a Wife. You are fortunate in having a mother truly worthy of you; she is doubly so in living with a Daughter as perfect as the Signora Chiara M. B. May this union last for ever! and may your grandchildren recompense you for all the griefs you have received elsewhere!

These are the most ardent wishes of your ailing but sincere, very humble and obedient Servant,

M. Wortley Montagu.

Text (p. 288 above)

To Mme Chiara Michiel 8 *May 1762*

I am literally (my Beautiful Lady) in despair at your situation. Would to God that it depended on me to relieve all your anxieties; but of what use are vain wishes? and sad Alases?—Let us say no more about them.—

Mr. Mackenzie is still one of the most charming and worthy Men in the world. We have a thousand plans to serve you. Meanwhile, God give you Health; take care of it yourself, my dear Friend, and do not let yourself be crushed by griefs of which everyone has a sufficient share.

Lord Northampton says he is furious that the day of his departure is not yet fixed. I would be very glad if the Trifles that I have left in the Convent of Murano could be sent to me, if possible, among the equipage of your Ambassadors; if not, at least have them addressed to one of their Excellencies. I am ashamed to enter into these petty details with you, but your Kindness is as universal as the Light of day. I flatter myself that I shall not die ungrateful.

Our Great King (who can literally call himself the well-beloved) has just purchased a Fine House at the end of St. James's Park, which he intends, it is said, to be the Marly of London. He will put there Books and Curiosities of all kinds. You should see how people run to look at the Walls they have seen a thousand times. These are the little attentions that reveal the Heart; it seems that all his subjects are in love with him. It is a Sight I never thought to see in England. What a change! Perhaps we shall see the Nutmeg flourish in our fields; I should hardly be more surprised. Meanwhile we are dying of cold this present month of May. God keep you, dear Friend. I am with an eternal attachment entirely yours,

M. W. Montagu.

May 8, 1762
Great George Street, Hanover Square

They say here that your Doge is dying, and that the Beautiful Giustiniana is going to give the world some new Offspring.

Text (p. 291 above)

To Mme Chiara Michiel *18 May 1762*

My dear and most esteemed Friend,

On no other occasion would I take up a pen, but when it is a question of thanking you for a Kind Letter and relieving you of a burden, I am willing to forget myself, although it is rather difficult to forget a heavy Head, and dizzy spells which overwhelm me. An epidemic Illness reigns in this unhappy Isle; it is said that no one dies of it;

meanwhile everyone is out of sorts. The Duke of Kingston was forced to postpone a Dinner to which I was invited the day before yesterday, not having among his numerous staff any Footmen to serve at Table. Marianne has suffered a terrible attack, Dr. Moro has had his share, and poor me, I suffer like a wretch.

It is impossible for me to send you by this post the inventory in question; fortunately it is not very necessary for the present, but the box is open and you have seen the trifles in it. They are a coffee-pot of silver, a small bowl of the same, and a cup of Silver-gilt. If Lord Tavistock is in Venice—he is my Nephew; everyone speaks very well of him—I am sure that he will take charge of them Willingly. He can put them in his baggage without inconvenience, and as for the Box, [he can] throw it away wherever he likes.

I do not know what I am saying; pardon all my Weaknesses, my heart is always the same. I express badly but I feel quite clearly that I am entirely yours.

M. W. Montagu

1762 May 18.
Great George Street, Hanover Square

Text (p. 292 above)

To Mme Chiara Michiel *11 June* [*1762*]

You must have an Angelic Goodness to forgive me for all the trouble I have been to you. When I begged you to consign my Trifles to Lord Tavistock, he had already left Venice. At last nothing remains for me except Patience to sustain me against all the vexations of life; no one is exempt from them. Weak Consolation!

I do not want to bore you with a Long Letter that cannot be diverting. My Heart is always the same, but my spirit is so greatly weighed down by the heavy air of this Country that I confess I no longer know myself.

Adieu my Beautiful and worthy Friend; be assured that I am with the most perfect devotion entirely Yours,

M. W. Montagu.

11 June

Text (p. 293 above)

Appendix II

ADDITIONS AND CORRECTIONS

VOLUME I

Page 19, *note* 3: Cresswell (not identified) is possibly Richard Cresswell, M.P. 1710–15, who m. (n.d.) Elizabeth, da. and co-heir of Sir Thomas Estcourt.

Page 19, *note* 5: Mrs. Cartwright (not identified) is possibly Armine (1679–1728), da. of 2nd Baron Crewe, who m. (1699) Thomas Cartwright, of an important Northamptonshire family.

Page 68, *line* 10: 'as soon': LM always writes these words as one, a standard usage of her time.

Page 120: second piece of verse from Matthew Prior, *Henry and Emma* (*Literary Works*, ed. H. B. Wright and M. K. Spears, 1959, i. 294).

Page 121: second piece of verse: ibid.

Page 149: The verse is quoted from Aphra Behn, 'To Damon', 1688 (*Works*, ed. M. Summers, 1915, vi. 346).

Page 177: verse: Prior, *Henry and Emma*, 1959, i. 289.

Page 178: second line of verse: ibid., 287.

Page 200: last line from John Sheffield, Duke of Buckingham, *The Temple of Death* (1709), lines 1–2.

Page 201: lines 13–15 contain three lines quoted from Pope's 'January and May' (lines 9–12), first published in the *Poetical Miscellanies* of 1709.

Page 214, *note* 2: W's 'On the State of Affairs' is W MS vii. 204–10.

Page 216, *note* 1: Bolingbroke was not dismissed until 31 Aug. 1714.

Page 224, *note* 5: Apparently Nulle is wrong; Lexington's interest was greater than Pelham's, and prevailed.

Page 247, *note* 1: A Place Bill was passed in 1705 (*not* 1701); or LM may mean that a petition against W's election was rumoured.

Page 252, *note* 1: The character in Jonson's play is Zeal-in-the-Land Busy.

Page 301: The line of verse is adapted from Cowley, *Davideis*, line 80, and Dryden, *MacFlecknoe*, line 73.

Page 322: verse from Matthew Prior, *A Letter to Monsieur Boileau Despreaux* (*Literary Works*, ed. H. B. Wright and M. K. Spears, 1959, i. 226).

Page 330, *note* 2: The Latin verse LM quotes had been translated by Pope in his *Ode for Music on St. Cecilia's Day* (1708), lines 111–16. The English verse comes from Dryden's 'To the memory of Mrs. Anne Killigrew'.

Page 333, *note* 1: Diana leads a chorus of dancing nymphs in 'the meads of cool Eurotas' in Charles Montagu, Earl of Halifax, *An Epistle to Charles Earl of Dorset . . . Occasion'd by His Majesty's Victory in Ireland* (1690), p. 10.

Page 346: To H. V: D[?]n probably Dresden.

Page 402, *note* 1 should read: Confirmed in Jean Ebersolt, *Constantinople byzantine et les voyageurs du Levant*, 1918, pp. 174–5.

VOLUME II

Page vii, *plate* 7: This plan is from the letter of 26 July [1748].

Page 20, *note* 3: The case is fully reported in *Select Trials at the Sessions-House in the Old Bailey*, 1742, i. 322–8.

Page 51, *note* 1: Baillie was replaced on 27 May 1725 (Robert Beatson, *Political Index*, 3rd ed., 1806, i. 339–40). An appointee of the Sunderland ministry, he had outlived his usefulness to Walpole. His pension was £1,600 per annum (Lady G. Baillie, *Household Book, 1692–1733*, ed. R. Scott-Moncrieff, 1911, p. xxiii, n. 1).

Page 81: The line of verse is adapted by LM from Aphra Behn, 'A Voyage to the Isle of Love' (*Poems upon Several Occasions*, 1684, p. 124).

Page 88:

From Henry Fielding [*Feb.* 1728][1]

To the Right Honourable the Lady *Mary Wortley Mountague*

Madam,

Your Ladyship's known Goodness gives my Presumption the Hopes of a Pardon, for prefixing to this slight Work the Name of a Lady, whose accurate Judgment has long been the Glory of her own Sex, and the Wonder of ours: Especially, since it arose from a Vanity, to which your Indulgence, on the first Perusal of it, gave Birth.

I wou'd not insinuate to the World that this Play past free from your Censure; since I know it not free from Faults, not one of which escaped your immediate Penetration. Immediate indeed! for your Judgment keeps Pace with your Eye, and You comprehend almost faster than others overlook.

---

[1] When he was twenty-one years old, Fielding's first play, *Love in Several Masques*, was produced at the Theatre Royal in Drury Lane, on 16 Feb. 1728, and ran for only four nights. Within a week it was published with this dedication to his cousin and patron Lady Mary (Wilbur L. Cross, *The History of Henry Fielding*, 1918, i. 61–62).

This is a Perfection very visible to all who are admitted to the Honour of your Conversation: Since, from those short Intervals You can be supposed to have had to yourself, amid the Importunities of all the polite Admirers and Professors of Wit and Learning, You are capable of instructing the Pedant, and are at once a living Confutation of those morose Schoolmen who wou'd confine Knowledge to the Male Part of the Species, and a shining Instance of all those Perfections and softer Graces which Nature has confin'd to the Female.

But I offend your Ladyship, whilst I please my self and the Reader; therefore I shall only beg your Leave to give a Sanction to this Comedy, by informing the World that its Representation was twice honoured with your Ladyship's Presence, and am, with the greatest Respect, *Madam, Your Ladyship's most obedient most humble Servant,*

Henry Fielding.

Text: *Love in Several Masques*, 1728

Page 119: This letter, actually dated 20 Aoust. V.S., should be headed 31/20 Aug. [1738].

Page 150, *note* 3: In 1732 Lady Grisell Baillie thought Browne 'a worthy honest Scots man' (*Household Book*, 1911, p. 398).

Page 239: line 15 is adapted from William Wycherley, 'To Mr. Pope, on his Pastorals', printed in the *Poetical Miscellanies* of 1709.

Page 316, *note* 3: The Cowley epitaph had appeared in *Spectator* No. 551 (2 Dec. 1712).

Page 338:

To Lady Mar 10 Aug. [1744]

Dear Sister,

I return you many thanks for letting me know the agreable news of Miss Evelyn's happy marriage. I saw Lord Goreing at Venice, and am of your Opinion that he is a very valuable Young Man.[1] I am glad you are likely to have so good a Neighbour.[2] I wish you all sort of Blessings. I suppose you have heard my Daughter ⟨is⟩ brought to Bed of a Son.[3] I hope he may live to be a dutifull Nephew to you. I beg you would be so good to make my Compliments to Lady F[rances] Erskine,[4] and beleive me ever Your most affectionate Sister,

M. W. Montagu.

Avignon, Aug't 10. N.S.

[1] For the marriage of LM's niece Evelyn Leveson-Gower to Lord Gowran, see ii. 326 and n. 1.

[2] Lord Gowran's mother had bought (in 1736) Ampthill Great Park and its mansion. Lady Mar and her daughter lived at Ampthill Manor House, lent them by another niece, the Duchess of Bedford, whose husband had purchased the 'honour of Ampthill' in 1738 (William Cole, *A Journal of My Journey to Paris in the year 1765*, ed. F. G. Stokes, 1931, p. 90; Walpole, *Corr.* xx. 281; David and Samuel Lysons, *Magna Britannia*, i, 1806, p. 38).

[3] John, eldest surviving son (see ii. 340).

[4] Lady Mar's daughter.

Text Mar and Kellie MS, Scottish Record Office, Edinburgh
Address The Rt Honble the Countess of Mar at Ampthill Bedford-
shire by way of London Angleterre par Paris   *Postmark* AV 13

Plate 7, facing p. 408: date should be 26 July [1748].
Page 505: The letter dated 20/9 Aug. [1738] should be headed 31/20
  Aug. [1738].

VOLUME III

Page 50: The song quoted by LM is 'The Old Man's Wish', with
  the refrain:

> May I govern my Passion with an absolute sway,
> And grow wiser and better as my strength wears away,
> Without Gout or Stone, by a gentle decay
> > (*Poems on Affairs of State*, iii, 1704, pp. 438–9).

Pages 63–64: Pope had used this image in the *Essay on Man*, Epistle
  iv, lines 360–72.
Page 121, *note* 1: A fragment of French verse on this fable is W MS
  vii. 309 *verso*.
Page 218, *last line of verse*: This is quoted from "Advice to a
  Painter, 1697" (*Poems on Affairs of State*, ii, 1703, p. 431.)
Page 219: The verse is quoted from her own (unpublished) "Epistle
  from Mrs. Y—— to her Husband, 1724" (H MS vol. 256).
Page 222, *lines* 15–16: This sentence is adapted from Thomas Parnell's
  'An Elegy, To an Old Beauty' (*Poems on Several Occasions*, 1726,
  p. 129).
Page 244, *line* 3: 'Queen *Bess* never thought it' is a line from 'A New
  Song of the Times, 1683', a poem about political degeneracy (*Poems
  on Affairs of State*, i, part 1, 1703, pp. 218–20). In her actual
  letter LM presumably quoted more than this line.

INDEX

TO VOLUMES I, II, AND III

By ISOBEL GRUNDY *and the* EDITOR

Peers and peeresses are listed under their titles; other married women under their husbands' surnames. At the beginning of each entry, any pages listed without captions indicate a mere mention of the subject. The two longest entries are Lady Mary's (under Montagu) and her husband's (under Wortley Montagu); and each is preceded by a 'table of contents'.

Grand Tour: ENGLISHMEN (*cont.*)
Oliver; Pitt, Thomas (later Lord
Camelford); Rosebery; Shrewsbury,
George, Earl of; Southwell; Strafford,
William, Earl of; Stuart, Mr.; Tor-
rington, George, Viscount; Walpole,
Horace; Wrey.
— — LM's opinion of, ii. 99, 177, 196,
221, 469, 495, iii. 148, 159, 166, 229,
234, 245, 276; pay court to LM in
Rome, ii. 228–9, 231, iii. 32; inhabi-
tants of Lovere eager to attract, iii. 55;
admire LM's cooking, iii. 136;
Murray and, iii. 137; do not visit LM,
iii. 151, 159, 166, 202, 245, 276, 278;
LM offers to tell Lady Bute about, iii.
270.
— TUTORS (*see* Anderson; Clephane;
Devismes; Hewett; Hickman; Law,
Mr.; Otway, Francis; Platel): their
social position, ii. 440; their imperfect
knowledge of Europe, ii. 495; considered LM a good influence, iii. 32;
fools or knaves, iii. 148; bad company,
iii. 166.
Grand Viziers (*see* Ali Pasha; Ibrahim
Pasha; Khalil; Köprülüzade Mustafa):
accept bribes, i. 348; subservient to
Kâhya, i. 349.
Grange, Lord: *see* Erskine, James.
Grant, Peter, Abbé: and LM in Rome,
iii. 32.
Granville, John Carteret, 2nd Earl: ii.
275; his wit, ii. 56; speaks well of
Wortley Montagu, junior, ii. 269; to
arrange commission for him, ii. 272,
287; power of, ii. 283; summons
Montagu to London, ii. 292, 295 n. 4;
to advise him, ii. 308; second marriage
of, ii. 327, 336; resigns from ministry,
ii. 354; recommends Montagu, ii. 356.
Granville, Sophia Carteret (Fermor),
Countess: ii. 154; recovers from illness, ii. 124; her beauty, ii. 124 n. 6,
198; gossips about LM, ii. 204 n. 1,
222 n. 1, 228 n. 6; Lord Lincoln and,
ii. 265, 284; receives legacy, ii. 294;
marriage of, ii. 327, 329; well known
to LM, ii. 327, 328; education of, ii.
336; death of, ii. 391 n. 1.
Gray, Arthur, footman: ii. 14 n. 1.
Gray, Sir James (as British Resident in
Venice): letters to be sent by, ii. 435,

465, 474; books to be directed to, ii.
441, 471; leaves Venice, iii. 17, 18;
LM's opinion of, iii. 60, 128; (as
Envoy to Naples): iii. 128, 262.
Gray, Thomas: at Herculaneum, ii.
215 n. 2, 220 n. 1.
Greece: LM and W sail past shores of, i.
416–24; Archipelago, i. 421, 428;
wine of, i. 444.
Greek language: i. 390; inscription in,
i. 418, iii. 84; to be studied by
women, iii. 21; Queen Elizabeth's
translations from, iii. 185.
Greek Orthodox Church: Rascian sect
similar to, i. 304–5; Koran mis-
represented by, i. 318, 375; ignorance
of priests, i. 318–19, 418; persecuted
by Roman Catholics, i. 319; super-
stitions of, i. 339, 375; images used by,
i. 361; close to Arianism, i. 411.
Greeks: at Philippopolis, i. 311;
gardeners near Adrianople, i. 332;
under Ambassadors' protection, i.
338; inoculation among, i. 339; not
slaves, i. 345, 367; antiquaries, i. 364;
characteristics of, i. 378; servants, i.
390; ignorance and prejudice of, i. 400,
401; adoption among, i. 409–10;
peasants at Sigeum, i. 419.
— WOMEN: iii. 104–5; use cosmetics, i.
327; dances of, i. 333, 366; acquaint-
ances of LM, i. 347, 349, 350, 351,
352, 361, 386.
Greeks, Ancient: i. 320, ii. 60, 68,
299.
Green, George Smith: *The Life of
Mr. John Van, a Clergyman's Son*,
sent for by LM, iii. 125.
Greenland: i. 308, ii. 69.
Greenwich, London: ii. 18.
Gregory, Saint: Armenians converted
by, i. 410.
Gregory, Mr.: carries letter for LM, iii.
202, 203.
Gremaud, Jean-François: *see* Fribourg.
Gresham, Sir Marmaduke: his financial
dealings with LM, ii. 199.
Greville, Frances (Macartney): in Venice,
iii. 127; her admirers, iii. 136; her pas-
time, iii. 137.
Greville, Fulke: LM's opinion of his
Maxims, iii. 136–7; admirer of Swift,
iii. 158.

Index

— ABSTRACT OF BIOGRAPHICAL EVENTS: his correspondence with LM, i. vi, xiii, xiv, xviii, xix, ii. x, 395 n. 2, iii. ix, 118, (his endorsements on LM's letters) i. 25 n. 2, ii. 147 n. 3, 154 n. 1; his education and Grand Tour, i. 4 n. 2; his friendship with Addison, i. 4 n. 2, iii. 65; LM's father learns of his courtship, i. 28; discouraged by relations from courtship, i. 29, 37–38; marriage treaty broken off, i. 51–52; Steele dedicates second volume of *Tatler* to, i. 51 n. 1; spends evening with Addison and Swift, i. 58 n. 1; marriage treaty to be renewed, i. 63; advises LM about her family's finances, i. 68–69; his suggestions for meeting LM, i. 74–82, 85–91, 127–33 *passim*; advises LM about her suitor's estate, i. 83; often in Steele's house, i. 87; Addison proposes sharing house with, i. 92 n. 1; at social functions, i. 100; reported a suitor of LM, i. 100, 102; offers to withdraw his suit, i. 101, 103, 106, 136; arrangements for eloping, i. 148, 156; gets marriage licence, i. 163 n. 1, 164; stays at same inn as LM, i. 166; suspected to be a highwayman, i. 167; marriage of, i.